A Place to Grow

Women in the American West

Arthur S. Link
Princeton University
General Editor for History

A Place to Grow
Women in the American West

GLENDA RILEY
Ball State University

Harlan Davidson, Inc.
Arlington Heights, Illinois 60004

Library of Congress Cataloging-in-Publication Data

Riley, Glenda, 1938–
    A place to grow : women in the American West : essays and documents / Glenda Riley.
        p. cm.
    Includes bibliographical references and index.
    ISBN 0-88295-886-0 (pbk.)
    1. Women—West (U.S.)—History. 2. Pioneer women—West (U.S.)—History. 3. Frontier and pioneer life—West (U.S.) 4. West (U.S.)—Race relations. I. Title.
    HQ1438.W45R55 1992
    305.42′0978—dc20   91-40984
                                                                                        CIP

Cover: Polly Bemis of Warrens, Idaho. Photograph #71-185.29
Courtesy of the Idaho State Historical Society, Boise, Idaho.

Book design by Alan Wendt.

Manufactured in the United States of America
96 95 94 93 92 1 2 3 4 5 ML

In memory of Sandra L. Myres
Supporter, critic, and friend who shared
my love of the past and its peoples

FOREWORD

In 1976, the Western History Association's annual conference included a session devoted to women in the American West. Since then, a burgeoning number of historians have analyzed western women's lives, roles, and contributions. The late 1970s and the 1980s were heady times for these historians. The saga of the West had long focused upon men, but during these years, with the contemporary feminist movement and their own intellectual curiosity spurring them on, historians made new discoveries about the role of women in western history. In the 1990s, this research on western women is rich, varied, and increasingly sophisticated. But answers to crucial controversies remain elusive. Did the American West offer women a place to grow? Did women find more economic opportunities in the West than elsewhere? Were western women more politically active and effective than their eastern counterparts? Did the West's reputed liberalism and democracy shape the lives of all western women for the better? Or did women of some social classes, races, and ethnic backgrounds find the West to be accommodating, while other women did not?

Over the last twenty years or so, my own professional growth, both as historian and as teacher, has been largely the result of formulating and attempting to answer such questions. From the articles I have written for publication, I have selected ten that I have found especially useful in explaining the nature and importance of these issues in the classroom as well as for audiences of both colleagues and laypersons. I have rounded out the selection with an essay written especially for this volume and with a large collection of primary documents. The result is a text that addresses these questions and, in the process, reveals both the complexity of research issues and the multiplicity of women's perspectives. These essays discuss and analyze a variety of topics concerning women's lives and experiences in the American West. Interspersed among the essays, the documents not only give the flavor of women's attitudes and reactions to issues of the day, but also demonstrate the importance of women's own words as historical evidence.

The selections presented here, which explore gender, race, class, region, and other variables, are arranged in five sections: 1) stereotypes of western women, 2) women and westward trails, 3) women migrants and Native Americans, 4) women and work, and 5) women, adaptation, and change. Almost every type of western woman is represented, although archivists and scholars have only recently begun to retrieve Native American, African American, Asian

American, and Mexican American women's words and documents. These sources are more difficult to locate than Anglo American women's writings. Other women's documents are almost impossible to find—those commenting directly on sexual matters, especially by abortionists, prostitutes, rape and incest victims, and lesbians.

In addition, although the selections included here concentrate on the late nineteenth and early twentieth centuries, many scholars are beginning to explore women's lives in the contemporary West. Published by the Center for the American West at the University of New Mexico in 1990, Pat Devejian and Jacqueline J. Etulain's *Women and Family in the Twentieth-Century West: A Bibliography* lists over eight hundred bibliographical entries. After years of neglect, the twentieth-century West is gradually becoming an accepted area for scholarly study.

A Place to Grow concludes with notes for each essay. They are included partly to illustrate the rich scholarship on western women, and partly to serve as a resource to readers who are interested in pursuing a particular topic. Each section also provides suggestions for further reading. The essays included in *A Place to Grow* have been revised slightly to observe current conventions in language and style.

A number of archivists and historians have given their time and expertise to this project and have contributed appropriate documents to it. I greatly appreciate the advice and assistance of Susan Armitage, Gordon Bakken, Jo Tice Bloom, Anne M. Butler, Richard Etulain, Bruce Glasrud, Joan Jensen, Barbara Jones, Margo Gutierrez, Arnoldo De León, Valerie Mathes, Sandra Myres, Alexa Nickliss, Gail Nomura, and John Wunder, as well as the skillful editing of Michael Kendrick. I am indebted to Marquette University and the Association of Marquette University Women for encouragement and research support during my tenure there as Visiting Professor of Humanistic Studies during the fall semester of 1990, and to Greg Lang, who served as my research assistant. I am also grateful to the University of Northern Iowa for funding a research internship at Pacific Lutheran University in Tacoma, Washington.

If this collection not only enlightens, but encourages further debate and investigation, it will have fulfilled my hopes for it.

Glenda Riley
Muncie, Indiana, July 1991

CONTENTS

INTRODUCTION

A number of themes pervade the articles and documents presented here. The selections discuss stereotypes of western women, the ethnic and racial backgrounds of western women, women's migration experiences, female migrants' relations with Native Americans, women's contributions inside and outside the home, including their struggle for legal and political rights, and women's paid employment including access to the professions. These essays and documents assess how race affected women's outlook and choices, how and when women's and men's realms and roles intersected, and how women were treated by men who sometimes cared more about the promise of the West than about their families' hardships. This book also examines a hotly debated question—how did the West affect women and their female descendants? In other words, was the West a place to grow?

In spite of western historians' massive attack during the past decade and a half on the stereotypes of Western women, such images continue to exercise a firm hold on the American mind. Scholars who attempt to rethink and restructure the traditional picture of the American West are frequently criticized for having a penchant toward extreme revisionism, political correctness, and an unnecessarily negative view of the nation's heritage. Many historians, however, have little desire to keep repeating the customary shibboleths in their classrooms; they feel they can far better serve their students and the nation's future by asking critical questions about the past.

One of the most persistent stereotypes has been that of the Saint in the Sunbonnet—the ubiquitous woman who supposedly helped "conquer" the American West. Modern researchers argue instead that western women were extremely diverse and thus reacted in different ways to events. These women were native-born Americans, African Americans, Native Americans, Asians, Europeans, and Mexicans. Thus, had we asked a white migrant from Boston if the West was a place to grow, she might have said yes, while an immigrant woman from China might have said no.

Western women were not a homogeneous entity or category. They reflected a variety of educational, racial, ethnic, and social class backgrounds. Their marital status, sexual preference, and religious affiliation also varied, as did their location, which could be rural or urban. Thus, each woman's circumstances shaped her perception and experience of the American West. An Anglo American woman migrating westward with her middle-class family, for example, might have found the West congenial in many ways. But an African American Exoduster fleeing the post–Civil War South only to discover blatant prejudice in Kansas or Colorado or Oklahoma may have thought the West a bitter disappointment. Perhaps a well-born Mexican woman deprived of her status, power, and wealth by the coming of American "conquerors" would have judged western life destructive rather than empowering. And certainly an Asian woman shunned by employers, shopkeepers, and Anglos would have felt that the American West was less than a promised land.

A good example of the conflicting testimony created by and about western women is Susan Shelby Magoffin's portrayal of Doña Tules, also known as Gertrudis Barcelo, who was a successful saloon-keeper and reputed monte dealer in New Mexico during the early 1800s. While Magoffin lived in Santa Fe, she wrote of Doña Tules as "a stately dame of a certain age, the possessor of a portion of that shrewd sense and fascinating manner necessary to allure the wayward, inexperienced youth to the hall of final ruin." She was further scandalized at the woman's flirtatious behavior at a ball and her habit of smoking cigarettes in public.[1]

Still, when a Mexican, Fray Angélico Chávez, analyzed Doña Tules, he came to a different conclusion. Chávez argued that Magoffin was a typical, puritanical American who saw gambling, smoking, and drinking as vices. "As opposed to the Puritan, the Latin mind saw these things in a different light," he continued. "To the Latin there was nothing in the law of nature, or in the Scriptures, that labeled tobacco, liquor, or gambling, as sins in themselves." He noted that while Latins opposed habitual drunkenness and gambling with improvidence, they did not see any need to prohibit drinking and gambling entirely. In his view, Doña Tules "made her living by running a house where open gambling, drinking, and smoking were enjoyed by all and sundry with no thought of being socially degraded."[2] Was Tules an immoral woman, representative of depraved Mexican morals? Or was she a savvy businesswoman who earned a good living without breaking civil or religious laws?[3]

Because the answers to such questions varied from individual to individual does not mean that they should be discarded. An Anglo American woman's perception of a Hispanic woman—or of an African American or Asian woman—discloses much about cultural values and intergroup relations of the time. Likewise an African American woman's comments on white women's clubs or their childraising practices offer rare insight into cultural values and misconceptions.

But such observations must be handled carefully. In particular, we must avoid the trap of "colonizing" types of women—older, single, religious, lesbian, women of color—that is, the trap of invariably grouping them and applying existing paradigms of Anglo American, middle-class women's history to them. Instead of marginalizing groups of women in this way, we need to recognize the diversity *within* groups of women and the validity of their cultures in their own right rather than as simply subgroups of the larger society. The "cult of domesticity," for example, was largely a white, middle-class phenomenon that had limited applicability to other groups of women.[4]

The idealized American woman was an invention—a model. Therefore, we cannot judge all women by her. Rather, as historian Elizabeth Fox-Genovese phrased it, we must attempt "to establish the cultural integrity of noncanonical culture" rather than consider minority groups "for their specific dynamics and in relation to the canon or dominant groups that excluded, oppressed, or ignored them."[5] Still, as we rethink the past, we must also consider carefully how to use our new findings. In particular, should examples from the past be used to support and advance feminist causes and other social change? If so, how, when, and where would such usage be appropriate and effective?

Today, historians themselves are divided concerning the proper use of the past. Some insist that researchers accept women's words and actions as they stand. If most women said that home and family dominated their lives and thoughts, then that is a reasonably accurate representation of the way women saw things at the time, or the way they chose to remember their lives as they aged.

These historians would probably agree that we cannot know the actual past but can only know the virtual past through written sources, artifacts, and other bits of evidence. Because we can only know the past through this evidence, researchers must interpret sources as accurately as possible. Of course, all historians have biases, but researchers should minimize their biases and present their findings with a degree of faithfulness to available source materials.[6]

This is a traditional view of what it means to "do history." Advocates of this position argue that academic and public historians must strive for at least a modicum of objectivity. To understand the past, to discover its meaning, we must let its inhabitants speak for themselves even if their words and actions fail to provide instructive lessons for those living in the present.

The catch in this approach is that historians cannot be objective; their eyes and brains cannot escape the individual perspectives of their minds. Are they, then, creating historical accounts without recognizing—and alerting us to—their own biases? Perhaps more important, are they failing to mine the past for lessons? If they were to study women's past experiences in terms of exploitation, or oppression, or liberation, or other contemporary concepts, the past might be more meaningful and helpful to people struggling to survive in the present and plan for the future.

Scholars who take this tack argue that because we cannot know the literal truth about the past, we can, indeed we must, interpret the past in light of current issues and understandings. We must read the past from the angle of today's needs and concerns. For instance, by bringing to light cases of women who performed heavy farm labor, worked at a "man's" job, or got involved in politics, historians can show that women did not always function in the domestic realm and can thus present far more identifiable role models to men and women of the late twentieth century. Moreover, deconstructing historical gender expectations by challenging the way they were constructed, legitimized, and maintained can provide insights into larger historical questions.[7]

One danger in this approach, however, is the possible devaluing of women's domestic labor. If "men's work" becomes the normative standard against which we judge the worth of women's tasks, do we not demean the historical kitchen? If we judge women by their ability to break into what was commonly regarded as a man's world, are we not denigrating their own world? Women were not rendered unimportant by gender expectations. To assume that women could be significant only when they expanded, or fled from, the domestic realm is to impute powerlessness to women, power to men. But women were already empowered and esteemable in their own world; women's contributions were worthy and satisfying in their own right.

We must acknowledge too that the female realm was not totally separated from the male. Although women were expected to focus on home and family, they were not excluded from the rest of the world, just as men were not excluded from the domestic realm. Women's activities often overlapped with men's; a domestically oriented woman might hold paid employment, or hold office as a school superintendent, or work to provide a library, playground, or medical care for her community. To judge women according to their participation in either domestic work or paid employment is to miss the complexity of the whole. This overlapping of roles was especially true of white working class women, immigrant women, and women of color, who performed heavier physical labor at home and had higher rates of paid employment than white middle-class women. For them, the worlds of home and work overlay each other. They worked outside the home out of necessity rather than as a way of enlarging their personal development. They became paid laborers to survive rather than to protest. When we take into account their numbers, the assumed separation of home and work, private and public, blurs and recedes.[8]

Nor should we conclude that traditional gender roles gave women no opportunity for growth or that their tasks had no worth. If women had not spent a good deal of time in their kitchens—which were the factories that transformed the raw materials produced by men into finished products—the western economy would not have grown as rapidly as it did. In a sense, sunbonnets and petticoats were the uniforms of a critically significant workforce.

Furthermore, some contemporary feminists do not see women working at traditionally male jobs as a manifestation of liberation. Rather, they argue that the male system of patriarchal capitalism has co-opted women by convincing them to accept male standards of productivity, value, and worthy work. To them, nothing short of a new system of government, cultural ideology, and economy will qualify as liberation.[9] The question of how the past should be used to support current changes would thus vary greatly from one reformer to another.

Before historians of western women can confidently use their data one way or the other, however, they must confront several important research problems. One of these is the currently changing view of the American West. For generations, historians have seen the West largely as a land of opportunity, change, and equality. It was in the American West that people found more satisfactory lives, earned better livings, and blossomed by virtue of its open spaces and nature. In this scenario, women's gains receive emphasis. Women's triumphs and breaks with the past are esteemed.

More recently, however, some scholars have begun to question this interpretation of the American West. Instead of opportunity and change, historians of a school called the new western history see despair and disillusionment, failed farms and unproductive mines, exploitation and destruction of the environment. Instead of an atmosphere of equality in the western environment, they see dominance by the wealthy, decimation of the native population, and prejudice against such groups as African Americans and Asians. New West historians emphasize women's subordination and play down their triumphs and breaks with the past.

To further complicate matters, western historians have no common definition of "frontier" and "West." To say that one is studying "frontierswomen" or "western women" conveys little exact information. One may be talking about women in colonial New England or women in late twentieth-century California. In this collection, I have chosen, as so many historians do, to focus on the trans-Mississippi West.

The meaning of "frontier" is not so easily resolved. Was a frontier a region with less than two people per square mile, as the U.S. Census Bureau defined it? Or was it the phenomenon of migrants pushing in among native populations? Was it, then, a place or a process? Some scholars have argued that it was a historical development, or perhaps a political unit, a cultural system, a concept.[10]

Not only is "frontier" an inexact term, it is often a pejorative one as well. The word often evokes an image of Anglo Americans bringing "civilization" to a western area and its peoples. Yet, surely neither Native Americans nor Mexicans considered themselves a primitive frontier folk in need of civilizing.

The fuzziness of the term "frontier" complicates any definitions of the American West. Did it begin in New England? Or after Americans crossed the Appalachian Mountains? Was it the Old Northwest, what is today the Midwest, the Great Plains, the Pacific Northwest, the Southwest, or all of these? Did it fade as the nation entered the twentieth century, or does it still exist? Is it a geographic region or a mentality?

"Frontier" is an outdated term, an idea that has outlived whatever usefulness it may have had. It encourages a we-versus-them mentality, an adversarial perspective on western migration. It seems to me, however, that the American West is a useful concept. It is a fluid term, evoking an image of region *and* mentality, of place *and* concept, that spans early Native American and Mexican development and the contemporary West Coast. It allows us to study women—or any other group—in frameworks other than that of vanquishing others and triumphing as the bearers of "civilization."

Another significant issue for western historians is that of continuity versus change in women's roles. Did traditional gender expectations hold sway in the American West or did they crumble? This question has been discussed at length for more than a decade. During the late 1970s, historian John Mack Faragher argued that well-defined gender divisions characterized men's and women's work on the westward trail. Similarly, historian Julie Roy Jeffrey maintained that customary gender expectations existed among migrants in raw western regions.

During the late 1980s, after comparing western women's lives in two regions and eras in *The Female Frontier*, I also concluded that while western men exercised an array of choices—to marry or remain single, to work at a huge variety of jobs, to be absent from one's wife and children for weeks as an itinerant preacher, laborer, or merchant, or for months as an argonaut, land-seeker, or explorer—women had fewer choices. As in the East, the South, and Europe, prevailing gender norms dictated that women should marry, regard homes and families as their primary jobs, and eschew thoughts of leaving their husbands and children to seek gold, land, or adventure on their own. Women who resisted these models were dismissed as exceptions or branded as deviant; social controls ranging from cultural sanctions to violence chastised them and attempted to force them into line.

In addition, women's lives changed less over time than did men's.[11] Quite often, while men worked the fields with the latest gasoline-powered engines, women continued to cook on wood-burning stoves and carry water to and from washing machines. Continuity more than change appeared to characterize the lives of women in the American West.

But other historians of western women disagree with this interpretation, sometimes sharply. One curious observer asked why scholars could not agree on events of the past. After all, he pointed out, the past was over; it was done with and settled. The answer is, of course, that although past events may be done and settled, their *meaning* is far from clear. The next logical question is *why* it is so difficult to agree on the meaning of the past, a question that requires an extensive response.

One important problem in studying the lives of western women is the lack of common definitions of "continuity" and "change." Both terms are absent from handbooks and dictionaries of feminist theory.[12] This lack of agreement makes it virtually impossible to determine whether western women's lives changed significantly or not. As an example, let us examine the situation of Minnesota women before and after the emergence of the market economy. After surveying the modifications that took place in these women's lives, we shall see how such modifications might be interpreted as continuity *or* as change.

Both before and after the introduction of the market economy, Minnesota women were a diverse lot. Their number included a large number of European immigrants. In 1870, Governor Horace Austin estimated that as much as three-fifths of Minnesota's population had been born in Europe. Finnish women, for example, formed a significant portion of Minnesota's female population.[13] African American women were present as well. Yet, despite this diversity, some general patterns can be detected in these women's lives.

Before the market economy developed in any given region of Minnesota, women worked as domestic artisans in their homes, which also served as their workplaces and factories. The technology in these workplaces ranged from basic to downright primitive. Early women's writings overflow with details about whitewashing cabin walls, making medicines and treating the ill, making candles and soap, processing foods, cooking in open fireplaces or on small stoves, making cloth and clothing, and washing clothes "on the board." A Steele County woman remembered, for example, that her mother made shoes with uppers of thick cloth and soles cut from the tops of worn-out boots. She also dyed and braided straw for summer hats, spun yarn and knitted socks, and hand-sewed clothes for ten people. Most of this work was done by the light of a candle. Despite the difficult working conditions, she also made hide gloves to sell for extra cash.[14]

Such production for both domestic use and the market was common. Mary Carpenter, who lived on a farm near Rochester, described one of her days. She rose at four A.M. to prepare breakfast, then "skimmed milk, churned . . . did a large washing, baked 6 loaves of bread & seven punkin [sic] pies . . . put on the irons & did the ironing got supper—besides washing the dishes, making the beds." In the same letter, she told of making 100 pounds of butter in June and selling "28 doz. of eggs at 10 c. a doz." later that summer. She proudly, and expansively, added that her butter-and-egg money paid for "everything" her family had.[15]

A paucity of raw materials further complicated women's work. Mary Burns, an inventive woman living near Ely Lake in 1892, embroidered burlap to create a cover for one "company" chair. She made pillows by filling gunny sacks with pine needles, and ground coffee by putting "roasted berries into a strong cloth bag, taking it to a rock outside and pounding it to the right degree of fineness." She told her friends and family about her strange new life in letters written on thin sheets of birch wood.[16]

During the pre-market years, even women who lived in towns performed demanding and exhausting domestic labor. Except for the fortunate few who employed help, town women often kept chickens, or even pigs and cows, carried their family's supply of water from wells a street or two away, and washed "on the board" just as did their counterparts on farms. Nor were early towns far ahead in technological improvements or social opportunities. During the early 1860s, one woman characterized the town of St. Anthony, today known as Minneapolis, as a "very quiet village" in a "sleepy condition."[17]

In addition to their domestic duties, some Minnesota women held paid employment outside their homes during the pre-market years. As a case in point, woman were among the first teachers in virtually every area of Minnesota.[18] Anecdotal evidence indicates that women often established some of the first schools in their homes. In these subscription schools, students paid fees, brought their own books, and in the first such school in Rochester, brought their own seats.[19] When communities erected log or frame schoolhouses, women taught in them as well.

Women were also active in providing assistance to neighbors and new migrants. They frequently established aid associations, joined together in quilting and work bees, and formed groups to help erect schools and churches. As a result, women had a long tradition of helping neighbors and friends, occasionally through organized groups.[20]

As the market economy reached various parts of Minnesota, it unquestionably altered women's lives. For one thing, women now labored in larger, better-equipped homes and work places. Still, their workloads appear to have modified more in nature than in amount. Instead of collecting tallow and making candles, women now spent hours each day trimming wicks and cleaning kerosene lamps. They employed treadle-powered sewing machines to make clothing that was becoming increasingly complex in design. One woman near Jordan explained that although her grandmother had spun thread on a spinning wheel and sewed clothes by hand, her mother had worked on a sewing machine after 1886. But a St. Cloud woman of the same era remarked that it now took twelve yards of material and numerous ruffles and tucks to make an acceptable dress; the task was harder on a sewing machine than it had been by hand.[22] Growing numbers of women also washed their families' clothes in washing machines, but they had to turn the agitators by hand and carry clean water to the machines and dirty water from them because they lacked such support technology as indoor plumbing and electricity.

Agnes Kolshorn remembered clothes-washing days on the family farm near Red Wing during the 1880s and 1890s. Equipment included "a bench for the two wooden tubs, washboards, the washing machine, the wringer to be clamped onto the tubs or the machine, the copper wash boiler, wooden clothespins, clothes line, clothes basket, pails and bottle of bluing." She heartily disliked the task of carrying water from the cistern to the stove to be heated and then to the washing machine and detested the job of removing frozen clothes from the line during the winter. The next day women customarily ironed clothes with flatirons heated on the stove. Kolshorn recalled that her family owned the latest technology in flatirons: each had a separate handle that was clamped onto it before it was lifted from the stove.[23]

After the arrival of the market economy, women continued to produce domestic goods for sale. In fact, the market economy often expanded women's work, for it offered them the opportunity to sell in greater quantities to larger markets. During the late nineteenth century, farm woman Lydia Sprague Scott sold butter, milk, and eggs to customers in nearby Mankato. The Kolshorn women also made butter and eggs to sell in town. Agnes remembered butter-making "as an exacting, time consuming task" that culminated in packing butter into two- or five-pound earthenware jars to be transported to Red Wing.[24]

Even after the Kolshorn family moved to Red Wing in 1901, women's work continued to be difficult and tedious. Because their house lacked indoor plumbing, the Kolshorn women carried water from an outdoor cistern equipped with a hand-operated pump or from a well located in a nearby street. They got their milk from a son in Red Wing who kept a cow. And they emptied the drip pan of their new icebox several times a day and depended upon a man in a horse-drawn wagon to bring ice several days each week.[25]

As the market economy developed, a growing supply of raw materials became available. As early as the 1850s, the pages of the Minnesota *Pioneer* advertised such exotic foodstuffs as oysters at "$1.00 a quart for family use," a treat for former New Englanders. Another advertisement announced that steamships from New York and Europe had brought a stock of the latest American, French, and English dry goods. Women's account books and diaries indicate that many women took advantage of the increasing availability of products. During the 1880s, Lydia Scott noted purchases of calico, velvet, thread, buttons, lace and braid edging, hats, shoes, a parasol, a fan, and a corset.[26]

Another notable change was the increasing numbers of women who sought paid employment outside their homes. Gazetteers, city directories, and newspaper advertisements of the period demonstrate that growing numbers of women worked for pay as the century progressed. Although women usually worked as domestics, nursemaids, and in the needle trades, some women became teachers, nurses, doctors, and at least one was a minister.[27] After 1870, more information became available regarding women employed in Minnesota because the United States census stopped categorizing women as "Not Gainfully Employed" and asked them about their paid employment. In 1870, 10,860 Minnesota women worked as compared with 121,797 men; in 1890, 65,625 women worked as compared with 403,461 men; and in 1910 145,605 women worked and 689,847 men did so.[28]

By 1870, when the United States census began to list women and men teachers separately, women far outnumbered men. In Minnesota in 1870, there were 1,274 female teachers compared to 460 men; in 1890 there were 7,371 women teachers as opposed to 2,085 men; and in 1910 there were 17,078 women teachers and 2,452 men.[29]

Women entered other fields at this time as well. For instance, a growing number of Minnesota women began to write about domestic matters, travel, and other nonpolitical topics for newspapers and magazines during the late nineteenth century. In 1870, there were no female journalists in Minnesota as compared with seventy-seven male journalists. In 1890, however, there were sixteen female journalists and 550 male journalists. And in 1910, one hundred women worked as journalists (including editors and reporters), while 753 men did so. Women who were correspondents for newspapers and authors of sketches, stories, and essays for newspapers and journals frequently used pen names to protect their privacy and reputations.[30]

Homes and families were still the focus of women's lives; many insisted that they enjoyed managing homes.[31] Still, more women, including rural women, were becoming involved in the world outside their homes and farms than ever before. Women increasingly believed that it was their responsibility to create and improve societal amenities and supplement the efforts of men. As one Dundas woman poetically phrased it: "Those men believed they built that church, pointing it out with pride, nor realized it was the Ladies' Aid who really stemmed the tide."[32]

Minnesota women also became involved in the women's club movement of the late nineteenth century and were active in an incredible variety of service organizations. During the early 1870s, for example, Jewish women living in and around St. Paul formed the Hebrew Ladies' Benevolent Society to provide food and other supplies to needy Jewish families. In 1877, the Minnesota chapter of the Women's Christian Temperance Union was organized. Soon such local organizations as the Scandinavian Young Women's Christian Temperance Union sprang up. Other women's associations were cultural groups. The Schubert Club, for instance, sponsored musical performances.[33] In 1895, Margaret Jane Evans Huntington became the first president of the newly formed Minnesota Federation of Women's Clubs.[34]

Especially for urban women of the middle and upper classes, accessibility to women's clubs, reform organizations, and other urban refinements became more available than for rural women. New technology also freed urban women from time-consuming chores, and domestic help took over part of their work loads. As a result, the common ruralness of Minnesota women's lives began to dissipate.

During the late nineteenth century, women also became more interested in furthering their own education, in part to take advantage of opportunities offered by the enlarged economy. In June 1875, Helen Ely of Winona was heralded as the first woman to graduate from a four-year program at what is now the University of Minnesota.[35] Although formal statistics are unavailable, anecdotal evidence indicates a marked increase in the number of women attending college during this era.

Minnesota's women also talked of their rights far more than they had in pre-market days. Some women believed that increased power lay in obtaining the vote. They also attempted to break down gender segregation in Minnesota politics in other ways. During the 1920s, Susie Stageberg, long-term president of the Red Wing WCTU, ran for Minnesota secretary of state on the Farmer-Labor ticket.[36]

This abbreviated case study leaves little doubt that the work and thinking of Minnesota women altered with the introduction of the market economy. What is less clear is whether these alterations reveal a basic continuity or a meaningful change in women's lives.

One historian might interpret these alterations as slight in the overall scheme of things, as minor improvements in women's activities and roles, which continued to be determined largely by gender expectations. For example, although the number of working women increased, the kinds of roles open to them expanded very little. Also, women's work continued to be viewed as supplemental to the "breadwinner's" income.[37] Even as women came to dominate teaching, they were still regarded as supplemental earners and were thus routinely paid less than men. Women's education and clubs, which still concentrated on women's "interests," are another example of this continuity. Women still lacked economic resources, political and military power, and the status that were the tools of male control and dominance in the prevailing system.[38] In other words, a historian could argue that although technology changed, values remained much the same. Although women's material culture now included machines, ideas of what a woman should or should not do continued to determine her work and activities.

Another historian, on the other hand, could make a strong case for the argument that women experienced distinct changes. He or she might maintain, for example, that post-market wives' incomes brought them increased power in the family, that they were knocking down the psychological walls of their homes by seeking employment and education and by forming women's groups, and that they were beginning to manifest their disgruntlement with domestic work loads and traditional gender expectations.[39] In other words, this historian could argue that as technology helped women expand their roles and activities, women were escaping the confinements of gender and challenging the wielders of power. It was not simply women's material culture that altered, but also thinking about what was proper for women.

Perhaps the key to whether an event constitutes continuity or change is its effect on women's own consciousness and identity. Let's take the case of women who produced clothing. Women who sewed by hand or by machine in their homes, sewed by hand in a sweatshop, or sewed by machine in a factory were performing the same task with different technology in different locales. It would appear that the woman who sewed by machine in a factory had a vastly different experience than the woman who sewed by hand at home. But what if both of these women defined themselves as primarily wives and mothers and described their work as a female task? What if the factory woman did not see herself as a full-fledged worker, a significant contributor to the economy, an individual with an identity in addition to her role as wife and mother? What if she continued to see herself as a supplemental producer whose "real" job was at home? Perhaps, we would conclude, the locale of her work had changed, but her consciousness and identity had remained continuous with that of earlier women.[40]

But not all western working women accepted their status. Instead they engaged in lobbying, protests, and strikes. They refused to comply with society's expectation that they work in needle trades and accept less pay than male tailors. Consequently, their consciousness appears to have undergone significant modification.

Obviously, we need to know more about women's personal gains; we need to know what happened or did not happen to their personal autonomy. Did paid employment bring women increased power in their relationships with men? Did women who became active in community and political activities also assume more control over their bodies in sexual relationships and childbearing and over their marriages by an increased willingness to divorce?

One last hurdle in studying western women is the lack of comparative data regarding women in the northeastern and southern United States and in other countries. Without comparative studies, it is impossible to determine whether western women expanded their realm and rights faster than northern or southern women did. Certainly, western women received the right to vote before those in the North and South, but this achievement fails to demonstrate a priori that western women were more politically conscious than their counterparts in other regions. We also must ask if African American, Asian American, and Hispanic women in the West received the suffrage, and if so, under what conditions. Numerous western women also became entrepreneurs in businesses ranging from millinery to prostitution, but this fact does not prove that western women were more business-minded than their northern and southern sisters. We simply do not know how western, southern, and northeastern women *compare*.

Among other scholars, political scientist Virginia Sapiro cautions us to avoid overemphasizing easily apparent differences among groups of women. We may, she warns, overlook commonalities. As a case in point, she notes that "although employment rates of women in the United States are among the highest in the industrialized non-Communist world, the degree of occupational segregation is similar, and in some countries—for example, France and West Germany—the earning gap between women and men is smaller than in the United States." Sapiro adds that even in Scandinavian countries, "which are generally considered more progressive than the United States, feminists are quick to point out how much job segregation remains."[41]

Only comparative regional studies will allow us to understand differences between, and commonalities among, groups of women in different geographical regions and countries. During the past decade, scholars have increasingly studied the effects of race, class, and gender on the lives of American women and men. In fact, these three variables are occasionally referred to as the "holy trinity." It is time to add region to the litany.

Clearly, rising to the challenge implied by the title of this book is more difficult than it first appears. Was the West a place to grow only for Anglo American, middle-class women, while poor women and non-Anglo women found it oppressive? Or did women of all racial, ethnic, and other groups find opportunities of some sort in the western environment? And whether women's ability to alter the prevailing order was more extensive and significant in the

American West than elsewhere in the United States—or in the world—remains to be seen.

These, then, are the major issues that guided the selection of the following essays and documents. In Section 1, stereotypes and images of western women are examined with the intent of demonstrating the vast diversity of their existence. Included are narratives of Native American, Asian, African American, Mexican, and Anglo American women. Section 2 shows that the celebrated overland trail was not the only route women took to the West. Rather, routes were many and a woman's migration experience often depended upon her status: free, slave, married, single, migrating at her own volition or against her will, seeking better opportunities, or fleeing some form of oppression. Section 3 analyzes the differences between women travelers' perceptions of "westering" and what it meant to Native Americans. That each had their own side of the story is thrown into sharp relief. Section 4 reveals some of the expected and unexpected ways in which western women supplemented family incomes or supported themselves or their families. Although many pursued socially acceptable jobs and professions, others challenged accepted norms by entering nontraditional areas. Finally, Section 5 argues that while the prescribed sphere for woman was highly idealized and limited to certain roles and duties, western women actually participated in every aspect of the world. Through adaptation and innovation, some of these women inadvertently, and others purposely, began the long process of redefining women's roles in nineteenth- and early twentieth-century society.

Did, then, the American West offer women, regardless of race and background, a place to grow, or did the region offer opportunity to some and not others?

SECTION

1

Women and Stereotypes

Stereotypes regarding western women abound in both the myth and the history of the American West. Western women have been portrayed as either white women or as Indians; other ethnic and racial groups in the West have been overlooked. For example, Mexican women, who were native to the Southwest, are often invisible. African American and Asian women, who migrated to the West as settlers, also receive short shrift or appear only in specific guises, such as the kindly servant.

The following essays focus primarily on three of these groups—Native American women, white women migrants, and African American women migrants. They explain how and why European and American observers, novelists, and historians often misinterpreted, misrepresented, or overlooked the reality of these women's lives. Interspersed among the essays are women's documents demonstrating that the stereotypes were often inaccurate or misleading and that a wide variety of women, including Hispanics and Asians, made up the category "western women."

1.1
Some European Misperceptions of
Native American Women

During the late 1970s and the 1980s, scholars and laypeople became much more aware of the stereotypical roles and status that American society has traditionally assigned to women, including Native American women. This essay

1.1: Adapted from *New Mexico Historical Review* 59 (July 1984), 237–66. Used by permission. Photo: This 1898 drawing by F. S. Church of a Nez Perce woman presents the idealized, heroic view of Native American women. Courtesy of the Museum of New Mexico, Santa Fe.

explores one source of these stereotypes: eighteenth- and nineteenth-century European views of American Indian women. What follows are reviews and critiques of the writings of European explorers, travelers, and novelists who were potent forces in shaping thinking in both the Old World and the New. These samples include a cross-section of writers from European nations, historical periods, and professions. Some were well-known, while others were obscure.

Rather than conduct their own thorough or objective investigations about the New World, most of these European writers tended to rely on images, rumors, and each others' writings. As a result, their work tends to reveal one dominant and enduring theme: the eventual triumph of Anglo American populations over inferior native inhabitants of America. Believing in the natural superiority of white people and their "civilized" world, these writers, like most Europeans, characterized white settlers as deserving conquerors of America's western regions.

This ethnocentric thinking often led European writers into curious interpretations of women—white and native. Typically, they admired white women as forces of progress and morality in the wilderness, as courageous victors over an untamed region and its barbaric residents.[1] But they frequently reacted negatively to Native American women. They were inclined to call Indian females "savages" and to place them on the other end of the continuum from white women. According to these Europeans, the saints would clearly triumph and the savages would vanish.

Like so many distorted European conceptions of the American West, these prejudiced images of Indian women resulted from what Europeans wished to see rather than what they actually saw. Even when writers derived their information from firsthand observation, they shaded, colored, and limned their views in such a manner that white women became slightly larger than life while native women were degraded.

Of course, many European writers simply subsumed Indian women in a general treatment of Native Americans. Those who specifically discussed Indian women, however, tended to describe them as either princesses or squaws. Given the inaccuracy of a word like "princess" and the unflattering connotation of the term "squaw," such diction by Europeans suggests a low regard for other cultures and reveals their ignorance of, and prejudice toward, Indian women.[2]

To understand these contradictory images of Native American women, one must recognize that understanding Native American behavior was a difficult, complicated endeavor for most Europeans. Confronted with opposing interpretations of the "good" Indian who was simple, pure, and virtuous and the "bad" Indian who was cruel, rapacious, and predatory, Europeans often recounted only one view or the other rather than try to reconcile such differences in a composite portrait.[3]

A number of Europeans staunchly defended the reality of the "good" Indian, but the greatest advocate of Native Americans was Karl May, a German writer famous for his novel *Winnetou* (1892). May argued that Indians had been denied adequate time to evolve from hunters to farmers to city dwellers. "What could the race have achieved given a chance?" he lamented.[4] More frequent, however, were critical European portrayals of Indians. As early as 1628, a Dutch minister described American Indians as "entirely savage and wild . . . uncivil and stupid as garden poles," a view repeated many times in subsequent eras.[5] As late as 1913, English commentator Rupert Brooke epitomized this line of thought when he proclaimed in the *Westminster Gazette*: "The Indians have passed. They have left no arts, no tradition, no buildings or roads or laws."[6]

Such contradictory accounts of "good" and "bad" Indians naturally influenced European interpretations of American Indian women. Were native women pure, simple, lovely princesses clothed in exotic attire or were they ugly, filthy, ragged squaws who deserved extermination? Most Europeans, far removed from the shores of America, were more comfortable with the first view. (Certainly these notions were easier to accept while reading a romantic novel and sitting by a warm fire on the Continent!) Europeans who arrived in the New World with specific ideas about how women, even those of a supposedly inferior race, should look and act were frequently dismayed and puzzled by what they saw.

Those writers who actually traveled to the American West and observed Native American women initially judged them in the same manner that they apprized European women—on the basis of attractiveness and dress. While some observers grudgingly portrayed native women as "seldom ugly," others described them as "quite lovely."[7] Still others noted the beautiful women of specific tribes. For example, a French naval officer thought that Louisiana Indians had "beautiful wives," a German writer that Choctaw women had "beautiful figures," and a French traveler that Lake Erie Indian women were "the most comely savages I had yet seen."[8] In the 1840s the English author Frederick Marryat depicted Comanche women as "exquisitely clean, good-looking, and but slightly bronzed."[9]

These comments, however, represented a minority viewpoint. Indeed most Europeans seemed convinced that Native American women were dirty, ugly, unattractive creatures. They shared the view of French author Alexis de Tocqueville that there were no "passable" Indian women and offered a variety of explanations for their unsightliness.[10] Many thought that the hard work Indian women performed was the cause of early aging.[11] In the 1790s an Englishman, Isaac Weld, declared, "I never saw an Indian woman of the age of thirty, but what her eyes were sunk, her forehead wrinkled, her skin loose and shrivelled, and her whole person, in short, forbidding. . . . This is chiefly owing to the drudgery imposed on them by the men. . ."[12] Uncleanliness and filth were also suggested as reasons for what some viewers described as women's "disgusting" appearance.[13] During the 1840s, a German scientist, Prince Maximilian of Weld, described women of various tribes in the upper Missouri River region as having ugly dress and repellent personal hygiene.[14]

Another early nineteenth-century traveler was more succinct: "As to personal appearance, with very few exceptions, I can only specify three degrees—horrible, more horrible, most horrible."[15]

When Europeans turned their attention to the dress of Indian women, however, their descriptions did not match those of ugly, filthy females. Weld, for example, reported that native women wore many ribbons, jewelry, and other ornaments.[16] Other Europeans noticed ribbons, shells, feathers, beautiful dresses, delicate moccasins, and ornaments.[17] In addition, observers frequently commented on carefully arranged hairdos.[18] "Their hair is very beautiful," Hungarian naturalist John Xantus wrote of women in Missouri, "always dressed with great care and falling softly on the shoulders."[19]

Meanwhile, back in Europe, novelists produced in their works a plethora of lovely young maidens and princesses. Because most writers had not traveled the West themselves, they relied upon secondhand accounts for their information. In a novel published in 1845, one author visualized his heroine in an elegant sheepskin cloak, porcupine quill work, and elks' teeth ornaments.[20] Beads, tinkling silver bells, wampum belts, scarlet leggings, partially nude bosoms, and hair that reached almost to the ground were part of other novelists' descriptions.[21] Then, in 1878, the French novelist Gustave Aimard created a prototype of Indian maidens when he introduced Ova, the daughter of a chief, who wore "a tunic of water-green colour, fastened around her waist by a wampum-belt, with a large golden buckle."[22]

European novelists also produced their share of drudges and squaws, women who performed all the domestic and agricultural chores and undertook tasks that were thought to be too menial for even European servants. In these authors' descriptions, such women were lower even than peasants and gipsies. Far from being adorned with ribbons or ornaments, these women dressed in tatters and rags or were nearly naked.[23]

In time, Europeans got around to probing deeper than Indian women's appearance and dress. Sexual relations between Native American women and white men especially evoked a spectrum of reactions. Beginning with John Rolfe and Pocahontas, Europeans exhibited a willingness to believe that European men were sent by Providence to guide and uplift native women in a way that their own men were incapable of doing.[24] Observers also noted several practical reasons for an alliance between an Indian woman and a white man. A German traveler stated that a native wife insured a white man's safety while among the Indians.[25] Marryat argued that Indian wives "labour hard, never complain, are always faithful and devoted, and very sparing of their talk."[26] Others argued that Native American women were attractive only because of their lands and income.[27]

Still, many European men recoiled from establishing liaisons with Indian women. Some thought that such alliances were detrimental to the Indians. Weld, for example, believed that promiscuity among native women caused sterility and thus a decline in the native population, while Englishman Adam

Hodgson expressed concern during the 1820s that intermarriage between Indians and whites undermined native customs.[28]

Other Europeans opposed Indian-white relationships on the basis of traditional prejudices. A Hungarian traveler rejected the idea because he thought Indian women unattractive.[29] The protagonist of a Hungarian novel rebuffed the offer of an Indian bride because he thought native women were dirty, untidy wives.[30] And the hero of a Polish novel fled an impending marriage with an Native American woman because he found her customs repulsive.[31]

Other Europeans were repelled by what they considered a lack of moral compunction in Indian-white relationships.[32] Indians, one German traveler wrote during the 1850s, "know little of the pure feelings of shame and love."[33] Even German novelist Karl May, who favored American Indians, had trouble with this issue. In one of his works, an Indian character asserts, "The great Spirit has cursed every red woman who loves a white man; therefore the children of such a woman are like the worm." In another novel, May has Winnetou's sister killed to prevent further embarrassing affection between her and the hero, Shatterhand.[34]

Significantly, few Europeans analyzed *why* American Indian women became involved with white men. These commentators not only failed to consider that the chance for economic gain may have motivated Native Americans but also ignored Indian customs that prescribed sexual and marital behavior for women. Instead, they offered supercilious descriptions: "It is very curious to see that at each of the trading posts there has been started a manufactory, so to speak, of half-breeds. Every petty clerk or apprentice has his squaw."[35]

Polygamy was an especially perplexing issue to Europeans. Travelers commented at length upon polygamy, and many novelists suggested it was a commonplace in Native American life.[36] The usual interpretation suggested that polygamy demonstrated Indian men's disdain for women. Louis-Phillippe claimed that polygamy rendered women contemptible in men's eyes, while von Raumer argued that polygamy failed to establish mild, happy relationships.[37] Some travelers recounted dramatic tales of women's responses to polygamy, including stories of wives who violently fought the admittance of another wife into their homes, or committed suicide rather than tolerate such indignity.[38]

The seeming liberality of premarital sexual practices among native groups also upset many Europeans. "When an unmarried brave passes through a village, he hires a girl for a night or two, and her parents find nothing wrong with this," French naval officer Jean-Bernard Bossu remarked during the 1860s.[39] Paul Wilhelm simply assumed that native women entered into involvements with such men-children because they were outgoing, kind, and overly fond of ornaments.[40] Still others maintained that many Indian women were little more than prostitutes who were sold by their mothers, fathers, or themselves.[41]

To European eyes, the sexual behavior of many Native American women not only appeared immoral and dangerous, but also contradictory, for few women had a voice in the selection of marriage partners. Traveler Fredrika

Bremer declared that one of the worst features of Indian women's lives was their inability to choose mates.[42] The practice of arranged marriages also provided raw material for hundreds of nineteenth-century romance novels, which often ended with one or both partners committing suicide.[43] Only a few commentators looked deeper into the situation, as did one Polish writer in the 1870s, to see if women's lack of choice was perhaps not as absolute as first appeared: "If you take her against her will you are brewing yourself a whole pot of trouble. The maiden will sulk, bite, throw herself on you with a knife, hide away, malinger, and after a few days will flee back to her father . . ."[44]

Many Europeans also seemed baffled that Indian women—sexually unrestricted before marriage—were expected to be chaste afterwards.[45] One eighteenth-century commentator remarked that "liberal to profusion of their charms before marriage, they are chastity itself after."[46] Others noted that native women who violated standards of matrimonial fidelity might receive harsh punishments, including such physical disfigurement as the severing of an ear.[47]

These expectations of women's chastity in marriage did not seem to jibe with another Indian custom: offering wives as bedmates to guests. John Smith of Virginia was one of the first Europeans to maintain that Native American men did not consider a sexual alliance between their wives and other men promiscuous if they themselves had sanctioned it.[48] In later years, others also pointed out that a woman's sexual liaisons were not judged immoral when approved by a husband, father, or brother.[49]

Other Europeans commented on additional aspects of native women's behavior and status that bewildered them. Bossu noted that Choctaw women left their homes during their menstrual periods, seemingly to placate men who believed a menstruating woman would cause illness and bad luck in battle. Choctaw women went into the woods alone and bore babies without assistance. They also disciplined female children, but never males.[50]

Still other Europeans recorded similar customs among other Native American groups, but added that once a wife became a mother she was accorded a degree of respect.[51] "A crime considered frightful and unheard of among the Indians is that of a son rebellious to his mother," wrote François René de Chateaubriand in 1827.[52] According to Bremer, native men especially esteemed the mothers of distinguished warriors.[53]

The division of work among native women and men was another matter for concern. Reportedly, women were expected to take part in all domestic and agricultural labor, while men were expected "only" to hunt, fish, care for their animals and weapons, and conduct warfare. Although the list of men's duties appears demanding and dangerous, most Europeans, who were products of settled agrarian or industrial backgrounds, saw men's tasks as light, incidental, and even amusing. As a case in point, French traveler Edouard de Montule depicted Indian males as hunters and fighters because they were "by nature very lazy in cultivating the land or in working as do civilized people."[54] Rare indeed was the perspective of a traveler such as Friedrich Gerstacker, who argued that "in a state of society where the lives of the family depend upon the success of the hunter, he must have his arms free and unencumbered for action at every minute, and dare not toil under a heavy load, for it would make his aim unsteady."[55]

Nearly every traveler lamented the plight of women, explaining that they carried out all domestic chores, labored in the fields, and tended the family and its housing while their mates did little or nothing (that is, they hunted, fished, fought, and took care of religious duties).[56] Some writers even reached the extreme of claiming that Indian men did no work and sometimes had to be carried on their wives' backs because they were too indolent to walk home from hunting.[57]

This portrait was drawn so often that it became a truism. "The man smokes peacefully while the woman grinds corn in a mortar," Louis-Phillippe wrote. "The men in domestic life are exceedingly slothful," traveler John Davis stated.[58] "The squaw has to toil," Pulzsky observed, "the man but to fight, to hunt, to play, and to speak in council."[59] And according to Hodgson, "The women were hard at work . . . [while] the men were either setting out to the woods with their guns, or lying idle before doors."[60]

Many European onlookers thus concluded that Native American women were animals or slaves. Indians "look upon women in a totally different light from what we do in Europe, and condemn them as slaves to do all the drudgery," one explained during the 1790s.[61] "The women are forced to do the hardest work, and are treated like slaves," emphasized another in 1845.[62] "The wife of an Indian is his marketable animal," yet another maintained in 1847.[63] English botanist John Bradbury claimed that as a result of their drudgery, "mothers frequently destroy their female children, alleging as a reason, that it is better they should die than lead a life so miserable as that to which they are doomed."[64]

These inaccurate accounts occurred because observers usually saw only village life. While they had many opportunities to watch native women carry out domestic chores, they seldom had a chance to witness native men engaged in a demanding buffalo hunt, deadly warfare, or various rites such as a sweat lodge ceremony. Since Europeans came from an industrialized society where hunting and fishing had become little more than a leisure sport and warfare a matter for a trained few, they had little conception of the skill and peril entailed in such pursuits. Thus, in their eyes, native women got the worst of the bargain, while men got the best.[65]

Another complicating factor was observers' lack of direct contact with Native American women. Even trappers and missionaries who became acquainted with native women frequently allowed self-interest and prejudice to bias their reports.[66] In addition, most Europeans overlooked especially accomplished women. Although some Indian women became exceptional equestrians, daring warriors, revered medicine people, and venerated religious leaders, only a few anthropologists, historians, and native women serving as tribal, family, or personal historians have passed on their stories. European observers were apparently oblivious to such Indian women as Elk Hollering, Running Eagle, and Old Lady Drives the Enemy.[67] Still other problems distorted the perception of white Europeans. Because most Europeans regarded the roles and positions of white women as inferior, it was difficult for them to understand the view of many native groups that men and women were separate but equal.[68] They failed to see that men and women were proud of their duties, which they performed faithfully and well. An American Indian woman could insult another by saying, "You let your husband carry burthens [sic]," yet, to European ears, this sounded like a complaint.[69] Neither could Europeans understand that an American Indian male walking in front of a female did not indicate inferiority of the female; rather, because the male was expendable, he placed himself in front to protect the valuable female who propagated and cared for the race.[70] Nor did the visitors see that separate dances and amusements did not indicate male disdain for women.[71] In addition, European observers apparently did not realize the irony in their descriptions of native women beribboned and bedecked with ornaments, beads, and finely worked clothing, since such women hardly epitomized contemptible, degraded slaves.[72] Further, Europeans exclaimed upon the exquisite basketry, ingenious quillwork, and fine weaving of Indian women.[73] Maximilian, for example, admired the porcupine quill work, leather dresses and shirts, and buffalo robes produced by Crow women he encountered.[74] Europeans seemed unable to realize that such skills could not be achieved or such crafts produced by slave-like beasts with no leisure time to develop the marks of a cultured, productive society.[75]

Clearly, Europeans appear to have been terribly inaccurate reporters and image-makers of Indian women in the American West. This occurred as a result of several basic attitudes and occurrences. First, those Europeans who actually traveled in the West were often disconcerted because their observations failed to confirm inaccurate and unrealistic expectations they had derived from novels and other biased sources. Disappointment was common, in part because Europeans had been almost obsessed with information about American culture and character from the founding of the first colonies.

Viewing America as a child who would fulfill their thwarted wishes and dreams, Europeans had marveled at American space, land, abundant food, progress, and freedom, characteristics that their narrow and impoverished environment seemed to lack.[76] As a result, European expectations were derived through a filter that not only shaped but often distorted vision. In other words, they were willing to believe almost anything. As one late nineteenth-century writer explained it, most Europeans "judge by what they have read and their opinion would be perfectly justified, were it not that with few exceptions authors have seemed to centre their attention on the careful collection of as many instances of barbarism and crime as their pens could lay hold of . . ."[77]

Moreover, this European tendency toward wish fulfillment was encouraged by successive American settlements. Each wave of expansion appeared to be one more promise, one more opportunity for the redemption of the decayed world that Europeans inhabited. Many commentators thus reached new heights of exaggeration and inaccuracy as time passed, even if they had seen very little of the West. As English writer Isabella Bird approached Rock Island, Illinois, she rhapsodized, "On we flew to the West, the land of Wild Indians and Buffaloes."[78] Others who waxed eloquent despite limited exposure included William Cobbett, who visited Indiana in 1818, Alexis de Tocqueville, who traveled over New York and Michigan in the 1830s, and Albert Koch, who toured the easternmost area of Iowa in the 1840s.[79]

Also, Native American women were perhaps often seen as primitive and crude because they were symbols of opposition and challenge to Anglo expansion. While they could occasionally be credited with a spark of beauty, warmth, or creativity, in the final analysis they had to be grouped with their men as poor, degraded people meant for subjugation and extinction. The willingness of so many Europeans to see Native American women as savages was a logical outcome of their pervasive belief that white people were destined to inherit the earth and, most immediately, the American West.

The writings of American authors also shaped Europeans' vision of the West. James Fenimore Cooper's Leatherstocking Tales, for example, not only provided idealized notions of Indians and settlers, but also created a vast market for other dramatic western literature, including the widely read dime novel.[80] By the early twentieth century, formula novels regaled European audiences with western character types, including Indians characterized as "savages," "pesky redskins," "red devils," "cussed redskins," and "bloodthirsty wretches" who could speak only broken English.[81]

European authors quickly recognized the widespread popularity of such themes and exploited them fully. In Germany, for example, popular novelists developed a deep and continuing affinity for western motifs, including wilderness, violence, and the American Indian. Such authors as Charles Sealsfield, Friedrich Gerstacker, Friedrich Armand Strubberg, and Balduin Möllhausen presented adventure novels that featured German-born protagonists as heroes of the American West. The German fascination reached its apex in the writings of Karl May, who was often called Germany's Cooper, but who did not visit the West until he had already written most of his western adventures. He was an expert at combining his own imagined "facts" with bits and pieces of information to produce tales that well-served the wishes and needs of his readers.

Finally, these European writers were largely middle- and upper-class, well-educated, and usually male. Consequently, they were unprepared by background or experience to serve as accurate reporters of the West and its peoples. Whether they analyzed early settlements in New England, the Midwest, or the Far West, their perceptions were so permeated by image and myth that objectivity was nearly impossible. Given this situation, how could European interpreters of the American West possibly write with anything approaching accuracy?

Unfortunately—at least from today's perspective—the result was too often superficial, biased descriptions of Indian society and culture, descriptions that were nevertheless read and taken as accurate accounts of Native Americans. The negative view of American Indian women that resulted persuaded generation after generation of Europeans and Americans to believe that American Indian women were either princesses or squaws.

The following excerpts from an interview with an Indian woman living in Vinita, Oklahoma, during the 1930s offer a necessary corrective to Europeans' narrow and often negative perceptions of Native Americans. Her story demonstrates that many native women were neither pampered princesses nor degraded squaws:

I was born on a farm, near Welling, now Cherokee County, of Tahlequah on September 16, 1858. . . .

My grandfather . . . and [his] brother . . . both married full blood Cherokee sisters [in Tennessee]. . . . About 1831 he and his brother rigged up a small steamboat and with their families and thirty other families, they set sail for the Indian Territory and landed at Barren Fork, near Fort Gibson. Here they built cabins and established their residence for four years before the "Old Settler" Cherokees arrived from Georgia. At Barren Fork, they established "New Hope Mission," with the Reverend Mr. O'Brien, a missionary, in charge. . . . My grandmother, at the age of sixteen, had joined the Presbyterian Church at Brainard Mission in Georgia, January 31, 1819. She wrote the first hymn ever written by a Cherokee. This hymn came to her in a dream. . . .

When the Civil War broke out, my father took his family to the Choctaw Nation which was headquarters for the Southern Army. He built a cabin for us to live in and then joined the army. . . . When we returned after the war our house was burned and all of our stock . . . had been shot or stolen. My grandmother's house was still standing, near Wauhilla, in Tahlequah District and we moved into her house. . . .

My father thought it unsafe to remain longer in the Tahlequah District and moved his family farther to the northwest, to what he termed "The Great Wide Prairie," where he could find peace and quiet for himself and family. We landed in the Pheasant Hill District seven miles northwest of the present town of Vinita in 1872.

My mother graduated with the first class that graduated from the [Tahlequah] Female Seminary in 1855 and she taught school before the Civil War. . . . I received my education at the Female Seminary in Tahlequah and the Moody College, Northfield, Massachusetts, being a graduate of both schools. When I finished school, I went to the Creek Nation and taught three years, then I returned to the Cherokee Nation and taught in the Cherokee Orphan Asylum, under Joseph F. Thompson, as superintendent. I went from there to the Female Seminary and taught a number of years. . . .[82]

Buffalo Bird Woman's description of courting and marriage customs reveals that Hidatsa Indians had strict rules that were probably difficult for outsiders to understand. Here she recounted some of her people's practices in North Dakota before the U.S. government relocated her nation on the Fort Berthold Reservation in the mid-1880s:

My great-grandmother, as white men count their kin, was named Ata'kic, or Soft-white Corn. She adopted a daughter, Mata'tic, or Turtle. Some years after, a daughter was born to Ata'kic, whom she named Otter.

Turtle and Otter both married. Turtle had a daughter named Ica'wikec, or Corn Sucker, and Otter had three daughters, Want-to-be-a-woman, Red Blossom, and Strikes-many-women, all younger than Corn Sucker.

The smallpox year at Five Villages left Otter's family with no male members to support them. Turtle and her daughter were then living in Otter's lodge; and Otter's daughters, as Indian custom bade, called Corn Sucker their elder sister.

It was a custom of the Hidatsas, that if the eldest sister of a household married, her younger sisters were also given to her husband, as they came of marriageable age. Left without male kin by the smallpox, my grandmother's family was hard put to it to get meat; and Turtle gladly gave her daughter to my father, Small Ankle, whom she knew to be a good hunter. Otter's daughters, reckoned as Corn Sucker's sisters, were given to Small Ankle as they grew up; the eldest, Want-to-be-a-woman, was my mother. . . . smallpox again visited my tribe; and my mother, Want-to-be-a-woman, and Corn Sucker, died of it. Red Blossom and Strikes-many-women survived, whom I now called my mothers. Otter and old Turtle lived with us; I was taught to call them my grandmothers.

. . . Our tribe's customs in such things [courtship and marriage] were well understood. The youths of the village used to go about all the time seeking the girls; this indeed was almost all they did. Of course, when the girls were on the watchers' stage [guarding ripening corn from theft] the boys were pretty sure to come around. . . . If there were relatives at the watchers' stage the boys would stop and drink or eat; they did not try to talk to the girls, but would come around smiling and try to get the girls to smile back.

To illustrate our custom, if a boy came out to a watchers' stage, we girls that were sitting upon it did not say a word to him. . . . He would smile and perhaps stop and get a drink of water.

Indeed, a girl that was not a youth's sweetheart, never talked to him. This rule was observed at all times. Even when a boy was a girl's sweetheart, or "love-boy" as we called him, if there were other persons around, she did not talk to him, unless these happened to be relatives. . . . In olden days, mothers watched their daughters very carefully.[83]

The responses of a Yavapai Indian woman to a white interviewer in 1967 poignantly reveal a spiritual and moral depth that would have surprised many

Europeans. She also explained why whites and Indians must always be at odds. Nellie Quail was born in 1882 and raised on the San Carlos reservation near Prescott, Arizona:

When we went to school, the government said, don't teach them the bible because they wouldn't understand. There are too many churches, but give them hymn books, let them sing, so I don't know nothing about the bible, but I do know, from my Indian[s], about the great spirit. They teach just this: thou shalt not steal. That's what the mother tells the daughter, and the father tells the son. That covers everything, you know that. Covers everything. Don't steal somebody's wife or husband or horse or blanket or shoes or what. That's what they mean, see? That one commandment covers all, I always say, from our Indians, but [the whites] have ten. . . . it comes from heaven, they say, but they learn it, and they don't do those things. . . .

You know, sometimes white people don't like Indians very well, and we don't like white people very well. We are different tribes, that's how we are. We have our own ways to live, everything, we live our own way. We're given the way we should live. . . . It's better to keep it away from them, and them have better keep theirs, and you run your own way. Maybe God did that, we don't know, see, because we'll never get along if we mingle with our religion and yours, and our ways of life in living and all that. You don't like the way we live. I don't like it, now, the way you dress, see? The way you dress is, I don't like it, see. That's the way it will be, we'll never get along. . . .[84]

That women were esteemed among many Native American groups is revealed by their myths. Unlike European and American settlers, some Indians believed that a woman created the world or that a woman was the savior of their people. This story is still frequently repeated by Sioux Indians:

Eons ago, my people lived in a sad state of affairs. They knew little and didn't understand how to communicate with the Great Spirit. Also, they were starving. They didn't have horses and their hunters were unable to find game to kill. Every day hunters went out from the camps, but returned empty-handed. Then one day, two young hunters ventured far from camp in search of animals. Finally, they saw something coming toward them. But instead of an animal, it was a woman—a holy woman floating along just above the ground.

The woman seemed to draw the sun so the young men could not see her form. But as she drew near, they saw that she was young and beautiful. She was dressed in white buffalo calfskin that shone in the sun, reflecting its glory into the two men's eyes. Her dark hair hung loose down her back and her black eyes glistened with knowledge and power.

When one of the young men desired her, he became nothing more than a pile of bones on the ground. To the other, who was pure of heart, she gave a message. "Return to your people," she said, "and help them prepare for my arrival. I have come to bring knowledge and salvation to them."

The man did as he was told and the people rejoiced. They prepared the village for her arrival, making everything holy to receive her. After a few days, she entered the camp, her white calfskin dress gleaming as before. The people greeted her and asked the White Buffalo Calf Woman to instruct them. Then they noticed she carried something wrapped in skin. They prepared a holy altar to receive her gift.

When all was in readiness, she opened her sacred bundle and revealed a pipe. She lifted it with her right hand on the stem and her left hand on the bowl. She filled the pipe with tobacco and lit it with a coal from the fire. She indicated that the sacred smoke would carry their messages. She showed them how to pray and chant and gesture to urge the smoke and its entreaties on its way toward the sacred sky. She then bowed toward the sacred earth and toward the four corners of the world.

White Buffalo Calf Woman spoke to the men and boys about their responsibilities as hunters and warriors and to the women and girls about their duties as workers who produced fruits from the earth and from their bodies. She reminded the men and women that they were equally important, and that they were to make the sacred pipes together in a spirit of love and harmony.

She told the people that the Great Spirit would now be with them. As she walked off toward the setting sun, she turned first into a black buffalo, then into a brown one, then into a red one, and just before she disappeared into the horizon, she became a white female buffalo calf. Sometime later, White Buffalo Calf Woman sent the buffalo to us. They gave us their meat, skins, and bones so that we might live and flourish.

After that holy time, my people honored the Buffalo Woman Calf with dances and ceremonies. They chose a respected woman of the tribe to represent her and thanked her for her teachings and her gifts. But then the white settlers came and destroyed the buffalo and most of the Indians. Perhaps someday White Buffalo Calf Woman will come to us again.[85]

1.2
European Views of White Women in the American West

European observers of the American West were legion; a collection of their works would consume incalculable thousands of feet of shelf space. Yet, despite the torrent of words that spectators expended on describing, analyzing,

1.2: Adapted from *Journal of the West* 21 (April 1982), 71–81. Used by permission. A bibliographic essay accompanied the original article; it is available by writing Glenda Riley, Department of History, Ball State University, Muncie, Indiana.

and criticizing the people who so fascinated them, it is impossible to derive a clear picture of western Americans from European writings. The portraits that Europeans drew tended to be ones of extremes, truisms, and fantasy. In addition, they focused on Anglo settlers while overlooking African Americans, Hispanics, and Asians.

White westerners, as seen through European eyes, frequently loomed larger than life. As inhabitants of a strange, new region characterized by danger and opportunity, these people often seemed to be atypical specimens of humankind. The vices as well as the virtues of white western Americans were magnified by many curious Europeans who attempted to fathom the reality of western life.

In addition, most of these European commentators had poorly defined impressions of the American West. The popular French writer, Chateaubriand, traveled only briefly in the United States in 1791. Although he only went as far west as upstate New York, he confidently produced a series of "Indian" novels, a detailed commentary on his experience in America, and a string of observations regarding inhabitants of the West. The American West was clearly more of a mythical image than a geographical region to many Europeans.

Most European commentators were middle- or upper-class; to them, the absence of a candle snuffer seemed a barbarity, and a person who blew his or her nose without a handkerchief an affront. Moreover, women travelers experienced considerable physical discomfort and social disapproval. Their numbers were few, so assessments of westerners were left largely to males and their gender-associated values and biases.

As a result, whether they commented upon early settlements in New England in the 1600s, the Midwest of the early nineteenth century, or the Far West of the late nineteenth century, Europeans' ideas were so permeated with image and myth that factual reporting was elusive at best. Yet European observations about white settlers are worth exploring, for they presented westerners to generations of Europeans who were extremely curious about the mysteries of the American West. European views also helped shape the ways in which white westerners thought about themselves, thus contributing further to the myths and inaccurate images.

European interpretations of white western women also reflect the confusion generated in many Europeans' minds when their traditional values clashed with new, liberal, and innovative ones. Given their customary and conservative ideas regarding women's "place," what could Europeans possibly think when they confronted relatively independent, free, even gun-toting women? Yet, when one recalls their belief that Anglos were destined to conquer the West and its native populations, it is not surprising to learn that they also accepted the notion that white women were heroic conquerors.

This dichotomous manner of thinking resulted in contrasting judgments regarding white women settlers; they ranged from shock and outrage to paeans of praise. The one view that European observers generally agreed upon was that white women, shaped in the crucible of the western environment, were unique among women. To many Europeans, these women were a distinct and superior breed of females.

Of course, as products of a male-dominated era, many Europeans neglected specifically to mention the experience of women in their commentaries. They either subsumed women in a discussion of men or ignored them. Thus, when Francis Grund stated that nine-tenths of the immigrants to the West were farmers, one might reasonably assume he meant that women also engaged in agrarian-related pursuits. But when Charles Dickens noted that western men of any grade could climb the social ladder, when Brissot de Warville asserted that men were brave and aggressive, and when W. Faux declared that nine-tenths of the adult population in the West owned land, it is likely that they were omitting women because they did not regard them as having social status. Such men also believed that women could not be brave or aggressive and that they were not personally or legally qualified to own land.

Other Europeans may have ignored white women settlers because they were relatively few in number. Those Europeans who commented upon women frequently mentioned their scarcity. An Italian traveler estimated the ratio of men to women in Colorado during the 1870s as 15 to 1, while one British traveler placed it as high as 20 to 1. "The cry is everywhere for girls; girls; and more girls," he wrote in 1869. Another British traveler reported that a Denver man was willing to pay "a ten-dollar piece to have seen the skirt of a servant-girl a mile off," while the British newspaper, the *American Settler*, reported that a Durango newspaper claimed that "the greatest want in Colorado is women, especially those who can get themselves up in good form; who will go to Church and Bible-class on Sunday; who can wait at table" and "above all . . . for sweethearts."

Despite the scarcity of white women, at least during the early years of settlement, many Europeans did frequently include women in their remarks. But they often looked at women primarily as sexual and ornamental beings. Consequently, many commentaries concentrated upon such superficial factors as physical appearance, beauty, and dress. A few reporters were graphic in their descriptions. A Frenchman, Edouard de Montule, declared that white women were "on the whole very pretty and shapely" but that he had encountered only one woman who had "truly lovely breasts (which American women rarely have)." Western women were, he wrote, "generally pleasing; and, with due respect to the amiable ladies of Philadelphia, they are much more attractive in the West than in the regions bordering the coast."

Some Europeans concurred with Montule. Charles Sealsfield asserted that western women were "considered very handsome" and Fredrika Bremer that "one seems to meet nothing but handsome faces, scarcely a countenance . . . may be called ugly."

Other observers disputed these judgments. Some thought that few women were beautiful; rather, they believed that women grew old prematurely, their beauty faded, and their health disintegrated. They attributed this to a harsh climate, heavy labor, and poor diet. One British traveler, William Shepard, thought that women displayed dull, expressionless faces due to hard work, poverty, and cheerless lives. Tocqueville believed that despite "fever, solitude, and a tedious life" in a "comfortless home" in the "Western wilds," most women had not lost "the springs of their courage." To him, "their features were impaired and faded, but their looks were firm: they appeared to be at once sad and resolute. I do not doubt that these young American women had amassed, in the education of their early years, that inward strength which they displayed under these circumstances."

European observers were in closer agreement concerning the style of these women's dress. Friedrich Gerstacker stated that white women "even of the lowest classes . . . were simply but tastefully dressed." During a Fourth of July celebration he was startled that the women changed their dresses four or five times between noon and the following morning. He concluded that since they had little chance to display their wardrobes, they had to seize any opportunity to do so. Some commentators mentioned Sunday church services as an occasion for women to flaunt their apparel. According to Frances Trollope, women attended church in "full costume," while Montule explained that "confined within the small, cleared spaces in the midst of this wilderness, they impatiently await Sunday, the only day when they can see each other, and be seen; therefore, they make the most of the occasion." Others recalled seeing stylish women in other circumstances. Tocqueville considered women walking along the streets of Albany to be "well turned out," Moritz Busch thought Kentucky horsewomen dressed "in modish costume," and Theresa Pulszky judged women standing in the doors of log houses in the Allegheny Mountains to be elegantly dressed.

Although many Europeans discussed only the physical appearance of white western women, some were curious about how these women were treated by reputedly rough and unpolished western men and about the status of white women in western society. They were generally impressed that men extended a great deal of courtesy and respect to women, but tended to attribute this respect to the efforts of women themselves. Gerstacker argued that women inspired respect by their energy and grace, while Charles Sealsfield agreed that they were "well entitled" to chivalrous attention.

Yet others felt that male chivalry was a sham and limited in practice. Harriet Martineau derided it as a poor substitute for justice. In her eyes, "ungentle, tyrannical" men fell below their own democratic principles in their treatment of women. Another woman, Frances Trollope, also doubted the value that western men placed upon women. As she watched women "amusing" themselves in exercises at religious revival she asked, "Did the men of America value their woman as men ought to value their wives and daughters, would such scenes be permitted among them?" Other criticism came from Gerstacker, who disliked the custom decreeing that women could eat only after men had finished, and from Henryk Sienkiewicz, who thought it grossly uncultured for men not wearing coats or even boots to talk with ladies.

But many others Europeans found contrasting examples. Charles Lyell stated that women always seated themselves at the table before men, Charles Dickens that "no man sat down until the ladies were seated," and Gottfried Duden that women were always served before the men. Alexander Mackay was astounded that men were willing to forego spitting and chewing in the presence of women; this constituted a "gallant self-denial" in his view. And Eilert Storm marvelled that in the West "where a woman has all rights over against a man, while the latter has none over against her, a judge finds it very difficult to sentence a woman, and for a jury that is even more difficult."

Clearly, these onlookers were not grappling with the issue raised by Martineau and Trollope: did men's outward respect toward white women stem from a deeper, more lasting esteem? Most observers did not consider this question; they tended to assume that a woman's pedestal automatically connoted progress and freedom. Consequently, many travelers, men and women alike, appeared to be disproportionately awed by the safety with which a white woman could travel in the West. Von Raumer emphasized that women could travel alone through the "whole country" because even men who were rough in relations with other men extended courtesy to women; Gerstacker maintained that "often one will see young girls and women who undertake long journeys alone and without protection, for they find in every companion a protector and friend . . . we know here in the forest of nothing more cowardly and mean than the mistreatment of a woman."

Since most European travelers toured America for a short time and derived their opinions from limited contact with white women on steamboats and stagecoaches, it is perhaps understandable that they drew conclusions from surface evidence rather than by delving into women's situations, as Martineau might have preferred. As a result, steamboat and stagecoach stories regarding the preferential treatment of women assumed the proportions of legends. A Norwegian traveler described one captain's table as having empty chairs separating the ladies and the captain from the male passengers. John Xantus seemed amazed that when a stagecoach was filled and a lady wanted to board,

> the last gentleman who got on will give up his seat, get off and wait for
> the next coach, which sometimes may take a week; or he may have to
> proceed on foot or horseback. This happens so many times that it
> does not even occur to the party involved to grumble about it, even
> though it may be raining hard when he casually gives up his seat as if
> it were the most natural thing in the world.

While so many European spectators of the western scene seemed enamored with the public treatment of women by men, there were those who attempted to examine other aspects of white women's lives, such as education. They tended to agree that women's education was pervasive and of high quality. Pulszky pointed out that women's schools were common and that home education was rarer in the West than in the East. Busch, upon viewing a Cincinnati ladies' school, was pleased that such "an offspring of fashionable refinement does exist and is flourishing," while Trollope was impressed that it had "higher branches of science." Ranging further west, Bremer visited a ladies' school in Wisconsin whereupon she remarked that "an important reformation in female schools is taking place in these Western States at the present time under the guidance of a Miss Beecher."

Other visitors were struck by westerner's penchant for coeducation. Although Charles Varogny wrote that it was "strange instruction, and strange schools . . . in which girls and boys sat together," he concluded that such schools produced women who were sure of themselves, able to compete with men, and capable of eliciting respect from men. William Bell had a similar response to the coeducation movement in Kansas. To him it was little wonder that there was scarcely a political contest in Kansas in which "petticoats are not well to the front; and that woman's suffrage and equal rights form part of each platform in every election." He added that it would take a particularly bold Kansas man to oppose "openly the phalanx of political Amazons."

But were these observers impressed by the existence and unusual formats of these women's schools or by their quality? Several remarks suggest that some commentators confused academic education in such subjects as English, history, and science with "female accomplishments," including fancy needlework, pianoforte playing, and cultivation of literary interests. For instance, Sealsfield stated that Cincinnati women evinced "a high taste for literary and mental accomplishments" and had originated the *Literary Gazette*. Another traveler noted that women living in boardinghouses in western towns filled their hours with reading and attending public lectures. Yet another explained that women were given more time to cultivate accomplishments than men; as a result, they were more civilized than men.

Several female critics of women's schools believed that confusion did exist in many people's minds between the existence of ladies' schools and meaningful education for women. After visiting backwoods New York in 1818, Frances Wright declared that although there had been strides in women's education, it was still puerile. Until it became "the concern of the state," she argued, women's education would provide little of real use. Martineau believed that women's education tended to be rote rather than based on intellectual activity. She was particularly incensed by a young ladies' school she visited in New Madrid, Missouri, in the late 1830s. "There are public exhibitions of their proficiency, and the poor ignorant little girls take degrees," she wrote scathingly. "Their heads must be so stuffed with vain-glory that there can be little room for anything else." Fredrika Bremer was even more vitriolic on the subject. Visiting St. Louis in 1850, she stated in disgust that women were physically weak due to their "effeminate education" and lived a constricted "harem life" as pampered sultanesses with male subjects. "The harems of the West," she continued, "no less than those of the East, degrade the life and the consciousness of women." According to Martineau, the only possible life course open to women educated in this manner was marriage.

Of course, women *were* in demand as wives. European analysts carried on at length regarding the need for wives. Assuming, as did most people of the era, that all women desired matrimony as soon as possible, one Norwegian declared that the West was an "El Dorado" for women. Another advised his hometown newspaper in Norway to publish the advice, "Go west, young woman." Another insisted that even those women who "crossed the line," a Norwegian folk expression for those who strayed from the straight and narrow, were marriageable in the West.

Many Europeans were also fascinated by the early marriages that population imbalances seemed to encourage. As early as 1698, an English farmer stated that American women usually married before twenty and soon "hath a child in her Belly, or one upon her Lap." The following year another Englishman said that women thought they were ready for husbands by age thirteen and were "very Fruitful, which shows the Men are Industrious in Bed, tho' Idle up."

This trend toward early marriage seemed to move westward, for accounts of thirteen to fifteen-year-old brides commonly appeared in traveler's journals, immigrant's accounts, and novels. Not only did white women supposedly marry young, but according to onlookers, they immediately remarried after the death of a spouse. "Matrimony, like death," charged one writer, "spares neither age nor condition. I have seen young girls of thirteen and hideous old girls of fifty snapped up eagerly as soon as they arrived in the country."

Europeans thought it unusual that young white men and women selected their own mates, decided on marriage before consulting their parents, and eschewed a dowry. A few disapproved of the freedom to marry without parental consent or the usual formalities. One traveler was particularly horrified when he saw a young couple meet on a riverboat and decide to marry. When the minister could not reach them due to ice, they knelt on the deck and were wed despite the distance between themselves and the shore-bound minister.

Travelers were also amazed how little time was spent on courting. According to Pulszky, a man simply paid a few calls to a neighbor with an eligible daughter: he "places himself in a chair before the chimney, chews, spits in the fire" and eventually offers a proposal of marriage. A German traveler described the process in a similar way.

> The American is abrupt; he has no time to beat around the bush. He meets a girl in a shop, in the theater, at a ball, or in her parents' home. He needs a wife, thinks this one will do. He asks the question, she answers. The next day they are married and then proceed to inform the parents.

Many Europeans believed that such practices created social problems. One was the breakdown of the family because children departed at such young ages to form their own families. But many felt that the great power that accrued to wives was the most pernicious ill. A husband could go nowhere without his wife, the *American Settler* reported in 1892. Worse yet, wives expected their husbands to be extremely affable for, as one young western woman quipped, "if he don't there's plenty will." Such wives purportedly refused to do barn work, negotiated prenuptial agreements, and even ordered servants to flog errant husbands.

If women were displeased with their marriages, they reputedly sought divorces with little hesitation or social recrimination. In 1830, Simon O'Ferrall noted that three divorces were granted during his brief stay in Marion, Ohio. All three were brought by women: one for desertion, one for physical abuse, and one for general neglect. O'Ferrall added that women were seldom refused a divorce in the West; dislike of a husband was considered a sufficient reason for granting a woman her freedom.

Stories of such behavior caused many immigrants to conclude that such women were so spoiled that a proper wife had to be imported. This reputation was perhaps undeserved, for when critics turned their attention to women's domestic labors they were usually complimentary. Although an occasional visitor depicted wives as living in "sloth and inactivity," others were pleased that women were not as lazy as rumored. Still others presented women as very diligent indeed. According to Sealsfield, a farm woman was "in motion from morning till evening." William Blane was even more laudatory. In his view, these women were "the most industrious females" he had seen in any country.

These women reportedly never worked in the fields, however. As early as 1656, an English farmer pointed out that "the women are not (as is reported) put into the ground to worke, but occupie such domestique employments as in England." Similar accounts followed as white settlements spread across the continent. British travelers consistently characterized white women as hard workers in the home who were spared "unwomanly employment" in the fields. In 1841 one Englishman emphasized that "every man here, rich or poor, seems on all occasions sedulously to give place and precedence to females, and the meanest of them are exempt, or I might rather say debarred, from those masculine or laborious tasks which are commonly enough assigned the sex, or assumed by them, in our country."

Other European observers confirmed these reports. During the 1820s, a German traveler said that "not even the poorest farmer allows his wife or daughter to work in the fields." In 1860, a Swedish immigrant wrote that "the women never work in the fields—not even milking cows." Various reasons for many white women's exemption from field work were suggested. Most analysts believed that the high regard paid women explained the situation, but one suggested that the cost of imported British textiles caused women to be "chiefly employed in making articles of domestic clothing."

It is interesting that observers assumed that restriction to domestic labor meant a relatively easy life for women. They often characterized migrants' wives and daughters as "ladies" who would not condescend to draw their own water from a well. In 1848, a Swedish farmer in Illinois wrote that "women do not have to do any other work here but wash clothes and cups and keep the house tidied up and at some places also cook food." A Frenchman traveling in Kansas in the 1870s also presented white women's lives as easy: "An American woman's only job is to make a home and to make little Americans; we were never able to make the women there understand that country women in France work on the land and know how to do it almost as well as their husbands."

Some European women who had recently chosen to become westerners themselves presented another side to the picture. Elisabeth Koren felt that women did nothing but cook, thus having little time for other chores, much less for leisure. Gro Svendsen pointed out that, although women were supposed to have much leisure time, she had not met any who thought they had time or energy to spare. And Rebecca Burlend said she worked in the fields because her husband was unable to find a hired hand.

These comments suggest that white women not only worked long and hard hours within their homes but labored in the fields whenever necessary. Other accounts indicate that women refused to limit themselves to traditional tasks and responsibilities. Women, for example, did not hesitate to take up arms in their own defense. Busch remarked that in the early years of settlement "everyone was a soldier, and even the women know how to handle a rifle," while Gustave Aimard said that women often "take a rifle in their delicate hands, and fight boldly in defense of the community." He added that "women fight by the side of the men, and forgetting the weakness of their sex, they can, on occasion, prove themselves as brave as their husbands and brothers."

Other Europeans related stories of white women moving into what were believed to be male areas. Women who ran businesses or who served as judges or as university professors were among the cases mentioned. Not constrained by gender or social class distinctions as in Europe, women apparently achieved some latitude in their roles.

European responses to women's endeavors ranged from shock and surprise to dismay and puzzlement. Most observers appeared to feel more comfortable with women who used their talents in traditional female ways, particularly as civilizing forces in western areas. Women exercising their moral powers were something most Europeans could understand and applaud. British visitors seemed delighted to observe that many women exerted a stabilizing force in the West. According to one, women were second only to religion in helping refine the new society. Another writer was enthusiastic in his description of women's salutary influence:

> A lady is a power in this country. From the day when a silk dress and a lace shawl were seen on Main Street, that thoroughfare became passably clean and quiet; oaths were less frequently heard, knives were less frequently drawn; pistols were less frequently fired.

Other spectators said that women were judges of decency, guardians of humanity, cement of a society that "without woman, is like an edifice built on sand." Henryk Sienkiewicz insisted that women so softened the brutal habits of one western town that "the men argued still, but quietly. Bowie knives remained in their sheaths and revolvers in the pocket. Cards were not played so fiercely and only cocktails were drunk, instead of the usual enormous draughts of whiskey."

If these portraits of western women seem to embody superior beings, it is perhaps because many Europeans believed that these women were in fact superior. Despite the contradictions and disagreements regarding women's lives, roles, and actions, the overall assessment that emerged was that these American women enjoyed a superior situation and knew how to use this advantage fairly and well.

Europeans were very fond of comparing western women's lives with those of women in other countries. They stressed again and again that western women received more respect than women anywhere else in the world; they also emphasized that women wielded more power in their homes and in society than did women in other regions of the world. One Dutch traveler, Tutein Nolthenius, wrote that western women "are different from our womenfolk, who are kept inferior female animals from force of habit and superstition." Moreover, Europeans often pointed out that western women faced more opportunities within the institution of marriage, in the schools and colleges, and in employment than did other women.

Many Europeans credited women for taking the fullest possible advantage of these conditions. The *American Settler*, for example, complimented women for making "good use" of the "free field" they found in the West. Others concluded that women's salutary situation resulted from a combination of environmental factors and women's own abilities. Challenged by the openness of the environment, western women responded by mustering strength that proved them the equals of men in almost every way. As Charles Varogny explained, a woman was relieved of her "chains" by the western setting, but "her duties won for her the equality with him which she sought."

Despite these glowing statements, there was little agreement regarding the status of women's rights in the West. Except for a few onlookers, such as Harriet Martineau and Fredrika Bremer, Europeans did not seem to see discrepancy between this vision of sexual equality and women's lack of legal rights. As a result, their descriptions of the women's rights movement in the West were contradictory and confusing. One observer, for instance, said that women did not "clamour" for their rights, but failed to explain why. Another castigated aggressive women who pushed to become "more than equal." Yet another lectured women that they should adhere to their "providential mission in this world." And another benignly remarked that those women who already exercised the right of suffrage were not creating social upheaval.

In light of their conservative view of women's rights, it is not difficult to understand why many Europeans evidenced confusion, concern, and disparate interpretations of women's political situation in the West. It appears that, due to their backgrounds and values, most European commentators were not yet ready to grapple with the realities of women's equality and rights, but were more interested in molding the myth of western women to meet their own needs and expectations.

Hemmed in by social convention and functionally unequal in most areas of life, Anglo western women did face a number of restrictions and problems.

Yet most Europeans did not see it that way. Compared to the tradition-bound situation and restricted status of European women, western women *appeared* to be free and equal. As inhabitants of the wonderfully progressive American West, women were thought to have been recipients of the human rights and pervasive spirit of equalitarianism that "enlightened" white people were supposedly cultivating in western settlements. To most European analysts, western women lived in a promised land indeed.[86]

The following reminiscence of Sarah Thal of Nelson County, North Dakota demonstrates that many women worked hard to make a success of their western venture. Sarah Thal was a German Jew whose life as a settler was far from idyllic:

When a child attending the religious school, the story of the sojourn of the Israelites in the Wilderness stirred my imagination. I too longed for a sojourn in the wilderness. I did not know that my dreams would become a reality, a reality covering long years of hardship and privation. I grew to womanhood in the town of Ellingen in the Saar Valley, and when I married Solomon Thal in 1880, I went to live in the picturesque village of Berg in the Mosel Valley. I remember this country as quiet and picturesque, where life was pleasant and peaceful.

My husband had brothers in Milwaukee who sent home glowing reports of conditions in America. We wished to try our luck in that wonderful land. When my daughter Elsie was fourteen months old we left to make our fortune, fully confident of our undertaking. We sailed from Antwerp and landed in Boston. I brought with me my linen chest, feather beds, pillows, bedding, etc. I have some bits of these things today. As most of the immigrants of that time were German, we reached Milwaukee without difficulty. Here my brother-in-law met us and took us to his home. I had become ill during the last part of the journey. I went to bed at once to learn I had typhoid.

My brother-in-law Sam Thal advised us to go to Dakota Territory. He had been out there and thought highly of the prospect. In fact, he had a large farm out there only twenty-eight miles from the railroad. My husband was anxious to get started and as soon as he could leave me he went out there. Six weeks later I followed. The only English I knew was "Yes" and "All right," and when my fellow passengers admired my baby and asked, "Is it a girl?" I said "Yes," and when they said "Is it a boy?" I said "Yes." I didn't know why they looked at each other and smiled. . . .

We had few neighbors. At Harrisburg there was a little settlement and owing to the large tract of land the farm stood on, we had only one near neighbor, the Seligers, and another Jewish family. We received mail rarely. A stage ran from Harrisburg to Larimore. The service was not dependable and getting mail was a big event. . . .

In the spring of '83 we homesteaded land in Dodds Township along the supposed railroad right of way. A Mr. Anderson, long since dead, built a four-room house. The lumber was hauled by ox-team from Lari-more. The nearest store was in Bartlett. We drove there to get some things we needed. Money was scarce and prices were outrageous. I paid $3.00 for a set of flat irons. . . .

That fall I would look out of the window and see [prairie] fires in the distance. These I believed were far off factories. I was still unable to real-ize the completeness of our isolation. . . .

That fall my second baby, Jacob, was born. I was attended by a Mrs. Saunders, an Englishwoman. We couldn't understand each other. It was in September. The weather turned cold and the wind blew from the north. It found its way through every crack in that poorly built house. I was so cold that during the first night they moved my bed into the living room by the stove and pinned sheets around it to keep the draft out and so I lived through the first child birth in the prairies. I like to think that God watched out for us poor lonely women when the stork came. All but two of my neighbors survived their many confinements and lived to see their children grown. . . .

One year all the Germans of the community were asked to a Fourth of July picnic at the Gutting Grove. We looked forward to this with great anticipation. I had just finished ironing the last piece for the next day's outing when I saw it clouding up, a greenish gray. The storm broke and with it came a terrific hailstorm, the worst in my memory. When over, our beautiful wheat was cut to the ground. The next morning the sun came out. We couldn't disappoint the children, we drove to the picnic, a distance of twenty-two miles, each way, around the lake and up and down the steep hills, a heavy day for a team. Each foreign colony cele-brated in their own fashion, loyal to the traditions of the old land and faithful to those of the new. . . .[87]

In recent years, historians have seriously grappled with the question of women's diversity. The following excerpts from Mary Annetta Coleman Pomeroy's life story offer a first-hand view into one variety of woman settler. As a Mormon woman who in 1881 moved from Utah to Mesa, Arizona, Pomeroy's life was similar in most respects to other women's, but her polygamous family situation differed from most:

I was born November 21, 1862 in Pinto, Utah. . . . My father had another wife, Elizabeth Eagles. She was the mother of Willie, who died when he was a baby; Willard died 1897, in August, at Alpine. He was struck by lightning. Della, who died also; Sue, Doll, John, June, died June 1893 at Springerville, of typhoid, and George. When George was born (1882) his mother died and our mother took the children. George was then only twelve hours old. This was a lot of trouble for her, but she cared for the children as if they were her own.

Mother and father's other wife lived in the same house; each had a separate apartment, however. Ma often left me with Aunt Lizzie but she always took Lell with her because no one would take care of her. She had a terrible temper. She has changed now. . . .

My father was a good dairyman. He took the dairy three miles from Pinto for one summer. (1870) The next year we lived on a ranch but before the summer was over the water began to fail and we moved back to town for the winter. That summer two good friends stayed with us; Lide Pomeroy and Sophy Gerry. During the summer we went to Camp Valley, Nevada. We were there two years. . . .

In 1872 we gave up the ranch and moved to Spring Valley where Evans was born. Mr. Heywood came from Washington, Utah, to teach school. He taught one summer and two winters. He began to make loving eyes at Lell. . . .

In 1875 Pa moved Aunt Lizzie out to Spring Valley and that same year Lell and Mr. Heywood were married. A very exciting year for us. Neal, Lell's first baby was born January 12, 1876. . . .

July, 1877, we moved to Upper Kanab [Utah]. My father cared for the Cannan herd of cattle. Cannan was the name of a company which dealt in cattle. . . . We milked a hundred and fifty cows. We made butter and cheese and in the fall took them to Salt Lake or Silver Reef to trade for wearing apparel. I do not know how my parents endured that life. My mother was interested in higher education and a better way of living, so I can easily guess how she felt about it.

When Lide [Pomeroy] came back to Utah in July neither my mother nor I thought anything about it. He was an old friend of the family and Pa enjoyed having him work about the farm because he was so careful. We had 150 milk cows and several corrals. Lide and I milked in the same corral and we often drove our cows together so we could talk while we milked. We went on several hay-rack rides and we had a very good time all that summer.

One night in October, 1878, a big thunder-shower came up. Lide and I had just finished washing the milk buckets. When I heard the thunder and saw the lightening I became frightened. Lightening had struck a tree not far from me once, and it had always terrified me since. I told Lide that I was frightened and he said, "Well, we'll just stay behind the kitchen door until it stops." Then he asked me to marry him! I do not remember what he said but I remember that my heart went pitter-patter and I could hardly say "Yes". . . .

October 12, 1879 Lide and I started to St. George to get married in the Temple. . . . We got to St. George on the 15th and were married on the 16th. . . .

July 4, 1880 a little girl came to take her abode with us. We called her Emma Charlotte. . . .

October 30, 1880 all of us started for Arizona. We went to Mesa and the others went to Bush Valley. We went about half a mile together, then separated. It was hard for me because I had never been away from the family for more than a month before. I didn't see them again until eight years had passed. . . .

Our wagon was very comfortable. My husband got a sheet-iron stove with two holes and an oven. He fixed the pipe so it would not come down when we were traveling. We had a double bed in the wagon and a shelf over it for our baggage. . . . We did all our cooking and baking on the stove. When we rested for a few days, Lide took our large brass bucket, put it on a stick between the spokes, and made a fire under it so I could wash. I had a small tub and board to wash with. I also had a small iron with which to iron the baby's clothes. . . .

I had always lived in a cold climate and I couldn't get used to such warm temperature when it was the first of March. It was so warm that we had to raise the wagon cover. . . .

Mesa was a very small town. A few rough adobe houses with dirt roofs and no windows. Some had no floors. They nailed cloth over the windows to keep out the dirt and flies.

John and Emily Pomeroy had one room made of saguaros and covered with dirt. In it were one six-paned window, and a door. (Besides the furniture, of course.) The house had a brush shed on three sides where they cooked and ate. We moved in their granary which was half full of wheat. We had our little sheet iron stove, a bed on a platform off the floor, a chair and a stool. Lide made a small table, put up shelves for a cupboard and nailed a cloth over the window.

We lived there seven months, sleeping on the ground when it became too hot, then we moved four blocks southwest on what is now Robson Street. We got a tent to cook in and slept in the wagon. Lide made adobes and William Newell built a house for us. The house had two rooms and a dirt roof. It had one six-paned window and one twelve-paned window. The kitchen had two holes covered with screen and two wire doors. Lide had some cattle which he sold in Tempe. With the money he bought a bed, one large rocker, three chairs, a gate-legged table, a clock and a stove. I was certainly surprised when he brought them home. We had rags enough for a carpet which we had woven. The carpet covered the floor of the room. We put straw under it and tacked it down. The kitchen had a dirt floor so I sewed gunny-sacks together and held them on the floor with wooden pegs. The house was white-washed and curtains were put up. I was never so happy in my life. I sat in the rocker, listening to the clock tick and watching the baby play on the floor and thought I should burst with pride. . . .

We were surely blessed! On October 11, 1882 a son was born. We called him Thales Coleman. . . .

In December 1882 Brother Thatcher, one of the twelve apostles, came to Arizona. The wards were organized and officers for them were appointed. . . .

In September, 1884 we decided to enter into the order of celestial marriage and started to St. George. Lucretia Phelps was the woman my husband chose. It was a great trial to me. Nobody but one who is in it knows the many heartaches which one goes through while living that order.

January 1, 1885 Elijah Haskell was born. It was a wonderful gift. He was such a good boy. . . .

Nothing but the dreary routine happened until November 20, 1886, when a bouncing baby girl, Irene Ursula, came to live with us. She weighed an even twelve pounds. . . .

December 13, 1888 another girl came to make her home with us. We called her Francelle Aeolia after our sisters. . . .

In 1890 the U. S. Government began serving warrants for all polygamists. Of course my husband had to go to Mexico. He was gone two years. Only those who have experienced this know what I went through. I had a lot of public work to do and took care of my family too so I was kept quite busy.

On Christmas morning 1890 a wee little lady came to take her abode with us. We called her Minnie Linnfitt. . . .

In August 1892 my husband came home. The children were very happy, but I didn't know whether I wanted to live with him again or not. Finally, under the circumstances we decided to let by-gones be by-gones and to live for the future. The winter passed very quietly. . . .

May 15, 1893 Sceva came to make her home with us. She was the fifth girl. We were a little disappointed for we thought our next one would be a boy but we loved her just the same. . . .

March 21, 1895 another girl, Jetta, was sent to us. She weighed 15¾ pounds. My, we were proud of her. . . .

My health was so poor that I had to wean Jetta when she was six months old. For ten months all I could eat was hard, dry graham bread, oysters and melon juice. . . . I wonder how I lived, but I'm thankful I was permitted to raise my large family. We have our ups and downs in life but we can look around and find someone who is worse off then we are.

December 20, 1896 we were blessed with our seventh daughter. Ida Ione we called her. Of course, the children all said we spoiled her. . . .

In October, 1899 we bought eighty acres two miles southwest of Mesa. Soon after we moved the farmers asked Lide to put up a building and start a dairy. It was certainly hard work. I did the testing once a week. . . .

It is now the summer of 1934 and I am staying in Flagstaff. I intend to meet Lell in a few months and we are going to take a trip around Utah. We intend to visit all the towns that we used to know. . . . I am very satisfied with my life. I have nine children, eight of whom are living, nineteen grandchildren, and twelve great-grandchildren.[88]

Another type of female migrant who contributed her energy and labor to the development of the American West was the Mexican American woman. In her reminiscences, Doña Jesús Moreno de Soza of Tucson, Arizona, described a life of determination and hard work:

My parents were married in California. My father's name was Benito Moreno; we were all born in California, four living and two dead before we left there. My father cultivated some land he had, but a big flood came along once and everything was carried away and destroyed. My father lost all, became desperate, and left for Sonora at that time, where the family remained until my mother died in 1860, then we were brought here with my sister who had married an American. I lived with them until I married.

My husband's name was Antonio J. Soza, a rancher and farmer. We made our home by the San Pedro River and raised a family of fourteen children. After my husband died, June 15, 1915, I remained here [in] Tucson. . . .

Once when my husband was a child of twelve years the Apaches raided Tubac. . . . the town was abandoned and the family came to Tucson that consisted of what we now call Main Street, only it was walled. They lived across the way from "El Ojito" (a spring that used to be north of the Elysian Grove) until we were married. . . .

My husband farmed the land very successfully, raised wheat and barley in abundance. On one occasion when they could not go to the store nearby to bring the necessary flour on account of the big flood making it impossible to cross, I shed many a tear thinking my children would starve. My husband got busy, started cleaning the wheat and then ground it so we might have something to eat. I continued to be in a flood of tears, but tried to assist him. A man at the ranch carved some stones to be used in grinding the wheat, so we had flour and lard in abundance as I had the hogs well fed on bran. . . .

In 1890 an immense flood washed our adobe house away and we had to find shelter in the stables; hogs, mill and everything were washed away, all that we ever saved was one hog. It was at the time that we moved to the next ranch where later we built a house. We had a wagon for ranch needs, and a canvas-top carriage for the family. The farm was enclosed within a brush fence, and then we started to milk the cows and made cheese to sell. . . .

Another incident was the earthquake which occurred May 3, 1887. I remember distinctly, we were living at San Pedro, I was sewing, had baby in cradle, was scared, and could not understand. The result at the ranch was that where the water flowed on the surface, the ground opened making a deep river. . . .

Her daughter added that the ranch complex also contained an adobe church and a school. All those who visited the ranch or crossed its lands were fed generously. The ranch, however, was also a setting for tragedy. According to Soza's daughter:

Once my mother was drawing a bucket of water at the well, she heard a shot, my brother disappeared, could not be located, he laid dead on the ground for two months at the San Pedro ranch before he was found. A man working for my father knew he had money and shot him; after a two months disappearance his body was found by a man who accidently happened to be crossing the hills. It was intact, never touched by a single animal nor by ant, but completely dried up. Father dug a grave there where the body was and buried him. His burial started the cemetery there. . . . A cross over him [the grave] reads "Manuel Soza—killed."[89]

A very different type of female migrants, Asian women, began to arrive during the mid- and late-nineteenth century. During the early twentieth century, some women, as indicated by the following comments of a Japanese immigrant, came to marry Japanese men already living in the United States:

At that time [1919] ships were coming into Seattle every week from Japan, carrying one or two hundred Japanese brides. So there was a store set up especially for these new arrivals. There was a hotel run by a Japanese and also Japanese food available. The Japanese couldn't go to the stores run by whites, so there were stores run by Japanese to deal with Japanese customers. We did all of our shopping there. . . .

I was among the lucky ones, coming to America as I did. . . . In Japan, the woman doesn't go out hunting for a husband. We used a go-between. The marriage arrangement offer from Mr. Sugihara came a week before the one from a person going to Manchuria.[90]

It is also becoming apparent that women migrants in the West included many African Americans. Although some came to the West before the Civil War, their number increased considerably after the war's end. Their source materials are elusive, but they do exist:

1.3
African American Women in the West

In 1946, a lively, highly informative autobiography of an African American woman effectively challenged the prevalent stereotype that female settlers in the American West were primarily white. Few, if any, observers of the American

1.3: Adapted from "American Daughters: Black Women in the American West," *Montana: The Magazine of Western History* 38 (Spring 1988), 14–27. Used by permission.

West had thought that the strong, conquering Saint in the Sunbonnet or the delicate, dewy-eyed Madonna of the Prairie might occasionally be dark-complexioned rather than fair. Era Bell Thompson's *American Daughter* disputed the usual conception of the lily-white western women.

Yet, over four decades later, our knowledge of African American women in the West has increased relatively little. Western black women still suffer from an unfortunate case of near-invisibility in the historical record.[92] It is time to look at some of the inclusions and omissions of African American women in the nineteenth-century trans-Mississippi West. And it is time to suggest some of the reasons why these women have been overlooked and what might be learned about them, their lives, and their contributions.

An immediate, but inaccurate, reaction to this objective might be that the necessary source materials do not exist. In fact, census materials contain much information about African American women, and their diaries, letters, and memoirs are numerous. Many literate women left written materials behind them. Others, both literate and not, have participated in oral interviews. With a little effort, the interviews can be found in archival collections, oral history projects, and in published form. The Montana American Mothers Bicentennial Project of 1975–1976, for example, housed in the Montana Historical Society Archives in Helena, includes a short biography of "Aunt" Tish, a African American settler who ran a popular dining room and boardinghouse in Hamilton, Montana, during the early years of the twentieth century.[93] In the University of Wyoming's American Heritage Center in Laramie, there is a transcript of an interview with Sudie Rhone, who talks about a black women's club movement on the Great Plains.[94]

State, county, and local history also contain tidbits of information concerning African American women in the West. For instance, in the pages of an article describing African Americans in South Dakota history there is mention of black brothels that catered to black troops stationed in the area during the 1880s, of land promoter Mary Elizabeth Blair, who was active professionally during the early 1900s, and a number of other working and entrepreneurial women during these periods.[95]

If African American women's sources exist, then why have they been largely overlooked? Clearly, such records are not easy to find. A researcher must hunt them out and then supplement them with newspapers, statistical data, legal documents, police registers, wills, marriage certificates, bills of sale, property inventories, contracts of emancipation, and a wide variety of other records. But these problems are not unknown to the historian. It is more likely that prejudice is also responsible for the virtual absence of African American women in western history. Because blacks in general, and black women in particular, have not been highly regarded by most Americans, their documents have not been widely or systematically collected. Few investigators have protested the situation or tried to remedy it. Once recognized, however, such attitudes and resulting dearth of scholarship can be changed.

Concerned historians who have attempted to explore the lives of African American women in the West have demonstrated that writing their history is both possible and desirable. In 1977, for example, Susan H. Armitage, Theresa Banfield, and Sarah Jacobus published a study of black women's communities in Colorado. Arguing that Colorado was the "most promising destination for blacks" during the late nineteenth century, the authors pointed out that Colorado's black population began to increase after 1880, largely as a result of an influx of disillusioned Exodusters from Kansas. By 1910, African Americans in Colorado numbered 11,453, most of whom were located in ghettos within white towns and cities. Black women not only lived and worked there, but they also pursued reform within their communities through a sizable and active black women's club movement. These women also struggled with discrimination. The six interviews with Colorado women that make up the bulk of the study whet the reader's desire for more information.[96]

A few years later, historian Lawrence B. de Graaf made an admirable attempt to unscramble census data regarding African American women in the Rocky Mountain and Pacific Coast states between 1850 and 1920. He found that black women in these western areas bore fewer children, were of a higher median age than their counterparts in the South, and tended to live in urban rather than rural areas. Like the women in Colorado, these women also noted the difficulties created for them by pervasive racial prejudice manifested in segregation policies, denial of their civil rights, exclusion from land purchases, and attempts to harass African American settlers or drive them away entirely. As a consequence, black women workers often had to work at low-paid and extremely exhausting domestic and agricultural tasks. While de Graaf offered some answers, he also raised many questions that few investigators have followed up. De Graaf's conclusion that "black women would long remain an invisible segment of western society whose lives and accomplishments would remain known only within the confines of their race" is unfortunately still largely accurate.[97]

In a study of Iowa women published in 1981, I also concluded that the recreation of the history of African American western women would be a difficult and long process. Although the people of Iowa were generally antislavery in philosophy, white citizens still harbored noticeable prejudice against blacks. During the early settlement years, for example, Iowa did not countenance slavery and claimed to enforce fugitive slave laws, yet newspaper advertisements seeking for information about runaway black indentured servants suggest that slavery existed under other guises. Prejudice also flared when African Americans received jobs. Even in Grinnell, a liberal abolitionist town, a violent mob protested the arrival of four black male workers in 1860.[98]

More recently, historian Sandra L. Myres attempted to include African American women in her study of westering women. She mentioned a few notable women and the community efforts of black clubwomen and also explored the prejudicial attitudes of the time that helped make such women "an almost invisible part of the mythology of westering women." She explained that although African Americans were "part of the westward migration rather than a native people encountered on the frontier, they were most often regarded, like Indians and Mexicans, as an alien influence." She noted that following the Texas Revolution of 1836 the government of the new republic passed legislation to enslave or expel free blacks in Texas. Myres added that in 1851 Indiana prohibited blacks from entering the state, as did Illinois in 1853, and that colonization societies dedicated to sending blacks to Africa dotted the Midwest. She concluded that all over the West, African American women endured discriminatory treatment and isolation.[99]

All these studies suggest that prejudice and discriminatory treatment of African American women were long-standing. They support a harsh assertion posited some years ago by black historian William L. Katz. In assessing antiblack attitudes in such western areas as Iowa, Katz observed that "the black laws moved westward with the pioneers' wagons." He declared that statements made during the 1844 Iowa constitutional convention were clear examples of blatant racism. According to Katz, many Iowans argued that white citizens "should never consent to open the doors of [their] beautiful state" to African American settlers because these people "not being a party to the government, have no right to partake of its privileges" and that "there are strong reasons to induce the belief that the two races could not exist in the same government upon an equality without discord and violence." Such sentiments dispute the notion that enlightenment and liberation characterized the West. Katz concluded: "The intrepid pioneers who crossed the western plains carried the virus of racism with them."[100]

Not all western migrants deserve Katz's indictment, however. Thousands of whites aided slaves fleeing to freedom via the Underground Railroad, brought free African Americans home with them after the Civil War, welcomed them as settlers, and worked for their civil rights.[101] Such evidence as a county manumission record showing that Mommia Travers's master freed her at Fort Vancouver in 1851, and the Iowa court case involving a free African American woman married to a white man indicate that black women occasionally received positive sentiments and actions.[102]

An additional factor that is often cited for historians' neglect of African American women is the relative scarcity of blacks in the western population. But this observation raises questions. Is the smallness of a group sufficient reason to dismiss it from the annals of history? Is a group's size always proportional to its importance and contributions? And is it true that African American women were indeed scarce in the West? Although the answer to all three queries would appear to be "no," only the last can be clearly proven. Census figures indicate that the number of black women in western states, particularly after the Civil War, was not minuscule. Thousands of them lived in most western states, and their ranks increased over the years. Census data for seven selected Plains states during the fifty years following the Civil War document the absolute numbers, relative proportions, and increase of African American women.

Federal census figures can be supplemented by county records that often include both population figures and personal information. A Missouri county registry of free African Americans between 1836 and 1861 listed approximately ten women and twenty men, but the records unfortunately gave little additional information about them. Another Missouri county, however, not only counted free blacks but noted age, gender, occupations, and places of origin. In 1850, sixteen free blacks lived in this county of over one thousand families. Five were female, of whom two were cooks while three had no paid occupations. In that same year in McLean County, Illinois, the population totaled 1,594, of whom 777 were white females, 777 were white males, 17 were black females, and 23 were black males. Among the African American women were cooks, servants, and a twenty-year-old schoolteacher born in Kentucky.[103]

Compiling census figures, particularly on the county level, is a time-consuming and exhausting means of gathering information, but such data are a rich source of information. Given the dearth of material regarding African American women and the frequent omission of them in western history, which is partially a result of this lack of information, census records are a resource well worth mining.[104]

Historians and writers have also tended to overlook female participation in historical movements. African American women, for instance, came to western regions very early in the settlement period. As early as June 24, 1794, a marriage between Jean and Jeanne Bonga was recorded in Mickilmacknac Parish, later part of Minnesota. Many African Americans entered the area as part of fur-trading expeditions, exploring forays, and the military. Beginning in 1820, officers and their families stationed at Fort Snelling in what is now Minnesota brought slaves, both male and female, with them. By that time, there were already an estimated 2,000 to 3,000 African Americans, both slave and free, in the upper Louisiana country.[105]

During the early nineteenth century, settlers from southern states also brought slaves into western regions. In 1822, a party of settlers traveling from Virginia to Missouri included four white men and their four black valets as well as "Mammy," a woman servant ensconced in the cook and supply wagon. This family spent its first years in a log cabin, with Mammy helping out inside while the white and black men broke the prairie sod outside.[106] Many other settlers also relied on slave or free black women for help in raising children, doing domestic chores, and running inns and other family businesses.[107]

Even western states that loudly proclaimed themselves to be antislavery had their share of trappers, traders, soldiers, miners, and settlers who brought slaves with them. The Iowa census of 1840 listed ten female and six male slaves, even though the state had outlawed slavery. Although no slaves appeared in the Iowa census after that year, slave-holders circumvented the law. Some held African Americans as indentured servants. As late as 1850, an advertisement in Iowa's *Burlington Tri-Weekly Telegraph* asked for the return of such a servant. Described as black, thirteen or fourteen years old, and with five years left to serve of her indenture, the girl was said to have been "decoyed" away by some "meddling person." Her owner claimed that "it would be an act of charity to her could she be restored to him."[108]

Throughout the pre–Civil War years vestiges of slavery continued in Iowa. Female indentures served as cooks, nursemaids, and domestic servants.[109] Despite the antislavery movement and the activities of the Underground Railroad, proslavery sentiment ran strong, especially among the many migrants from southern states who had moved into southern Iowa seeking land.[110] The proslavery sentiment in these districts made them less amenable to the entry of free African Americans and clearly challenged the egalitarian reputation of western regions. But even antislavery Iowans were afraid of cheap black labor and the difficulties they believed would result from living and working with African Americans. These whites supported the passage of laws that excluded blacks, denied their civil liberties, and regulated their behavior. A certificate of freedom was required of any free black entering Iowa, and the state often forced free blacks to post monetary bonds of $500 to ensure their "good behavior."[111]

In neighboring free Minnesota, both slave and free African Americans, including women, entered the region during the decades preceding the Civil War. Abolitionist sentiment, however, seemed to be more rife there than in Iowa, perhaps partly because of a smaller proportion of African Americans in Minnesota's population. The residence at various army posts of a slave woman named Rachel from 1831 to 1834 led to her successful suit for freedom in 1835. The two-year stint of Dred and Harriet Scott at Fort Snelling from 1836 to 1838 eventually resulted in the Dred Scott case of 1857. In 1849, the first territorial census recorded forty free blacks, thirty of whom lived in St. Paul. But during the 1840s and 1850s, both free blacks and fugitive slaves continued to enter Minnesota. This migration alarmed those who feared cheap labor and "inundation." Yet, in 1860, when Eliza Winston accompanied her master on a vacation to Minnesota, she was able to enlist the aid of local abolitionists in seeking her freedom.[112]

Although African American women evidently lived and left their marks in Iowa and Minnesota, little is said of them in the complex and sometimes voluminous historical accounts of these regions and of the African American people living in them. Beyond the occasional mention of a female fugitive slave, a woman involved in a marriage or court case, or a free black woman employed as a domestic helper, washwoman, or day laborer, there is no systematic discussion of their roles or of the contributions of African American women to the early development of these western regions.

The history of the Exodusters, an African American group that migrated in great numbers from the South to Kansas, Oklahoma, and other areas after the Civil War, is another example of historical neglect of female participation in a major movement. Even though the census figures clearly demonstrate the presence of relatively large numbers of African American women and a constant increase in the size of the black female population in Kansas and Oklahoma, these women generally appear only incidentally in historical accounts of the Exoduster movement.

The flight of the Exodusters to midwestern and Plains states during the latter decades of the nineteenth century is well documented. During these years, thousands of southern African Americans traveled up the Missouri River and along other routes in an attempt to escape the evils of sharecropping, tenant farming, and prejudice. Seeking a better life in the "promised land," they sought employment in the cities or on farms, worked as cowhands, homesteaded, or created both rural and urban African American communities. In the Midwest, Pulaski County, Illinois, contained a sizable black population by 1900. Plains colonies included Nicodemus, Kansas, established in 1877, Langston, Oklahoma, in 1891, and Dearfield, Colorado, in 1910.[113]

The part played by women in this migration has not been researched and recorded even though diary entries, letters, and memoirs of both white and black women indicate that many Exodusters were female. Anne E. Bingham, for instance, recalled that she and her husband hired a family of six Exodusters, two adults and four children, to help on their Kansas farm in 1880. Bingham remarked that the two adult Exodusters were reliable and diligent workers. She was particularly pleased to have the woman's services as washwoman. "She would carry a pail of water on her head with one hand to steady it," Bingham remembered, "and something in the other hand, and carry the clothes basket that way, too." Bingham was very sorry when the Exoduster family "got lonesome and finally went to town."[114]

The memories of several female Exodusters also offer enough information to make the reader eager to learn more about them and their lives in the "promised land." According to Exoduster Williana Hickman, at the end of an exhausting railway journey from Kentucky to Kansas in 1878, her husband pointed to "various smokes [sic] coming out of the ground and said, 'That is Nicodemus.'" African American families were living in dugouts almost at ground level, Hickman remembered. She reacted to the scene in much the way many of her white counterparts did: "The scenery to me was not at all inviting, and I began to cry." According to another newspaper story about early settlers in Nicodemus, a woman who also arrived in 1878 began teaching a class of forty-five children in her new dugout home.[115]

Moreover, African American women among homesteaders who settled throughout Nebraska, the Dakota Territory, and other Plains states have yet to be studied. In North Dakota, for example, a group of black male and female homesteaders attempted to establish a farm community near Alexander in the southwestern part of the state around 1910. Numbering only ten families at its peak, the settlement was not a success. Within a decade, all its residents dispersed to nearby towns and cities. More successful were the homesteading families of Ava Day in Nebraska and Era Bell Thompson in North Dakota. Day and Thompson both grew up on the Plains, far from the South their parents had known. But the difference that relocation made to these women and others like them remains unexamined. Furthermore, we do not know whether black women homesteaded on their own as did so many white women during the 1890s and early 1900s. Nor have African American women's contributions to the overall homesteading experience been noted.[116]

Although historians have not intentionally omitted African American women from western history, the implication remains that these women led puerile lives. There is a great deal of available information and there are tremendous insights to be gained about African American women in the American West. But how should we proceed? A place to begin might well be African American women's domestic lives, a highly revealing area in the study of any group of women. Women's writings point to great similarities between black and white women's daily existence in the West. Home and family were the focus of black women's lives, just as they were for white women, and they went about the care of both in similar ways.

From the pioneer years in Minnesota comes the example of settler Emily O. G. Grey who joined a growing African American community in St. Anthony in 1857. Like many white women, Grey set up housekeeping in a converted barn and created cupboards and bureaus from packing boxes covered with calico.[117] Three decades later in neighboring St. Paul, Amanda Jennie Lee Bell married a barber and established a home. Her experiences in housekeeping, raising her family, and assisting with her husband's business also closely resembled those of white women living in other pioneer western towns. And in North Dakota during the early 1900s, women in the family of Helen Johnson Downing followed traditional work patterns for girls and women and relied on books to ease their isolation just as white women settlers did.[118]

The employment patterns of African American women are another rich area for investigation. Their work experiences, however, diverged widely from white women's, especially in pay and terms of employment. A higher percentage of black women than of white women worked outside of their homes. Between 12 to 25 percent of all teenage and adult white women were employed in paid professions, but the figures for black women were much higher—40 to 50 percent. Black women's relatively high employment level was largely due to economic necessity. Although both whites and blacks believed that women should work within the home, black women actually remained in the home far less than white women did. The hardships of scarce and low-paying jobs for black men typically forced black women to contribute to family income. Racial prejudice, however, kept them from holding all but the more menial jobs. Burdened by the poor wages, exhausting conditions, demeaning status, and heavy labor that these jobs usually entailed, African American women sacrificed their own ambitions and took the positions most readily available to them.[119]

Most commonly, African American women worked as domestics in western areas, although after the Civil War white western women, especially native-born women, began leaving domestic service for retail, sales, and clerical work as well as a variety of professions. Employing African American women as cooks, washwomen, dressmakers, nursemaids, and maids seemed to many white employers logical and appropriate extensions of the roles these women had fulfilled as slaves. Often called by such names as "Nigger Ellen," African American servants received minimal wages, sometimes supplemented by leftover scraps of food or cast-off clothing.[120] These servants were frequently described by their white employers as loyal, willing, and competent, while white—especially immigrant—women often evoked their employers' enmity. Anna Ramsey of St. Paul wrote to her daughter that Martha, her African American maid, performed many duties well, from housecleaning to packing the family's clothes for trips. Referring to her servant as "beloved" Martha, Ramsey regretted that old age necessitated Martha's retirement. On the other hand, a Bloomington, Illinois, woman did not think much of her maid's abilities as a housekeeper, but this young bride was delighted that her mother had sent the servant along with her as a companion on her journey to the West.[121]

In other cases, African American women earned local reputations as skilled workers when they carried their domestic talents out of the home and into the public arena. In Sioux City, Iowa, two cooks during the 1860s vied with each other for the acclaim of their patrons. Another cook referred to as "Black Ann" not only received the kudos of passengers on Mississippi steamboats, but she also earned enough money to buy her own freedom and that of her children. And in St. Paul, Minnesota, during the years following the Civil War, customers praised the skills of a family of African American seamstresses.[122]

Despite the huge odds against African American women progressing very far beyond employment as domestics, a considerable number parlayed their energy and abilities into such relatively high-status positions as hotel and boardinghouse keepers and restaurant managers and owners. The most famous African American boardinghouse keeper was Mary Ellen "Mammy" Pleasant, a Californian who was also known for her charitable acts of assistance to needy blacks.[123] Other women became entrepreneurs in a variety of businesses, including millinery shops, hairdressing establishments, and food stores. The most eminent of them was Sarah Breedlove Walker, better known as "Madame" Walker. She developed "The Walker Method" of straightening African American women's hair in St. Louis in 1905 and moved to Colorado in 1906.[124] Many women were real estate brokers, including Biddy Mason of Los Angeles, Clara Brown of Denver, and Mary Elizabeth Blair of Sully County, North Dakota. Biddy Mason, most prominent of the group, not only amassed considerable wealth, but she also spent huge amounts of time and money helping the less fortunate. Because of her charitable work she was called "Grandmother" Mason.[125]

A number of African American women also became successful in a variety of professions. Young women showed an interest in and talent for education, in spite of state and local attempts to prohibit them from attending school and laws that assigned them to often poorly funded segregated schools. Ironically, because black women often lived in towns and cities, they gradually gained access to better schools than those available to white rural women, resulting in a high rate of school attendance and graduation among black girls in the

West. In addition, African American families sometimes chose to educate daughters instead of sons to protect the girls from domestic service and starvation wages.[126] A number of these educated women entered teaching, probably the profession most accessible to them because of the establishment of an increasing number of black schools around the turn of the century. As teachers in segregated schools or as founders of their own schools, black female educators usually outnumbered black male educators in most western areas.[127]

Other achievement-oriented women struggled to become nurses, doctors, journalists, and editors, but they were far fewer in number than women who became teachers. Charlotta Spears Bass of Los Angeles particularly distinguished herself. In 1912, she became editor of *The California Eagle* (published from 1879 to 1966), the oldest African American newspaper on the West Coast. Through its pages she waged a fierce crusade for over forty years against racial segregation and discrimination. In 1952, she became the first African American woman to run for the Vice Presidency of the United States.[128]

Prostitution was the one "profession" left open to and, in fact, often urged on African American women. Both economic necessity and negative societal images pushed them toward criminal occupations, but it was a pressure that they frequently resisted.[129] Thompson recalled being told by a white man in Mandan, North Dakota, that all black women were prostitutes.[130] Yet, neither observers nor census takers noted large numbers of black prostitutes in the West. Occasionally, black brothels did coexist with sizable populations of cowhands or soldiers, but other black women in the area commonly scorned and reviled these prostitutes and madams.[131]

Racism was the condition and circumstance that most clearly alienated African American women from their white counterparts. During her high school and college days in Mandan, North Dakota, Era Bell Thompson frequently became the victim of prejudicial treatment that threatened to impair seriously or end her education. Eventually, she fled to Chicago in hopes of "blending in" with the African American population there. Similarly, Dr. Ruth Flowers, who in 1924 was the first black woman to graduate from the University of Colorado, spent her teenage years working as a dishwasher in a restaurant, resisting persistent racism that barred her from even enjoying an ice cream cone or a movie and studying until early morning hours to get an education she hoped would free her from such trials.[132]

The prejudice and discrimination encountered by African American women in the West demonstrate how pervasively race and racism shaped their experiences. Yet we know little about the development of racism in the West. Ava Day, whose family settled in the Overton area of Cherry County, Nebraska, in 1885, claimed that she met with very little prejudice during her childhood in the Nebraska Sandhills, where her family raised cattle, brood mares, and mules. She recalled that her grandfather was white and her grandmother black. As Day explained, "Color never made a difference to Grandpa. You were a person and a man and a lady." She added that the family's neighbors felt much the same about the race issue, for they were friendly and helpful: ". . . everybody asked did you need anything from town—and brought it back by your house or left it at your gate."[133]

Era Bell Thompson also had some pleasant memories of white neighbors during her very early years in North Dakota. She claimed that when her family moved to the Plains shortly before World War I they met with little discrimination. As she commented years later: "I was very lucky to have grown up in North Dakota where families were busy fighting climate and soil for a livelihood and there was little awareness of race." She recalled that neighbors befriended her family, especially a Norwegian family who brought supplies to the Thompsons at critical times. Thompson believed that North Dakota's high percentage of ethnic residents encouraged migrants to look on each other as equals, a situation that apparently changed as migration increased, judging from the educational and career limitations placed on Thompson by racist attitudes and policies later in her life.[134]

Other African American women had different memories of prevailing attitudes. An urban woman, Sudie Rhone of Cheyenne, Wyoming, contradicted Thompson's view of race relations during the pre–World War I era. She noted that the Searchlight Club, founded by African American women in 1904, was the only service group for black women at that time, adding that while black women could have joined white women's clubs, they seldom chose to do so. She believed that widespread prejudice and nonacceptance of blacks by whites kept the two groups of women segregated in this and many other activities.[135]

Rhone's observations about western women's service clubs pinpoint not only the racial prejudice that divided white women from black, but also lead us to investigate the activities and attitudes of African American women reformers and civic activists. How widespread were African American women reformers and clubwomen? Did they typically attack the same social ills as did white women reformers, or did they attempt to solve race-related problems? And did they ever join with white women, or did they work only within groups of black women?

So little material exists on African American women reformers in the West that it is impossible to give definite answers to any of these questions except the first one. Numerous African American women did become reformers and community activists. One Colorado woman stated that in black western communities where men worked long hours or were away seeking work, women served as the "backbone of the church, the backbone of the family, they were the backbone of the social life, everything."[136] Other women also wrote or spoke of the considerable amounts of time and energy that they and their friends devoted to community improvement projects.[137] And records of African American organizations, such as the Pilgrim Baptist Church of St. Paul, founded in 1866, and the Kansas Federation of Women's Clubs, organized in 1900, reveal the number and diversity of women's charitable organizations that existed from an early stage in westward expansion.[138]

Whether African American women reformers attacked "black" problems and worked only with black women is not quite clear. Charlotta Pyles, a free African American living with her family in Keokuk, Iowa, was a reformer. She and other family members joined together in a fund-raising effort to buy their relatives out of slavery. During the 1850s, Pyles launched a speaking tour in the East to raise funds and converted her Keokuk home into a station on the Underground Railroad. To advance her cause, she joined with white abolitionists and helped many fugitive slaves escape to Canada.[139]

Unlike Pyles, numerous reform-minded African American women chose or were forced by racial prejudice to cooperate only with other black women in reform activities.[140] Many of these joined the rapidly proliferating ladies' aid groups, charity associations, and missionary societies often associated with African American churches. Reformers Emily Grey of St. Anthony and Amanda Bell of St. Paul, for example, attacked problems that particularly plagued African Americans, including inadequate health care, poverty, and substandard education.[141]

The General Federation of Women's Clubs' long-standing policy of accepting African American women's organizations only as segregated locals pressured black women all over the United States to maintain their own service groups. African American clubwomen formed a parallel organization, the National Association of Colored Women, in 1896, and by 1915 it had 50,000 members in 28 state federations and over 1,000 individual clubs. Should an investigator take the time to explore them, the records of these clubs might yield an abundance of information about such African American clubwomen in the West as Josephine Leavall Allensworth of California, who helped organize the Women's Improvement Club that provided a public reading room and built playgrounds for children.[142]

There are many other topics in the history of African American women in the West that are rife with unanswered questions. Little is known, for example, about western black women's participation in the women's suffrage movement. Because many African American women in the South and the East organized their own suffrage groups, it is reasonable to believe that western women did so as well. Because suffrage for women first became a reality in western territories and states, it might be significant to know if race had any influence at all in this development. African American women's roles in temperance reform, the Grange, and Populism, and the lives of those women in army forts are other subjects that need investigation. The African American woman's relationship to Native Americans and the physical environment of the West is virtually unexplored.

Historian Susan H. Armitage cautions that it is also necessary to consider regional differences in the lives and experiences of African American women. In an unpublished paper and a bibliography of sources on black women in the Pacific Northwest written with Deborah G. Wilbert, she explores domesticity, employment, racism, reform, and other germane topics but notes that the experience of an African American woman in Kansas might vary greatly from that of a woman in Oregon. Her point regarding regionalism is a highly significant one; era, class, and urban or rural residence are other important variables to be included in any study of African American women in the West.[143]

Perhaps the ultimate issue to be raised here is why the history of African Americans in the West should be recovered. One obvious answer is that only by analyzing the history of all types of western women can their history and the history of the West itself ever be understood. Comparisons between black and white women will yield valuable insights about each group and about the larger group of women of which they were a major part. Moreover, despite racial prejudice, there were many ties between black and white women. Anna Ramsey not only employed an African American servant but also found herself strongly drawn to the enthusiasm and verve of the Tennessee Jubilee Singers who performed in the St. Paul Opera House to raise funds for education. In Missouri, some women owned slaves while others, like Susan Vanarsdale, felt great sympathy for a female fugitive slave.[144] African American women, on the other hand, had to confront and interact with white women in almost every area of their lives, including employment, education, and social life. How, then, can the history of one group be written without the other?

Probably more crucial, however, is the issue of justice in restoring a historical heritage to African American women in America. As Era Bell Thompson argued so well in *American Daughter*, black women were an integral part of the western and American traditions. It both impairs a sense of identity and unbalances the historical record to continue to overlook the role of African American women in the development of the American West.

As we enrich the saga of western women by adding the history of African American women to the mix, we need to remember that thousands of slave women also helped settle the American West. This slave woman who lived on a plantation near Georgetown, Texas, during the 1850s and early 1860s had relatively pleasant memories:

From what I's larnt by talk with other slaves, we's lucky slaves 'cause dere no sich thing as whippin' on our farm. . . . We all lives in one big family, 'cept us have dinin' room for de cullud folks. Grandpappy am de carpenter and 'cause of dat us quarters fixed fine and has reg'lar windows and handmade chairs and a real wood floor.

Mammy and my grandma am cooks and powerful good and dey's larnt me and dat how I come to be a cook. Like everybody dem times, us raise everything and makes preserves and cure de meats. De hams and bacons am smoked. Dere am no hickory wood 'round but we uses de corncobs and dey makes de fine flavor in de meat. Many's de day I watches de fire in dat smokehouse and keeps it low, to git de smoke flavor. I follow de cookin' when I gits big and goes for myself and I never wants for de job.

When surrender breaks all us stay with Massa for good, long spell. When pappy am ready to go for hisself, Massa gives him de team of mules and de team of oxen and some hawgs and one cow and some chickens. Dat gives us de good start. . . .[145]

Another Texas slave woman, however, recalls a drastically different scenario:

I's born right down in Rusk County [Texas, c. 1848], not a long way from Henderson, and Massa Andrew Watt am my owner. My pappy, Hob Rollins, he come from North Carolina and belong to Dave Blakely and mammy come from Mississippi. . . .

Massa Watt lived in a big log house what sot on a hill so you could see it 'round for miles, and us lived over in the field in little log huts, all huddled together. They have homemade beds nailed to the wall and holding sack mattresses, and us call them bunks. Us never had no money but plenty clothes and grub and wear the same clothes all the year 'round. . . .

The hands was woke with the bit bell and when massa pulls that bell rope the niggers falls out them bunks like rain fallin'. They was in the field 'fore day and stay till dusk dark. . . . Massa Watt didn't have no overseer, but he have a nigger driver what am jus' as bad. He carry a long whip 'round the neck and I's seed him tie niggers to a tree and cowhide 'em till the blood run down onto the ground. Sometimes the women gits slothful and not able to do their part but they makes 'em do it anyway. They digs a hole, 'bout body deep, and makes them women lie face down in it and beats 'em nearly to death. . . .

I stay mos' the time in the big house and massa good but missy am the devil. . . . You see, I's massa nigger and she have her own niggers what come on her side and she never did like me. . . . If I have a dollar for ev'ry cowhidin' I git, I'd never have to work no more. . . .[146]

Another African American woman living in Eufaula, Oklahoma, during the 1930s remembers her slave background, but ties her personal history far more to Native Americans and Oklahoma Territory:

My mother was a slave of Mr. Lee Stidham's father before the Civil War. When the war began Mr. Stidham moved to Texas and carried all of his slaves with him.

When Mr. Stidham moved to Texas my mother went with him and about the same time Mr. Lee Stidham was born. Mrs. Stidham died when Lee was an infant and my mother nursed him and my brother too, and raised Lee until he was grown. Mr. Stidham moved back to the Territory after the Run and my mother came back to the Territory with him.

My father was a Cherokee Indian by birth but registered in Muskogee with the Creeks. He was a relative of James Ross of Muskogee. My father and mother lived near here until they died.

I married a Creek Indian. . . . He had an allotment west of Eufaula and we have lived all the time with Creek Indians. . . .

When I was a girl I went to an Indian school about four miles west of Eufaula called Tullewache, which means "dark night." Some man from Eufaula taught there then, but there is no school there now, it has been abandoned for years. Our stomp ground is gone too. We used to go to the Hickory Stomp Ground for stomp dances and there was an old Indian church there too, but it is all torn down and gone.[147]

The usual stereotypes of western women not only omit African American women, but many others as well: Asian, Hispanic, Jewish; single, widowed, divorced, older, working, and professional women; army wives and daughters, prostitutes, miners, and homesteaders are some important examples. Throughout the following sections, be aware of the great diversity of women who helped develop the American West.

For Further Reading

Blackman, Margaret B. *Sadie Brower Neakok: An Iñupiag Woman.* Seattle: University of Washington Press, 1989.

Bush, Corlann Gee. "The Way We Weren't: Images of Women and Men in Cowboy Art." *Frontiers* 7 (1984), 73–78.

Cabeza de Baca, Fabiola. *We Fed Them Cactus.* Albuquerque: University of New Mexico Press, 1989.

Castañeda, Antonia I. "Gender, Race, and Culture: Spanish-Mexican Women in the Historiography of Frontier California." *Frontiers* 11 (1990), 8–20.

de Graaf, Lawrence B. "Race, Sex, and Region: Black Women in the American West, 1850–1920." *Pacific Historical Review* 49 (May 1980), 285–313.

Deutsch, Sarah. *No Separate Refuge: Culture, Class, and Gender on an Anglo-Hispanic Frontier in the American Southwest, 1880–1940.* New York: Oxford University Press, 1987.

Dysart, Jane. "Mexican Women in San Antonio, 1830–1860: The Assimilation Process." *Western Historical Quarterly* 7 (Fall 1976), 365–75.

Glenn, Evelyn Nakano. *Issei, Nisei, War Bride: Three Generations of Japanese American Women in Domestic Service.* Philadelphia: Temple University Press, 1986.

Godfrey, Kenneth W., Audrey M. Godfrey, and Jill Mulvay Derr, eds. *Women's Voice: An Untold History of the Latter-Day Saints, 1830–1900.* Salt Lake City: Deseret Book Co., 1982.

Hafen, Mary Ann. *Recollections of a Handcart Pioneer of 1860: A Woman's Life on the Mormon Frontier.* Lincoln: University of Nebraska Press, 1983.

Ichioka, Yuji. "*Amerika Nadeshiko*: Japanese Immigrant Women in the United States, 1900–1924." *Pacific Historical Review* 49 (May 1980), 339–57.

Jameson, Elizabeth. "Toward a Multicultural History of Women in the Western United States." *Signs* 13 (Summer 1988), 761–91.

Jensen, Joan M., and Darlis A. Miller. "The Gentle Tamers Revisited: New Approaches to the History of Women in the American West." *Pacific Historical Review* 49 (May 1980), 173–214.

Lee, Mary Paik. *Quiet Odyssey: A Pioneer Korean Woman in America.* Seattle: University of Washington Press, 1990.

Malone, Ann Patton. *Women on the Texas Frontier: A Cross-Cultural Perspective* (Monograph #70, *Southwestern Studies*). El Paso: Texas Western Press, 1983.

Myres, Sandra L. "Mexican Americans and Westering Anglos: A Feminine Perspective." *New Mexico Historical Review* 57 (October 1982), 317–33.

Scadron, Arlene, ed. *On Their Own: Widows and Widowhood in the American Southwest, 1848–1939.* Urbana: University of Illinois Press, 1988.

Stauffer, Helen Winter, and Susan J. Rosowski, eds. *Women and Western American Literature.* Troy, New York: The Whitston Publishing Co., 1982.

Trulio, Beverly. "Anglo-American Attitudes Toward New Mexican Women." *Journal of the West* 12 (April 1973), 229–39.

Wilson, Gilbert L. (transcriber). *Buffalo Bird Woman's Garden.* St. Paul: Minnesota Historical Society Press, 1987.

Thompson, Era Bell. *American Daughter.* St. Paul: Minnesota Historical Society Press, 1986.

Underwood, June O. "Western Women and True Womanhood: Culture and Symbol in History and Literature." *Great Plains Quarterly* 5 (Spring 1985), 93–106.

Yasui, Barbara. "The Nisei in Oregon, 1834–1940," *Oregon Historical Quarterly* 76 (1975), 225–57.

Yung, Judy. *Chinese Women of America: A Pictorial History.* Seattle: University of Washington Press, 1986.

SECTION

2

Women and Westward Trails

Trails criss-crossed western lands but also utilized lakes, rivers, and oceans. In a quest for health, wealth, freedom, a better future or to join friends and relatives, all kinds of women migrated with their families or on their own: Spanish-speaking women moved northward from Mexico and other parts of Central America; white and black women traveled westward from the northern, eastern, and southern United States; European women sailed the Atlantic Ocean to trek westward; and Asian women sailed the Pacific Ocean to reach the American West. Because white women traveling overland routes left thousands of trail accounts, their migration has received the most popular and scholarly attention. Rather than being a reason to abandon the study of western trails, this limitation must spur scholars to expand their conception of what constituted a trail and to collect the accounts of many different kinds of trail women.

The trail experience is crucial to understanding the western experience, for it was the trails that brought Anglo, African American, and Asian settlers into the western regions originally held by Native Americans and Mexicans. Women's time on the trail was often critical because it shaped the way they would interact with their neighbors wherever they settled. The following essays explore white women's reactions to two different routes and to the native people along one of those routes, while the documents attempt to enlarge existing ideas of western trails and the kind of women who traveled over them.

Photo: The diversity of female migrants who journeyed to the American West is indicated in this photograph of an African American migrant in Mantorville, Minnesota, c. 1905. Courtesy of Minnesota Historical Society, St. Paul.

2.1
The Trail as Process

During the nineteenth century, the western portion of America exploded into an unbelievable multitude and variety of additional settlements. Some sprang up overnight while others disappeared; most, however, were created gradually and peopled incrementally. There was no neat line or pattern to these developments. Migration did not march in an orderly manner across the western portion of the continent from the Ohio Valley to the Pacific Ocean. They appeared wherever there was land, gold, lumber, or some other asset attractive enough to draw people. Signing a deed or pounding in a claim stake might mark a migrant's arrival, but it did not mark the beginning of his or her western experience. On the contrary, this process began sometime during the transitional phase between the old home and the new. That transitional link was the trail—the time spent and the space crossed by settlers in order to reach their chosen region of the promised land. As they traversed this link, migrants were not living in suspended animation. Those who came by land did not board their wagons and descend a few hours later on the edge of a verdant prairie or a raw gold field as a modern jet traveler might. Rather, they invested in the journey many weeks or months, as well as untold amounts of physical and psychic energy. The trail was not a pleasure trip, a joyride, or a vacation. It was difficult work for people to transport themselves from the known to the unknown. It was even more difficult for them to create the necessary metamorphosis in themselves that changed them from the settled into migrants. In short, the trail was not just a prelude to relocation or something that suddenly began when a river was crossed or an artificially drawn boundary line reached. The trail was a temporary community in movement, in the process of becoming.[1] The trail experience was serious business because it was the first chapter of western life. What the migrants did, said, thought, and learned on the trail helped shape the outcome of their own personal dramas.

Migrants had to apply their energies to four basic areas of endeavor while on the trail: 1) performing the chores connected with daily living, with the duress of the trail environment added; 2) physically moving themselves, their families, and goods; 3) learning, practicing, and honing the skills that would aid survival in their new homes; and 4) reshaping their psychological mindset from looking back to their former homes to looking forward to the West. Some migrants were successful in these areas, others were less so. Some were enthusiastic about the venture, others were not. But for good or ill, once on the trail migrants were already part of the surging and demanding American West.

2.1: Adapted from "The Frontier In Process: Iowa's Trail Women as a Paradigm," *Annals of Iowa* 46 (Winter 1982). Used by permission.

What did the rigors of transit mean to women in particular? As casual observers and serious scholars tried to fathom the ways the trail affected the women who tackled it, a predominant generalization emerged. This image pictured a forlorn, beleaguered woman forced to leave her comfortable home by a husband blind with wanderlust. Due to her supposedly inherent weakness and domestic nature she begged her husband at every opportunity to turn back. She choked in the dust, became weathered in the sun, and continuously bemoaned her fate and that of her poor children in a primitive land.[2]

Somehow this portrait, although widely accepted and certainly supported by cases of women who did suffer, does not ring quite true. Its generality is cause alone for suspicion. But how can this image be tested? Obviously there were many trails to many destinations over many decades. Clearly, it can only be tested, in a sense, trail by trail. If it is found wanting on even one trail then the conclusion is evident: other trails during other times to other places must also be examined more thoroughly and objectively. In many ways, the Iowa-bound trail was typical of other overland westward trails, especially of those to family-farm regions. As such, the Iowa trail is a useful case study. It was an episode that began with early white squatters in Iowa's Half-Breed Tract in 1828 and had more or less vanished by 1870, the United States Census Bureau's official closing date for Iowa's settlement period. The trail's travelers, largely white men and women, originated primarily in the farm areas of the Ohio Valley, with others from the southern states, the middle Atlantic states, the New England states, and other countries. Many people came seeking a better climate, improved health, richer land, or a more promising future for their children. Others set out to escape inordinate taxation, slavery, or personal financial problems. Most travelers migrated in extended family units which often included, or were supplemented by, both single men and women. Although there were no census-takers on the trail, later territorial and state census data indicate that most migrated to take up land and become farmers.[3]

From these facts several additional characteristics of the Iowa trail can be intuited. The abundance of families indicates that a high proportion of women and children journeyed on the trail. The capital needed to make the trek, purchase seed and tools, and invest in land suggests that, despite popular belief, the very poor were not common among migrants. That most migrants had farmed means they already had some training in the skills needed to make the westward move.

In other ways, the Iowa trail was less representative, particularly of overland routes to the Far West. Most Iowa-bound migrants traveled over parts of the country that were comparatively well settled, a situation that created a certain amount of ease for them in that they could occasionally buy supplies along the way and could sometimes stay at inns or campgrounds. References to fresh produce, friendly shopkeepers, and campgrounds established specifically for covered wagon people abound in the diaries and letters of Iowa migrants. This is not to argue that their time on the trail was easy, but there is little in their history or mythology to compare with the tragedy of those trapped for a winter at Donner Pass.

Because of the settled countryside through which they traveled, Iowa-bound migrants had relatively little to fear in the way of confrontations with Native Americans. Land treaties, President Andrew Jackson's removal policy, and outright genocide had essentially cleared the portion of the United States lying northeast of the Mississippi River of native populations. Indians valiantly resisting white encroachments were noticeably absent from the Iowa trail saga.

Moreover, besides moving through populous countryside, these migrants were moving westward in a time period marked by increasing industrialization and technology, which supplied them with a variety of modes of transportation. Legend to the contrary, the covered wagon was not the only means of travel in mid-nineteenth-century America. Given the widespread media image of migrants, it is rather startling to learn that many of them chose other means of conveyance. Riverboats, for example, were one widely-used type of transportation. When the Harris family came to Iowa from Pennsylvania they traveled virtually the entire way by river. A daughter wrote that the boats carried them "first down the Allegheny to Pittsburgh; thence down the Ohio River on the steamboat, 'the Diadem,' to Cairo; thence on the 'New England' up the Mississippi to Keokuk." She commented that although they traveled in deck passage to save money, they remembered it as a speedy and enjoyable trip, often made pleasurable by the company and song of other passengers.[4]

Rail routes were another possibility. Leaving New Hampshire in 1855, the Motts chose a rail route all the way to the Iowa boundary line. They began their journey going by railroad first to Boston, then on to Niagara Falls where they crossed the suspension bridge into Canada. They continued on the railway until the end of the line on the Mississippi River across from Dubuque. On the last lap of the trip they took a steamboat to Lansing in northeastern Iowa and finally engaged stage passage to Decorah, their final destination.[5] In 1858, the Newtons tried a slightly different combination. They began their trip with a stagecoach ride from their Connecticut home to Fair Haven, where they boarded a steamboat to New York. There they boarded "the cars" for Chicago, and after visiting the city for a few days, they again boarded the cars for Davenport. They then rode to the end of the rail line in Louisa County, Iowa, where they hired a driver and team to transport them to their new home in Keokuk County.[6]

As the various steamboat and railroad companies increased their services, improved their facilities, and multiplied their routes, more migrants selected them as quick and easy means of moving to Iowa. But despite these attractions, both the boats and "cars" had some serious disadvantages. Space limitations curtailed the migrants' ability to move household goods, farm implements, seed, stock, and even clothing. Because such goods were more in demand and thus more expensive in Iowa than back East, the unequipped migrant could expect difficulty in obtaining goods as well as expense in paying for them. In addition, boat and rail fares were expensive and often prohibitive if more than two or three members of the family were making the trip.

In the face of these drawbacks, the overwhelming majority of Iowa migrants elected to use covered wagons. Although they had the deserved reputation of being slow and awkward, their unwieldy bulk accommodated family members, goods, equipment, and animals. The journey took considerably longer than one by boat or rail, but the migrants enjoyed the advantage of having their belongings, seed, and stock with them in a territory with few surplus goods. If necessary, the prairie schooner could even become a temporary home for the settlers when the trail finally came to a welcome end.

Realizing the magnitude of their undertaking, migrants focused their mental and physical efforts on each minute detail of the trip ahead. They already knew from emigrants' guides, word of mouth, and personal accounts that any small oversight or lack of attention to a petty detail could make the difference between success and failure, between survival and destruction. So family members worked on the necessary preparations as a team, but like any effective team they divided the labor according to the skills of the individuals involved. This meant a traditional division of labor. Because of their long experience with machinery and livestock, the men took responsibility for the wagon and its team. The women worked long and hard to prepare the needed clothing, bedding, kitchenware, and foodstuffs for the trip.

In practice, however, the division was not this clear. Men and women helped each other whenever possible, overlapped duties, and shared tasks. The men usually made the final selection of the wagon. They chose from two basic types: the large Conestoga wagon, which was approximately fifteen feet long, five feet wide, and five feet deep or the smaller, lighter Emigrant wagon which measured about ten feet in length, four feet in width, and two feet in depth.[7] Their choice was based on how much they wanted to carry and how fast they wanted to travel. In either style they looked for a sturdy, well-constructed box which would not shake apart on some desolate stretch of trail. Once the wagon was selected, the men equipped it with running gear and trained suitable animals to haul it and its contents hundreds of miles through sun, dust, rain, mud, and snow.

At this point, the women took over. The final segment of the wagon consisted of a cloth top, produced by the women of the family, who had familiarity with fabrics and sewing skills. This was a long, difficult job because the top was frequently stitched by hand. In planning a wagon cover for one of their journeys, Kitturah Belknap explained that she would "make a muslin cover for the wagon as we will have a double cover so we can keep warm and dry; put the muslin on first and then the heavy linen one for strength. They both have to be sewed real good and strong and I have to spin the thread and sew all those long seams with my fingers." According to Belknap, energy and expertise by the woman or women were the two essential ingredients needed to produce a roof which would successfully shelter the travelers from inclement weather during their long journey.[8]

While the production of the cover was progressing, women, aided by the men and children, were also giving much thought to the equipping of the wagon box. The degree of thoughtfulness and efficiency expended on this task could spell disaster or success for the migrants. A family's entire future had to be assembled and packed in limited space. Every item they owned or purchased had to be critically examined for its potential usefulness. Equipment had to include all clothing, food, cooking utensils, bedding, medicines, and tools that might be necessary to sustain family and animals along the trail as well as seed, farm implements, and furniture to carry them through the beginning phases of establishing a home.

Although equipping the box was a chore involving both men and women, they still divided the labor along customary lines. The men readied such items as firearms, tools, and furniture. They also utilized every possible space on the outside of the wagon box to hang buckets of grease for the axles, barrels of water for the stock, and spare parts for the wagon. Then they busied themselves training the team and preparing the family's other stock for the long journey ahead. Women took primary responsibility for food, clothing, and medicine, which they began to prepare well in advance of departure. Kitturah Belknap left a detailed account of preparations which consumed all her spare moments during an entire winter:

> I have to make a feather tick for my bed . . . the linen is ready to go to work on, and six two bushel bags all ready to sew up . . . have cut out two pair of pants for George. . . . I have worked almost day and night this winter, having the sewing about all done but a coat and vest for George. Will wash and begin to pack and start with some old clothes on and when we can't wear them any longer will leave them on the road.[9]

Despite exhaustion and ill health, she also dipped enough candles to last a year; prepared a complete medicine chest; packed home-sewn sacks with flour, corn meal, dried fruits, and other foodstuffs; assembled dishes and cooking pots; and cooked enough food to last the first week. Finally, she put together a workbasket of sewing so that she wouldn't spend any idle moments during the trip. Meanwhile, her husband George built an ingenious camp table, practiced with the oxen, and readied the other stock for travel. Belknap was delighted with the camp table; it perfectly complemented the ambience she was determined to maintain on the trail. She had already decided to start off with "good earthen dishes," although she was realistic enough to bring tin dishes as a back-up in case the earthen ones were broken. She also had made "four nice little table cloths." With these accoutrements, she declared that she was "going to live just like I was at home."[10] This cooperative venture between men and women in readying themselves, their families, and their goods for the trail resulted in a fully loaded prairie schooner that must have been an impressive sight. It has been estimated that they ranged from 1500 to 2000 pounds, not counting the additional weight of their human passengers.[11] Many wagons had an assortment of farm animals tied to the back end or dangling in crates tied to the sides. Moreover, many men and women worked together to incorporate individualized refinements, depending on their own needs and inventiveness. The Belknaps prepared a secure spot for Kitturah's rocking chair so she could ride comfortably while sewing. They also arranged a minuscule play corner for their young son and devised a clever folding bed that would allow them to sleep in the relative comfort of their wagon. The Shutes family arranged their wagon to accommodate Ann Shutes and her infant at night. A common practice, which soon became an accepted part of trail lore, was sewing canvas pouches to the inside of the wagon cover. Catherine Haun found their "pockets" invaluable for small items which needed to be kept in easy reach, including cooking knives, firearms, and toilet articles.[12]

People who chose a smaller wagon usually had a shorter distance to cover, but they too were experts at utilizing every possible inch of space. Mary Moore McLaughlin described her family's wagon as "a low, long-coupled, straight-box, two-horse wagon, made roomy and comfortable by an extension of the wagon bed over the wheels." Although it was relatively limited in size, it was crammed with many items, including some things that were apparently family treasures. McLaughlin especially remembered "mother's little cane seated rocker, our family pictures and books, one bureau, and a jar of honey." Like most other families, the Moores made every effort to create additional space. They hooked a small table upside down on top of the feed box at the back of the wagon to hold "the cooking utensils, the dinner box, the stove rack used for campfire cooking, and two splint-bottom chairs." When it was unhooked, it quickly converted into a convenient, comfortable dining area.[13] These various refinements and additions indicate that effort was made to provide a minimal amount of comfort.

Of course, the physical provisions for the journey were only a part of migrants' total preparations. They also had to begin the process of psychologically separating from their families, friends, and neighbors. The trauma of parting cannot be overemphasized. Unlike modern society, where the average person moves many times in his or her life, most nineteenth-century people were accustomed to being part of a region, a town, a neighborhood, and a kinship network. These people shared value systems, social life, customs, and traditions. They shared the joy of births and weddings and the sadness of deaths. They called upon each other for help in times of crisis. And they gathered together to pray or to celebrate a holiday.

There is little evidence that the emotional wrench of leaving was any harder on women than men. Popular myth to the contrary, both men and women seemed to share the pain. Granted, it was more socially acceptable for women to show it; while Hiram Shutes stole away for a secret farewell with his mother, Kitturah Belknap openly refused to attend a last church service because of her emotional state.[14]

A family's decision to leave was not only traumatic for them, but for those left behind. An announcement of impending departure thus initiated a transition period during which both the soon-to-be travelers and those remaining at home attempted to adjust to separation. The rituals accompanying the parting included dinners, dances, family visits, and special church services, all designed to wrap the migrants in a warm cloak of good wishes and friendship. Despite brave attempts to ease the farewell with a festive air, the morning of departure usually presented a heartrending scene. In the murky early morning light, people gathered around the migrants to help them load their wagon, serve them breakfast, grasp their hands one last time, and wish them luck in the new country. Sleepy-eyed Mary Alice Shutes peered through the dim light of a pre-dawn bonfire to discover that a great number of relatives and friends had come to see her family off and to cook breakfast as a "final display and effort of friendship." She sensed the strain in the air: "The younger kids know something unusual is going on but don't understand it like the older folks do. . . . Some of the older ones seem to welcome the solitude away from the fire . . . they have said their goodbyes and are just waiting." She sympathized but did not really understand. From her perspective as a thirteen-year-old, she was thinking more of the excitement of the "good lark ahead of us" than of those left behind.[15]

It was a common practice for friends to ride along with the migrants and their wagons for the first few miles in an extended goodbye ceremony. As the outskirts were reached, these riders gradually dropped back and returned home, leaving the wayfarers to begin their expedition. As they waved one last farewell to their friends and the life they had known, the travelers confronted the trail that would transform them into westerners.

Scary, exciting, intimidating, promising—these and many other words must have flowed through travelers' minds as they assessed the scene unfolding before them. Their trepidation may have been allayed somewhat because they did not lack for company in their trek towards Iowa. One observer even portrayed Iowa migration as a mass movement. As early as 1836 he claimed:

> The roads were literally lined with the long blue wagons of the emigrants slowly wending their way over the broad prairies, the cattle and hogs, men and dogs, and frequently women and children, forming the rear of the van, often ten, twenty, and thirty wagons in company. Ask them, when and where you would, their destination was the "Black Hawk Purchase."[16]

The huge, distended wagons forced their iron-covered wheels into the earthen trail, leaving tracks that were reinforced by thousands of wearying footsteps of people and animals. By the time the migrants converged on Iowa, the marks of their passage were etched on the prairie. Recalling her family's move in the 1860s, McLaughlin later wrote, "I can see now the two tracks of the road, cut deep by the wagon wheels and washed out by the rains."[17] These tracks became a kind of map for those who followed and a testimonial of those who had already completed the demanding journey.

Whenever they had the opportunity, migrants joined with another group to swap information, exchange bits of trail lore, or travel together for as long as their routes coincided. McLaughlin remembered that at times they traveled alone, but when possible, they joined with other "movers." She remarked that they "were always glad to have company, especially when fording swollen streams, for then we could double up teams and take turns in making the crossing." Her explanation of this gregariousness was perhaps too simplistic. Joining with others, comparing points of origin and destinations, and making new friends was a tie to a past filled with friends, an attempt to maintain identity in a world that reduced everyone to a common denominator, and practice for a future that would demand the establishment of many new contacts. Hiram Shutes, for example, was enthusiastic when he met someone from his home region or a person who planned to settle in the same area as his family.[18]

Some migrants, perhaps anticipating the anonymity of the trail, traveled in groups. When the Willises announced their intention to relocate in Iowa, they were surprised and pleased to learn that "most of the immediate relatives soon sold their homes, loaded their goods into wagons, and started for Iowa" with them. They helped each other by "fording streams, wading through mud, and enduring untold hardships" together. The Harris family put together a similar kind of caravan. Numbering ten people, they moved in two huge covered wagons pulled by yokes of oxen and a two-seated buggy pulled by a team of horses.[19]

What neither of these chroniclers articulated was the hedge the family caravan formed against the onset of loneliness, the disintegration of family unity, and often stark aspects of the trail. Furthermore, neither they nor many other Iowa women writers specifically discussed why they had placed themselves in such a threatening, albeit potentially fulfilling, situation. Of the few that mentioned motivation, Mary Ann Ferrin stated that she "was fond of adventure and preferred to go with my husband." Similarly, McLaughlin said that her mother liked to move: "father always said that whenever he wanted to move he had only to tell mother of his plans and she was ready and willing to go."[20]

According to the traditional image, however, a woman was simply an appendage to a man; her husband, father, or brother made the decision, and in the manner of a "True Woman" of the nineteenth century, she accepted that decision. This stereotype clouds attempts to understand the motivation of the unmarried woman migrant. It has been assumed that the unmarried female relocated only so that she would become an appendage; in other words, she moved to marry one of the surplus male migrants already in Iowa. Such thinking was common in a society in which all women were expected to marry, and the preponderance of women did so. Despite the emergent feminist movement of the 1840s, marriage was still seen by most Americans as the appropriate be-all and end-all of a young woman's life. It is not surprising, then, that many young women capitalized on the West's gender imbalances to further their marital aspirations.

Regardless of the stereotypical thinking of the era, many ambitious single women headed west as laborers, missionaries, and teachers. Catharine Beecher encouraged women teachers to choose western careers because she saw employment opportunities for them and because she regarded women as civilizing influences necessary to a new society. In addition, some unmarried women moved, as did men, to take up land, although the data on them are incomplete. Unfortunately, such evidence as Newhall's 1846 guide to Iowa, which listed only the occupation of dairy maid as a possible job for a woman, and gazetteers and almanacs that categorized women primarily as seamstresses and dressmakers frustrate the curious historian. Worse yet, some Iowa census reports listed women as "not gainfully employed."[21]

If assessing the motives of the single woman is difficult, the task of discerning the motives of married women (or women otherwise part of a family unit) is nearly impossible. Because they were dependent members, their part in the decision-making process was usually obscured by the aggregate family decision. As a result, some rather tenuous suppositions have been formulated. One argues that many women had no motivation beyond obeying or pleasing their husbands. Another holds that because income production was the husband/father's ascribed duty in nineteenth-century society, he made the decision how and where that income would be produced; the rest of the family had to acquiesce.[22]

Certainly, nineteenth-century society cast men in the role of breadwinners, initiators, and decision-makers, but Iowa women's writings fail to uphold the theory that they were repressed. Rather, the feelings of women in family units ran the gamut: they accepted, identified with, supported, or initiated the idea of migration. As women described their feelings, one detects that their emotion was more often optimism rather than bitterness. Like men, they too were sensitive to the pushes and pulls that caused friends, neighbors, relatives, and ultimately themselves to decide to uproot their lives and families. These pushes and pulls, after all, tended to be oblivious of gender. Women were not dumb; they could see exhausted lands, the poor health of a family member in need of restoration, or the richness of the West.

Whatever their initial motivations, Iowa women tended to respond to the demands of the trail with hard work, buoyant spirits, and few complaints. In the four areas of enterprise, they usually made sincere, and often successful, attempts to achieve and excel.

The first area, the performance of regular chores connected with daily living, was not only time-consuming for women (whether at home or on the trail), but it was made even more troublesome by primitive trail conditions. To the credit of most women, they cared for the needs of their families in as homelike an aura as they could create during the time when the wagon was their only home and the trail their only backyard.

One of the easier problems to resolve was the families' sleeping arrangements. The wagon was an obvious "bedroom," and many of the wayfarers took advantage of its minimal protection. The Titus party was delighted that its two wagons "were roomy enough for all," but they did not remark on the comfort or the space. Most groups found that all members would not fit into the wagons, so they turned them over to the needy members: the aged, ill, small children, or women with infants. The Harrises developed another alternative: whenever they located a tavern, they boarded the women of the party there, while the men slept nearby in the wagons.[23] Others utilized tents, deserted houses, or simply slept outside, using quilts, feather ticks, or corn husk mattresses to shield them from the chill air and the unrelentingly hard ground. Most campers combined a night watch with an all-night fire to protect their camp. Shutes mentioned that "the men folks arranged about turns for night watch to watch the stock and keep the fire going as a warning for intruders to keep away." Later, she reported that they had a "nice campfire going to keep wild animals away—mostly the small kind." The eerie shadows created by the flickering fire combined with the noises of a wilderness night must have provided a frightening backdrop. Recalling a night she spent in the wagon, McLaughlin vividly remembered that, "as the twilight settled into darkness, the wolves came slinking around the camp; and while they howled we children snuggled closer together in our beds in the wagon box, begging father to build the fire higher."[24]

Occasionally, some travelers were afforded shelter for a night by a friendly family who remembered its own trek west. For Kitturah Belknap, one instance of hospitality was particularly welcome. The Belknap party crossed an eighteen-mile stretch of prairie in the freezing snow; Kitturah drove the team so her husband could herd the stock. "I thought my hands and nose would freeze," she related. "When I got to the fire it made me so sick I almost fainted." Luckily, they were taken in by a family of eight people living in a tiny, isolated cabin. Belknap thawed out her frozen provisions for dinner and then, sick with a toothache, bedded down on the floor with the other five members of her party. They arose at four A.M. to eat breakfast without disrupting their hosts and set off for more miles of snow-covered prairie.[25]

The Shutes' situation was not so desperate when they met with a hospitable family who had come to Iowa in the 1840s and had been helping migrants ever since. They had just been chased out of a deserted log cabin by what the children called "striped kitties," but which their father identified as skunks. After their close escape, they were happy to spend a night in the host family's barn and be treated to a breakfast of buckwheat cakes, fresh side pork, and coffee. Mary Alice was pleased with the meal because "you could eat your fill with no smokey taste."[26]

Mary Alice's observation highlights the fact that women had a much harder time feeding their families than they did figuring out where they would sleep. Women tackled the arduous job of meal preparation by developing a trail-craft, the ingenuity of which rivaled the woods-craft or plains-craft of their male counterparts. Using reflector ovens, prairie stoves, or campfires, they concocted meals that ranged from adequate to wonderfully unforgettable. Lydia Titus was particularly adept at campfire cooking. She "fried home-cured ham or bacon with eggs," while she "boiled potatoes or roasted them in the hot ashes." The Lacey family settled for a cold lunch from the big barrel that Sarah had packed, but at night she insisted upon cooking them a hot meal. She prided herself on offering them "meat or eggs and a warm vegetable for all, as well as pie or cake." McLaughlin recalled a homey scene with prairie chicken as the centerpiece: "father would bring water, build a fire and take down the little green table and splint-bottom chairs from the back of the wagon, while mother prepared the meal. We were at home on the prairie with prairie chicken for supper!"[27]

Another woman's diary referred to cooking over an open fire, cooking in the rain, and cooking food on Sunday to be eaten during the first part of the following week. One Sunday her project of fixing beans was interrupted by a rain shower. "Wasn't it a shame!" she lamented. "Mine were almost done when a shower came up and drove me into the wagon. The beans taking advantage of my absence burned up. Nothing was left for me but to cook more." Like many trail women, she augmented her facilities with whatever resources came to hand. At one camp spot she made biscuits after obtaining permission to bake them in a nearby house; at another she prepared eggs on a borrowed camp stove.[28]

As the migrants neared Iowa, the task of food preparation became more difficult due to decreasing fuel supplies. Because prairies did not readily yield wood, the travelers often had to purchase it. They also twisted hay, prairie grass, or slough grass into "cats." This created an extra job for the women and children, who spent hours collecting and twisting the hay or grass, but it was perhaps more agreeable than the other widely employed option of collecting dried animal excrement, euphemistically called cow-chips or buffalo-chips, for use as fuel.[29]

Another problem, limited water supplies, made it increasingly difficult for women to wash clothing and bedding. When the rain barrels were full, when a farmhouse with a well was located, or when a stream was reached, the women and girls seized the opportunity to refresh garments dirtied and worn by traveling in heat and dust. Gould's note was typical. "At four p.m. I commenced and did a real large washing—spreading the clothes on the grass at sunset." At a later point, she expressed shock because, while they were "laying over because it was the Sabbath," she discovered that "the women were doing up their week's washing!"[30]

Gould's observation offers a critical insight into women's work on the trail: their tasks were often out of pace with the rhythm of other trail work. Rest periods for the men and younger children, such as meal stops or evenings, were the times women began their chores. Complicating matters was the ever-present task of child care. Any attempt to determine the proportion of children on the trail is thwarted by lack of census data. Although their numbers remain a matter of conjecture, mention of their existence is liberally scattered throughout women's sources.[31] Moreover, there is little indication that anyone thought it unusual for children to make the demanding trip, even at very tender ages.

The story of Lydia Titus is representative. In 1869, when she and her husband resolved to make Iowa their new home, her younger sister and her husband announced they were going along. Both couples sold their farms and stock, "keeping only a wagon apiece and four horses," to transport themselves and their four children. Lydia had an eight-year-old daughter, a three-year-old son, and a ten-month-old girl, and her sister had a six-week-old baby girl, yet neither woman thought that moving young children was an extraordinary undertaking. They soon learned that they were not alone. There were many others, such as the Archer family, who with four wagons were moving nineteen people; thirteen were children who ranged in age between two and the early twenties.[32] For trail women, the problem of physically protecting the children was the most distressing aspect of child care. Despite their constant vigilance, children often got off to the side of the road or lagged behind the train, causing their parents more than a few anxious moments. Furthermore, the possibility of accident, illness, and disease constantly hovered over women. Although they carried medicine, they knew that the services of a doctor would be virtually unobtainable in case of serious trouble. Elisha Brooks always remembered the starkness of the situation when illness hit him and other children of his party. "A picture lingers in my memory," he said, "of us children all lying in a row on the ground in our tent, somewhere in Iowa, stricken with the measles, while six inches of snow covered all the ground and the trees were brilliant with icicles." Similarly, Shutes recorded the terror she faced when sleepy young Archie bounced off the wagon and barely escaped having his head crushed by its wheel. When she learned that Archie was dazed but otherwise uninjured, she sighed with relief: "Am sure luck is with us."[33] Evidently, migrants did not see these hazards as much greater than those of their former lives, for they persisted in undertaking the trip with babies and children. In some cases, optimism offset the threat of adversity. One couple traveling with two infants was described as "young and full of hope and made light of the hardship." In other cases, a spirit of necessity prevailed. As "Grandmother" Brown summed it up, "then I never thought about its being hard. I was used to things being hard."[34]

These tasks were aggravated because women were expected to help in the second objective, that of physically moving the group to the new area. When the caravan was on the move, women were not relieved of duties. Child care continued, but women also contributed to such "male" tasks as driving the team and herding stock. Haun called it lending "a helping hand." She explained that "the latter service was expected of us all—men and women alike." Belknap, for instance, frequently took over the lines and drove the team to free her husband to tend the unruly stock. And Lyon's mother routinely drove the wagon part of each day so that her husband could stretch his legs. When their wagon became mired in mud, she mounted their horse and, with "the baby in her arms" and her small son astride behind her, guided the horse in rescuing the wagon.[35]

Women also engaged in the battle against sun-scorched prairies, biting snow storms, mud sloughs, and wide streams and rivers. The latter could often be forded or ferried across with comparative ease, but in some cases their depth or flooded condition presented a barrier to migrants, wagons, and animals. There were some classic tales of groups pushing ahead with the help of their women. In 1832, for example, Caroline Phelps and her husband were stymied by flooded Sugar Creek. They crossed by swimming on horseback and floating on driftwood. In the process, Phelps, who suffered with an eye swollen shut by an infection, was knocked down and kicked in the forehead by a frightened horse. She roused herself sufficiently to pick up her baby and get across the creek; the men of the party brought their wagon across in pieces. Her comment on the affair demonstrated her vigor: "we had a good supper and a good bed. . . . the next morning I was quite refreshed."[36]

Even if they escaped such perils, Iowa-bound migrants had to confront the Mississippi River. Railroads and highways ended on the east bank, leaving the settlers to traverse the river by boat or ferry. Because bridges across the Mississippi were not constructed until the late 1860s, due to bitter opposition by steamboat companies and ferry operators, settlers had to deal with this impediment to their progress.

For most people, crossing was a time-consuming but interesting event. When the Shutes family reached the Mississippi, they learned they had just missed a flood which had prevented crossings for several weeks. "Not just too much water," they were informed, "but too much trash and big trees that would smash anything in their way." Fortuitously, Hiram had been advised to arrive ahead of his party and get their name "in the pot," so they had to wait less than a day. When they left their camp and approached the ferry, they were quickly caught up in the excitement of throngs of people, escalating noise levels, animated talk of high water, and piercing blasts from the whistle of the steam-powered ferry. As they gradually edged up the loading plank, the men took responsibility for the wagons, the children led the blindfolded horses, and the mother shepherded the small children. Once out upon the swirling waters, Shutes felt that her mother had "the real job sitting on a chair holding the baby and Howard."[37]

For some women, the crossing was not this easy. In the mid-1860s, a woman who had already managed moving herself and four children under age eleven to join her husband, was appalled to learn that cracking ice on the Mississippi River prevented teams from transporting any more migrants it that winter. She was told she would have to wait until the ice cleared for the ferries to run again. Faced with four exhausted children and a diminished cash reserve, she decided to join others who were walking to Iowa over the groaning ice floes. She picked up the baby, distributed the luggage among the older children, and set out. Her daughter later recounted their perilous crossing:

> I can see yet, as in a dream, that great expanse of gray ice. Even then it was cracking, and as we went on there was a low grinding sound. . . . we were constantly warned not to crowd together or we would break through. Mother who, with all her burdens, was clipping along with the rest would call out cheering and encouraging me to come along. I don't think she had realized how wide the river was, how far the distant shore.

When asked what had given her the courage to keep going across the splitting ice, she replied, "I was thinking of your father and all he had been writing about you children growing up in Iowa."[38]

Obviously, time on the trail was far from dull for most women; neither was it uninstructive. As they carried out chores and helped with other trail work, they were developing themselves in the third area—sharpening skills that would serve them well both on the trail and in new homes. Since they were predominantly farm women, they were not naïve about what would be required of them: food processing, cooking, spinning, weaving, and other skills were already in most of their repertoires. Yet, on the trail, they demonstrated creativity, and at times pure genius, in the way they adapted these skills to the conditions at hand. Kitturah Belknap was a perfect illustration. Using a Dutch oven, a skillet, a teakettle, and a coffeepot, she devised meals just like "at home." These featured her salt-rising bread, which she worked at between her other chores:

> When we camped I made rising and set it on the warm ground and it would be up about midnight. I'd get up and put it to sponge and in the morning the first thing I did was to mix the dough and put it in the oven and by the time we had breakfast it would be ready to bake. Then we had nice coals and by the time I got things washed up and packed up and the horses were ready the bread would be done and we would go on our way rejoicing.

Butter was not a problem for Belknap either. When the cows were milked at night, she strained the milk into buckets which were covered and set on the ground under the wagon. In the morning, she skimmed off the cream, put it in the churn in the wagon, and after riding all day she had "a nice role of butter." Kitturah further supplemented their meals with foodstuffs bought along the way. She kept her eye out for a farmhouse where she might purchase a head of cabbage, potatoes, eggs, or other fresh foods. She soon became trail-wise: "where there were farms old enough to raise anything to spare, they were glad to exchange their produce for a few dimes."[39]

Despite the prevalence of such grit, some women never made it in the last area—changing their mindset from an eastern orientation to a western one. Some of these women, regretting their decision or finding themselves unable to cope with the demands of migration, voluntarily turned back. Like every society, the trail had a number of misfits. These were not only women, for some men also decided to terminate the venture. As one woman pointed out, "some liked the new country, but others . . . returned to their native States."[40]

Some scholars have argued that the work which women performed and the mental anguish they endured on the trail was not repaid by a bond of inclusion in what was essentially a male-directed undertaking. They have claimed that in consequence women soon became alienated and disheartened by the migration experience.[41] If Iowa women experienced these feelings, they generally avoided recording them. Perhaps they realized that any domestic routines they could recreate, any assistance they could offer, and any supportive feelings they could extend were necessary to the preservation of their families and themselves under the duress of migration. Most seemed to understand that their tasks, whether physical or psychological ones, were absolutely essential in subduing the trail and getting their families to new settlements. Rather than complain, these trail women often expressed a sense of equanimity. This was apparent in Gould's remark that it was "decidedly cool camping out and cooking by a campfire, but we must do as we can." It was also reflected in Shutes's statement that "we have a lot of weary miles behind us. Glad to have done it but would not care to do it over again, or very soon anyway." Furthermore, the harshness of the trail environment was often leavened by fun. Singing, dancing, and good-natured courting were frequently part of the scene. The following diary notation was not uncommon: "I hear the merry notes of a violin. A general cheerfulness prevails."[42]

Had these women been hardened and bitter, they could not have been as awed and as pleased as they were by the prairie country that gradually enveloped them. One exulted that "the prairies were just one great flower garden." Another remembered how her family learned to love the open prairie as they traveled across its broad expanse. Another emphasized that she could not adequately describe "the magnificence of the wild flowers that made the prairies for miles in all directions one gorgeous mass of variant beauty." And yet another called it "a perfect garden of Eden."[43]

It appears then that in challenging the trail, many Iowa-bound women also challenged the nineteenth-century stereotype that women were weak, emotionally insecure, and capable of existing only within the confines of a home tucked away from the realities of a harsh world. Although the westward journey broke and embittered some women, so many emerged from it intact or even strengthened that it is unconscionable to generalize any longer. Many trail women were strong because, in reality, life for most nineteenth-century American women was difficult whatever the location. As one woman put it, her parents survived the crude conditions of the road because "their early lives had been spent amid such surroundings."[44] That their lives were not easy, or even satisfactory at home, was the very reason that most people were on the trail. It was tough, but at least it offered the hope of increased rewards for their deprivation and toil.

Many of these trail women not only survived the journey, but they went on to become settlers, to live to tell about it, and to recount many happy times as well. A great number became trail women again, this time tackling the overland route to the Far West. Kitturah Belknap, Lucy Cooke, E. Allene Dunham, Eliza Ann Egbert, Catherine Haun, and Virginia Ivins were only a few of the Iowa women who eventually crossed the Plains to the Far West just as they had traveled to Iowa. And on the overland route, as on the trail to Iowa, they recorded positive impressions of their trek.

As one might expect from previous descriptions of Kitturah Belknap, her mettle and spunk survived the long route to Oregon in 1848. She prided herself on having the only dinner table in the train with a cloth on it. She industriously sewed and mended in her spare moments, and she became an adept trader with farmers, emigrants, and Indians. Although she noted her fear of Indians and Mormons, a quarrel in the next wagon caused by a husband's refusal to give in to his wife's demands to turn around, and her son's serious illness, her own spirits remained high. Her description of the journey was sprinkled with comments such as: "the road is good and I am standing the riding fine," "it is a fine spring morning," "have had fine weather, good roads and all have been well," and "I have washed and ironed and cooked up a lot; find our appetites improve the longer we are out."[45]

A similar mood emanates from the trail letters of Lucy Cooke, a young mother with a year-old baby who emigrated to California with her husband and his parents in 1852. Her mother-in-law's lamentations about the trip, frequent outbreaks of cholera, and the rigorous mountain crossings failed to intimidate her. She too was able to find "luxuries" along the trail: candy and preserves from Ft. Laramie, a fine dinner in a boardinghouse in Salt Lake City, and an impressive collection of furs garnered from trading some of her goods with Native Americans. At Salt Lake she wrote her sister in Iowa that "so far as we have come, there's nothing to fear on the road. Two-thirds of the distance has been good as a turnpike road. . . . I wish I were seated in your snug parlor, telling the wonders of travel."[46]

Her husband, William, was depressed by the trip, however. Lucy told her sister that "William often wishes we were back, and says so soon as he gets any more than he started with he'll be with you. If I were very anxious I think William would send me back to you in the spring, and he go on alone to California; but it looks best we journey together." During their next lap—four months to California—she wrote, "so far enjoy ourselves. . . . We live first rate." When they finally sighted Lake Tahoe, she rejoiced that "our trials would soon be of the past, whilst the future, oh, where was the limit?"[47]

Because E. Allene Dunham crossed the trail to California as a young girl with her family in 1846, her remembrances are of a slightly different nature. She did, however, mention amenities such as camping at a farm, her mother and the baby boarding in a hotel, staying in an emigrant campground, and buying milk from farms along the way. She remembered a few unfriendly Native Americans, but said the majority were pleasant, asked for food, and invited the emigrants to their camps. Dunham's other recollections focused upon gathering wild flowers, playing on rocks, hiding in the sagebrush, and the highlight of the trip was being taken to mountain peaks by some young women of the train who "took their revolvers and we had a fine time." Her conclusion: "We children knew nothing only to enjoy ourselves, and we surely did."[48]

Like Dunham, Eliza Ann Egbert crossed the Plains in 1852 as a girl. Although she noted accidents, deaths, "impudent" Indians, and loss of stock, she did not dwell upon them. Instead, she noted her appreciation of "a beautiful camp ground near a little stream on the prairie," "fair weather today and good road," "delicious water," and "good grass." Her son was later to say of her, "No doubt the young emigrants endured many hardships, but if so, they are not stressed in the diary, nor do I remember that they were ever mentioned by my mother in the many times I have heard her speak of the trip. To them it was the big adventure and the hardships were accepted as part of that adventure."[49]

Catherine Margaret Haun, on the other hand, made the trip as a young bride in 1849 due to family financial trouble and her own poor health. She maintained that the hazards of the trail did not frighten her. "Indeed," she wrote, "as we had been married but a few months, it appealed to us as a romantic wedding tour." Overall, the trail proved therapeutic for her: "In my case, as in that of many others, my health was restored long before the end of the journey." The first few days, however, she found to be extremely tiresome and she described herself "dazed with dread." She avoided confiding in her husband because she didn't want to add to his burdens. She believed that "he would certainly have turned back for he, as well as the other men of the party, was disheartened and was struggling not to betray it."[50]

From that point on, Haun's frame of mind improved, and she surprised herself by offering, despite her lack of experience, to do all the cooking for her party when the cook quit. She found her companions to be "a wonderful collection of people," the youngest of whom was a six-week-old baby. Like the other women, she helped drive the wagon, cared for the children, and caught up with her washing and mending on Sundays. Although they were passed by many discouraged emigrants returning home, she urged her husband onward. She was pleased that they were among the dozen or so people out of the original 120 in the train that reached Sacramento as scheduled.[51]

The last tale of the overland trek was written by Virginia Ivins, a Keokuk woman who left for California in 1853 with her husband, one-year-old son, aunt and uncle, five drovers, and a German cook named Carl. Around the time they neared Ft. Laramie she noted that "on the whole we were having a rather good time; were all well, were becoming inured to privations, and things were moving along quite satisfactorily." She was aware that Indians were frequently around, but said they never bothered the camp. Although only twenty years old, she cheerfully helped with the heavy cooking chores. Near the end of the journey, when she fell seriously ill, she stated that she "simply endured without complaint" but "made the best of the somewhat difficult situation and was quite cheerful when my husband was with me." When foul weather and broken-down wagons beset them, she went to the aid of her husband because he was "altogether discouraged, hardly knowing what to do and seemed to depend on me for advice.[52]

When, near California, Ivins's husband was offered several lucrative jobs, they decided to continue on their way. According to Ivins, "ease had no charms for us then." She basked in the limelight created by the scarcity of women, remarked on the lovely weather, and congratulated herself for having remained "perfectly cool in every danger we had encountered." When the end was finally sighted, she found herself "almost jubilant" to have survived a "most trying and tedious journey" successfully.[53]

Here, then, are the stories of six representative women who crossed the most feared trail of all—the route across the Plains to the Far West. Yet the conditions they recounted and the emotions they expressed were very similar to those women on the Iowa trail. There was a hardiness, a creativity, a buoyancy of spirit in these women that makes one wonder if the trail was as detrimental to women as myth would have us believe. The similarities they shared were more than coincidental: the goods purchased along the way, the enjoyment of scenery and climate, the lack of serious problems with Native Americans, the shoring up of tired and discouraged men, and the determination to reach the intended destination were recurrent themes which cannot be ignored. The replacement of the image of beleaguered trail women with a more balanced picture is clearly long overdue.

Many women's treks were relatively short because migrants commonly moved to one western area, then to another. Rumors of richer land, better climate, and more peaceful conditions drew them away from one destination to try yet another. Here, a woman recalled her family's journey from Texas to Oklahoma in 1892:

When we left our home, which was twenty miles from Weatherford, Texas . . . there were three families and their stock, and their household goods. Each family had a covered wagon, which held all their belongings such as bedding, clothing, cooking utensils, and food and family. . . . There were 350 head of cattle, forty head of horses and about sixty head of sheep.

When we left Texas, several neighbors and their families prepared lots of good things to eat and went with us as far as the Brazos River; there we all ate dinner together. The river was up and we had to ferry the wagons and sheep across, but the cattle and horses swam the river. Our neighbors returned to their homes and we three families set our face toward the unknown land and we never saw any of our friends again.

We met and overcame many obstacles. There wasn't room to sleep in the wagons, so we slept on the ground under and around the wagon, and sometimes we would have to set up in the wagon all night when it was raining or storming. Sometimes we would sleep in a schoolhouse. The rain and storms bothered more than anything else, as the men had to ride around the cattle all night. Once when it was storming and raining very hard the cattle stampeded and we had to camp there until they were rounded up, that is all the cattle which could be found. Not all were found. The women drove the wagons and men looked after the cattle. . . .

When we came to Pear River, it was very narrow and shallow. I remember holding to the stirrup of the saddle on the horse. My mother rode across the river and I waded all the way across. When we got across, it was late in the day, and we camped close to a man's house by the name of King. That night a terrible storm came up and it stormed hard all night, and Mr. King came out and invited all the women and children to come in and spend the night in the house. Oh! how nice it was to be in out of the storm. . . .

Well, the next river we came to was Red River at Doan's Crossing. The river was up and had been several days, so we camped there a few days and the river went down enough that my father thought if he drove the cattle and horses across first, that it would pack the sand enough that the wagons could cross without much trouble, which they did. The next place we came to was Navajo, where my father's brother lived. We rested two days and then we started on. The next river we came to was the North Fork of Red River and it was up, but not so bad but what my father thought we could make it across, and we did, but the mules went under all but their heads and some kettles and pans that were in the feed box of our wagon floated out. After we got across North Fork we came on this way and when we got to Big Elk Creek we saw our first Indians and their tepees and papooses. . . .

We arrived at our new home on a beautiful day the 29th of June. We camped under a large oak tree until my father could make us a dugout, which was the most comfortable thing we had been in for days. . . . That summer this part of the country was so beautiful, just as far as you could see was a sea of grass, and so many wild flowers and every stream of water had trees on each side of the bank. . . .[54]

Of course, the rigorous overland route across the Plains to California received a tremendous amount of publicity, especially when catastrophes occurred. The most memorable of these calamities struck the Donner Party, who spent a harsh winter in the Sierra Nevada in 1846–47. Virginia Reed Murphy described her family's experience as part of the Donner Party:

I was a child when we started to California, yet I remember the journey well and I have cause to remember it, as our little band of emigrants who drove out of Springfield, Illinois, that spring morning of 1846 have since been known in history as the "Ill-fated Donner party" of "Martyr Pioneers". . . .

Our wagons, or the "Reed wagons," as they were called, were all made to order. . . . We had two wagons loaded with provisions. Everything in that line was bought that could be thought of. My father started with supplies enough to last us through the first winter in California, had we made the journey in the usual time of six months. . . .

Nothing of much interest happened until we reached what is now Kansas. The first Indians we met were the Caws, who kept the ferry, and had to take us over the Caw River. I watched them closely, hardly daring to draw my breath, and feeling sure they would sink the boat in the middle of the stream. . . .

. . . we came to the Big Blue River, which was so swollen that we could not cross, but had to lie by and make rafts on which to take the wagons over. . . . As the river remained high and there was no prospect of fording it, the men went to work cutting down trees, hollowing out logs and making rafts on which to take the wagons over. . . . Finally the dangerous work was accomplished and we resumed our journey.

The road at first was rough and led through a timbered country, but after striking the great valley of the Platte the road was good and the country beautiful. . . . Traveling up the smooth valley of the Platte, we passed Court House Rock, Chimney Rock and Scott's Bluffs, and made from fifteen to twenty miles a day, shortening or lengthening the distance in order to secure a good camping ground. . . .

At Fort Laramie was a party of Sioux, who were on the war path going to fight the Crows or Blackfeet. The Sioux are fine-looking Indians and I was not in the least afraid of them. . . . On the sixth of July we were again on the march. The Sioux were several days in passing our caravan, not on account of the length of our train, but because there were so many Sioux. . . . Some of our company became alarmed, and the rifles were cleaned out and loaded, to let the warriors see that we were prepared to fight; but the Sioux never showed any inclination to disturb us. . . .

A new route had just been opened . . . called the "Hastings Cut-off," which passed along the southern shore of the Great Salt Lake rejoining the old "Fort Hall Emigrant" road on the Humboldt. It was said to shorten the distance three hundred miles. Much time was lost in debating which course to pursue. . . . My father was so eager to reach California that he was quick to take advantage of any means to shorten the distance, and we were assured by Hastings and his party that the only bad part was the forty-mile drive through the desert by the shore of the lake. . . . The greater portion of our company went by the old road and reached California in safety. Eighty-seven persons took the "Hastings Cut-off". . . . These are the unfortunates who have since been known as the "Donner Party."

. . . a few days showed us that the road was not as it had been represented. We were seven days in reaching Weber Canyon, and Hastings, who was guiding a party in advance of our train, left a note by the wayside warning us that the road through Weber Canyon was impassable and advising us to select a road over the mountains. . . . There was absolutely no road, not even a trail. . . . Worn with travel and greatly discouraged we reached the shore of the Great Salt Lake. It had taken an entire month, instead of a week. . . . This desert had been represented to us as only forty miles wide but we found it nearer eighty. . . .

The stock, scenting water, had rushed on ahead of the men, and had probably been stolen by the Indians, and driven into the mountains, where all traces of them were lost. . . . my father and his family were left in the desert, eight hundred miles from California, seemingly helpless. We realized that our wagons must be abandoned. The company kindly let us have two yoke of oxen, so with our ox and cow yoked together we could bring one wagon. . . .

Before leaving the desert camp, an inventory of provisions on hand was taken, and it was found that the supply was not sufficient to last us through to California, and as if to render the situation more terrible, a storm came on during the night and the hill-tops became white with snow. Someone must go on to Sutter's Fort after provisions. A call was made for volunteers. C. T. Stanton and Wm. McClutchen bravely offered their services and started on bearing letters from the company to Captain Sutter asking for relief. We resumed our journey and soon reached Gravelly Ford on the Humboldt. . . .

On the 5th day of October, 1846, at Gravelly Ford, a tragedy was enacted which affected the subsequent lives and fortunes of more than one member of our company. . . . Milton Elliott, who was driving our wagon, and John Snyder, who was driving one of Mr. Graves's, became involved in a quarrel over the management of their oxen. Snyder was beating his cattle over the head with the butt end of his whip, when my father, returning on horse-back from a hunting trip, arrived and, appreciating the importance of saving the remainder of the oxen, remonstrated with Snyder. . . . Hard words followed. . . . springing upon the tongue of the wagon, Snyder struck my father a violent blow over the head with his heavy whip-stock. One blow followed another. Father was stunned for a moment and blinded by the blood streaming from the gashes in his head. Another blow was descending when my mother ran in between the men. Father saw the uplifted whip, but had only time to cry: "John, John," when down came the stroke upon mother. Quick as a thought my father's hunting knife was out and Snyder fell, fatally wounded. . . . My father regretted the act, and dashing the blood from his eyes went quickly to the assistance of the dying man. . . .

The members of the Donner party then held a council to decide upon the fate of my father, while we anxiously awaited the verdict. They refused to accept the plea of self-defense and decided that my father should be banished from the company and sent into the wilderness alone. . . . Then came a sacrifice on the part of my mother. Knowing only too well what her life would be without him, yet fearful that if he remained he would meet with violence at the hands of his enemies, she implored him to go, but all to no avail until she urged him to remember the destitution of the company, saying that if he remained and escaped violence at their hands, he might nevertheless see his children starving and be helpless to aid them, while if he went on he could return and meet them with food. It was a fearful struggle; at last he consented, but not before he had secured a promise from the company to care for his wife and little ones. . . .

It was apparent that the whole company would soon be put on a short allowance of food, and the snow-capped mountains gave an ominous hint of the fate that befell us in the Sierras. Our wagon was found to be too heavy, and was abandoned with everything we could spare, and the remaining things were packed in part of another wagon. We had two horses left from the wreck, which could hardly drag themselves along. . . .

On the 19th of October, while traveling along the Truckee, our hearts were gladdened by the return of Stanton, with seven mules loaded with provisions. . . . Hungry as we were, Stanton brought us something better than food—news that my father was alive. . . .

We now packed what little we had left on one mule and started with Stanton. . . . looking up with fear towards the mountains, where snow was already falling although it was only the last week in October. Winter had set in a month earlier than usual. All trails and roads were covered; and our only guide was the summit which it seemed we would never reach.

Despair drove many nearly frantic. Each family tried to cross the mountains but found it impossible. When it was seen that the wagons could not be dragged through the snow, their goods and provisions were packed on oxen and another start was made, men and women walking in the snow up to their waists, carrying their children in their arms and trying to drive their cattle. . . . Stanton went ahead with the guides, and came back and reported that we could get across if we kept right on, but that it would be impossible if snow fell. He was in favor of a forced march until the other side of the summit should be reached, but some of our party were so tired and exhausted with the day's labor that they declared they could not take another step; so the few who knew the danger that the night might bring yielded to the many, and we camped within three miles of the summit. . . .

. . . In the morning the snow lay deep on mountain and valley. With heavy hearts we turned back to a cabin that had been built by the Murphy-Schallenberger party two years before. We built more cabins and prepared as best we could for the winter. That camp, which proved the camp of death to many in our company, was made on the shore of a lake, since known as "Donner Lake". . . .

The misery endured during those four months at Donner Lake in our little dark cabins under the snow would fill pages. . . . The storms would often last ten days at a time, and we would have to cut chips from the logs inside which formed our cabins, in order to start a fire. We could scarcely walk, and the men had hardly strength to procure wood. We would drag ourselves through the snow from one cabin to another, and some mornings snow would have to be shoveled out of the fireplace before a fire could be made. Poor little children were crying with hunger, and mothers were crying because they had so little to give their children. . . .

Time dragged slowly along till we were no longer on short allowance but were simply starving. . . . We now had nothing to eat but raw hides and they were on the roof of the cabin to keep out the snow; when prepared for cooking and boiled they were simply a pot of glue. When the hides were taken off our cabin and we were left without shelter. Mr. Breen gave us a home with his family. . . . Death had already claimed many in our party and it seemed as though relief never would reach us. . . .

On his arrival at Sutter's Fort, my father made known the situation of the emigrants, and Captain Sutter offered at once to do everything possible for their relief. He furnished horses and provisions and my father and Mr. McClutchen started for the mountains, coming as far as possible with horses and then with packs on their backs proceeding on foot; but they were finally compelled to return. . . . [then] a party of seven . . . were sent to our relief . . . On the evening of February 19th, 1847, they reached our cabins, where all were starving. . . . strong men sat down and wept. For the dead were lying about on the snow, some even unburied, since the living had not had strength to bury their dead. . . .

On the 22nd of February the first relief started with a party of twenty-three men, women and children. My mother and her family were among the number. . . . The men wearing snow-shoes broke the way and we followed in their tracks. At night we lay down on the snow to sleep, to awake to find our clothing all frozen, even to our shoe-strings. At break of day we were again on the road, owing to the fact that we could make better time over the frozen snow. . . . when we reached the place where a cache had been made by hanging the food on a tree, we were horrified to find that wild animals had destroyed it, and again starvation stared us in the face. But my father was hurrying over the mountains, and met us in our hour of need with his hands full of bread. . . .

Most of the survivors, when brought in from the mountains, were taken by the different relief parties to Sutter's Fort, and the generous hearted captain did everything possible for the sufferers. Out of the eighty-three persons who were snowed in at Donner Lake, forty-two perished, and of the thirty-one emigrants who left Springfield, Illinois, that spring morning, only eighteen lived to reach California. . . .[55]

Not everyone was satisfied with California, however. Minnie Lee Cardwell Miller told of her family's migration from their home on the Sacramento River in Colusa County to Washington Territory in 1885. Because her father's death had left the family with a meager estate, her brothers were anxious to "try their fortune" in the new country:

The date fixed for our departure was May twenty-seventh and many were the friends and neighbors who gathered that morning to bid us

God-speed. Tears fell like rain as lifelong friends clasped hands in farewell. . . .

We now settled ourselves inside the covered wagon where things had been arranged as comfortably as possible for mother. There was a feather bed as well as a rocking chair, so that she might change from one to the other when tired. . . .

Our road followed the Sacramento River and though somewhat dusty, was about the average. . . . we were going to Washington Territory and nothing else mattered. . . .

Mother seemed better, so on this our second day we gained new courage and pressed onward. Still following the river we soon crossed the boundary line of Colusa County into Glenn County. It seemed now we were getting far from home. I had a strange feeling of loneliness as I watched the white line posts recede from view. . . .

I recall that about this time we came to Red Bluff Tehama County, head of navigation of the Sacramento River. Here we left the plains and entered a wooded, hilly country. . . . Occasionally we came to creeks, wide and shallow to be forded. Bridges were few and far apart. Sometimes we stopped amidstream and the horses would quench their thirst. . . .

Very well do I remember our camp on Pitt River near an Indian ranch. . . . The Indians came over to visit. They talked to us in Spanish which we were able to understand to some extent. At that time the Indians lived where they chose, and had not been relegated to the different reservations. My brother cut a long pole and went fishing with one of the Redskins and when he stayed rather too long, mother and I were somewhat worried. It was almost dark when they appeared with a long string of speckled trout, and what a treat when they were fried brown, for breakfast. These Indians gave us nuts and chewing gum from the sugar pine, and we, in exchange, gave them bread. . . .

. . . There were hills and more hills—up one and down another, we bumped along. The red dust covered our faces already brown with tan. No wonder the Indians were so friendly. We certainly were of the same complexion. It was the day of the straight bang and with my red checkered dress, I resembled one of their race to a marked degree.

. . . Directly ahead of us Mt. Shasta loomed snow white—immense. The climate in this higher altitude was very cool and toward evening we felt the chill in the air. Mother had gained rapidly and was now able to climb into the wagon without assistance. Her appetite was whetted by the cool pine scented atmosphere. She was cheerful and courageous. . . .

The country was sparsely settled. A few wood cutter's shacks and a lumber camp occasionally. Often we spent a night near these woods-people and found them very congenial. I remember one such camp by a small saw mill almost at the very foot of the Great Mountain and near where the town of Weed now stands. The people of this small settlement were of an assortment as to race and color, but being in this isolated place, it was—"hale fellow well met." They circled around the huge bonfire, and I am positive they enjoyed us....

At last we emerged from the mountains to an open valley. There were scattered farms and slightly better roads. Mt. Shasta directly East and Yreka was our next town. It was great to be in civilization and to be able to ride again. We camped early at Yreka and shopped for groceries which had begun to run low. I recall that by way of luxury, we invested in a loaf of baker's bread and a wedge of cheese....

We had looked forward to crossing the state line, and high in the Siskiyou Mountains—there it was. A pine tree limbed high with a banner floating from the top. We rested longer here, as if loath to set foot on the soil of a foreign state. We looked backward over the tree-covered mountain tops with a tinge of that something for which there seems to be no name. I remember mother saying, as she climbed into the wagon, "Goodbye California, I shall never see you again." Which, indeed, proved true.

Our expense fund, which had been small at the beginning, was rapidly becoming depleted.... So the beanpot was brought out more often now. Good old brown bean soup, seasoned with smoked bacon and garnished with slices of red onion, became our principal menu....

We crossed the Rogue river on a wooden bridge at Grants Pass and, although the roads were better, yet the inevitable hills were still with us.... It was pitiful to see our faithful beasts, how they would flinch at the slightest touch. There was nothing else to do but "lay-by" for awhile to rest and doctor them. We managed, however, to reach Roseburg. Our money was low. We could not afford to stop and yet it was impossible to go on. We were told there was a wonderful camping place in the oak grove down by the Umpqua river. Mother led the team while Tom and I pulled the wagon for probably two hundred yards. In the morning instead of the [horses'] sores being better they had become badly swollen and much worse. After some inquiry, we found a pasture and turned the horses in. To them it was Horse-heaven. We had not counted on this delay and there was just one thing to do. Tom must inquire for work. We would spend most of each day down on Main street, where he could meet the farmers. We all began to feel rather disheartened—at last admitted—homesickness. Would have turned back had it been possible.... I can remember the first evening Tom came home after he began to work. The lady sent a pat of butter. I never knew, before, how delicious buttered bread tasted. Each evening she would send some little delicacy to us....

Three weeks passed and it became evident that one of the horses had developed a lameness. About this time a man—one Pete McKinney—came to our camp looking for someone to run his header. My brother said, "I am your man." We hurriedly gathered our traps and swept them in the wagon. The lame horse was able to travel but slowly for the six miles, and we reached the McKinney ranch at sundown, where a savory meal awaited us. There was a small vacant house back of the orchard in which we made our home for two months. We found Mr. McKinney and his maiden sister exceptional people. . . .

The horses traveled fairly well after the long rest. . . . The third day we reached the Coquille Valley and our kin. We found ourselves now in a country that was different. A people that were different, living in a small world of their own. They were odd, old-fashioned, contented—mossbacks indeed. Here you would see men driving oxen, working in the fields, and the women spinning and knitting yarn. They also made soft soap and some still cooked their meals by the fireplace. Their dresses were devoid of style and very quaint. Their language a mixture of Missouri, Tennessee and plain old Oregon. . . . We soon fell in with these strange people; adopted their singular ways and became one of them. Mother carded some wool and started her knitting, saved ashes and made soap, she was reminded of her early life. I parted my hair in the middle and tucked it up—learned to dance the Virginia Reel. . . .

How we longed for spring so that we might resume our journey northward. . . . The mud was slow in drying up and it was July first before we were able to start. We left Coos Co. without a single regret. We had made friends—they had entreated us to stay but our mind remained unchanged. It was "Washington Territory or bust."

After reaching Roseburg, we turned north and headed toward Willamette Valley. After several days travel we came to Eugene. There were three routes across the Cascades. The McKenzie, the Santiam, and the Barlow route. We were advised that the McKenzie was the best. So at Eugene we crossed the Willamette river and took a northerly course, thus leaving the main road. . . .

The farms grew farther apart, ceased altogether. We had reached the mountains, the timber and the McKenzie River. A swift rough stream breaking over a rocky bed. Close to the bank we kept now, at water grade, until late evening brought us to the McKenzie bridge, a well known camping spot. . . . The bridge had large rails at the sides which were literally covered with initials and dates. We added ours, of course. A crude way of registering.

As I remember, the road left the river here and a steep climb to the summit began. . . . We approached the summit of the Cascades toward noon. . . . Just a few miles further on were the long-dreaded lava-beds. A stiff pull, of perhaps fifty feet, and we were up on them. For all rough roads here was the climax. The lava had been broken in pieces, not so small, to form a road bed. . . . Pots and pans rattled and banged. The horses crept along carefully picking their way step by step. It was so horrible that it finally became laughable. . . .

Going along the eastern crest of the Cascades we had a splendid view of the snow-covered peaks, the Three Sisters and Mt. Washington. . . . We left the Cascades, the pines, the wooded hills and came down into the Junipers. Eastern Oregon was so vastly different from the west side. . . .

Our journey now became more and more tiring. Every day practically the same kind of scenery. The sun beating down to the tune of 110. Our wagon sheet once so white and clean was now travel stained and brown with dust.

Time passed on. Each night found us only a few miles from where we stayed the night before. . . . Indians were numerous. We found them to be very different from those we had known. They chatted to us in Chinook, a strange jargon. Instead of saying "no savy," We learned to say, "Halo cumtux." They traveled in long train pack-trains. Roaming from one tribe to another, ignorant, idle and perfectly contented. . . .

If in our inmost hearts we bemoaned this fate there was no outward sign. Often viewed the situation from a comical standpoint, laughed in the face of starvation. . . .

Our course turned abruptly west, coming into the old Oregon Trail. The first wagon road in the northwest, established in the thirties by immigration to the Oregon country. The feet of their oxen and heavily tired wheels had ground deeply. The wind carrying the dust away, leaving great trenches still visible, though it had been fifty years. . . .

Next morning, to our surprise, there were Indians all around us strapping their pack-horses. It being dark the night before, we had landed almost in the midst of their camp. These were the Umatillas and very friendly. . . .

A small town occasionally, Adams, Centerville (Athens) Weston, Milton. One by one these villages fell behind us and then we crossed the line into Washington Territory. Although we were still some distance from our destination, it was a great satisfaction to know that at last, we were in Washington Territory. . . .

Then we came to Snake River Canyon. . . . Each curve in the descent grew rougher than the last. . . . There was an Indian village down on the sandy point. There teepees gleaming white against the dark basalt cliffs. It was a relief to, at last, be down to the water level and the old pioneer crossing, Lyons Ferry. . . .

Now that our last grand barrier had been crossed, we rallied our courage and strength for the nearing goal. . . . We estimated that two more days would finish the trip. So, this was Washington Territory! In vain we looked for trees, flowers and green grass. In vain we looked for people, farms, but all that greeted us was a few homesteaders' shacks, most of which were deserted. Sage brush, scab rock, yellow dust. Oh! for the sycamores and the oaks of my California! . . .

While traversing the last twelve mile stretch, all rejoiced that the long tedious journey was about to end, after one and one fourth years of Gypsy life, and all said, "Never again." The last pot of beans had been baked, the pone of bread baked, the last sup from the old black coffee pot. . . . The sun was low on the western hills when we rounded the last bend. There was a cabin in the draw. An old man with a long gray beard, waved a battered straw hat. It was Uncle John. We had come to the end of the trail.[56]

Nor was the westward trail easy for determined Mormons who pulled handcarts toward Utah. Mary Ann Hafen recalled how her family migrated from Switzerland to Nebraska where they began pulling their handcarts to Utah:

When we reached Florence, Nebraska, near present Omaha, we were forced to stop for a while because there were not teams enough to take us across plains to Salt Lake City. The men set to work making handcarts and my father, being a carpenter, helped to make thirty-three of them. Ours was a small two-wheeled vehicle with two shafts and a cover on top. . . .

Our company . . . contained 126 persons with twenty-two handcarts and three provision wagons drawn by oxen. We set out from Florence on July 6, 1860, for our thousand-mile trip. There were six to our cart. Father and mother pulled it. . . .

After about three weeks my mother's feet became better so she could wear her shoes again. She would get so discouraged and down-hearted, but father never lost courage. He would always cheer her up by telling her that we were going to Zion, that the Lord would take care of us, and that better times were coming.

Even when it rained the company did not stop traveling. A cover on the handcart shielded the two younger children. The rest of us found it more comfortable moving than standing still in the drizzle. . . .

Our provisions began to get low. One day a herd of buffalo ran past and the men of our company shot two of them. Such a feast as we had when they were dressed. Each family was given a piece of meat to take along. My brother John, who pushed at the back of our cart, used to tell how hungry he was all the time and how tired he got from pushing. He said he felt that he could just sit down for a few minutes he would feel so much better. But instead, father would ask if he couldn't push a little harder. Mother was nursing the baby and could not help much, especially when the food ran short and she grew weak. When rations were reduced father gave mother a part of his share of the food, so he was not so strong either. . . .

At last, when we reached the top of Emigration Canyon, overlooking Salt Lake, on that September day, 1860, the whole company stopped to look down through the valley. Some yelled and tossed their hats in the air. A shout of joy arose at the thought that our long trip was over, that we had at last reached Zion, the place of rest. We all gave thanks to God

for helping us safely over the Plains and mountains to our destination. . . .[57]

*Although Anglo women's writings dominate archival and published collections
of trail accounts, women of other groups left occasional descriptions as well. The
note of triumph that so often concluded white women's reminiscences are often
sadly lacking in other women's memories. Slave women, for example, were often
transported under duress. A former Missouri slave woman recounted her trip:*

We stayed up all the night packing for the trip. . . . We rides the wagons
all the way, how many days, I dunno. The country was wild most of the
way, and I know now that we come through the same country where I
lives now, only it was to the east. And we keeps on riding and comes to
the big river that's all brown and red looking [Red River] and the next
thing I was sold to Mrs. Vaughn at Bonham, Texas, and there I stays till
after the slaves is free.

   The new Mistress was a widow, no children round the place, and she
treat me mighty good. She was good white folks . . . . When the word get
to us that the slaves is free, the Mistress says I free to go anywhere I
want. And I tell her this talk about being free sounds like foolishment to
me—anyway, where can I go! She just pat me on the shoulder and say I
better stay right there with her, and that's what I do for a long time.
Then I hears about how the white folks down at Dallas pays big money
for house girls and there I goes. That's all I ever do after that—work at
the houses till I gets too old to hobble on these tired old feets and legs,
then I just sits down. . . .[58]

*Eastern Indians also brought slaves with them when they migrated to Indian
Territory. This Oklahoma woman related her mother's trail story:*

My mammy belonged to white people back in Alabama when she was
born—down in the southern part I think, for she told me that after she
was a sizeable girl her white people moved into the eastern part of Alabama where there was lot of Creeks. . . . When mammy was about 10 or
12 years old some of the Creeks began to come out to the Territory in
little bunches. They wasn't the ones who was taken out here by the soldiers and contractor men—they come on ahead by themselves and most
of them had plenty of money, too.

   A Creek come to my mammy's master and bought her to bring out
here, but she heard she was being sold and run off into the woods. . . .
The Creek man that bought here was a kind sort of a man, mammy said,
and wouldn't let the master punish her. He took her away and was kind
to her, but he decided she was too young to breed and he sold her to
another Creek who had several slaves already, and he brought her out to
the Territory.

The McIntosh men was the leaders in the bunch that come out at that time, and one of the bunch, named Jim Perryman, bought my mammy and married her to one of his "boys," but after he waited a while and she didn't have a baby he decided she was no good breeder and he sold her to Mose Perryman. . . . my mammy got married to Mose's slave boy Jacob, the way the slaves was married them days, and went ahead and had ten children for Mr. Mose. . . .

We slaves didn't have a hard time at all before the War. I have had people who were slaves of white folks back in the old states tell me that they had to work awfully hard and their masters were cruel to them sometimes, but all the Negroes I knew who belonged to Creeks always had plenty of clothes and lots to eat and we all lived in good log cabins we built. . . .[59]

Other African American women chose to migrate westward after the Civil War. Texas was the promised land for this Alabama former slave woman:

I's hear tell of dem good slave days but I aint nev'r seen no good times den. . . . It seems impossible dat any of us ev'r lived to see dat day of freedom, but thank God we did. . . . after we knowed what it mean, didn't many of us go, 'cause we didn' know where to of went. . . .

But after ole marster dies we keeps hearin' talk of Texas and me an' my ole man, I'd done been married several years den and had one little boy, well we gits in our covered wagon wid our little mules hitched to it and we comes to Texas. We worked as sharecroppers around Buffalo, Texas 'til my ole man he died. My boy was nearly grown den so he wants to come to San Angelo [Texas] and work, so here we is. . . .[60]

Decades later, other women also traveled to the American West to work the land. Here a Mexican-American woman recalled her family's migration to Texas and other parts of the Southwest.

Mama often talked to me of Mexico. She loved that country. She lived in Saltillo. But times were hard there so she and my father left early in the 1890s. They went to Texas and became pickers. They picked fruit, vegetables, cotton, anything that needed people to break their backs picking it.

My mother and father followed harvests all over Texas and the Southwest, Mama having babies along the way. I was the last child, born in 1903. None of us had any schooling. We were never in one place long enough and Papa said we didn't need it to be pickers.

My mother cooked our own Mexican dishes whereever we lived, even when it was difficult to get cilantro and other ingredients. We spoke only Spanish to each other and to other Mexican pickers. Living conditions were usually bad and Mexican workers helped each other as much as they could. But it was impossible to make friends. As soon as I began to like someone, we were off following the crops again.

In most towns, Catholic priests and nuns tried to help us. They talked to us about the Bible and brought us food and medicine. I think that I survived that rough life only because of the church. I also learned that I wanted to read and write. A nun started to teach me once when I was six, but we left within a few weeks . . .[61]

But not all trails traversed land. Incalculable numbers of women migrated westward by water routes like the one that passed over the Atlantic Ocean, the Isthmus of Panama, and the Pacific Ocean:

2.2
Women on the Panama Trail to California
1849–1869

The Panama Trail was a major artery to California, but the women who followed it have not received the attention accorded to women who traveled the overland routes in North America.[62] This essay seeks to correct that oversight by examining the experiences of female migrants as described in the writings of two dozen Anglo women who chose the fast but often treacherous route across the Isthmus of Panama between its opening in 1849 and its decline after 1869 when the newly completed transcontinental railway offered a quicker, cheaper way to reach California.[63]

Though women on the Panama trail have received little attention, historians *have* noted their presence. John Kemble observed that the proportion of women and children gradually increased among shipboard companies,[64] while Oscar Lewis speculated that the trip, at least in the early years, was too severe to attract many women passengers. The women who did attempt it, he believed, were mostly prostitutes anxious to reap lucrative rewards from their timely appearance among male travelers. He added that Eliza Farnham of New York encouraged a group of single women to make the crossing as potential wives for male California settlers and that the steamship lines increasingly solicited the business of family groups. He also remarked that when hardships lessened after 1850, the number of women travelers increased slightly.[65] More recently, Sandra Myres ascertained that on the initial voyage of the *California* to San Francisco in 1849, fourteen of the 364 passengers who came by way of Panama were women.[66]

That women regularly journeyed via the Panama crossing, and thus have a story worth examining, is substantiated by a variety of sources. The presence

2.2: Adapted from the *Pacific Historical Review* 55 (November 1986), 531–48. Used by permission.

of women is reflected, for example, by passenger lists published in San Francisco newspapers as well as in more recent sources. The number of women on such rolls cannot be determined absolutely owing to the practice of listing most passengers by their initials rather than first names and because of the failure to record steerage passengers at all. But often women passengers can be identified by the titles Mrs., Miss, wife, lady, daughter, or even by a first name, making it clear that women were among the passengers of every Panama-bound steamer between 1849 and 1869. These women traveled with their husbands, with their children, or alone. On an 1852 voyage, for example, the *Golden Gate* carried seventy women and fifty children, figures that increased noticeably as the passage became easier and quicker.[67]

Women's diaries, letters, and memoirs also demonstrate that "respectable" women, both single and married, were among the passengers of virtually every steamship to Panama from the beginning. Illustrative is the diary of Mary Jane Megquier, who on February 18, 1849, wrote that she was about to board the *Chesapeake* for Panama, where she would take another steamer up the Chagres River, ride a "mule's back" for miles, and board the steamer *California* for its first voyage to San Francisco. "It is a long route, and a dangerous one," she confided, but she had "not regretted for one moment" the decision to make the journey.[68] She maintained that resolve despite later discomforts, including being seasick for four days. Nonetheless, she enjoyed the voyage more than she expected, noting that she was the only woman among two hundred men and thus "received every attention" and "enjoyed it finely." Writing again to her daughter from Panama City while awaiting passage with approximately 2000 other Americans stranded by a lack of coal for the steamers, Megquier claimed she was happy because of her ability to "endure almost anything and enjoy it."[69]

Other sources offer insight into women's roles on, and reactions to, the Panama route. One case is Jessie Benton Frémont, who crossed Panama in 1849. Her journey was not as pleasant as Megquier's. Although she avoided seasickness, she wanted to turn back at Chagres due to her distress over the increasing "separation from home." She rode in native dugout canoes and slept on the ground in native huts and a tent although she was "told at every turn" to go back because she could not survive the torture. She also endured a dangerous two-day mule trek to Panama City which she characterized as "a nightmare." Through the kindness of a friend, she stayed with a family rather than in a hotel in Panama City, a fortunate circumstance since she, like Megquier, was detained there for seven weeks because the steamer's crew had deserted to go to the California gold fields.[70]

Other women also braved the isthmian crossing during its earliest years. Jane McDougal traveled across Panama and boarded the dangerously overloaded *California* with her daughter and gold-seeking husband on its initial trip in 1849. In 1850, disillusioned by her husband's failure in California, she returned home across Panama.[71] During the spring of 1849, Margaret DeWitt wrote to her parents-in-law from the steamer *Crescent City* describing her good health, a pleasant captain and friendly passengers, and the fun she anticipated "riding the donkeys." A later letter assured her mother-in-law that she was safely and happily settled in San Francisco.[72] In her 1886 reminiscences, Mary Pratt Staples portrayed her forty-one-day trip from New York to San Francisco via Panama in 1850 as "full of interest from beginning to end."[73]

As the number of women making the crossing increased, so did the types of women multiply. "Foreign ships brought a few women," noted one traveler.[74] Another, Sarah Merriam Brooks, recorded that several African American women asked to accompany and serve her in California, where slavery did not exist. Although they could go for half fare, she declined their offers, for "the desire of this class to get to California was so great they would promise almost any terms to accomplish that end."[75] Very little is known of steerage-class women. Perhaps they seldom kept diaries and wrote letters, or such documents might not have been preserved. But other sources occasionally give brief insights into their situations. Brooks wrote of women in steerage who made the land portions of the passage on foot rather than mule-back.[76] Another traveler recalled that when she crossed Panama in 1864 "food was literally thrown down to the passengers" in steerage.[77]

The number of women who ventured on the Panama route can only be guessed; similar problems exist in determining the ethnic and racial makeup of these women. The diaries, letters, and other writings that have survived are largely those of white, middle- and upper-class women. What is apparent is that women were present, and they engaged from the outset in planning the journey. They were also largely ignored by guidebook writers, who directed their remarks toward men.[78] As a result, women relied upon hearsay, letters, newspaper articles, and the advice of friends.[79] Unfortunately, these sources of information were inadequate, and women frequently found themselves unprepared and overburdened to the point of having to either pay additional freight charges in Panama or to leave goods behind.

Armed with little useful knowledge, women nonetheless planned to the best of their ability. Mary Megquier had the foresight to make herself a durable gown of red calico for her crossing in 1849 and to include a sidesaddle that was a gift from her husband.[80] Three years later, Sarah Brooks departed with her three-and-a-half-year-old child on what she believed would be a "difficult and hazardous journey [even] for a man." When counseled to take expensive new clothes because they would last longer, she heeded the advice. She soon regretted her action and longed for some old clothes for the demanding trip. She was pleased with her specially prepared trunks, however, because they were designed to be an appropriate load for a mule. "They were made of light but strong wood," she explained, "covered with sheepskin, and bound with many bands of steel." She began packing the trunks a month ahead of time and as the contents settled, she added more to them.[81]

Knowing how much and what to take was a common problem. In 1855, Hester Harland's mother was almost over-prepared after engaging in "tremendous planning and packing" to insure taking everything she would need.[82] In 1857, because Lucy Sexton's father warned his wife and daughter to take only clothes due to the high cost of freight, they limited themselves to four trunks.[83] In 1861, Julia Twist and other passengers became angry upon learning that all trunks would be weighed before departure and each assessed ten cents for every pound over fifty. When told that she also had to deposit two dollars for keys, she declared, "It was a swindle from the beginning."[84] As with the overland journeys in North America, most female migrants tended to over-prepare, often taking too much rather than too little.

As troubling to women as the preparations for the journey were their intense fears of the actual trip. Whether heading toward the Panama or overland routes, they dreaded the unknown wilderness. In Panama, the jungle seemed frightening; in North America the plains, deserts, and mountains alarmed them. They feared that they and their children might not survive, and they were understandably concerned about the special complications posed by childbirth, child care, and heavy and inappropriate clothing. Also, a Victorian sense of modesty complicated bathing and toilet functions in this strange environment.

The nature of the Panama trip did little to allay women's fears. In 1849 and 1850 it involved taking a steamer from New York to Chagres, proceeding by native dugouts called bungos, enduring a mule ride from Gorgona or Cruces to Panama City, and being carried by natives to small steamers connecting with larger San Francisco–bound steamships. The trip consumed about six weeks if all connections worked and much longer if they did not.[85] While relatively short in duration, the demands of the trip on human energy, patience, and tolerance were huge. The Panama route was widely known for high prices, bad food, a chaotic and ineffective government, and such diseases as malaria and cholera. The rough boom town of Chagres posed another set of difficulties for women. Most women reacted with dismay when they experienced its brutal climate, saw its mud huts with thatched roofs, gaudily or scantily dressed natives of African, Indian, and Spanish descent, and primitive hovels purporting to be hotels. According to one historian, even after wharves and substantial buildings were constructed, Chagres remained little more than a "wild, roaring, American-run frontier town."[86] When hotels replaced tents, women were usually housed together in one room. If the room became overcrowded, hotel owners simply curtained off a section of the main room for them. Bars far outnumbered hotels and offered liquor at seven times New York prices. Moreover, the threat of death from yellow fever, malaria, typhoid, cholera, or a gunshot wound was always present. "Adventurers and North American soldiers arrived in Panama thinking and believing that here neither life nor property need be respected," another historian of Panama has commented. "Brothels and bars were like mines planted in the middle of the city," and "the dance of gold stepped parallel to the macabre dance of crime".[87]

By 1851, the first branch of the railroad moved the jumping-off place slightly west from Chagres to Aspinwall (later known as Colon).[88] Gradually companies, notably the Wells Fargo Company, took over the transportation of emigrants across the isthmus. By 1855, the railroad reached Panama City on the West Coast along a winding route through the Cordilleras Mountains.[89] Once in Panama City, however, weary travelers found a congested, decaying town overrun with migrants annoyed by a two-dollar landing tax and frequently stricken by tropical diseases. Here they often tolerated long delays because of the lack of steamships.[90] Although the terrors of the Panama passage approximated the blizzards, deserts, deaths, and other disasters of the North American overland route, the Panama Trail was short and the experience there too different to allow women to either make the transition to a new lifestyle or to learn the skills that they would need as settlers in California.

On neither the Panama route nor the North American overland trails did women express a generalized "female" response to their migration. Some intensely disliked the experience and even turned back, while others saw it as a great adventure. Like women on the overland roads, the reactions of female migrants to the Panama trip depended upon the conditions that they encountered. For women crossing Panama, the state of the railroad, hotels, and steamers colored their perspective. Like their overland counterparts, their observations were further tempered by their own personalities, hardiness, and determination.

Of these early female travelers, Mary Jane Megquier seemed nearly unflappable. She expressed distress only at poverty and squalor. When in Panama City, she was pained "to see so much misery, everything going to ruin, the most splendid cathedrals, of which there are six, all tumbling to decay. . . . No one can have any idea of the misery that is in the world until they have seen some of these old towns where everything speaks of misery and decay."[91] Jane McDougal, another migrant, escaped the unpleasant aspects of her trip in 1849 by engaging in such pursuits as reading, sewing, and watching porpoises and whales. She lightened the dreariness by indulging in some of the omnipresent champagne on board. She had little to say of her travel in a hammock suspended between two native men that was followed by a trip on mule except "very thankful that we were safe." After being drenched by a torrential storm and taking fright at "two parties of tigers & panthers," she noted her party's safe arrival. By the latter part of her trip, however, she was seasick and bored. When the captain caught a shark she remarked that she "watched it die for the sake of having something to do."[92]

Jessie Benton Frémont's story was much different, for after a trying overland journey, she contracted "brain fever" during her protracted stay in Panama City. Although the family with whom she lodged cared for her, she had not recovered when she finally boarded a steamship for San Francisco. Here she was one of 400 passengers on a ship designed for eighty, a situation that was met by marking off sleeping spaces on the deck with chalk.[93] Conditions had improved little by 1850 when another female diarist described her seasickness, "a nasty, filthy, drunken, gambling hole" that served as her hotel, and the mass "confusion and excitement" when the mules arrived at her door. On the other hand, the scenery along the Chagres River was "beyond description" and the mule ride pleasurable, an experience aided by the sidesaddle she had brought along. Although she rode from eight in the morning to eight at night and had "no use of her limbs" when she dismounted, she expressed delight in "the novel scene" before her.[94] Another woman of similar temperament noted after arriving in Panama City, "It was a hard road to travel, I can asshure [sic] you." Far from being discouraged, however, she spent her two weeks in Panama City earning twelve dollars by making trousers.[95]

A woman's physical reaction to the traveling conditions significantly determined her attitude toward the trip. In 1852, Sarah Brooks immediately fell ill when the sea "hit" during dinnertime. Neither she nor her young daughter left their berths for two days and nights. When the ship reached the Gulf Stream, they found their clothes much too warm. "I was wondering whether I should make an effort to get up and dress or lie quiet and just die easy," she complained. When she went on deck the sea air improved her health and outlook in spite of the crowd of 1600 passengers on a ship built for 1200. She spent the duration of the voyage sleeping on deck in a "standee" (a berth mounted in a framework of metal or wood). Her first night in a crude hotel was marked by the "crying of children with thirst and fever" and the moans of ill men dosed with liquor that "made the night hideous." In addition, there was the "chattering of monkeys, shrieks of night-owls," and large "numbers of flying and creeping things." She and her companions divided themselves into "sleepers" and "watchers," the latter to fight off insects.[96]

Sarah Brooks's lack of sleep and poor health made her more than a little cranky by the time the mules appeared. "Such broken-down, miserable beasts!" she exclaimed. "Hundreds of them, lame, blind, ringboned and spavined, big and little, mostly little, everything that could be gathered up in all the country, were brought into requisition to carry the army of people who every two weeks had to cross that mountain." Although she drew a horse and a sidesaddle, her disposition failed to improve, especially when her party's muleteer and baggage disappeared. Lunch she described as "a boiled ham, with the mouldy skin sticking to it, a large dish of very dirty-looking boiled rice, and some chunks of black bread." By the time she reached Panama City she was "hot, dusty and weary beyond expression." This experience was followed by a rowboat trip to a steamer that left her "nearly insensible" for the journey to San Francisco during which nine people died.[97]

Emeline Benson, like Brooks, had her trip in 1853 ruined by poor health. Her travel diary is a litany of illness and complaints, especially seasickness, made worse by unbearably hot weather that convinced her there was "no prospect of getting well till we get ashore."[98] During the same year, Emeline Day endured similar difficulties, but retained her health and exhibited a different attitude toward her experience. The saddles were "good" and the mules knew the road well enough to proceed without her guidance. "We had no difficulty" on the trail, she recorded, and as for the trip on the steamer *Golden Gate*, "all is peace. [A]m not much sick." When two male passengers died, both were "throwed over, with little ceremony. . . . Appears to have no effect on the passengers." She logged the constant card-playing and swearing on board without complaint, noting near the end of the her journey that "the time seems short, [but] in that month I have traveled almost six thousand miles."[99]

Although health was important, a woman's personality seemed to have been a more crucial influence on her attitude toward the journey. In 1854, one plucky women found that illness and heat were offset by "gayety and mirth, bustle and confusion, singing and dancing, on board that floating structure." Neither a crowded hotel nor a disrupted night's sleep due to continual singing and shouting dismayed her. She recounted "great frolicking and laughing with the ladies while fixing away on the mules." Nonetheless, there were less pleasant occasions. After several tropical rainstorms, narrow mountain passes, and the death of three people from heat and exhaustion, she admitted to having "cried sometimes, with fright!" Still, her overall attitude remained positive, and she continually expressed delight in the scenery and the beauty of the animals on which she rode.[100]

Also in 1854, Mallie Stafford, although at first intimidated by the "great world of waters," soon found ship life thoroughly enjoyable. When confronted with the "horrid" mules for which no sidesaddles were available, she adopted "a masculine mode of riding," which quickly proved both safe and wise. "Such a scene!" she remarked as she watched 900 passengers being paired with a like number of mules. But her own good nature shone through. "I sat an unobserved spectator, having accepted the inevitable with as good grace as I could command." When later carried to the ship by natives she quipped, "Previous to this, many of the ladies had thought that a mule-back ride comprised the realization of the horrible." After witnessing "the solemn and mournful ceremony of burial at sea" three times during the voyage, Stafford reached San Francisco, which she immediately accepted as "home."[101]

With the completion of the trans-isthmian railroad in 1855, traveling conditions improved, contributing to the positive outlook of women. Fannie Reading, Lucy Sexton, and Mary Ann Meredith described pleasant train rides and "uneventful" and sometimes "very pleasant" voyages to California.[102] Nellie Wetherbee was not so fortunate. First, her new husband became jealous over her friendship with a young lieutenant. Then followed a stern lecture by her husband because she had complained about their stateroom. When she reached San Francisco she spent the day unpacking and crying, feeling homesick and lamenting the necessity of becoming "a wife."[103]

During the 1860s, women continued to be more favorably disposed to the journey than earlier female travelers. In 1863, Angelina Harvey informed her cousin that she had had "a prosperous passage of 10 days to the isthmus; the crossing of which was truly an oasis in the desert of waters and another equally prosperous of 14 to the bay of San Francisco." To her, the scenery along the way was "magnificent," Panama City was "lovely, ruined, yet picturesque," and the coast of Mexico offered "much to enjoy and admire." She complained only about the crowds of passengers, a situation that had not been changed by improved facilities.[104] The following year, Hannah Ingalls found the trip a "delightful experience" with the rail segment offering "a lovely ride" with much "luxuriant foliage, beautiful birds," and striking landscape. She arrived in San Francisco in "health and safety."[105]

Although women's perspectives toward the trip improved over the years, there was no parallel improvement in their relationships with native peoples. Racism and prejudice, deeply instilled in them by myth and the media before departure, were as prevalent among women on the Panama route as they were among female migrants who had earlier gone overland from such "jumping-off" points as Independence, Missouri, and Council Bluffs, Iowa. Guidebooks published for Panama travelers emphasized the need to be "liberal to the men who work the canoe" and warned migrants to negotiate written contracts with native workers.[106] This less-than-encouraging advice was supplemented by newspaper accounts of confrontations between natives and emigrants. Though infrequent, such clashes received sensational treatment. Typical was the "Watermelon Riot" of 1856. According to the press, "excited savages" engaged in "a general melee" and "a general massacre" in which "Twenty-Five Americans [were] Massacred by the Natives." Native troops dispatched to quell the rioters reportedly joined their "fellows" in the attack on the migrants.[107] Such tales caused many women to develop an absolute terror of the land portion of the trip. "The papers had given accounts of the dangers to be met with there," observed Sarah Brooks in 1852, and these included "robbers."[108] Most women expected the Panamanians to be, as Ida Fitzgerald observed, "little above the animals."[109]

Like women on the overland trails, Panama migrants viewed the natives as curiosities and savages. They routinely described the near-naked state of the men and children, one observing that the men were "swarthy-visaged, half-naked Carthaginians. . . . a mongrel race of natives, whose appearance and features were equally as repulsive."[110] The native women fared somewhat better. Mary Ann Meredith thought they dressed "fantastically," although perhaps a bit "comically" with their ruffles and beads, and Emeline Day believed "the females were dressed quite fancifully" in their frocks of thin white gauze.[111]

Native housing was another matter. Female travelers wrote disparagingly of filthy huts, miserable thatched dwellings, and such overwhelming dirt and stench that they were, according to Mary Staples, "obliged to hold our noses and have cologne to go to sleep by."[112] Julia Twist was horrified by the shanties which were "occupied by a race of beings hardly fit to be classed as human. They are the nearest to the brute creation of any I have yet seen."[113]

Even the best-natured of women were generally harsh, cruel, and spiteful in their descriptions of the people they saw in the towns and villages who carried their luggage, led their mules, piloted their canoes, carried them on their backs from the steamers to shore, and performed a wide variety of other services. "Desperately ugly in looks," stated Sarah Brooks, "they proved equally so in character."[114] Mallie Stafford accused them of being greedy while another woman was convinced that they practiced such subterfuges as hiding mules and bribing boatmen "in order to secure as many pieces of money as possible."[115] To Mary Jane Megquier the natives were "simple, inoffensive people," who nevertheless "understand perfectly the getting of the dimes from the Americans."[116]

Panamanians were equally curious about the women traveling through their country. Like their Native American counterparts, they went out of their way to observe the visitors. Mary Jane Megquier was disconcerted by the natives' habit of invading hotels and other buildings to stare at female emigrants "in perfect astonishment" as if they were "one of the greatest curiosities in the world."[117] Other women were upset by what they considered the temperamental nature of the Panamanians. To Jessie Benton Frémont they were a "naked, screaming, barbarous" people.[118] Mary Ann Meredith considered "the natives . . . so impetuous and excitable that it was almost impossible to do anything with them."[119]

Unlike their sister migrants on the overland trails, these women seemed oblivious to any signs of creativity or energy in the natives they encountered. During the relatively short time it took to cross Panama, women had neither the opportunity nor the motivation to revise their preconceptions of the people. Rather, their prejudices intensified as a result of conflicts between themselves and Panamanians. In 1852, Sarah Brooks was involved in an altercation with "an ugly set" of boatmen, one of whom shed his breechcloth due to the heat and refused orders to put it on.[120] Two years later Mallie Stafford became frightened when a man in her party aimed a pistol at a mule driver who had told him to "go to hell." Her fright turned to terror when another native pulled her mule off the trail. She flailed at him ineffectually with her riding whip until rescued. To her, all vile rumors about the Panamanians were true:

> Men had been murdered for their money and clothing, and women had been stolen away and murdered for their jewelry. The natives appeared to be the lowest type of humanity, treacherous, malicious, deceptive, and avaricious, many of them being capable of committing the foulest murder for a small sum of money. Only a few months before the natives, armed, had waylaid a train of passengers, and robbed and massacred them in open daylight.[121]

Equally convinced of native perfidy was Hester Harland, who was among those caught in the 1856 riot in Panama City. "Families were separated . . . many were knocked down, beaten, left for dead in the streets, and some of the women had their earrings torn from their ears, and brooches from their dresses."[122]

Such conflicts, together with the rigor and shortness of the journey, prompted most women to express views similar to those of Mallie Stafford, who saw the Panama trip as a "ride over a wild, inhuman country on the back of a wild irresponsible mule driven by a wild, demoralized, irrepressible son of the tropics."[123] Observations about Panamanians became fewer following completion of the railroad in 1855, the construction of improved hotels, and the introduction of shuttle steamers that removed women from contact with natives.

Although female migrants crossing Panama seldom revised their negative views of Panamanians, women on the overland trails frequently rethought their anti-Indian biases, largely as a result of their interactions with those native groups. Otherwise the experiences of female migrants on the overland and Panamanian trails exhibited more similarities than differences. In both migrations, women constituted a significant proportion of the population. They undertook complex preparations and were fearful about the journey ahead. Once on their way, their responses were conditioned by the situations they encountered, their own personalities, and the state of their health.

Despite the widespread, grim view that women faced exploitation, ill health, and despair as a result of their westering, most women did not regret their action. Their views were similar to those of Emeline Day who in 1853 stated: "I am happy and contented. If I could return I would not."[124] If there is a larger point to be drawn from these observations, it is that assessments of westering women on many routes are necessary before any accurate insights or generalizations of trail women's lives, roles, and responses can fully emerge.

Other dangerous trails that involved crossing over land and water were those from Dyea, Alaska, across steep and treacherous Chilkoot Pass, and from Skagway, Alaska, across the even more daunting White Horse Pass. Travelers then sailed across lakes Lindeman and Bennett to Dawson City on the Klondike and Yukon rivers located in Yukon Territory, Canada. Like so many women who went to California, women who took the Chilkoot Trail hoped to reap profits from one of the gold rushes. The Klondike Rush, which peaked in 1898, attracted women from all over the world, married and single. Inga Sjolneth Kolloen was a Norwegian woman who described crossing the land trail through Chilkoot Pass with friends during the early spring of 1898:

Fr. March 18. Today we have taken all our supplies from the dock to the City of Dyea. Have now set up our tent on a sand bank near the river. It rained this afternoon. . . . The tent is full of wet sacks, boxes and clothing.

Sat. March 19. When we awakened, all of our clothes were frozen stiff. . . . All I could manage was to build a fire in the Klondike stove. . . .

Mar. 20, Sun. The sun is clear and warm over the high snowy and ice-clad mountains. . . .

Mon, March 21st. We got up at five this morning. . . . went for a load of our supplies. . . . I pulled three sacks on my sled, and it went pretty well. There are hundreds of people here dragging or carrying their supplies, all striving to reach the Klondike. Some have horses and still others have dog teams. . . .

Tues, March 22. We were up early today and dragged a load of our supplies to the next stopping place. I dragged one sack this time because

I was so weak that I could not do more than that. When we got home I was very tired, and after we had eaten I became quite sick although I remained on my feet until six o'clock. . . .

Wed, March 23. I felt better today when I got up, although I was not entirely well and therefore I did not go out. . . . I like it here, and am disappointed that I will have to move tomorrow.

Thurs, March 24. We moved a few miles further north and are now established in Canyon City. . . .

Fri, March 25. We took the last of our supplies up to Canyon today. I went along with the last load. . . . I long for someone to whom I could open my heart . . . who would understand me and give me a sympathetic smile. But there is no one. I am alone.

Sat, March 26. This has been a long day for me.

Sun, March 27. When I awakened this morning I was discouraged and did not have much enthusiasm about getting up and beginning the day's activities. I did, however, get dressed and went outside for a moment of peace in God's free nature. . . . I sat on a stone and prayed, asking Him to enfold me in His arms and protect me from all sorrow. . . .

Mon, March 28. . . . This is our last day in Canyon City. Tomorrow we shall leave here.

Tues, March 29. Today we moved from Canyon City to Sheep Camp. The trail in from Canyon is narrow and crowded, lying between two steep mountains. If one looks up one sees only mountains over one's head. The snow has turned to water, so progress has been very difficult. Ida and I pulled a loaded sled together though the canyon and heard many comments about it. We heard one man say he wished he had such a "tram" as we were. Some of the men took off their packs and laughed at us. . . .

Sun, Apr 10. Easter morning dawned clear and beautiful and the weather has been pleasant all day. This morning early I went out for some small fir twigs with which to cover the floor and fixed up everything as well as I could. . . .

Tues, Apr 12. Snow has been falling all day. I was on my way to The Summit, but had to turn back because of the storm. . . .

Wed, Apr 13. Strong winds today. . . .

Thurs, Apr 14. . . . The weather has been good today, but a change is coming. It began to rain this evening. . . .

Fri, Apr 15. There has been rain and snow. . . . I have not felt well today and have stayed in bed most of the time. . . . I am bored and weary with this place, and wish I could get away from this dirty Sheep Camp!

Sat, Apr 16. The weather has been bad today also. I have been inside the whole day. I do not feel well. Everything is so unpleasant around me. I am depressed and without courage. . . .

Sun, Apr 17. I have been ill today and have spent the day in bed. . . .

Tues, Apr 19. Beautiful weather today. I have accomplished very little—have not felt like doing anything. . . . I am going to leave Sheep Camp and go over The Summit tomorrow.

Wed, Apr 20. We got up early, had our breakfast, and packed our supplies. We were ready at 6 A.M. . . . It took a long time to get up there. We sat and watched those who scrambled over. They went up very slowly, but came down the chute again with great speed! Many sat down and slid most of the way. It took only a few minutes. It went so fast that I was afraid to watch. It was so late when my supply train went over that I was afraid to go over with it. I was really afraid. So I went down to Sheep Camp again. . . .

Thurs, Apr 21. Unusually beautiful weather again today. The sun is actually warm. I feel well and am quite satisfied and at peace here. . . .

Fri, Apr 22. I chopped fresh green twigs to lay on the floor. The bunks consist of sacks which I have arranged as best I can, and they look quite presentable. . . .

Sat. Apr 23. The weather was good today also. . . .

Sun, Apr 24. Snow and rain all day. . . .

Mon, Apr 25. Good weather today. The boys have packed all their supplies over The Summit. Tomorrow I shall go over also, if only the weather is good. . . .

Tues, Apr 26. I got up at five o'clock today to see how the weather was. I soon both saw and felt that it was rainy and blustery, so I hurried to get under my blankets again I slept until 7 o'clock, then got up and made pancakes for breakfast. It had been decided that we should go over The Summit today, but now, account of the weather, our plans have been changed. . . . The ice has melted so the ground is bare and muddy, and the snow that remains is very soft. The horses bog down in many places. People say a horse fell and couldn't get up again. It took two other horses to pull him up.

Wed, Apr 27. We left Sheep Camp about nine o'clock this morning, and arrived at Lake Lindeman around five. . . .[125]

Because Kolloen's party arrived at Lake Lindeman so early in the spring they had to spend long, weary weeks waiting for ice to break up. It was early June when they crossed the lake and shot the rapids toward Dawson City. Georgia White and her party of friends, however, arrived later. Although they took the chance of a tardy start in the gold fields, they had a relatively easy time getting to Dawson City via what was largely a water trail:

June 16. . . . Lindeman is a pretty place situated on a flat beside the lake and surrounded by mountains. . . .

June 17. Got up at half past ten ate a breakfast of ham and eggs. . . .

June 18. My day to cook at the camp. . . .

June 19. . . . I went skiffing and seeing the men build the boat.

June 20. . . . we all had dinner at Hotel Lindeman. . . .

June 21. We staid [sic] at Lindeman Hotel and in the morning played "Black Jack". . . .

June 22. . . . started on our journey. We had a pleasant trip to the foot of Lindeman where my trunk had got wet and red water was running from it. Our baggage was portaged to Lake Bennett and the boat went over the rapids 1½ miles in five minutes. . . . We started down Lake Bennett. The wind was blowing hard and we made quick time and went about 30 miles where we found a beautiful place to camp. . . .

June 23. Arose at 8, got breakfast and started again but very little wind but managed to get to Large Windy Arm where we found a beautiful place to camp. . . .

June 24. Started out again with a good breeze. Got across both Windy Arm. Other boats rested but we ventured and made many miles. Pitched tent at 8 on a sandy beach. Got as close to water as possible so as to be free from mosquitoes, as we had not slept the night before, they were so dreadful. . . . My face and eyes are all swollen with them.

June 25. Started with a good breeze but wind has gone down and the men are rowing—so far this has been a very pleasant trip and the gentlemen are kindness itself toward us in every way, but oh I miss my darlings [her children in California] so that it makes me quiet where I ought to try and be pleasant and cheerful but I can not—my thoughts are always on home. . . .

June 26. It was raining so did not get up until 2 P.M. Stopped raining and we are rowing down the river. It snowed all around on the mountains. We pitched camp early as it turned cold. . . .

June 27. We rowed until we came to the Canyon where it is necessary to employ a pilot to take the boat through Canyon and Whitehorse Rapids, so some of goods was taken out and sent by tramway over the Rapids. . . . We were compelled to walk around a distance of 3½ miles as an order had been issued where no women or children could "shoot the rapids." . . . Got the Kodak and took several photos. . . . We waited awhile until the goods came and packed in the boat. When we started out again but had not gone very far when we got stuck on a sandbank in the middle of the river (there were numerous banks there). The boys were obliged to get out and after hard work got off without damage being done. There were two other wrecks there so it must have been a bad place. Well after going a short distance it started to rain. . . . I fear very much that I am a damper on our company, I am so quiet and seldom if ever make fun or seem good-natured. Firstly, I think constantly of my little ones and God knows at times it seems more than I can bear but I must—for Oh deliver me from becoming insane up here. . . .

June 28. We got up late this morn and then got out our clothes to dry as it is a beautiful morning. Mostly everything at the bottom of my trunk is destroyed. . . . We left camp late in the afternoon and went down 60

Mile River with a good breeze. There are numerous sand banks on the way. We reached Lake Laberge and went about 15 miles and found a beautiful camping ground (free from mosquitoes). . . .

June 29. . . . Got up half past six, had breakfast and are sailing down Lake Laberge which is 31 miles long and very wide. We expect to reach Fort Selkirk today. A police station [Canadian Mounted Police] was not far from our camp and a policeman was on patrol. . . . We got out of Lake Laberge all right and when about five miles down the river we ran on a rock and knocked the bottom out of our boat. . . . The boys lost everything but a few sacks of provisions and we lost lots of our clothes and the boat is worthless (there were three wrecks on that rock today). . . . About 2 P.M. the boat got off the rocks and floated away. When we found it, it was miles down the river and one axe and a sack of bacon was in it.

June 30. A boat with five men came along. . . took us aboard so now there are nine of us. We are crowded and well loaded but all are pleasant. . . . We got on a sand bar and when off again pitched tent. . . . We slept well, considering we were shipwrecked. That is all we talk about. We passed the Old Glory at police station and now are sailing down the Lewis River.

July 1. . . . We got on several sandbars but got off safe. We found every so many boats in Little Salmon River so camped there at Police Station. . . .

July 2. A beautiful day and we are rowing down the river.

All is well. We got on a sand bank, but got off O.K. We went through a small rapids safe and sound. Stopped and had lunch and went along until we reached the Five Finger Rapids. They looked dreadful. The rocks or fingers, are very large and sea gulls are flying around there waiting for victims. . . . We camped and made supper, it being nearly 1 A.M.

July 3. . . . We ate breakfast of bacon and beans and started our trip with a little fear as we knew that within an hour we would have the Rink Rapids to shoot. They are 6½ miles from Five Finger Rapids. We shot the Rink Rapids fine and they were not as bad as we thought. Still, since the wreck we are in constant fear. We did not know what fear meant before the accident. We will be so glad to get to our journey's end. We heard there was a new [gold] strike. . . .

July 4. . . . A steamboat passed it being the third steamer which went up the river and all are reported to have a large amount of gold aboard. In the afternoon we all slept. . . . After supper, we had music and singing and at 10 P.M. was a most beautiful sunset, then we had coffee and retired.

July 5. Got up early as we wanted to make up for lost time. We reached Fort Selkirk about 9:00. . . . The Yukon River starts in at Fort Selkirk and the Pelly River runs in there. . . .

July 6. Left camp about 10:15. Rowed all day. Pitched tent at 10 P.M. Lots of mosquitoes. I inspected my trunk—everything wet.

July 7. Got an early start and got along nicely until we reached the White River where something must have occurred as the water just came in very muddy and full of driftwood. . . . When we landed high and dry on a sandbank and all the men were obliged to get out and lift the boat off. Then we walked around the tent and ate lunch and then started out again and got on another sandbank. The boys were obliged to get out again and lift the boat off. The banks are so numerous that it is difficult to navigate but finally we reached a camping place where the mosquitoes are bad and the water very muddy.

July 8. Left camp in good spirits and took on some wood and arrived in Dawson at 8:00 P.M. Looked around and finally found a corner to camp. Dawson is very dull and many disgusted men selling outfits and very hard to get work. Took a walk in the evening to top of hill and had a fine view of Dawson. Klondike City is across the Klondike River from Dawson.

July 9. . . . Looked around for work but without success. . . .

July 10. Everything quiet as no one is allowed to work on Sunday.

July 11. Looked for work without success. . . .

July 17. Very weary. . . . started out about 9 o'clock for 17 on Eldorado, a distance of 18 miles. . . . We arrived at our destination at 6 next morn.

July 18. Had breakfast and then went to bed until 2 P.M. Got up and had dinner and went down to see the men sluicing. It is wonderful the amount of gold that is taken out. The season cleanup was $225,000. . . .[126]

Asian women also traveled land and water routes to reach the promised land of riches and opportunity. A Japanese American woman relates her mother's words regarding her trail:

I did not want to leave my mother. We were very close. When I left, she wrote me a poem of sorrow and love. I have the parchment yet, although it is now difficult to read.

I traveled from my family home outside of Kyoto by wagon. I had only one trunk of my things with me. My mother said she would send the rest when I reached Hawaii. The ship across the Pacific Ocean provided an unhappy voyage. I traveled in steerage and there were many smells of cooking and of unwashed people. I was ill many times but I made some friends among the other women. We often told of our families in Japan and what we planned to do when we reached America. We had so many thoughts of the future.

I reached Hawaii in 1898, just before my eighteenth birthday . . .[127]

The multiplicity of trails traversed by women was clearly incredible, but there were still others whose history has been slighted. Mexican women moving into California, for example, or missionary women scaling the Rockies to reach po-

tential converts, or Japanese women sailing to Honolulu, San Francisco, or Seattle were also part of the trail saga. Also, the reverse trail has been ignored; thousands of women settlers left the West to return to their former homes, Native American women forged their own kind of trails in attempts to flee from encroaching settlers, and some Hispanic women fled to Mexico. As with women themselves, stereotypes have ruled our customary view of the westward trail. It's a larger story than has yet been told.

For Further Reading

Bledsoe, Lucy Jane. "Adventuresome Women on the Oregon Trail, 1840–1867." *Frontiers* 7 (1984), 22–29.

Conley, Frances R. "Martina Didn't Have a Covered Wagon: A Speculative Reconstruction." *The Californians* 7 (March–August 1989), 48–54.

Drury, Clifford Merrill, ed. *First White Women over the Rockies: Diaries, Letters, and Biographical Sketches of the Six Women of the Oregon Mission who Made the Overland Journey in 1836 and 1838.* Glendale, Calif.: Arthur H. Clark Company, 1966.

Faragher, John Mack. *Women and Men on the Overland Trail.* New Haven, Conn.: Yale University Press, 1976.

Holmes, Kenneth, ed. *Covered Wagon Women: Diaries and Letters from the Western Trails.* 7 volumes. Glendale, Calif.: The Arthur H. Clark Company, 1983–1990.

Mayer, Melanie J. *Klondike Women: True Tales of the 1897–1898 Gold Rush.* Athens: Ohio University Press, 1989.

Myres, Sandra L. *Ho for California! Women's Diaries at the Huntington Library.* San Marino, Calif.: The Huntington Library, 1980.

Perdue, Theda. "Cherokee Women and the Trail of Tears." *Journal of Women's History* 1 (Spring 1989), 13–30.

Schlissel, Lillian. *Women's Diaries of the Westward Journey.* New York: Schocken Books, 1982.

Schlissel, Lillian, Byrd Gibbens, and Elizabeth Hampsten. *Far From Home: Families of the Westward Journey.* New York: Schocken Books, 1989.

SECTION

3

Women Migrants and Native Americans

Many female migrants feared Native Americans, while others took a more sanguine view. Gradually, even many of those women who believed Native Americans to be the greatest terror of westward migration and who were almost hysterical about encounters with them came to realize that many stories and reports were exaggerated tales based on unreasoning fear and pure rumor. Women's trail experiences with Native Americans and their growing understanding of them as people who had been mistreated and pushed off their lands sometimes contributed to understanding and communication between female migrants and native women and men. Women migrants—including whites and women of color— often tried to soften the tragedy of conquest for Native Americans and help them adapt to the new situation.

3.1
The Specter of a Savage:
Rumors and Alarmism on the Overland Trail

That violent outbreaks and tragic confrontations occurred between Native Americans and migrants intent upon settling the American West is a widely known fact. But the theory that many "uprisings" and "massacres" were little

3.1: Excerpted from *The Western Historical Quarterly* 15 (October 1984), 427–44. Used by permission. Photo: A teacher with her Flathead Indian pupils in Montana, August 1910. Courtesy of the Montana Historical Society, Helena.

more than the work of overactive imaginations has received far less attention. In truth, overlanders' diaries and letters reveal that problems with Indians were frequently derived far more from migrants' own anxieties about what *could* happen than from what actually *did* happen.

Fears given voice became ubiquitous rumors, which in turn created a climate marked by anxiety and tension. While such a state kept overland travelers alert to possible danger, it also tended to make them incapable of dealing effectively with the native populations they encountered. With the specter of the savage always before them, trail people were frequently less than calm and rational in their dealings with Native Americans.

This state of affairs resulted partly from a contradictory portrayal of Native Americans by the press and popular literature in America and Europe. One source might regard native peoples as friendly, kind, and courageous; another might condemn them as bad, hostile, and vicious. Because the stereotype of the "bad" Native American dominated throughout the middle decades of the nineteenth century, which coincided with the peak years of westward expansion, the expectations of prospective migrants tended to be negative.

Travelers were all the more vulnerable to alarmism because the custom of storytelling reinforced media images of Native Americans during the months, or sometimes the years, before their departure for the West. This family lore often included an episode or two featuring "murderous savages" and left little to the imagination. As storytellers repeated details and twisted them into various shapes for the amusement of their listeners, they sometimes embellished them to the point of the macabre. Thus, many migrants had already served childhood apprenticeships as potential victims before they climbed on the wagon seat. Harriet Smith, migrating as a young girl during the 1840s, vividly recalled her grandfather's thrilling tales of Indians he had supposedly encountered during the War of 1812. "Naturally we were somewhat afraid," she commented when they spied their first natives.[1] During the same decade, Virginia Reed Murphy carried a similar terror instilled by her grandmother's frequent recitals regarding the "fearful deeds of the savages," including an aunt held captive for five years.[2]

Often family lore focused upon the imputed Native American custom of scalping victims. Going west as a child in 1861, Lucy Fosdick not only heard much about scalping, but had her hair cropped short by her mother before departure as a protective measure.[3] In 1870, Mabel Beavers was met upon her arrival in Oklahoma by "a couple of full blood Indians." "I just knew," she recalled, "that if one of those Indians had touched my hair, that my scalp would have come off without any pulling." Her explanation was simple and telling: "They were Indians. Horrors!"[4] Even as late as the end of the nineteenth-century, the rumor mills continued to churn, predisposing new generations to fear and hostility. Sixteen-year-old Mary Ellen Williams, for example, confessed that when she joined her father's family, consisting of a Choctaw wife and offspring, in 1895, she "was absolutely scared to death."[5]

Those folks who decided to move west despite such horror stories experienced little relief on the trek. Not only were emigrant guides filled with dire warnings about Native Americans, but jumping-off places roiled with rumor and gossip. One young traveler of 1852 wrote: "As we drew near Council Bluffs on the Missouri River, the cry of Indians, Indians, turned me into stone. . . . The air was thick at Council Bluffs with tales of Indian massacres."[6]

On the trail, migrants entered an even more intense climate of dramatic reports. They soon learned they could not escape terrible and often ill-founded portrayals of native peoples. Almost all trail accounts included mention of widespread rumor-mongering and what were termed Indian "depredations."

Some migrants objected to the natural tendency of travelers to tell stories and to speculate.[7] The after-dinner fireside especially encouraged such activity. In 1864, Mallie Stafford lamented the effectiveness of a fireside gathering she attended in the middle of "Indian country" in Colorado. Stafford declared, "The conversation naturally, under the circumstances, centered on Indian stories, Indian attacks, crossing the plains, etc., and as the night wore on they grew more and more eloquent—it seemed to me they were gifted with an awful eloquence on that particular subject."[8]

Whether fabricated by a fireside or founded on an actual occurrence, rumors of Indian troubles spread from train to train in ingenious ways. On her way from Wisconsin to California in 1850, Lucena Parsons noted that bones were used as bulletin boards to report Indian "depredations." "We see writing on bones every day stating the deeds of the Indians," she wrote. A few days later she added, "Here we saw a bone stating that Indians had run off 17 mewls & horses."[9] In that same year, Margaret Frink was disquieted by a more sophisticated alarm system: printed circulars were distributed to migrants. She was further distressed that natives and "their doings" were frequently the focus of camp conversation. She began "to think that three men, one woman, and one eleven-year old boy, only armed with one gun and one Colt's revolver, are but a small force to defend themselves against many hostile Indian tribes, along a journey of two thousand miles."[10]

For many other travelers, word-of-mouth reports created consternation.[11] By the time she reached Ft. Kearney in 1853, Helen Love could no longer sleep because she thought she "herd wolves howling and Indians screaming and all sorts of noises."[12] One acquired license to purvey Indian intelligence simply by asserting that one "knew" something, that one held information that could avert a disaster or save a life. As a consequence, all kinds of people became reporters. In 1861, Lucy Fosdick pinpointed drivers of teams as the source of her unease. "The teamsters, to be sure, generally ended their advice by telling us that if we were well armed we should probably get through all right," she explained, "but we naturally felt very uneasy, and from that time dated my fear and hatred of 'Lo, the poor Indian.' "[13]

Because migrants' nerves were honed to a fine edge by such reports, they mistook an incredible variety of occurrences for Indian raids.[14] Expecting to see Indians at every turn, they transformed the landscape, their stock, and their companions into threatening menaces. In one instance, Indians mounting a major offensive turned out to be a loose rope hitting the water. On other occasions, supposed Indians were a deer, a lost dog returning to camp, four little pigs that had escaped, and some jittery cattle.[15] Train members sometimes inadvertently generated scares in other ways as well. When two young women rushed through the dark toward a young man on the fringe of camp in repayment for his practical jokes, they watched, appalled, as he dashed into camp and raised an Indian alarm in unreasoning fright.[16]

People along the trail were also taken for Native Americans. Mary Warner remarked that Indians fired at a member of her train as he passed through a canyon, or rather, she explained, "he supposed it was them."[17] Soldiers sent to protect the migrants also suffered from mistaken identity. Ada Millington said that when the men of her party sighted wigwams and Indians firing guns in the distance, they immediately loaded their guns and regrouped the train. When the menace turned out to be tents and U.S. soldiers, she said, "We had a good laugh over our scare."[18]

In this high state of agitation, migrants tended to blame Native Americans for any misfortune or irregularity that occurred, whether it was their doing or not. Katherine Dunlap explained that when their stock wandered it was "natural" to think the animals had been stolen by Indians "skulking around the camps."[19]

When natives were spotted, resulting reports were often blown out of proportion. One man rushed into camp shouting that Indians were chasing him. He raised fifteen to twenty armed men to pursue the Indians. But upon tracking the Indians down, the natives explained they had intended to beg for food. The whites remained convinced that a full-scale attack would be launched upon them that very night.[20] In case after case, trail reports were punctuated with impending crisis and predictions of doom, but the day's events often ended on an anticlimactic, peaceful note. Margaret Chambers's remark that "we had no trouble with the Indians—only some scares" during a hegira to Oregon in 1851 was typical.[21]

In time, many migrants became skeptical of the Indian rumors flying around them. When Charlotte Pengra heard a "frightful tale" about four hundred revengeful Indians blocking their party's path, she understandably reacted with concern. But she soon noted, "Have seen no Indians and conclude the tale we heard was false." Some days later, a "hostile" Indian village again caused her distress, but, she wrote, "We anticipated some trouble but realised none." By the end of her chronicle of this move in 1853 from Illinois to Oregon, she declared, "I have heard lots of bugbear stories about the Indians. . . . I conclude the stories are about as true as they ever will be."[22] Apparently, rumor was worse than reality. Most migrants suffered more from their own angst than from Indians.

There were, of course, violent and tragic interactions between migrants and Native Americans. But it does appear that folktales and popular media overemphasized such calamities to the point of distorting the historical nature of contact between migrants and natives. Moreover, it is evident that some trail folk were not above exaggerating or inventing incendiary tales to feed the interest of their contemporaries. In turn, newspapers, hoping to expand their subscription lists, published these fabrications with their own embellishments.[23]

While both men and women both reacted to and spread such exaggerated stories, women were usually expected to be more vocal, and more hysterical, than men. As a result of nineteenth-century dictums concerning a woman's weak, nervous nature as opposed to a man's strong, calm disposition, it is not surprising that migrants believed the threat of Indian troubles was more debilitating to women. When a train on its way from Illinois to the Willamette Valley in 1845 heard the cry of Indians, the men armed themselves and formed a corral while the women cried, wrung their hands, and prayed in near panic.[24] During her trip from Texas to California in 1853, Maggie Hall commented that the "groundless scares in the night" were merely "very exasperating" to her father, but "they made the women nervous and sick."[25]

Furthermore, trail documents indicate it was often these supposedly excitable females who raised alarms—often to the scorn or amusement of men. In 1853, on her way from Iowa to Oregon, Catherine Washburn jotted in her diary that "some of the women were very much allarmed to night they thought they herd the Indians coming to attacht us which turned out to be the ferry rope splashing in the water."[26] When men attempted to offset women's propensity to panic by holding drills, some women reacted to the drills themselves. In 1849, the captain of Catherine Haun's train called a drill, only to watch women go into a frenzy. "Some screamed, others fainted, a few crawled under the wagons," Haun wrote. "All of us were nearly paralyzed with fear." She added that seeing "nothing living but Indians, lizards, and snakes" for weeks was "trying, indeed, to feminine nerves."[27]

Still, in other cases, women maintained their composure. They neither cringed in terror nor fell into a state of hysteria. Rather, they conducted themselves admirably in the face of danger and lent aid to other women whose nerves were not quite as steady. In one such altercation in 1853, Harriet Ward claimed that several women were not frightened at all. She tellingly added that "I hardly think we ever suffer quite as much when anything of this kind really happens as we do in the anticipation."[28]

By being constantly reminded that they were weak and nervous, women were also being told that they were expected to behave in a panicky fashion and that it was socially acceptable for them to do so. That such behavior was both expected and allowed created a climate in which even self-possessed, plucky women could succumb to pandemonium created by their sisters. To maintain one's composure as Indians were about to invade was difficult enough; to remain calm while one's companions were creating bedlam was near impossible.

It should also be noted that trail women had at least two gender-related reasons to fear native assaults. One of these was the sexual threat, the unreasoning dread that almost every woman harbored of being raped (or to use the nineteenth-century euphemism, of being "passed over the prairie") by native molesters. The other danger women particularly feared was the seizing of their children by Indian captors. Responsible for child care and frequently lectured about their maternal sensibilities, women reacted with horror to stories of Indians who stole children and perpetrated atrocities upon them.

Naturally, men recognized these potential menaces to women and children. Consequently, they tried to avoid leaving them alone. In many circumstances, however, this precaution proved impractical. If necessity dictated their absence, men sometimes left women with a recourse. One woman, traveling with her small children, wore a locket on a thin gold chain which, beautiful as it appeared, was lethal, for it contained a folded paper containing small pellets of cyanide for her and her children to consume if they were faced with certain capture.[29] In this case, as in many others, the threat came to naught and the pills were never taken. Yet the terror experienced by women was crushingly painful to them, even though it was more frequently inspired by imagination than reality. Women's anxieties cannot be dismissed or belittled. Rather, women who took to the trail despite its dangers, who eschewed alarmist thinking, and who were able to maintain equanimity when a threat materialized deserve admiration.

Furthermore, despite nineteenth-century stereotypes regarding the excitability of women and the stability of men, trail accounts reveal that not all men were as imperturbable as reputed. Despite social beliefs that imputed steady hands and stout hearts to men, their supposed courageousness occasionally displayed significant cracks. The imaginations of numerous male migrants were prone to multiply a few Native Americans into hordes. In one case "hundreds" turned out to be fifteen, and in another, "thousands were actually forty Indians."[30]

This propensity to exaggerate on the part of some men was viewed with scorn by other migrants. Byron McKinstry, member of a train headed toward the California goldfields in 1850, jeeringly wrote his journal about one of his fellow travelers; when this man's Indians "vanished" so did his fears of them. He wished that "the Indians had Potts and a half a dozen more of our co. that I could name, then our Indian trouble would be at an end, at least the imaginary part of them."[31]

Apparently, men who behaved in a scaremonger fashion became the objects of derision. Charged with the protection of train members, wagons, and stock, and possessing a supposedly stronger nature, men were expected to demonstrate bravery and equanimity. They were supposed to stand implacable in the face of danger, and not surrender to the luxury of panic as women were allowed to do. Accordingly, most men attempted to live up to expectations. Most claimed they did not fear Indians and were confident in the strength of their own arms.[32] They organized protective associations, appointed military "captains" to lead trains, armed and drilled, and posted guards.[33] This aggressive stance on the part of men should have allayed the women's distress, but women frequently seemed unimpressed by either the good sense or the physical abilities of their men. Indeed, they were often doubtful, even caustic, in their statements. They seemed to sense too much braggadocio in the air. As Lydia Waters declared, "I should say we had some mighty men of valor with us. The Indians would die of fright as soon as they saw them! These mighty men could fire forty shots out of their wagons without reloading!"[34] Other women joked about their men's military might. Surveying her well-armed husband with his bowie knife and pistols, Lucy Cooke remarked, "Hope he won't hurt himself."[35]

Such remarks suggest a tension between men and women. The men clearly expected the women to be nervous and silly, but surprisingly, given nineteenth-century maxims regarding male strength, many of the women appeared to anticipate ineptness and irrationality from men. Barred by social custom from taking matters into their own hands, they could express their dissatisfaction only through jibes.

In addition, women often blamed men who created a hostile climate by mistreating Indians. Women indicted male migrants who slaughtered buffalo so that Indians, robbed of subsistence, would become dependent upon whites and thus vulnerable to becoming "civilized."[36] Other women noted that many men, convinced of their inherent right to invade native lands, refused to pay tolls to cross bridges the Indians had built; rejected entreaties for tribute to compensate Indians for destroyed grazing lands, exhausted game reserves, and depleted water supplies; and even captured Indians, whom they forced to serve as guides.[37] In one particular instance, Pauline Wonderly criticized some male emigrants who first refused to pay a "reasonable" toll to Indians who had constructed a bridge across the Elk Horn River, and then killed eleven Native Americans in the ensuing fight. Later parties, she prophesied, would have to pay for the "meanness of the men of that train."[38]

Some men devised a variety of schemes and scams to amuse or profit themselves at Indians' expense. Lavinia Porter noted with disgust that some men of her train who swaggered and bragged that they could whip Indians also treated them contemptuously on a personal basis. "It was their usual custom whenever the Indians approached our camp or sat by our camp fires," Porter complained, "to tease and play various tricks upon them."[39] A common prank involved fleecing an Indian in a trade, an occurrence that seemed to elicit delight from many professed Christians. Mary Hopping bitterly termed two men "smarties" who paid an Indian counterfeit money for moccasins.[40]

In other cases, leaders of wagon trains who believed that Indians would see them as easy marks refused to give aid or allow any conversations with natives who approached train members.[41] In 1857, Helen Carpenter recorded that a party of Pawnees came to their camp while they were "nooning." The captain ordered train members to refrain from giving them food. "It was thought," she explained, "that they would follow and be a nuisance if shown any kindness." But Carpenter discovered that she could not eat her lunch "with those poor wretches watching every mouthful like hungry dogs." Her mother seized an opportunity to slip food to the pitiable beggars, but the Indians did not follow the train nor give its members trouble. "We do not coincide with all of Uncle Sam's views," Carpenter added, "but he is the 'boss' of the train and as such his views must be respected."[42]

Other women complained that some men in their parties even transformed their fear and dislike of Indians into violent action. They reported that men physically abused and assaulted Native American women and took potshots at men.[43] As such events escalated, as they often do, they caused bitterness, hostility, and frequently the death of natives.[44] Also, women often reacted negatively to male migrants' willingness to intimidate Native Americans from attacking and to punish them harshly when they did. Many men were not above taking scalps, captives, and hostages, nor did they refrain from torturing and killing natives.[45]

Evidently, tensions between migrants and natives on the westward trail often translated into tensions between female and male migrants as well. Migrants not only feared and blamed Native Americans for their troubles, but they feared and blamed each other. Such external and internal pressures created groups of anxiety-ridden travelers whose attitudes and actions did little to encourage peaceful coexistence or harmonious interaction between migrating and native groups.

Perhaps the most unfortunate aspect of the situation is that travelers' apprehensions often had little to do with real Indians. Having absorbed ex-aggerated accounts before leaving home, and collecting more rumors, scares, and alarmism once on the trail, the migrants were primed for conflict. Rather than regard Native Americans as human beings much like themselves, they were well-prepared to despise and fear what was essentially a fabrication: the specter of the savage.

After migrants became settlers, miscommunication and conflict between invaders and natives continued. This antagonism seemed to exist in every century and in every region. Here a Mexican woman, whose family emigrated to Monterey, California, during the 1790s, described her reaction when Chief Solano and his followers visited Monterey, probably around 1820:

At the time Solano visited Monterey I was residing with Madam Pruden-cia Amestí and I took particular notice of the tall figure of that dark col-oured savage, who was dressed like the people of my race; his many fol-lowers, however, were dressed like Indians, and wore feathers round their heads, many of them were tattoed round their wrists, arms and legs. Their presence we disliked very much because their conduct was really overbearing. Solano and his Indians were all mounted on fine horses. . . . they wore long hair, carried their bows and arrows, and their appearance was such as to inspire fear. I really believed them to be devils let loose from hell. . . .

I heard my mistress say, that the arrival of these savages in Monterey, was a plague sent by God for the purpose of punishing us for our sins. Solano did not remain long in Monterey, he was prevailed upon to return to Sonoma. . . .[46]

Prejudice and misunderstanding could also lead to pathetic and humorous situations. Woman after woman recounted incidents that revealed the lack of communication between migrants and Indians. Ella Bird-Dumont of Texas described a humorous situation that occurred during the early 1880s:

We were talking and laughing when all of a sudden the dogs set up an unusual raving and barking. We stepped into the yard to see what was the matter; and oh horrors! what do you think met our gaze? Those Indians were coming. They were within less than fifty yards of the house. We stepped back into the house. I hid my gun for fear they might take it and so I could get it if needed. Mrs. Jones said she would stand in the door and maybe they would not come in. They dashed up and were dismounted in a moment almost. The chief led the way to the door. Mrs. Jones did not move. He pushed her aside and six others followed him. Now imagine our plight. This house was about twelve feet square with two beds, five children, three women, and seven Indians in it. We did not have standing room, nor could we understand a word they said.

The old chief was very friendly and tried to talk to us. . . . The object of their visit seemed mainly to trade clothing for groceries. This clothing was given them by the government of which they used but little, preferring to wear buckskin instead. Our grocery stock was short and we could not accommodate them much. They began prowling through the house as soon as they came. We did not know what they wanted until they found some groceries. Then they began showing us some clothes, holding up different garments, then pointing to the groceries. We understood but shook our heads; nothing doing! They kept on prowling and found my gun. They set up an excited palavering and talking; everyone had to look at it. The Chief took quite a fancy to it. He had a new Colt 45 pistol, which he offered to me for my gun. I shook my head. He then began showing me the clothes he had on, first touching his coat, vest, shirt, and so on. I did not understand him, and did not make any reply, so he began laying off his clothes, one by one.

Mrs. Jones and I looked at each other in helpless dismay. . . . the truth dawned on Mrs. Jones, just before it was everlastingly too late; she said, "He thinks you have traded your gun for his clothes." I began shaking my head, saying, "No, no." He laughed and proceeded to put on his clothes again.

She tried to explain to him why I would not part with my gun, that it was a present to my husband from the State. I wanted to add that it was given for killing Indians but thought it might be good policy to leave that part of it off. However, they did not understand anything she said. She also told them the men folks would be in that evening. She showed them their clothes to make them understand. They finally all moved out doors and sat down with some others beside the house and began talking in low serious tones, we thought. Mrs. Jones became very frightened and said she believed they were planning to kill us, but the Jones men came in that evening. . . .[47]

Even women living among the Five Civilized Tribes of Oklahoma during the late nineteenth and early twentieth centuries harbored unreasoning trepidation. This Oklahoma woman recalled her first contacts in 1893 with Native Americans:

I would be working, and would turn around and there would be one or two Indians sitting on the floor, or on chairs. They were so quiet that I never would hear them come in. The first time that occurred I was almost paralyzed with fear, when I discovered them, in fact, I was too frightened to make an outcry, or move, but just stood staring at them. They were an old couple and really seemed to enjoy my discomfiture, for they both laughed, then the woman said, in broken English, "we good Indians, come to see little white squaw. You maybe got tobacco?" I nodded my head for I could not possibly have spoken as my tongue seemed frozen to the roof of my mouth. I went into the next room and got some of my husband's tobacco and when I came out into the kitchen, there the old squaw stood turning my very sharp bowie knife, over in her hands. She tested the blade, then grunted and turned to me. I said a little prayer, for I sincerely thought my time had come, but no, all she wanted was the knife. "You give Indian nice knife?" she asked. "Yes, yes, you may have it," I answered quickly and gladly. She could have had anything in the house, I was so relieved that it wasn't my scalp this squaw had in mind. After looking around a bit more and taking some beads, which were lying on the table, they left as they had come without ceremony or saying "thank you" or "good bye."

I sank limply into a chair and cried from sheer nervousness and when my husband came home that evening, I told him of my experience and added that he simply had to put a screen on the door with a latch so that I would at least know when I had a visitor. This he did, and I had no further surprises.[48]

Unscrupulous people were not above taking advantage of migrants' fears of Indians. Jonaphrene Faulkner, a Texas settler during the 1850s, explained that such schemes and stories were as hurtful to settlers as they were to people on the trail:

Sometimes a report would come, vague enough as to its origin, but startlingly well defined in detail, of a massacre that had occurred somewhere twenty five or thirty miles away, in which whole communities were wiped out. . . . And as there was no way of disproving the rumor, or of investigating it, there could not fail a grim effect upon even the stoutest courage.

As the process of time failed utterly to substantiate these reports it is most probable that the whole disturbance was caused by one or two small bodies of Indians coming into the settlements for horses, or it is just as probable that there was not an Indian among them, but simply a band of horse thieves who took this disguise to cover their lawless deeds, and were not averse to a murder now and then, when it could be perpetrated in some out of the way place, where they could do it with safety to themselves. . . .

However, as far as the influence upon the minds and fortune of the people was concerned, the rumors might as well have been true to the letter. Certain it is they destroyed much of the contentment of the present and hope of the future in the life of our colony. . . .[49]

Both unscrupulous and unthinking people capitalized on women's fear of Indians. Flora Spiegelberg recalled a practical joke played on her shortly after her arrival in Santa Fe, New Mexico, in 1875:

One day my sister-in-law—I was a guest in her home—said to me, "Flora I am taking my children for a walk and will be home for lunch." I was sitting in my bedroom which faced the large porch, when I heard soft footsteps, then the old-fashioned doorbell rang loudly and incessantly. I ran to the door and called out, "who is there?" Imagine my fright when a number of men shrieked, "WHISKEY, WHISKEY," and then kept on ringing the bell, pounding on the door and jabbering away in a language I did not understand. Although greatly excited I had presence of mind and ran back to my bedroom window, peeked out from behind a corner of the shade, to my great astonishment saw a lot of almost naked Indians in war paint and feathers dancing on the porch. Meanwhile two old bucks were beating their tom-toms shrieking their wild war songs so that the dancers might keep on dancing.

Presently the bell began ringing again, loud pounding on the door and shouts, "Whiskey, Whiskey,". . . Although finding myself alone and scared, yet the strange sight of the dancing Indians fascinated me to the extent that I could not resist the temptation to peek at them again and again. After dancing awhile and ringing the bell and no whiskey they departed.

Shortly afterwards my sister-in-law returned, still much excited I ran to meet her, and as I started to tell her about the scare, she took me in her arms, saying, "I know all about it, it is only a joke my husband has played on you because you wanted to see and speak to live Indians. He has paid them very generously for this performance . . ."[50]

Of course, real incidents of violence between migrants and Indians did occur. These gave weight to the rumors and kept everyone in a constant state of agitation. A Nisqually, Washington, settler described a common scenario of good relations deteriorating into violence during the mid-1840s:

Father selected his farm at the junction of the Shonadaub and Squaquid Creeks. . . . The farm was situated upon the council grounds of the Nisqually tribes, the old chief Syonnatco, politely relinquished it to father. . . . At last [the Indians] came and told us, "We cannot stand much more imposition and if it is not stopped we will have to go to the woods." This meant they would go to war. It was about this time that Governor Stevens arrived, a brave and noble man, liked by all, both whites and Indians. He with a few others realized the situation and tried to make peace, but was too late. The Indians had been preparing for several years and were much better prepared than the whites thought. . . .

History tells us the Indian war was brought on by the whites taking their lands, but the old settlers know better. One among the many causes was the treatment their women received. A man perhaps with a wife in the east, would come here and marry an Indian girl or woman. According to the white man's law it was not legal. Those women and girls thought themselves as legally married as their white sisters, and so things went from bad to worse. The whites came in greater numbers. The wrongs the Indians endured were more and more, and liquor (the curse of man) but a far worse one to the Indian. The Indians grew to distrust and hate all newcomers, but were still kind to all the old settlers.

Some years before, when the soldiers were stationed at Steilacoom, a young officer had wooed and won the only daughter of Chief Yanatco, and like many others he had married her according to Indian rules. The soldiers were required to move from place to place and it became necessary for this officer to go. He couldn't take his wife according to the white man's laws and she had better go back to her father. Brokenhearted, she came home and told her story to the chief. He was brokenhearted, too, and fell to the ground in his terrible affliction. He crept in his degradation, refusing to walk upright. . . . Yanacto now abdicated in favor of his son, Leshi. Poor old man, he only lived a few months after his terrible grief. . . . Knowing Leshi as I did, I know he would never have gone to war except for this incident. He immediately went to the mountains and all his braves followed. . . .

Knowing of the strong friendship between father and Leshi, the whites appealed to him to carry a peace commission to Leshi, for him to sign. If anyone could do so it was father. The whites offered and father accepted the commission as First Lieutenant in the Puget Sound Volunteers. Still he didn't think the Indians would fight, so kind and docile they had always been. . . . His going away increased the anger of the Indians, as they had asked him to remain neutral. . . .

One morning in October, I was awakened at the break of day by a most piercing scream and heavy fall, we all ran out into the sitting room. . . . Indians now began to appear as though they had sprung from the earth, the room was soon filled with painted Indians, who went from room to room peering into everything. The house and yard were full. . . . Ugly faces were pressed against the window panes peering at us. The wildest orgies were going on outside, loud and boastful threats were made of "what they would do when they got us.". . .

The two youngest boys now slipped out to look for a team of some kind to try and make our escape with. . . . The long day passed and night came again. We had some food brought to us, but were too frightened to eat. . . . The long night wore away at last, as morning came, cold and chilly. . . . The boys returned early in the evening with the joyful news that they had found a wild, half-broken yoke of oxen, and had secured and hidden them far away. . . .

The boys talked to the Indians, trying to get them to permit us to go, the Indians did not know we had the team and of course thought we would have to go on foot to Fort Nisqually, and once out of the house would be very easy prey for them. . . . There was an old cattle road leading to the prairie and we decided to take it, hoping that, it being so little used, that they would not think it worthwhile to guard. . . .

We left the house and walked through the crowd of Indians. They gave way for us to pass. We went east, across the Squaquid Creek towards Fort Nisqually. The Indians did not attempt to follow us, thinking it wasn't worthwhile, as it was on this road that they had so carefully planted their best ambushes, so turned their attention to looting the house. . . . we turned abruptly to the south and followed the cattle trail through the woods some distance. We re-crossed the creek and were soon where the boys had hidden the team and wagon. They had placed a chain across the wagon box for the little ones to hold on to. . . . The oxen were so wild that the boys had to put ropes on their horns and ride by their sides to keep them in the road. Mother and the younger children were placed in the wagon, sitting flat upon the bottom and told to hang on to the chains. After much plunging, twisting, and turning, now backward and forward, we got started to the fort. . . . The cattle would run until they were tired out, then stop short almost pitching us from the wagon. When they felt like going they went at neckbreak speed. . . .

At last we rounded a point of timber and came in sight of the fort, about three miles away. . . . We were seen from the fort and a government wagon came to meet us. . . . So tight had been our grasp upon the chain across the wagon box that the soldiers had to unclasp our hands from it, as we were unable to do so ourselves. Our little bodies were so bruised and bleeding that we were not able to stand upon our feet. They lifted us from the wagon and soothed us with kind hands and gentle words. Every kindness possible was shown us and we were taken to the fort. . . .[51]

American entry into Mexican regions also created unrest among Native Americans. Some Indians who had pledged allegiance to Mexican rulers, rancheros, and mission priests switched loyalties to the Americans and frequently attacked their former friends. A California woman described such occurrences at the Mission of San Diego during the 1840s and 1850s:

The Indians had come intending to fall upon the mission; all appearances were suspicious. In the evening, we were dining when Doña Juana Moreno knocked at the door. . . . She informed us that a little Indian, a friend of her son, had told him that they should go away because the Indians were going to fall upon the mission and kill all the white people that they found in it.

Then the son of Señora Juana Moreno, an Indian named Santiago who cooked for us, and the little Indian of whom I have spoken before went out to where the horses were corralled to leave for Santa Margarita where Servulo Varelas and thirty men who that morning—or better near mid-day—had been at the mission, and I had fed them. . . . The Padre sent him a message to come at once as an Indian uprising against the people of the region was imminent and that they were plotting to kill us.

Varelas with men came to the mission at dawn. . . . Varelas sent two or three men to Guanjomito to learn if the Indians were there. They found them there. Varelas summoned them the following day. . . . When the Indians came, Varelas addressed them, scolding them for having declared themselves hostile to those of the region and saying that that was done without reason as those of the region and they were one. The Indians promised to do as he advised them. . . .

In those times, there were many Indian uprisings. . . . In the valley of the canyon (between the mission and El Cajón), the Padres had a milking place wherein they made cheese. One day, the Indians fell upon it and killed a vaquero, a boy who helped him, and an Indian shepherd who cared for a sheep ranch. . . . Another boy who was there escaped and came to give information. They killed the cows and carried off the meat, and they also carried off the wife of the vaquero who was an Indian and all the horses. They handed the woman over after about fifteen days. . . .[52]

Despite such confrontations, many non-Indian women learned more about Native Americans, observed the injustices done them, and became less fearful of them. As a result, many began to change their minds. They started to see the Indians' side of the story:

3.2
Women Migrants' Changing Views of
Native Americans in the Trans-Mississippi West

Women who migrated to the West during the nineteenth century held deeply ingrained images and preconceptions of Native Americans in the trans-Mississippi West. As women, they also labored under nineteenth-century images and preconceptions of females that in turn influenced and shaped their views of Indians. As a result, they tended to emphasize and react to certain aspects of Indian culture, society, and value systems. Most white women and many women of color responded, at least initially, in the ways expected of properly indoctrinated nineteenth-century women.

A crucial change in these responses often appeared as women interacted with various Native American peoples and as they realized their own resilience in facing the harsh demands of life in the West. Both experiences often challenged the prevailing view of what constituted "real" Indians and "true" women. Many women began to eschew these stereotypes in favor of a more authentic relationship with Native Americans. They began to trade and to interact socially with Indians; sometimes they even expressed affection for, and sympathy toward, some of them. Contemporary American and European writers, however, failed to record these changes. Journalists and novelists fed the anti-Indian prejudices of their reading public with fictionalized accounts of brutal and primitive savages who preyed especially on women who dared to venture into their domain. When women's own accounts were printed they were usually "penny dreadfuls" or captivity narratives that further inflamed hatred of Native Americans.[53]

Encouraged by profitable sales and enthusiastic readers, authors willingly responded with increasingly dramatic accounts of what were termed Indian "depredations," particularly those perpetrated upon women. One anthology of women's horror stories, for example, waxed eloquent on the subject: "The very sight of Indians were terrible to many women. . . . The savages could not be looked upon without calling to mind the horrid work of the tomahawk and the scalping-knife—the desolated home and the butchered relatives.[54] An Iowa woman, Abie Gardner-Sharpe, wrote an inflammatory account of the "massacre" of her family, which she sold in the souvenir shop that she established in the cabin where the "depredations" occurred.[55] Even James Fenimore Cooper contributed to the tradition with captivity segments such as those found in *The Last of the Mohicans*.[56]

But in women's personal writings a much different portrait of women migrants and Indians emerges. Western realities forced women to examine them-

3.2: Excerpted from "Frontierswomen's Changing Views of Native Americans in the Trans-Mississippi West," in *Montana: The Magazine of Western History* 34 (Winter 1984), 20–35. Recipient of the Palladin Writing Award. Used by permission.

selves, their roles, their views of Native Americans and their culture in a new light. As a result, women related to Indians in ways that were ignored or blurred in captivity narratives and sensationalized fiction of the day. In their daily lives, women acted in ways that contradicted the stereotypes of western women created by popular writers.

Reading women's own diaries, journals, letters, memoirs, and reminiscences is the only way to learn how women migrants perceived themselves and their relationships with Native Americans. Women's personal documents were seldom written for publication. They were daily records of significant events, usually expressing on-the-spot feelings and reactions, and had no reading public other than the writer or perhaps her family "back East" or in Europe.

The diaries women kept on the overland trail, the journals and daybooks of women migrants, the accounts by army wives, and the records of female missionaries mentioned in this essay represent experiences throughout the trans-Mississippi West from the mid-1830s to the end of the nineteenth century and include several unpublished statements of women who were involved in violent conflicts with Native Americans. Not written to describe Indians for a public audience and with no particular interest to promote, these documents reflect the attitudes and feelings of a cross-section of western women who typically had casual and intermittent contact with Indians as well as the prolonged, intense experience women missionaries and teachers had with native groups. Trail diaries especially illuminate how women's reactions to Indians changed as they moved westward, while women missionaries' accounts, for example, express deeply ingrained and fairly inflexible perceptions of Indians, which derived from their sense of mission; such remarks were clearly unrepresentative of women migrants in general.

Before turning to these women's statements, it is essential to understand the prejudicial attitudes that influenced most of them. That era's strong anti-Indian ideology originated during America's colonial years when attempts to enslave, acculturate, or assimilate Native Americans faltered because natives resisted or tended to sicken and die in slavery, leaving many white Americans to conclude that these peoples should eventually be exterminated. Later generations of Americans elaborated on that thought. They created the generic category "Indian," which lumped together over 2,000 native cultures, and described Native Americans as savages, infidels, heathens, and barbarians. Many people believed that these Indians were "bad"; naked, dirty, mean, rapacious, and hostile, they fully deserved destruction by the progressive and civilized white society.[57]

At the same time, some observers pointed out that native peoples possessed admirable qualities—bravery, courage, simplicity—that "civilized" society often lacked, and that some Indians could be friendly and courteous toward invading migrants. There must, then, be at least some "good" Indians. This sentiment, however, failed to offset the impulse for exterminating Native

Americans. Too many people believed that Indians were impossible subjects for acculturation or even coexistence.[58]

Europeans also developed an ambivalent image of Indians. As historian Ray Allen Billington explained, European writers defined "good" and "bad" Indians by their allegiance: "good" Indians were friendly to whites, and "bad" Indians were not. Racist depictions of Native Americans by whites, however, encouraged Europeans of the nineteenth century to believe that "the Noble Savage was a myth; the true red man was more beast than man, unfit to associate with Civilized Christians." As Europeans increasingly visualized the West as a land of savagery, they began to agree with those Americans who advocated the extirpation of Indians. Stories of Native Americans pervaded nineteenth-century American and European literature, providing European readers with vicarious thrills. Coopermania, as Billington termed it, became powerful on both sides of the ocean.[59]

In the nineteenth century, women migrants who viewed Native Americans through this prejudicial veil also had to contend with their own gender conditioning. Society attributed to women, as it did to Indians, constrasting superior and inferior natures. The superior side of women's character derived primarily from their supposedly exceptional moral sensibilities, qualities that cast them in the role of moral guardians of the home and family. Women had a cluster of other ascribed traits: they were kind, gentle, passive, religious, domestic, pure, and refined. On the other hand, women were inferior because of their obvious physical weakness and assumed intellectual limitations. They had small brains and weak muscles, and they were helpless, childlike, unassertive, indecisive, and unable to protect themselves.[60] Having listened all their lives to these descriptions of the female character, many women, both white and of color, internalized them and carried them westward. Their self-image as the protectors of ethics and civilization tended to shape their perceptions of Native Americans as uncivilized, morally deficient, and brutalized by their primitive existence while reinforcing their understanding of themselves as the harbingers of civilization.[61]

Women's imputed superiority often encouraged them to emphasize, and even become obsessed with, the Native Americans' supposed inferiority. Accordingly, disparaging views of Indians frequently dominated the early pages of most women's diaries and journals. The women often expressed disappointment when they met their first Indians and disillusionment at the ragged, unkempt appearance of these people that did not match the befeathered image they expected. Kate Furness wrote that they were "very ugly," and Sarah Herndon dismissed her first Indian as being "very disappointing as the 'Noble Red Man' we read about." The Indians' lack of clothing often shocked women. Mary Sandford recorded that "the Indians were nude save for a throw over one shoulder, and a strap around the loins." Mary Staples noted that their "clothing was very scant," Sallie Maddock that they were "mostly naked," Margaret Hecox that they frequently came "to our camp in a perfectly nude state," and Harriet Smith that she was "a little streaked for he had nothing on but a blanket and great earrings and bracelets, all brass."[62] Even when the Indians were dressed, women's assessments tended to be derogatory. After seeing her first Indians, Caroline Richardson wrote that they were "drest in their 'peculiar costome.' " Another woman observed that although "some are nearly naked, some dressed most fantastically," and another that they were "decorated in the extreme of Indian dandyism." When the Indian attire resembled white styles, however, women viewed it more positively. A group of Sioux who were "neatly dressed" in an approximation of white fashion struck Hecox as "clean and wholesome in appearance." When Maria Norton encountered Native Americans dressed "with pants and caps," she judged them to be "the most respectable that we have seen."[63]

Women migrants frequently disparaged various Native American groups for being unclean, dirty, and even filthy. To Maddock they were "disgusting and dirty looking," to Staples "a filthy set," and to Mary Jane Guill "a filthy and dirty set of Indians."[64] As one women put it, "the romance of Indian life will not bear a closer inspection—they are neither more or less than filthy savages."[65] Many women associated uncleanliness with some Indians' disconcerting habit of eating insects. When Angeline Ashley observed Utah Indians pulling wings off locusts and harvesting them in sacks, she decided that "they are very low Indians and very ugly looking." Another woman, watching an Indian woman eat lice from her husband's head while feeding him a few of the choice ones, wrote that the Indians were contemptible objects due to the "extreme indolence of their nature, the squalid conditions in which they live . . . and the general imbecility of their intellects." Helen Stewart indicated that she preferred that visiting Indians avoid her camp altogether. "They are the durtyist creatures I ever saw," she wrote. "They will pick the lice out of there head and eat them."[66]

Many female migrants also seemed to associate peculiar odors with Native Americans. They noted smelling a nearby Indian camp, or said that their horses and dogs responded with fear to the smell of an Indian.[67] One woman phrased it delicately when she wrote that the "effluvia arising from their persons is none of the sweetest." Another was more direct: "they were simply, and only painted, dirty and nauseous-smelling savages."[68]

Even though they were already of the opinion that Native Americans lived a life deficient in certain areas, many women were shocked to discover that many Indians spoke little or no English. With obvious dismay, Ellen Adams remarked, "Some of the Indians could not understand a single word of English." And when a Native American could manage a few words of English, women often recorded it, sometimes with derision.[69] "They do not understand any of our language," one woman reported, "and when they can speak a word of it they seem to think that they have done something very smart."[70]

Puzzlement, derision, and outright racism characterized many women's assessments of Native American customs. The sight of Indian villages moving on pole carts pulled by dogs or with the sticks of wigwams on ponies amused some, and other women found curious the Indian custom of burying their dead above ground. Marie Nash called the burial custom a "sad sight," but others minimized its significance, seeing it as simply a practical means to protect graves from being pillaged and bodies from being mutilated by wolves. Some women had so little respect for the Indian customs that they entered burial grounds to collect beads to string and wear as ornaments.[71]

Native American mating practices drew attention as well. Some women seemed obsessed with a need to chronicle every French trader they met who had an Indian wife and "half-breed" children. Amused by such intermarriages, Mary Fish quipped that "the Frenchmen go for amalgamation." When she met another with a dozen wives she joked that he was "fond of a plural number." Another woman wrote that the children of one such marriage seemed "playful and happy," but Maria Norton found the idea an abomination: "the greatest absurdity," she penned, " . . . was for a white man to live with black dirty squaws."[72]

Erroneously concluding from their superficial observations that Indian males crassly traded ponies and goods for wives, many women travelers became further distressed. "I was somewhat shocked to think of such a loose state of morals," Mary Bailey wrote in 1852. Yet, if a Native American male attempted to trade ponies for white women, they generally took the matter lightly. In response to an Ottawa Indian's proposal Emily Horton sarcastically wrote: "I was too unsophisticated to appreciate the honor." In a similar situation, Harriet Smith jested, "I thought I would wait untill some one would give Unc a lot of ponies for me and I would go and stay awhile with them then run away, and then we would have some ponies." Mary Warner jokingly noted in her diary that "Uncle Chester traded Aunt Lizzie off for two ponies but she would not go." And Catherine Bell wrote home that "there was an Indian chief offered Charlie two of his best ponys for me, dont you think he ought to have traded?"[73]

Despite occasional amusement, women generally deplored the manner in which Indian men treated Indian women. When they witnessed men taking money from women who had earned it by selling their handiwork, riding while women walked, or expecting women to carry the load while they went un-burdened, they judged Indian men to be detestable and contemptible.[74] These inaccurate perceptions of the low status of Indian women also added a new dimension to female migrant's forebodings regarding captivity, and they nervously guarded themselves and their children. "I have no desire to go among the Indians in that way," one asserted, and another confessed that she had her son watch her when she fetched water so that Indians would not carry her off. She also protectively gathered her children in her arms whenever Indians approached. Similarly, when Mary Caples saw Indians "dressed in their long macinaw blankets, with eagle feathers in their hair," she worried that "they would kill us all, and take my baby in captivity."[75]

Given these negative and usually imprecise interpretations of Native American ways, it is little wonder that many women travelers initially concluded that the Indians' character had to be of the lowest order and deserved a harsh assessment. Epitaphs such as "hard-hearted & cruel people," "too devilish for any human being," "most treacherous mortals on earth," and "too indolent to exert themselves much" were typical.[76] Although the Pawnee she met appeared friendly, Georgia Willis Reed insisted that "they are noted cowards, but if they get you in their power, your situation is critical." When Lucy Sexton saw a band of peaceful Pawnee routed by a small number of Sioux enemies, she resorted to sarcasm: "A brave nation, truly. One hundred and fifty of them vanquished by 13." A peace treaty with the Sioux, Helen Carpenter believed, was not worth the paper "once an Indian begins to feel ugly, and aching for a 'scrap.'" Another woman harshly concluded that Nebraska Indians were unfit "to inhabit such beautiful soil as we are now traveling through."[77]

Even when female migrants learned that most Native Americans did not intend to seize them, their children, or their scalps, their indignation toward Indians continued. It irked many women that Native Americans were, in Sarah Royce's words, "evidently desirous of getting something out of us if they could." Complaints were legion against Indian groups who begged and stole from migrants.[78] Although Native Americans often asked for sugar, meat, flour, coffee, other foodstuffs, and tobacco, apparently women seldom questioned why once self-sufficient groups needed to beg. Instead of attempting to understand the Indians' conceptions of hospitality, they more often viewed natives as sly, disgusting, or pesky.[79] One caustically wrote, "They are the greatest beggars I ever saw. I do wonder if they are hungry."[80] Other women were more acrimonious. "The better Indians come to camp to pay us a visit," wrote Mary Jane Guill, and "always stay till after supper. I suppose it is fashionable for them to stay." Mallie Stafford scornfully noted: "Two large powerfully built warriors, in all the glory of red paint, buckskin, beads, feathers, dignity and general magnificence, condescended to honor our humble camp with a call— a call long enough to eat up and devour everything we had cooked, that being an immense pot of beans and bacon."[81]

Paradoxical as it seems, women travelers who disparaged Native Americans were able to recognize the presence of "good" Indians. Women migrants had a special reason to search out superior characteristics in the Indians they met. Women had learned to think of themselves as weak, helpless, and incapable of protecting themselves. Their men, of course, could defend them to a certain degree, but many women seemed to feel dependent on the nobility and strength of character of the "primitive savage." Because Native Americans could injure women through thievery, sexual assault, or outright warfare, many women sought out a glimmer of nobility, a hint of kindness, an indication of intelligence in the native peoples they confronted. In this way, women occasionally found admirable qualities in the physical appearance, character, and customs of some Native American people.

Even women travelers who were most vitriolic regarding the ugliness, filth, and odor of Indians also described some of them with such phrases as "an imposing sight in the wilderness," "good-looking, fine-looking," and "noble-looking."[82] Other women depicted some Native Americans as "grave" and "stately," with "the appearance of wealth and independence," and as "tall, strongly made" with "firm features, light copper color, cleanly in appearance, quite well dressed in red blankets."[83] A few women punctuated even derogatory character assessments of Indians with such words as "industrious" and "intelligent," and one spoke of "mannerly conduct" and "a degree of refinement" that she had not expected to find among "just Indians."[84]

Women migrants also praised the Native Americans' abilities, commenting on the ingeniousness of their underground wigwams, the beauty of their needlework, and the high quality of their handiwork. Susan Magoffin went so far as to suggest that Indian postnatal practices were wiser than those of "ladies in civilized life."[85]

A large number of women migrants believed that Indians would respond to fair treatment. Many whites credited their respect, courtesy, friendliness, and willingness to share food with the Native Americans as important elements that insured the safety of their party. "Evidently our hospitality and courteous treatment won their hearts," Lavinia Porter wrote, "for they showed no signs of hostility to us. In fact from their general demeanor they rather inspired us with a confidence which seemed to sanction our presence in their midst."[86]

This ambivalence in women migrants' attitudes toward Indians was grounded, at least in part, in their perceptions of their own weakness and the danger Indians posed. Ada Vogdes's journal reflected such equivocalness. An army wife at Fort Laramie in the late 1860s, she repeatedly wrote in her journal that she was "frightened to death." One night she awoke to imaginary Indian war whoops—actually two drunk cooks—and repeatedly declined her husband's invitations to explore the area surrounding the fort. Yet, during a council meeting with Native American leaders following a dramatic false alarm of attack, she noted Red Cloud's "pleasant smile," Big Bear's "most splendid chest, and shoulders, I ever laid my eyes upon," and Red Leaf's "fatherly looking countenance, & one to whom you would go in trouble, were we in different circumstances." Although Vogdes remained in "constant fear" whenever she left the fort, she also enjoyed becoming "quite a belle amongst the red men of the Plains."

When Vogdes moved to Fort Fetterman, she again complained that western "life is terrible for a nervous excitable person as I am, and it seems as if I could not endure it much longer. For nearly two years the Indians have been the bane of my existence." At Fetterman she mistook a soldier returning late from one of the laundresses' quarters as an attacking Indian, and she shuddered with fear at the sight of Cheyenne Indians outside her windows. Yet Indian leaders who came into the fort impressed her. Of Red Dog she wrote: ". . . [he] had nothing on but the skin in which he was born . . . I never saw such shoulders, arms, & legs, & hands . . . his legs were equally as fine looking." After sitting with him at a small table she commented that although it would seem strange to an easterner to see her with "this naked man," it did not seem strange to her at all. "I am not shocked if I see them with no clothes on," she added.[87]

Ambivalence toward Native Americans, partly the result of indoctrination that contrasted Indians with non-native women, paradoxically also resulted from the gradual erosion of those societally induced attitudes. Women migrants who interacted with Native Americans soon learned that they were neither as "good" nor as "bad" as stereotypes suggested. Harriet Ward not only overcame her dread of Indians but also maintained that other women experienced a similar reaction. "I have conversed with many ladies," she declared, "and they all appear happy and in good health."[88]

These alterations in women migrants' attitudes toward Native Americans coincided with changes in their attitudes about themselves. They learned that their imputed ability to bring order was only one of myriad skills demanded of them in the West. Moreover, they discovered that neither they nor society suffered disaster if they could not fully exercise their role of cultural conservators. They washed clothes on the Sabbath, listened to oaths, and came into contact with gambling, drinking, and polygamy, yet life went on. Women quickly realized that their value to society did not erode under these circumstances; it took a different direction. Many accepted new functions and roles: driving teams, performing trail work, walking for miles over rough terrain, handling weapons, helping make decisions, and making significant economic contributions.[89]

Women migrants began to suspect that natives' ascribed inferiority was just as questionable as their imputed superiority was proving to be. There was not one recorded case of a woman's brain swelling and cracking from new demands, as had been supposed. Instead, most of these women grew strong, assertive, and confident. They realized that they might play some role in shaping their lives, protecting themselves and their children, and determining their survival in the West.

If women were ceasing to believe that their primary value was as civilizers, then they no longer felt a need to emphasize the inferior traits of Indian character. And if women were not weak and incompetent, then their safety did not depend on the Indians' benevolence and superior qualities. These realizations, added to their discovery that Native Americans were people rather than demons, created further contradictions in women's assessments of Indians. As a result, women migrant's interaction with Native Americans was vastly different from the story usually told.

Most women migrants learned to discriminate between Native American groups, realized that each possessed different qualities, and rejected the blanket categorization of "Indian" as an amorphous category.[90] They also learned that Native Americans not only varied from tribe to tribe and from region to region, but also from era to era. A group of Indians who were friendly to migrants in the 1840s might have experienced the ravages of migration so thoroughly by the 1850s that they had become belligerent instead.[91] Mary Pelham recorded a frequent complaint that migrants voiced as relations with Native Americans deteriorated: "How these Indians have changed. Not simple and childlike any more."[92]

Some women recognized that the invasion of growing numbers of migrants caused such alterations in Indians' behavior, a pressure that increasingly drove native groups into armed combat with each other over dwindling resources as well as into violent attempts to stem migrants' incursions. Intertribal wars often worked to the migrants' advantage because Indians attacked each other rather than encroaching travellers.[93] But when Indian groups turned to opposing expansion or exacting compensation, not all women migrants meekly accepted Indian demands.[94]

There are numerous recorded cases of newly confident women resisting Indian intrusions. Lavinia Porter refused a request for bread, only to have bleeding scalps thrust under her nose for her to count and admire. When she refused to retreat, her would-be oppressor muttered "white squaw no fear" and departed. On one occasion, Susanna Ede evicted a native interloper from her kitchen by threatening to pour hot grease on him, and on another by raising a pot of boiling water to throw on the trespasser. Another woman simply tore her belongings out of the hands of pilfering Indians.[95]

Many women went beyond resistance to violence in repelling impositions. Barsina French's mother took turns standing guard with the men to protect the party's stock from Indians. Another woman defended her horses and mules by spending a long night on the roof of her stable shooting at a band of Pimas. Eliza Egbert guarded some wagons by brandishing an empty pistol in the faces of some Pawnee and ordering them to depart or be shot. Mary Ann Davidson threatened an abusive Indian with a poker. And when Susie Van De Weile's husband asked her if she was afraid of the Indians surrounding their camp she calmly replied, "No, give me a pistol."[96]

Not all women migrants, of course, became involved in altercations with Native Americans. Many routinely traded trinkets, clothing, and foodstuffs with Indians, engaging in somewhat of a collegial relationship in their mutual attempt to wrest sustenance from the western environment. Female travelers exchanged needles and thread, foods they had processed, articles of clothing, and trifles with Native Americans, who bartered fresh foods in return. Women frequently mentioned Native American men and women bringing them butter, eggs, potatoes, corn, pumpkins, melons, strawberries, blackberries, venison and other fresh meats and fish, and dried salmon.[97]

Some women migrants also became interested in obtaining specialized native products and crafts. Lucy Cooke, at first in awe of Indians, became an expert trader and collected a fine cache of furs. Other women grew skillful at bartering for buffalo hides and robes, trousers made of antelope and elk hides, moccasins, baskets, and beadwork. Cynthia Capron was delighted with a watertight Indian basket she purchased for a dollar, and Eveline Alexander considered a war shield she bought "quite a valuable trophy." Even Ada Vogdes, who had spent so much time being fearful of Indians, learned local dialects and successfully traded with natives. "I rushed around all day to get a blanket worked with beads which I succeeded in doing," she wrote triumphantly.[98]

Many women migrants also hired Indian men, women, and children to perform household chores, such as chopping wood, drawing water, and washing dishes and clothes.[99] Despite the common rumor that Indians would take non-native children captive, numerous women entrusted their children to the care of Native American women and men.[100] Rachel Wright believed that the key to favorable relations with Indians rested with the migrants themselves. Indians were "an advantage rather than otherwise," she explained, "as they were not only willing but glad to work if they were left free, well treated and properly paid for their labor."[101]

In time, social intercourse flourished among some women migrants and Indians. Accounts by women who initially had been apprehensive frequently described pleasant visits to Indian settlements.[102] "We often visited Indian camps," Allene Dunham wrote. "They always treated us to a piece of dried buffalo, or venison, or some other kind of meat." Another reported that the Indians she visited were "really friendly." We had "quite a dish of conversation," she noted after visiting some Indian women.[103] These developing relationships, business and social, often fostered among women migrants an acceptance of Indians and genuine admiration of and affection for them. Harriet Ward clearly contradicted her earlier attitudes when she jotted in her diary how "surprised" her acquaintances would be "to see me writing so quietly in the wagon alone . . . with a great, wild looking Indian leaning his elbow on the wagon beside me, but I have not a single fear except that they may frighten the horses."[104] Often, as women relaxed enough to genuinely like some Indians, they expressed happiness at their arrival and sorrow at their departure: "We have parted with white folks that we did not regret so much," one woman insisted.[105]

Gradually, some female migrants made fast, personal friends with some Indians. When Mary Hodgson began trading with and entertaining her Native American neighbors, they responded by bringing "beautiful baskets and elaborate moccasins worked with beads and feathers" as presents. Similarly, when Alice Baldwin helped Indian women crimp and wave their hair, she discovered that "thereafter the Indian women were my firm friends, and rendered me various favors and kindnesses." A native man, whom Caroline Phelps took into her home as a nurse for her children, gained her family's love. After his death, they "cryed for poor John . . . as much as though he had been a relative."

Close friendships with Indians were possible, Leola Lehman believed, once migrants realized that Indians were afraid of them because of the terrifying stories they had heard. She befriended one Indian women and came to "like and respect her as one of the best women" she had ever known. When Lehman left the Indian region, she wrote, "I . . . had learned to like the Indians. I was no longer afraid and understood that many of their ways that seemed strange to me were caused by fear of white people."[106]

Even women who had suffered violent conflicts or captivity expressed positive feelings toward individual Native Americans. Some migrants claimed that "friendly" Indians had saved them from harm, and others wrote of Native

Americans who treated them decently and respectfully during a violent outbreak. Minnie Carrigan, taken captive in the New Ulm conflict in 1862, fondly
wrote of two Indian women who cared for her. "It seems wrong for me to call
those two Indian women squaws," she wrote, "for they were as lady-like as
any white women, and I shall never forget them." Of another Native American
family who aided her she wrote, "Their conduct toward me was so considerate
that I really liked them."[107]

Considering the evolution of some women's emotional ties to Indians, it
is little wonder that many migrants began to feel sympathy for the Indians'
plight and dwelled on these peoples' unjust treatment. "Is it right," Miriam Colt
queried, that men paid Indians "three dollars for a buffalo robe, worth twelve
at home?"[108] Many women believed that repeated foolish and thoughtless
actions by male migrants turned Indians into "demons" driven to "avenge
grievances or broken promises."[109] And Mary Tatum grumbled: "The heart
grows sick with the repeated tale of wrongs and broken promises by the whites
& government why must it be so why must the poor untutored redmen suffer
so from the whites who feel that they are so much further along."[110]

Many female migrants, upset that Native Americans often lacked adequate
food and clothing, pitied them and gave them what they could. After attempting
to help twenty hungry Indians, Vogdes lamented, "I did pity these poor things
paddling around in the cold & snow." A hungry Indian coughed so hard when
Lois Murray refused his begging that she later wrote, "If I could have called
him back, I would have given him bread." Claiming that she never turned a
needy Indian away again, Murray railed against migrants who abhorred and
mistreated Indians.[111]

Like Murray, many women blamed unprincipled white men for difficulties
with Indians, but they indicted others as well; they accused government agents,
renegade Frenchmen, Union and Confederate soldiers, Catholic priests, and
particularly Mormons of corrupting or inciting Native Americans.[112] Sympathetic women migrants also considered possible solutions to the dilemma of
migrant-native relations. Some argued for U.S. government intervention, but
others believed that as teachers, missionaries, and advocates they themselves
could help solve the problems.[113] Less optimistic women, like Margaret Carrington, held that the Indian had few options: "abandon his home, fight himself
to death, or yield to the white man's mercy." After the attack in 1866 on Fort
Kearney, Carrington disparaged anti-Indian newspapers that hastily judged the
situation "with all the embellishment and accuracy which wood engraving af-
fords while theories of blame were devised by those who never saw a live
Indian out of a city show."[114]

Despite this evidence to the contrary, nineteenth-century eastern American
and European literature, poetry, drama, informational books, textbooks, newspapers, magazines, sermons, and lectures supported the traditional image of
the fierce, rapacious Indian and the weak, victimized woman migrant. Yet, of
the one hundred and fifty diaries, journals, memoirs, and letters studied here,

one hundred and thirteen recorded no trouble with Indians, and twenty-two noted minor problems. Only fifteen reported major difficulties.[115]

In addition, over two-thirds of women migrants' writings chronicled process and change—from negative attitudes toward Native Americans to positive, sympathetic views.[116] But women migrants' diaries and letters were not sought out and published as men's accounts were, nor were women asked to become newspaper correspondents or authors. Nor were they welcome on the lecture platform or the lyceum circuit. Moreover, the interviews, sketches, and essays cranked out by male writers largely ignored women.

During an era when numerous Americans considered females and Indians inferiors, it is not surprising that women's personal perspectives of western events would be ignored. But there might be a deeper reason why many Americans clung so tenaciously to a deprecating view of these two groups. Most nineteenth-century Americans could not replace their prejudicial images of females and Native Americans with an accurate one that recognized them as rational and capable beings. Such a revision would have upset not only prevailing concepts, but also would have questioned those related discriminatory actions that society inflicted on these two groups. Therefore most nineteenth-century Americans would not observe nor accept what was transpiring between women migrants and Indians in the trans-Mississippi West.

Consequently, the nineteenth century bequeathed to the twentieth century a selective interpretation of the experiences of women migrants and Indians. That many twentieth-century people must have shared the needs and prejudices expressed by nineteenth-century people is indicated by their willing acceptance and continued perpetuation of these myths. Many people would agree, particularly those who are female or Native American, that the time is past due for a reassessment of this frequently inaccurate chapter in the history of the American West.

Although few people were interested at the time, Indian women had their own interpretation of the growing antagonism between migrants and Native Americans. In 1874, Isidora, a ninety-year-old Chiuructo Indian living in Sonoma, California (who was Chief Solano's widow) related her view of the situation:

My father's tribe lived near Cache Creek [Woodland]. . . . I drink a lot of liquor and I do this because I no longer have a land full of cows as the fair ones stole everything; nothing was left for poor Isidora. . . . I drank in order to forget. . . .

Before the whites arrived here we had much food and very good without much work; as there were many animals for hunting, and much wild onions. . . . In my country all my people had skin like mine, that is to say very red, all women were very tall, I was perhaps one of the smallest; many of us lived past one hundred, but the hair of the women doesn't become white; men yes, it changes; our Indians don't have big feet and big hands like blonde German or Mexicans. . . .

In winter when the white man came we did not know liquor, but Sutter forced the Jienguinero Indians to exchange hides for liquor, skins, fresh fish; Sutter had an Indian woman, not a Californian, she was a Canacha Indian who arrived in a boat with him. I do not like the white man much because he is a liar and a thief, my compadre Peralta and friend Bernales had many cows, Sutter lied to everyone, took everything and paid nothing. . . .[117]

Nellie Quail's family, Yavapai Indians in Arizona, related a similar tale. In 1967, eighty-five-year-old Quail related the story of her people's removal to the San Carlos reservation during the 1860s:

[The soldiers] started with the western Yavapai. They promised they were going to issue food, clothing, and about in the afternoon, maybe two or three [o'clock], they did give out some unbleached muslin, and some flour and beans, and then they started shooting. . . . my daddy was a young boy then. He said he run around this way in the bushes, and went way around, and he hid back of the soldiers' camp, and he stayed there. . . . he saw with his own eyes that his mother was killed and his aunt. . . . children, men, and women, just everywhere, he said. And then, they moved on to a next place. . . . after they killed many of the western Yavapai, they almost wiped them out, just piled high, so they call it today Skull Valley. . . . And then they move on to Camp Verde, and the storm was made. It just rain sleet of ice across the air, and everybody got sick, even the soldiers, and the Indians, of course, didn't have much clothing on.

They tried to get the northern Yavapai, they can't get them because of too many woods . . . cedar trees, just thick. . . . they heard that they were coming, and so they didn't get many, but, anyhow, they got some, and they slaughtered the cattle. . . . that was in 1872. . . .

They tried to get the southern Yavapai, [but] they couldn't find them. They found a few, but southern Yavapais said, they're not going to take us and starve us to death. We're just going to kill ourselves, so there's a ravine. . . . and so they went over there with their children, and they just drop in themselves and died there. . . .[118]

During the 1870s and 1880s, a Nevada Paiute woman named Sarah Winnemucca used the lecture platform and the press to carry the Native American's story to the American public. In 1883, she wrote Life Among the Paiutes: Their Wrongs and Claims:

I was born somewhere near 1844, but am not sure of the precise time. I was a very small child when the first white people came into our country. . . . My people were scattered at that time over nearly all the territory now known as Nevada. My grandfather was chief of the entire Paiute nation, and was camped near Humboldt Lake, with a small portion of his tribe, when a party travelling eastward from California was seen coming. When the news was brought to my grandfather, he asked what they looked like. When told that they had hair on their faces, and were white, he jumped up and clasped his hands together, and cried aloud, "My white brothers,—my long-looked for white brothers have come at last!" He immediately gathered some of his leading men, and went to the place where the party had gone into camp. Arriving near them, he was commanded to halt in a manner that was readily understood without an interpreter. Grandpa at once made signs of friendship by throwing down his robe and throwing up his arms to show them he had no weapons; but in vain,—they kept him at a distance. He knew not what to do. He had expected so much pleasure in welcoming his white brothers to the best in the land, that after looking at them sorrowfully for a little while, he came away quite unhappy. . . .

The next year came a great emigration, and camped near Humboldt Lake. . . . During their stay my grandfather and some of his people called upon them, and they all shook hands, and when our white brothers were going away they gave my grandfather a white tin plate. Oh, what a time they had over that beautiful gift,—it was so bright! . . .

The third year more emigrants came, and that summer Captain Frémont, who is now General Frémont. My grandfather met him, and they were soon friends. They met just where the railroad crosses Truckee River, now called Wadsworth, Nevada. Captain Fremont gave my grandfather the name of Captain Truckee, and he also called the river after him. Truckee is an Indian word, it means all right, or very well. . . .

This reservation, given in 1860, was at first sixty miles long and fifteen wide. The line is where the railroad now crosses the river, and it takes in two beautiful lakes, one called Pyramid Lake, and the one on the eastern side, Muddy Lake. No white people lived there at the time it was given us. We Paiutes have always lived on the river, because out of those two lakes we caught beautiful mountain trout, weighing from two to twenty-five pounds each, which would give us a good income if we had it all, as at first. Since the railroad ran through in 1867, the white people have taken all the best part of the reservation from us, and one of the lakes also.

The first work that my people did on the reservation was to dig a ditch, to put up a grist-mill and saw-mill. Commencing where the railroad now crosses at Wadsworth, they dug about a mile; but the saw-mill and grist-mill were never seen or heard of by my people, though the printed report in the United States statutes, which my husband found lately in the *Boston Athenaeum*, says twenty-five thousand dollars was appropriated to build them. Where did it go? The report says these mills were sold for the benefit of the Indians who were to be paid in lumber for houses, but no stick of lumber have they ever received. . . . Is it that the government is cheated by its own agents who make these reports? . . .

In 1865 we had another trouble with our white brothers. . . . soldiers rode up to the encampment and fired into it, and killed almost all the people that were there. . . . It was all old men, women and children that were killed; for my father had all the young men with him, at the sink of Carson on a hunting excursion, or they would have been killed too. After the soldiers had killed all but some little children and babies still tied up in their baskets, the soldiers took them also, and set the camp on fire and threw them into the flames to see them burn alive. I had one baby brother killed there. . . . This almost killed my poor papa. Yet my people kept peaceful.

That same summer . . . two white men were killed over at Walker Lake by some of my people, and of course soldiers were sent for from California, and a great many companies came. They went after my people all over Nevada. Reports were made everywhere throughout the whole country by the white settlers, that the red devils were killing their cattle, and by this lying of the white settlers the trail began which is marked by the blood of my people from hill to hill and from valley to valley. . . .

Now dear readers, this is the way all the Indian agents get rich. The first thing they do is to start a store; the next thing is to take in cattle men, and cattle men pay the agent one dollar a head. In this way they get rich very soon, so that they can have their gold-headed canes, with their names engraved on them. The one I am now speaking of is only a sub-agent. He told me the head agent was living in Carson City, and he paid him fifteen hundred dollars a year for the use of the reservation. Yet, he has fine horses and cattle and sheep, and is very rich. . . .

I was asked to act as interpreter to the Shoshones by a man called Captain Dodge, agent for the Shoshone Indians. He was going to issue clothing to them at a place called Battle Mountain. My brother Natchez went all about to summon the people there. . . . It took three days for the people to come up. Oh, such an issue! It was enough to make a doll laugh. A family numbering eight persons got two blankets, three shirts, no dress-goods. Some got a fish-hook and line; some got one and a half yards of flannel, blue and red; the largest issue was to families that camped together, numbering twenty-three persons: four blankets, three pieces of red flannel, and some of blue, three shirts, three hooks and lines, two kettles. It was the saddest affair I ever saw. . . .

Since the war of 1860 there have been one hundred and three of my people murdered, and our reservations taken from us; and yet we, who are called blood-seeking savages are keeping our promises to the government. Oh, my dear good Christian people, how long are you going to stand by and see us suffer at your hands? Oh, dear friends, you are wrong when you say it will take two or three generations to civilize my people. No! I say it will not take that long if you will only take interest in teaching us; and, on the other hand, we shall never be civilized in the way you wish us to be if you keep on sending us such agents as have been sent to us year after year, who do nothing but fill their pockets, and the pockets of their wives and sisters, who are always put in as teachers, and paid from fifty to sixty dollars per month, and yet they do not teach. . . .

When I went to Carson City in 1870, to see about my people's affairs, I was sent by the officials from one to another. At last we went to San Francisco to see General Schofield, and he sent me back to see Senator Jones. So brother and I went to where he was living in Gold Hill. I told him how my people were treated by the agents. He said, "I will see to it." He then put into my hands twenty dollars, which I took gratefully, for we were always poor, and brother and I went away. I have never seen or heard from him since. . . .[119]

Many Indians attempted to learn white ways and help other Native Americans adapt to the changed situation. Aitkala-Sa was a young Indian woman who decided to teach in an Indian school in the East during the 1890s. After visiting her mother on the reservation and reflecting on the education given Indian children, she became dismayed and disillusioned. In 1900, the Atlantic Monthly *aired her complaints:*

On an early morning I was summoned to the superintendent's office. For a half hour I listened to his words. . . . He was sending me West to gather Indian pupils for the school. . . .

Within a couple of days I started toward my mother's home. . . . At a small station, consisting of a single frame house with a rickety board walk around it, I alighted from the iron horse, just thirty miles from my mother and my brother Dawee. A strong hot wind seemed determined to blow my hat off, and return me to olden days when I roamed bare-headed over the hills. After the puffing engine of my train was gone, I stood on the platform in deep solitude. In the distance I saw the gently rolling land leap up into bare hills. At their bases a broad gray road was winding itself round about them until it came by the station. Among these hills I rode in a light conveyance, with a trusty driver. . . .

All the morning I looked about me, recognizing old familiar sky lines of rugged bluffs and round-topped hills. By the roadside I caught glimpses of various plants whose sweet roots were delicacies among my people. When I saw the first cone-shaped wigwam, I could not help utter-ing an exclamation which caused my driver a sudden jump out of his drowsy nodding.

At noon, as we drove through the eastern edge of the reservation, I grew very impatient and restless. Constantly I wondered what my mother would say upon seeing her little daughter grown tall. . . .

One black night mother and I sat alone in the dim starlight, in front of our wigwam. We were facing the river, as we talked about the shrinking limits of the village. She told me about the poverty-stricken white settlers, who lived in caves dug in the long ravines of the high hills across the river. A whole tribe of broad-footed white beggars had rushed hither to make claims on those wild lands. Even as she was telling this I spied a small glimmering light in the bluffs. . . . As I became accustomed to the night, I saw more and more twinkling lights, here and there, scattered all along the wide black margin of the river.

. . . "My daughter, beware of the paleface. It was the cruel paleface who caused the death of your sister and your uncle, my brave brother. It is this same paleface who offers in one palm the holy papers, and with the other gives a holy baptism of firewater. He is the hypocrite who reads with one eye, 'Thou shalt not kill,' and with the other gloats upon the sufferings of the Indian race". . . .

Leaving my mother, I returned to the school in the East. As months passed over me, I slowly comprehended that the large army of white teachers in Indian schools had a larger missionary creed than I had suspected. It was one which included self-preservation quite as much as Indian education. When I saw an opium-eater holding a position as teacher of Indians, I did not understand what good was expected, until a Christian in power replied that this pumpkin-colored creature had a feeble mother to support. An inebriate paleface sat stupid in a doctor's chair, while Indian patients carried their ailments to untimely graves, because his fair wife was dependent upon him for her daily food. I find it hard to count that white man a teacher who tortured an ambitious Indian youth by frequently reminding the brave changeling that he was nothing but a "government pauper."

Though I burned with indignation upon discovering on every side instances no less shameful than those I have mentioned, there was no present help. Even the few rare ones who have worked nobly for my race were powerless to choose workmen like themselves. To be sure, a man was sent from the Great Father to inspect Indian schools, but what he saw was usually the students' sample work made for exhibition. . . .

Alone in my room, I sat like the petrified Indian woman of whom my mother used to tell me. I wished my heart's burdens would turn me to unfeeling stone. . . . On account of my mother's simple view of life, and my lack of any, I gave her up. I made no friends among the race of people I loathed. . . .[120]

During the early twentieth century, other Americans became increasingly interested in the plight of Native Americans. In 1929, Century Magazine *published the recollections of Iron Teeth, a Cheyenne woman born in the Black Hills of South Dakota. She presents an Indian view of white ways and of Indians who took captives:*

The first issue of government presents to the Cheyennes was when I was fifteen years old. The place was near the fork of what we called Horse River and Geese River. Soldier houses had just been built there [Fort Laramie, 1849]. We were given beef, but we did not eat any of it. Great piles of bacon were stacked on the prairie and distributed to us, but we used it only to make fires or to grease robes for tanning. We got soda, but we did not know what to do with it. The green coffee looked to us like some new kind of berries. We boiled these berries just as they were, green, but they did not taste good. . . .

We got copper kettles, coffee-pots, butcher knives, sewing-awls, colored calicoes, bedticking cloth and boxfuls of thread for sewing. The thread was in skeins, not on spools. We were given plenty of brass buttons, colored beads, brass finger-rings, and red and blue face-paints. Blankets, of pretty colors, were issued to all of us. Our chiefs told us, "These presents are given to us so that we may become civilized, like the white people. . . ."

I was married to Red Ripe when I was twenty-one years old. But the Indian women of the old times did not change their names on account of marriage; so all throughout my lifetime I have kept the same name, Iron Teeth. My husband was a good hunter and did not need my help for gathering meat for his family, but I often went hunting with him. . . .

One time, when we were running away from the Pawnees, I and another woman stayed behind to help a friend bring her new baby. We hid in some timber and stayed there three days. Then we put the mother and her baby upon a travois bed made by stretching a buffalo robe across two lodge-poles dragged by a horse. By short cuts, we rejoined our band a few days later. If the Pawnees had found us it is not likely they would have killed us. Indians rarely killed each other's women and children. They captured them and kept them, to add them to their own tribe.

But white people did not spare us in this way. I know of one case where a young woman and an older helper stayed behind and hid themselves. At that time we were only moving camp, not fleeing from enemies. Two days later, the husband of the sick young woman went back to see how she was getting along. He found that she and her companion woman and the baby had all been killed. Horse trails showed that white men had done this. The husband was crazed by grief and anger. He vowed he never after that would have pity for any white people. . . .

All Indians liked to get women and children from other tribes. Captives were treated kindly, to make them feel contented. The women became wives, the children always found many people anxious to adopt them. From time to time we lost some of our Cheyennes in this way, but we brought many additions from other tribes. I recollect a young Crow woman being brought to us eighty-seven years ago. She married a Cheyenne man, and a son of theirs was Crazy Head, who became a great chief among us. . . . A white woman stayed with us through one summer, about sixty-five years ago. She used to cry, and I pitied her. I was glad with her when two Sioux men and a Cheyenne man took her to the soldier fort [Fort Laramie], so she might go back to her own people. When they got to the fort, the soldiers kept the three Indians and hanged them.

A white girl about four years old came for a time into my keeping. That was about eighty years ago. We were camped on Turkey River [the Solomon River, Kansas]. One of our women out digging turnips had been found dead, with many bullet wounds on her body. Some white men on horses had been seen near our camp. Our young men wanted to go out and fight them, but the chiefs decided we should move into the hills.

As I was packing to go, a woman brought to me the little white girl. "I am afraid I may be killed if white people find her with me," the woman said. "If you are not afraid, you may have her. If the white men get too close to you, you can turn her loose for them to find or you can throw her into the river." After a short time for thought, I replied, "If you promise not to ask her back from me, I will take her." The woman promised. It was raining hard, and the night was beginning to come. I made a blanket-sling and swung the child in it from my shoulders, on my back. She slept there while I walked and carried her almost all night. . . . This white girl grew to womanhood as one not knowing any language but the Cheyenne. She married a Cheyenne man, and they had several children. She kept her skin always stained to a brown color, so that white people might not be trying to persuade her to join them. . . .

Soldiers built forts in our Powder River country when I was about thirty-two years old. The Sioux and the Cheyennes fought against them. After a few years peace was made. The Cheyennes settled at the White River agency, in our favorite Black Hills country. This was to be our land forever, so we were pleased. But white people found gold on our lands. They crowded in, so we had to move out. . . .

Many Cheyennes and Sioux would not stay on the new reservations, but went back to the old hunting grounds in Montana. Soldiers went there to fight them. In the middle of the summer we heard that all of the soldiers had been killed at the Little Bighorn River. My husband said we should go and join our people there. We went, and all of our people spent the remainder of the summer there, hunting, not bothering any white people nor wanting to see any of them. . . .

Soldiers came [November 29, 1876] and fought us there. Crows, Pawnees, Shoshones, some Arapahoes and other Indians were with them. They killed our men, women and children, whichever ones might be hit by their bullets. We who could do so ran away. My husband and my two sons helped in fighting off the soldiers and enemy Indians. My husband was walking, leading his horse, and stopping at times to shoot. Suddenly, I saw him fall. I started to go back to him, but my sons made me go on, with my three daughters. The last time I ever saw Red Ripe, he was lying there dead in the snow. From the hilltops we Cheyennes saw our lodges and everything in them burned.

We wallowed through the mountain snows for several days. Most of us were afoot. We had no lodges, only a few blankets, and there was only a little dry meat food among us. Men died of wounds, women and children froze to death. After eleven days of this kind of traveling we found a camp of Ogalala Sioux. They fed us, but the rest of that winter was a hard one for all of us. When the spring came, I went with the band of Cheyennes who surrendered to Bear Shirt [General Miles] at Fort Keogh.

I was afraid of his soldiers, at first. These were the same kind of men who in past times had killed our people and burned our villages. I had in mind particularly a time, twelve years before this, when they had killed and scalped many of our women and children, in a peaceable camp near Mexico. At that time I had seen one of our women crawling along on the ground, shot, scalped, crazy, but not yet dead. After that, every time I saw white soldiers I thought of her.

From Fort Keogh we were sent to Dakota, and from there we were sent on to Oklahoma, to be joined with the Southern Cheyennes. In Oklahoma we Northern Cheyennes all got chills and fever. When we were not sick we were hungry. We had been promised food until we could plant corn and wait for it to grow, but most of the time the prom-ised food was not given to us. . . .

After about a year, our chiefs told the agent: "We are going back to the North." The agent replied, "Soldiers will follow you and kill you." My two sons joined the band determined to leave there. I and my three daughters followed them. I think that, all together, there were about five hundred Cheyennes in this band. Soldiers came after us, from every di-rection. Seven different battles we fought with them.

I still was having chills and fever. At night, when we had a chance to sleep, my daughters and I made willow-branch shelters for ourselves. Day after day, through more than a month, I kept my youngest daughter strapped to my body, in front of me, on my horse. I led another horse carrying the next-youngest daughter. The oldest girl managed her own mount. The two sons always stayed behind, to help in fighting off the soldiers. I do not know how many of our grown-up people were killed, but sixty of our children were missing when we got to the end of our journey. As we got near to the Black Hills my younger son and the oldest daughter joined a few others and went on to Pine Ridge agency. I and my younger son and the two younger daughters stayed with Dull Knife's band that went to Fort Robinson.

The soldiers at Fort Robinson took from us all of our horses and whatever guns they could find. They said then that we must go back to the South, but we told them it was better to die by bullets. After a few weeks of arguing, they put our men into a prison house. We were told

that women and children might go to Pine Ridge agency. Some of them
went there, but most of us went into the prison with the men. In the one
room, about thirty feet square, were forty-three men, twenty-nine women
and twenty or thirty children. . . .

The quantity of food given to us became less and less, every day, until they gave us none at all. Then they quit bringing water to us. Eleven
days we had no food except the few mouthfuls of dry meat some of the
women had kept in their packs. Three days we had no water. . . . The
men decided to break out of this jail. The women were willing. It was
expected that some of us would be killed, but it was hoped that many of
us would escape and go to join other Indians somewhere. Women cut up
robes to make extra moccasins. Packs were made ready. I gave to my son
the six-shooter I had. He was my oldest child, then twenty-two years of
age.

After the night bugle had sounded, my son smashed a window.
Others broke the other window and tore down the door. We all jumped
out. My son took the younger of the two daughters upon his back. The
older daughter and I carried a pack. The Indians scattered in different directions. A bright moon was shining upon the snow [January 9, 1879].
Soldiers were right after us. . . . I and the daughter with me found a cave
and crawled into it. We did not know what had become of the son and
his little sister. . . . Each day after that there was an occasional shot. We
stayed there seven days and nights. It was very cold, but we were afraid
to build a fire. We nibbled at my small store of dry meat and ate snow
for water. Finally, some soldiers found our tracks where we had gone out
of and back into the cave each day. They took us back to Fort Robinson.

My toes and fingers were frozen. Many other recaptured Cheyennes
were in worse condition than I was. I watched for my son and the
youngest daughter. After a while she came to me. I asked about her
brother. It appeared she did not hear me, so I asked again. This time she
burst out crying. Then I knew he had been killed. . . .

All of us were put again into the prison house. The number of us
now was only half what it had been. The soldier chief came. We were
mourning for our dead, so we had no ears for what he might say. The
interpreter said that the soldiers pitied us and did not want to kill any
more of us. He then asked us if we were willing now to go back to Oklahoma, so that no more of us would be killed. Everybody said, "No, we
will not go back there." . . . After a few days we were taken to Pine
Ridge. Twelve years later, almost all of the old Northern Cheyenne tribe
were brought together again, on this Tongue River reservation, in Montana. . . .[121]

*The tempestuous relations between migrants and Native Americans reinforce
the old shibboleth that there are always two sides to every story. But only recently
have Americans begun to take seriously the Indians' side. There are many lessons*

to be learned by citizens, policy-makers, and presidents alike. In the 1990s, marked as they are by continuing racial and ethnic strife, some of these lessons might well be applied to avoid another legacy of guilt similar to the one the nation carries regarding its past treatment of Native Americans.

For Further Reading

Albers, Patricia, and Beatrice Medicine. *The Hidden Half: Studies of Plains Indian Women.* Washington, D.C.: University Press of America, Inc., 1983.

Bataille, Gretchen M., and Charles L. P. Silet. *The Pretend Indians: Images of Native Americans in the Movies.* Ames: Iowa State University Press, 1980.

Buffalohead, Priscilla K. "Farmers, Warrior, Traders: A Fresh Look at Ojibway Women." *Minnesota History* 48 (Summer 1983), 236–44.

Black, Nancy B., and Bette S. Weidman, eds. *White on Red: Images of the American Indian.* Port Washington, New York: Kennikat Press, 1976.

Canfield, Gae Whitney, *Sarah Winnemucca of the Northern Paiutes.* Norman: University of Oklahoma Press, 1983.

Hurtado, Albert L. "'Hardly a Farm House—A Kitchen Without Them': Indian and White Households on the California Borderland Frontier in 1860." *Western Historical Quarterly* 14 (July 1983), 245–70.

Mathes, Valerie Sherer. *Helen Hunt Jackson and Her Indian Reform Legacy.* Austin: University of Texas Press, 1990.

Oshana, Maryann. "Native American Women in Westerns: Reality and Myth." *Frontiers* 6 (Fall 1981), 46–50.

Riley, Glenda. *Women and Indians on the Frontier, 1825–1915.* Albuquerque: University of New Mexico Press, 1986.

Smith, Sherry L. *The View From Officers' Row: Army Perceptions of Western Indians.* Tucson: University of Arizona Press, 1990.

Unruh, John D., Jr. *The Plains Across: The Overland Emigrants and the Trans-Mississippi West, 1840–1860.* Urbana: University of Illinois Press, 1979.

Williams, Carol. "My First Indian: Interaction Between Women and Indians on the Trail, 1845–1865." *Overland Journal* 4 (Summer 1986), 13–18.

SECTION

4

Women and Work

Everywhere in the world, women are expected to do domestic work or oversee the hired help, servants, or slaves that do it in their place. In the American West, domestic labor was especially crucial to survival because most homes were factories that produced the necessary foodstuffs and other goods. Women were the artisans and managers of these domestic factories, but they often engaged in other work as well. In mining regions, for example, women cleaned equipment and helped with other mine-related tasks. Because so much of the work in the West was related to agriculture, however, many women combined domestic and farm duties.

4.1
Farm Women's Roles:
Inside and Outside the Home

Rural women's lives were shaped to a large degree by a complex of political, economic, and social factors. Three constants, however, affected nearly all farm women: the character of the region in which they lived, the similar nature of their tasks from area to area, and the continuity of their tasks and concerns from the early years of the nineteenth century into the twentieth. Because the

4.1: Adapted from "Farm Women's Roles in the Agricultural Development of South Dakota," *South Dakota History* 13 (Spring/Summer 1983), 83–121. Used by permission. Photo: Alaskan working women—prostitutes during the gold rush era of the 1890s—pose in front of their cribs. Courtesy of the Alaska State Library, Fairbanks.

Dakotas were thought to be the heart of the West during the latter part of the nineteenth century, the impact of these three influences upon Dakota women will be examined here from the arrival of the migrants in the late 1850s to the mid-1930s, when the Great Depression, industrialization, and modernization reshaped not only urban areas of the country but rural sections as well.

Character of the Region

Because early Dakota migrants lived in a distinctive part of the country, it is not surprising that their history differed from that of even their neighbors in nearby areas. Although squatters began pushing across the Mississippi River as early as 1828 in an effort to displace Native American inhabitants of the Iowa region, it was not until fully thirty years later that a similar aggression occurred along the Missouri River. Initial attempts at settlement on the Dakota side of the Missouri River in 1858 pressured the United States government into negotiating the Yankton Treaty. Like the Black Hawk Treaty of 1832, it was widely misunderstood. Indian resistance to the treaty was rife, yet the agreement eventually opened the Dakotas to migrants just as the Black Hawk treaty had opened Iowa.

When Dakota Territory was formed in 1861, however, it did not experience the land rush that Iowa had during the 1840s. Not only had the economic boom of the fifties ended, but the Civil War was imposing political and economic hardship on many Americans and slowing migration. Clearly, the development of the Dakotas from the beginning was dissimilar to that of the already settled states further east because they were influenced by different historical factors. Chief among these was the Homestead Act, passed by the U.S. Congress in 1862. This legislation offered a person a free quarter-section of land (640 acres) with the condition that he or she cultivate that land for a period of five years. The lengthy "proving up" period called for by the Homestead Act inadvertently fostered tenuous claims in the Dakotas. Author and Dakota migrant Laura Ingalls Wilder described the homestead venture as a huge gamble: "The government bets a man [or woman] a quarter-section of land, that he can't stay on it five years without starving to death."[1] As a result, talk of claim shacks and "proving up" was widespread, while discussions of abandoning the entire adventure contributed a pervasive feeling of temporariness.

The Dakotas were not particularly alluring to migrants. Historian Everett Dick observed that four elements of the Plains region made it less than attractive: "the perpetual winds, the absence of water, the terrific heat, the absence of trees." He also noted a fifth factor that was especially severe in the Dakotas: the "deadening cold."[2] Prospective migrants were further discouraged during the 1860s by droughts, grasshopper invasions, and continuing problems with Native Americans. These conditions were exacerbated by the early migrants' crude methods of cultivation and their lack of knowledge about crops that could be raised in this region.[3] According to historian Mary Hargreaves, during most of the nineteenth century the Dakotas were written off by most Americans as part of the Great American Desert, an inhospitable place for both migrants and crops.[4]

Consequently, the strong commitment to the land that characterized migrants in richer areas did not usually exist in the Dakotas. Rare were the stories of advance scouts carefully searching out fertile land or of people arriving with money sewn into their clothing to purchase their farmsteads. Rather, when migration to the Dakotas began in earnest after 1870, the tales told were of land rushes and lotteries, the unlawful possession of as many as five and six claims, an elaborate barrage of advertising to attract potential migrants, and rushes into such newly opened lands as the Rosebud Indian Reservation.[5]

The tension created by such transience and mobility affected most migrants, but it wore on women in gender-associated ways. Encouraged by nineteenth-century societal norms to value permanence and domestic order, female migrants were often disconcerted by the instability of their new environment. In addition, there was even more pressure upon these farm women than was usual in other agrarian regions to prove that people could endure and perhaps prosper on a Plains farmstead. Wilder wrote that she, like so many women, felt a pressing need to help demonstrate that "farming was as good as any other business."[6] Thus, women were expected to contribute to family survival in every way possible, including living on an isolated claim alone with their children for months on end to hold it while their husband worked elsewhere to raise the necessary capital for seed and equipment.[7] One Dakota woman succinctly summarized the demands placed upon women: "While a woman had more independence here than in any other part of the world, she was expected to contribute as much as a man—not in the same way, it is true, but to the same degree."[8]

Many single women also seized the opportunity to gain a free homestead. Although single women frequently migrated westward as teachers, missionaries, laborers, and potential wives, unmarried women homesteaders were lured by the possibility of acquiring land, customarily considered a male undertaking. One investigator who sampled the land office data in Colorado and Wyoming discovered that the number of female homestead entrants ranged between 11.9 and 18.2 percent. Moreover, the data indicated that 42.4 percent of the women succeeded in making a final claim to their homesteads while only 37 percent of the men did so.[9] The diaries and letters of Dakota migrants contain occasional mention of female homesteaders. Enid Bern, for example, wrote of a "strange malady" she called "Homestead Fever" that struck all manner of folks, including single men and women.[10]

One example of a woman homesteader was Grace W. Fairchild who, after watching both her mother and sister-in-law homestead on their own, eventually decided to homestead herself as a divorced woman. During the course of her marriage, she had become increasingly aware that her husband's incompetence was driving them into mortgage and debt. After one particularly upsetting business deal, she exclaimed, "This longhorn fiasco convinced me that if we were to make our goddamn claim into a ranch, I had to take charge of the whole thing." She finally did just that in 1930, when she divorced her husband and began running the ranch by herself. Within ten years, she had extricated herself from debt, accumulated 1440 acres of land, and acquired sufficient sheep and cattle to keep her "out of the poor house, and then some."[11]

Similar Nature of Farm Women's Tasks

Of course, the first rural women to live in the Dakotas were Native Americans. As women, they cared for homes and families. And as agriculturalists, they not only developed knowledge of crops and farming methods, but they demonstrated that agricultural production was possible in this austere land.

During the 1800s, Native American women were disrupted and frequently removed from the land by encroaching expeditions and colonies that often included diverse kinds of women.[12] For example, army wife Fanny McGillycuddy accompanied her husband to Fort Robinson in the 1870s to help divest the original inhabitants of their land.[13] At the same time, female missionaries tried to ameliorate some of the problems that this process created, and female preachers and such orders of women religious as the Presentation Sisters established educational, medical, and other social services for both the native and newly arrived residents.[14] These early waves of migrants were soon followed by both male and female farmers and homesteaders.

These rural women represented many different racial, ethnic, and religious backgrounds. From the scanty evidence available, African American women made up a small portion of this population.[15] Such source materials as letters and diaries suggest that women from European and other countries were a far larger element in the early Dakota population; Germans, Scandinavians, Czechs, and German-Russians were especially dominant. White women from the eastern states also made up a significant portion of female migrants. Among these groups were Catholics, Jews, and members of many Protestant sects.[16]

Although Dakota farm women represented a variety of heritages manifested in special foods, clothing, crafts, or value systems, these women shared a common bond in the nature of their tasks and roles. Men could be engaged in mining, ranching, or farming, but most women concentrated the home. Women became domestic artisans producing goods necessary for family survival; bore, cared for, and trained children; and perpetuated traditional values. In addition, many women also worked outside their homes in such jobs as herding cattle and breaking sod. It is true that most single farm women did not have to care for a spouse or children, but they had to tend to their land and sometimes held paid jobs as well.[17]

Especially during early years, farm women performed their labors in rudimentary workplaces. Frequently, a woman's workplace was a one-room claim shack built of rough boards, covered by black tar-paper and lined with either expensive, effective blue paper or a cheaper, inferior red paper. Furniture commonly consisted of a homemade bunk with rope springs, an oil stove, a dry goods box or two for cupboards, and a wooden table and chairs.[18] For other women, the home workplace was a structure of hastily cut laths. An migrant to the Dakotas in 1889 caustically described her lath home as the "finest house on the prairies." You could, she wrote, "see right through the walls of the three rooms, for they were made of laths—open in between. . . . Upstairs horse blankets were nailed over the laths."[19]

For yet others, the first dwelling on the Plains was a sod hut or dugout, a practical response to the lack of timber. Although the roofs of such structures dripped particles of dirt, they offered warmth in the winter and coolness in the summer.[20] One South Dakota woman wrote that her sod house might "pass" if "one isn't too spoiled." She explained that it was built of sod for "safety as well as warmth." Its floor lay below ground level and its windows sat at ground level. She was delighted with the interior, which appeared to her as a "fairy palace" comfortably furnished with family treasures.[21]

Typically, women worked hard to convert these crude dwellings into pleasant homes. Wilder dressed up her tiny parlor with a small rocker, a glass lamp, books of poetry, and potted geraniums.[22] The mistress of the lath house had her grand piano shipped from Philadelphia to stand, according to her daughter, "very big and black in the front room on the bare pine floor, against the wall of laths that you could see through."[23] One woman even studied plastering and secured the material to patch the many holes in the walls of her first home near Brookings, while she solved her storage problems by packing things into a "shanty," a lean-to addition over the back door. She commented that while early Dakota houses had drawbacks, they could be made neat and cozy with a little effort.[24]

Women also converted these dwellings into effective workplaces where, despite the additional handicaps of scarce water and limited fuel, they functioned as domestic artisans. Women's diaries, letters, and memoirs are replete with accounts of domestic life, including cleaning, sewing, cooking, baking, washing clothes in tubs of rainwater, and caring for the ever-present newborn baby.[25] A Norwegian woman of the 1880s told of baking bread in a small stove, converting milk from two cows into cream and butter, processing wild game into edible meals, filling the cellar with "potatoes, roots and milk," and butchering heifers and hogs.[26] Another Norwegian woman expressed pride in her skills, which included baking, drying fruits and berries, laundering, and sewing, while yet another was so proficient at soapmaking, dying yarn, knitting, spinning, weaving, and sewing that her daughter aptly called their home a "factory."[27]

Dakota farm women were also adept at candle-making, spinning, weaving, doctoring, food processing, and even twisting hay into "cats" for fuel. One young woman remembered that her mother was particularly adept at processing meat by smoking it or packing it in lard in stone jars and at converting flour sacks into family underclothing.[28] A Fargo woman claimed that she made fourteen pounds of butter each week in addition to her other duties.[29] Another woman mentioned doing a "big washing," finishing "some little sewing," and completing her regular household duties, all within days of bearing her first child.[30] Since factories and trained professionals have taken over most of these functions in modern society, it is difficult for us to realize how much skill and toil were involved. Moreover, we often overlook the prominent role that these woman played in the economy. At the time of marriage, a young woman's greatest assets were her abilities as a domestic manufacturer and artisan. According to one study of western marriage, "the choosing of a mate . . . was a matter of economic necessity far and above individual whim. Good health and perseverance were premium assets . . ."[31]

If a woman chose to remain single or became single through divorce or the death or desertion of a mate, her skills were still important. Census figures indicate that most unmarried women were absorbed by other households maintained by parents, children, or other relatives. Here, single women continued to pull their economic weight. Like their married sisters, single women were highly skilled laborers whose contributions to the rural economy were vital to its progress.

Although both married and single women were expected to supply a bewildering variety of goods and services, married women were also encouraged to produce children to aid population growth and provide future laborers for the family farm. One scholar believes that an average of ten children per woman is a conservative estimate.[32] A representative case from South Dakota was Ane Marie Jensen of Dell Rapids, who bore ten children as well as helping her second husband raise his seven children.[33]

While bearing and rearing children was clearly considered one of women's most important economic functions, it was also one of the most physically taxing. Not only were women to deliver children, but they were expected to take responsibility for their care, training, and eventual participation in the family labor force. Thus, in addition to being workers and producers, women also filled supervisory and managerial positions.

Dakota farm women also worked to preserve traditional values, folkways, and mores. Women celebrated holidays despite the paucity of resources available on the Dakota plains. Scrimping, saving, and working with scraps to create something resembling a present, while also providing a small tree devoid of but the sparsest decoration, these women did their best to recreate warm and happy holidays. Other women routinely defied their own exhaustion by playing the piano in the evenings or by entertaining as kindly as possible despite an often continual influx of guests.[34]

Women also engaged in what was normally considered "men's work." One investigator has argued that the typical rural woman was involved in between one-third to over one-half of food production on family farms.[35] They labored in kitchen gardens, chicken houses, and in the fields. But women also occasionally performed heavier field tasks, including driving a reaper, harvester, or hay wagon as well as planting seed and digging potatoes. Because hired help was often unavailable and because women were often the only other adults on the farms besides their husbands, they were required to do more than what might be regarded as their share if judged by the standards of other eras or places.[36]

The work women performed in the fields was often critical in staving off failure of the family farm, but women also helped deflect economic disaster by bartering or selling milk, butter, and eggs.[37] Women also "helped out" by selling beeswax, dried fruits, and cloth and by taking in boarders or doing washing.[38] One young Black Hills woman recalled that her mother sold butter, eggs, meat, vegetables, wild fruit, and garden flowers, did "some washing on the board" for people, and knitted socks and mittens for sale to nearby cowboys.[39] That such women recognized their economic importance is demonstrated by the recollection of a rural woman: "Frequently enough, while the men were learning to farm, the women and children actually supported the families. They raised chickens and eggs for the table, raised the vegetables and fruit, and made butter to sell in exchange for things not produced at home. The women were not unaware of this fact and were quite capable of scoring a point on occasion when masculine attitudes became too bumptious."[40]

Farm women's tasks seemed to be never-ending and exhausting. Thus, one might expect farm women's lives to be dominated by fatigue, bitterness, and despair. Certainly, according to most western literature, women were not only reluctant migrants, but despondent ones as well. Although such writers as Bess Streeter Aldrich, Willa Cather, Mari Sandoz, and Vardis Fisher have created in their novels portrayals of resilient women who stand in opposition to the depressed, one-dimensional figures favored by such novelists as Ole Rölvaag and Hamlin Garland, they have not succeeded in capturing the popular imagination.

Unfortunately, historians in general have been as culpable as most novelists in perpetuating inaccurate depictions. In 1921, for example, Emerson Hough described the "woman in the sunbonnet" as the "gaunt and sad-faced woman sitting on the front seat of the wagon, following her lord where he might lead, her face hidden in the same ragged sunbonnet which had crossed the Appalachians and the Missouri long before."[41] Ten years later, historian Walter Prescott Webb devoted only one-and-a-half pages of his classic *The Great Plains* to women. He concluded that while men were hardy and adventurous, women feared and distrusted the land.[42]

More recently, Everett Dick gave the lives of women more consideration, but his conclusions were just as conventional. He asserted that many were soon broken "in spirit and body." Another recent historian concurred: "More place-bound than men, more dependent on the company of other women, on the forms of settled social life, [western women] grew old and died before their time, on the trail, in a sod hut or a rude cabin pierced by icy winds.[43] Yet another scholar stated that women were "the most conservative of creatures, hating with a passion those three concomitants" of western life—"poverty, physical hardship, and danger."[44]

In recent times, the contemporary feminist movement has raised serious challenges to such assumptions. Moreover, historians of women have been locating and collecting women's source materials to learn what women said and felt about their situations. Enough women's writings are now available to make some tentative observations possible.

Like men, women migrants recorded their fears of Native Americans, mud, rain, wind, dust, prairie fires, blizzards, tornadoes, rattlesnakes, and epidemics.[45] As women taught to value domestic order, networks of family and friends, and leisure time devoted to such pursuits as reading and craft work, they lamented the prevalence of dirt and bugs, isolation and loneliness, and heavy, time-consuming work loads. Some of these women did spend part or all of their lives on the verge of despair, insanity, and even self-extinction.[46] And some of them, like Sarah Thal or Emma Plaisted of the lath house, packed up their pianos and other belongings and headed elsewhere.[47] But many more stayed and triumphed.

It must also be remembered that while western women endured demanding lives, they found some redeeming qualities about their new environment. For some women, the rigorous climate was offset by what one described as the "beauties of nature."[48] Another woman interspersed her frequent negative remarks about the Dakota climate with expressions of joy regarding the birds, wild roses, and other flowers: "The day is very beautiful and I have been out nearly all of it picking posies. . . . I think there is something fascinating about gathering wild flowers. . . . It gives one a childish delight." She also exulted in the sunrise: "The sun rose in great splendor as it does nowhere else except on these prairies."[49] Yet another woman claimed that in the Dakotas of the 1880s, "no one minded the hot sunshine or the hard winds" because "they were to be expected: a natural part of life." She maintained that "the freedom and spaciousness of the wide prairie land" compensated for its hardships.[50]

Many women also accepted the challenge of unending chores with equanimity. "Certainly I have had to work," wrote a Dakota woman to her family in Scandinavia. Unlike her days as a laborer in her homeland, however, she believed that she "was considered a human being" even though she was poor. "Have a good home here," she added, and "have no wish ever to return to Sweden."[51] Margaret Roberts of the Black Hills was also undaunted by heavy workloads. After supporting and raising five daughters as a widow on a homestead, she moved to yet another homestead after her last child left home.[52] And despite her heavy workload, Mary Dodge Woodward noted in an 1884 diary entry: "I have enjoyed my life here very much and have never wished to leave."[53]

Even isolation and loneliness often turned out to be less prevalent than formerly assumed. One investigator has demonstrated that farms were laid out in a pattern of adjoining farmsteads, with villages and towns located at regular intervals. Early neighborhoods were often small and close knit, being held together by such bonds as kinship, race, or ethnicity.[54] Another scholar has claimed that the average distance between farmsteads in Lawrence

County was about half a mile and that "in the early period of settlement some-times four families, each taking a quarter section as a homestead, built their temporary dwellings upon adjacent corners to be near together."[55]

Farm women regularly described the many social events available to them through their families, friends, churches, schools, and nearby towns. One Da-kota woman of the 1880s spoke of a ladies' aid society, gala Christmas cel-ebrations, choir and band concerts, festive Fourth of July celebrations, wed-dings, and dinners with friends and neighbors, while another recalled such pastimes as "home talent entertainments," horseback riding, roller skating, and dancing.[56] A researcher who surveyed Dakota newspapers found that as time passed, social opportunities increased. New Year's celebrations, recep-tions, balls, lyceums, theaters, performances by woman elocutionists, church festivals and fairs, women's clubs, euchre parties, camping, boating, Fourth of July observances, and circuses were all common in many parts of the Dakotas by the mid-1880s.[57]

Faye Cashatt Lewis, a Dakota migrant in the early twentieth century, sug-gested that life on the Plains seemed formidable primarily because many peo-ple exaggerated the hardships. They recorded them "with gusto," she re-marked, to emphasize their own "superior stamina." Even the problems faced by her own mother (whose dismayed statement about the Dakota landscape— "there's nothing to make a shadow"—has often been quoted as an epitome of women's disillusionment) were alleviated in Lewis's view by the huge amount of personal support her mother received from her husband and children. In addition, literary meetings, plays, musical performances, reading, checkers, card playing, and candy-making abounded. According to Lewis, adversities were balanced by dreams and satisfactions. "Our riches were," she wrote, "good health, ambition, hope, and pride."[58]

Another key to understanding farm women's lives can be derived from the statement of a Norwegian pastor's wife. She was quick to point out that "as time passed people's circumstances improved."[59] Most women were not condemned to a lifetime in a one-room soddie, a sparsely settled neighbor-hood, or to perpetual poverty. Larger houses were built and improvements made. With population growth came neighbors, churches, schools, and clubs. In time, crops and other products supplied the needs of the family and fre-quently provided a surplus that was taken to market and exchanged for cash and necessary items.[60]

Such transformations, which often became noticeable within two years, also contributed to larger changes. By 1889, population and economic growth in the Dakotas persuaded President Grover Cleveland to sign the Omnibus Bill, which created four new states: North Dakota, South Dakota, Montana, and Washington.[61] During the following decade, the era of open range drew to a close and an agrarian economy characterized by the use of new tech-nological devices took hold in the Dakotas.

Continuity of Farm Women's Tasks and Concerns

What did technological modifications mean to farm women? For example, were their lives changed dramatically by new technology within the home?

Those investigators who have studied the types and effects of domestic technology upon farm women believe that not only was technology slow to be embraced, but that its impact was limited. Some years ago, Mary Hargreaves argued that the cost of such conveniences as indoor plumbing was prohibitive for most people through the "lean years," which did not abate until 1940. Calling attention to a survey of six South Dakota farming counties taken in 1935, she pointed out that at least three-fourths of the homes in these counties still had an outside water supply while only one-fifth had electricity and only one-eighth had central heating. One of the counties examined still had many log cabins; another was dotted with sod huts and had more under construction.[62]

Another scholar has maintained that although the new technology lightened the physical work of women, it did not alter the gender orientation of these tasks. To use an example, water pumps made it easier to draw water, but drawing water was still a chore performed by women; they were also expected to operate the new sewing machines; and the first crude washing machines were used almost exclusively by women. The new domestic technology did nothing to extricate women from the domestic realm, nor did technology improve the status or prestige associated with domestic work.[63]

More recently, historian Susan H. Armitage has examined the effect of the first washing machines on women's work, roles, and power relationships in the farm family. She discovered that although the machines made the actual washing somewhat easier, the entire process required a lot of physical labor because such support technology as hot water heaters and drains was not yet available. Thus, women still spent many physically taxing hours carrying hot water to their new washing machines and carrying dirty water away from them. In addition, women often continued to follow traditional methods of washing clothes, including making their own soap, boiling clothes before washing, and running clothing through a rinse with bluing, even though these processes were now outdated. Armitage concluded that washing machines, in spite of the drawbacks, released some of the farm woman's time and energy for other pursuits but that traditional sex roles remained firmly in place. Most women were discouraged from using their released time to fully participate in the business of the family farm. In Armitage's view, most women internalized these customary sex-role prescriptions and expended their new leisure in enhancing the quality of life for their families, which society considered an acceptable female pursuit. Armitage hypothesized that the new technology actually stripped farm women's work of some of its esteem in that it now appeared easier, and that this lost status was not shored up with other meaningful roles and tasks.[64]

The documents historians have been able to procure uphold the idea that little basic change occurred in Dakota women's lives. When, for example, seventy-year-old Ane Marie Jensen was complimented for the many socks she had knitted from the wool of her own sheep as part of the World War I effort, she brushed it off with the comment, "Why, I've all my life raised sheep and knitted—that's nothing new nor extraordinary." She pointed out that she had made her living by raising sheep and knitting in Denmark and had naturally continued the practice after arriving in the Dakotas and well into her senior years.[65]

Faye Cashatt Lewis's description of her family's 1909 claim shack also revealed the continuity that this home had with women's homes and work-places of earlier decades. It was, she recalled a tiny structure divided into two rooms: "a bedroom and the slightly larger room that was used for everything else, including a bedroom for the two boys."[66] Her mother's work also varied little from the chores of earlier women. She prepared gargantuan breakfasts consisting of oatmeal, ham or bacon, eggs, home-baked bread, homemade jellies or preserves, fried potatoes, and home-baked pies left over from the previous night's dinner. Lewis's mother also planted and tended a vegetable garden, spent untold hours in housekeeping chores, devoted at least one afternoon a week to bread-baking, and constantly battled the bugs and other vermin that regularly invaded the shack.[67]

A Grand Forks woman who recalled a childhood spent with her Swedish grandmother in the 1920s painted a similar picture. She remembered her grandmother washing on the board, boiling clothes, ironing with flatirons heated on the wood stove, producing her own lye soap for wash days, and converting flour sacks into underclothing. She recalled that her grandmother cooked on a huge wood range. The cream separator held the place of honor in the kitchen, while butchering and rendering were done in the old-fashioned way. Kerosene lanterns were still used and created a lot of work for the women who cleaned and filled them. Housecleaning, too, was a tedious chore since "no vacuum cleaner or other labor saving device had been purchased." To her granddaughter, "it was a nightmare" when "the lace curtains were washed and stretched on a prickly frame; heavy woolen quilts were washed by hand. . . . the soot had to be cleaned out of the chimney. . . . and woolen rugs were strung over the clothes line." Apparently, the only bow that her grand-mother made to the new technology was the use of an incubator in hatching chickens. Even this device did not seem very advanced to her granddaughter, who commented that "the more fortunate people ordered their chicks from the catalog."[68]

Apparently, technology was slower in restructuring labor in the farm home than it was in revolutionizing the work in the barns and fields. The letters of a North Dakota farm woman, Effie Hanson, written between 1917 and 1923, mention such devices as an incubator for the chickens, a knitting machine, canning aids, a telephone, and store-bought clothing from the Sears and Mont-gomery Ward catalogues. Yet, closer examination reveals that Hanson's prev-alent themes and concerns differed little from those of earlier generations of women. She wrote about giving birth, worrying over her children, raising hens and selling eggs, tending her garden, sewing and knitting, butchering, milking and churning, selling butter and cream, preparing food for threshers, and performing such field work as digging potatoes. She frequently noted that she was busy, tired, lonely, isolated, homesick, ill, and involved in an unending round of chores. In reading Hanson's letters, one gets a sense of timelessness that is only occasionally interrupted by a notation about a sewing machine or automobile.[69]

Little significant change seemed to have occurred in women's political participation, even though a considerable number of Dakota women were interested in obtaining the right to vote as early as the 1870s. Women not only engaged in local, state, and national suffrage associations and meetings, but they also supported the appearances in Yankton and other towns of such suffragists as Mathilda Joslyn Gage, Susan B. Anthony, and Elizabeth Cady Stanton. In 1885, a woman suffrage amendment passed the territorial council and house of representatives. But it was opposed by Governor Gilbert A. Pierce, who feared that the amendment would interfere with the territory's application for statehood.

When statehood was achieved in 1889, the framers of the South Dakota constitution included a provision that allowed male voters to remove the word "male" from the document if they chose, thereby extending to women the right to vote. This constitutional provision attracted Susan B. Anthony to South Dakota in 1889. As president of the National Woman Suffrage Association, she was convinced that, with a little push from organized suffragists, South Dakotans would prove their dedication to democracy and equality by granting women the vote. Despite her efforts, and those of local suffrage organizers like General William H. H. Beadle, Rebecca Hager, Matilda Hindman, and Women's Christian Temperance Union chapters, male voters continually rejected woman suffrage bills. Although many more years of effort followed, South Dakota women did not receive the right to vote until 1918, only two years before the ratification of the Nineteenth Amendment to the United States Constitution in 1920.[70]

In spite of the long and active campaigns for woman suffrage, the writings of many farm women noted the issues of women's rights and suffrage only in passing. When Laura Ingalls Wilder accepted a proposal of marriage, she interrogated her husband-to-be about his feelings concerning the word "obey" in the wedding ceremony. When he asked whether she was for "woman's rights," she replied, "No, I do not want to vote."[71] The writings of most women did not touch on the matter of women's rights at all; they seemed much more concerned about daily matters relating to their homes, families, and work. Even when women were granted the vote, many farm women accepted it impassively. Effie Hanson, as a case in point, regularly recorded when she went into town to vote but ascribed little significance or meaning to the event.[72] Clearly, much additional study is needed before we can fully understand the political participation of farm women and their responses to increased rights and opportunities in the political arena.

At least on the surface, then, farm women's roles seemed to have changed little during the early twentieth century. But historian Joan M. Jensen has proposed some important topics that must be considered before this issue can be fairly assessed. By considering cycles of farm women's work as well as ethnicity, race, and demography (including fertility rates, use of technology, and distribution of social organizations) historians may discover some critical information that will help us flesh out the picture of farm women's lives.[73] In the meantime, we can only hypothesize that women's roles changed little despite the innovations of "progressive" farming.[74]

The study of farm women is both exciting and complex. Exploratory studies such as these also demonstrate that although source materials are often obscure, they are available. Letters and diaries of women involved in farming, farm inventories and financial records, wills and other family documents, and oral histories are all potential mines of information.[75] Some hard data exist as well. The U.S. census, for example, recorded that between 1900 and 1930, the sex ratio (number of males per one hundred females) dropped in the Plains states from 109.7 to 104.2, although the national ratio decreased only from 104.4 to 102.5 percent. It also shows that sex ratios in urban areas in the Plains states went from 102.8 in 1900 to 95.7 in 1930, while the ratios on farms fell from 112.5 in 1900 to 104.3 in 1930. An examination of why such demographic shifts occurred might reveal information regarding the changing lives of women. Also, census figures document a decreasing birth rate in the Plains region during the first decades of the twentieth century; during the same era, longevity increased. These figures would suggest some significant alterations in women's life cycles and work patterns. Researchers must examine further the increasing percentage of women who attended school, migrated to urban areas, held jobs outside the home, and sought divorces.[76] In addition, the role played by social class, ethnicity, race, and religious beliefs in shaping farm women's experiences demands further exploration.

What we can say with certainty about farm women is that information about them exists in varied forms, but questions regarding their lives and roles still abound. Farm women, often casually shunted aside by the inaccurate and demeaning designation "farmer's wife," are beginning to be recognized for their contributions. This emerging awareness can only lead to a heightened understanding of all farm women's countless contributions to the agrarian development of individual states and to the country.

As mentioned in the essay just concluded, Native American women were the first agriculturalists on the Plains. Buffalo Bird Woman, a Hidatsa born around 1839, learned traditional farming methods from the women of her family on land in what is now North Dakota. She was eventually forced, however, to adapt to new methods and crops dictated by U.S. government policy:

My mother and my two grandmothers worked at clearing our family's garden. . . . [They] began at one end of this field and worked forward. All had heavy iron hoes, except Turtle, who used an old-fashioned wooden digging stick.

With their hoes, my mothers cut the long grass that covered much of the field, and bore it off to be burned. With the same implements, they next dug and softened the soil in places for the corn hills, which were laid off in rows. These hills they planted. Then all summer they worked with their hoes, clearing and breaking the ground between the hills. . . .

My grandmother, Turtle, . . . was an industrious woman. Often, when my mothers were busy in the earth lodge, she would go out to work in the garden, taking me with her for company. . . . With her digging stick, she dug up a little round place in the center of the corner; and circling around this from day to day, she gradually enlarged the dug-up space. The point of her digging stick she forced into the soft earth to a depth equal to the length of my hand, and pried up the soil. The clods she struck smartly with her digging stick, sometimes with one end, sometimes with the other. . . . In breaking ground for our garden, Turtle always used an ash digging stick; and when hoeing time came, she hoed the corn with a bone hoe. . . .

Planting season having come, the women of the household planted the field in corn. The hills were in rows, and about four feet or a little less apart. . . . While the corn was coming up, the women worked at clearing out the roots and smaller stumps between the hills; but a stump of any considerable size was left to rot, especially if it stood midway between two corn hills, where it did not interfere with their cultivation.

As I grew up, I learned to work in the garden, as every Hidatsa woman was expected to learn; but iron axes and hoes, bought of the traders, were now used by everybody, and the work of clearing and breaking a new field was less difficult than it had been in our grandfathers' times. . . .

With our iron hoes we made hills along the edge of the field and planted corn; then, as we had opportunity, we worked with our hoes between the corn hills to loosen up the soil. Although our tribe now had iron axes and hoes from the traders, they still used their native made rakes. These were of wood or of the antler of a black-tailed deer. . . .

The government has changed our old way of cultivating corn and our other vegetables, and has brought us seeds of many new vegetables and grains, and taught us their use. We Hidatsas and our friends, the Mandans, have also been removed from our village at Like-a-fishhook bend, and made to take our land in allotments; so that our old agriculture has in a measure fallen into disuse. I was thirty-three years old when the government first plowed up fields for us; two big fields were broken, one between the village and the agency, and another on the farther side of the agency. New kinds of seeds were issued to us, oats and wheat; and we were made to plant them in these newly plowed fields. Another field was plowed for us down in the bottom land along the Missouri; and here we were taught to plant potatoes. . . . Other seeds were issued to us, of watermelons, big squashes, onions, turnips, and other vegetables. Some of these we tried to eat, but did not like them very well; even the turnips and big squashes, we thought not so good as our own squashes and our wild prairie turnips. Moreover, we did not know how to dry these new vegetables for winter; so we often did not trouble even to harvest them. . . .

I think our old way of raising corn is better than the new way taught us by white men. Last year, 1911, our agent held an agricultural fair on this reservation; and we Indians competed for prizes for the best corn. The corn which I sent to the fair took the first prize. I raised it on new ground; the ground had been plowed, but aside from that, I cultivated the corn exactly as in old times, with a hoe. . . .[77]

Native American women farmers were pushed off their land by migrants who combined old methods with new. Often, women's skills and labor made the difference between success and failures. Bertha Anderson was a Swedish milkmaid whose expertise was the salvation of the family enterprise near Glendive, Montana, beginning in 1889:

As I could milk and there were several companies of soldiers about twenty-five miles north of us at Fort Bufford, an Indian reservation, we soon figured out that we should buy cows and make butter and sell at the Fort. Therefore, we first bought ten milk cows. . . . It took most of two hours to have the milking done, the milk skimmed and carried up for the calves and the cows turned out to graze. I found that the churn was not big enough to hold the cream for one day, and therefore I had to churn three times every day. Then the butter had to be worked. . . .

As soon as the evening milking was done and a bite of supper consumed, I would start getting the butter ready. We had about one hundred pounds a week, and though it was all worked and put in big containers after churning, it had to be worked over again and put in one-pound wooden molds. Then it was set on slats or boards in boxes and placed on the platform of the buckboard, and then transported to the Fort.

I always had Peter [her husband] go to bed as early as possible, as he couldn't help with that work. I spent the night getting the hundred pounds of butter ready. Usually I had finished by three or four in the morning. I then called Peter, got his breakfast, and he was always off before five, as he had to be down at the Fort before it got warm, since we had no ice and the butter would melt. If it melted he could not sell it. I then had my work cut out for me at home, milking twenty-three cows, carrying the milk to the spring, skimming the milk and feeding the calves.

During the second summer we milked only fourteen cows and I made cheese instead of butter. We also started another industry, that of raising lambs. . . . It was quite a job to feed fifty lambs with a nipple which I made from some old leather, but they grew and by fall they were large. . . .

Another thing that was not so easy for me that summer was that we expected a baby. It was only one more problem that had to be met. . . . When the time came we got a woman, Mrs. Meadows, who lived about four miles from us and who had helped others. I was not afraid, but that afternoon when I first took sick, the cows had made up their minds to be troublesome. They usually went out to graze in a place called Cheney's Bottom, a low place where there was water. But this evening when Peter came out to get them, there were only a few of them there. The rest were over toward the hills a couple of miles beyond.

He rode home with the first ones, thinking if it were possible for me to milk them while he rode after the rest, I would, and I did, though it was very hard. But it was our living and it had to be done. Between the pains I milked. I had them all finished when he brought back the rest of them. By that time he could see he would have to get Mrs. Meadows as soon as possible, so he hitched the ponies to the buckboard and went. As for me, I went struggling on again, milking when I possibly could, for I knew that if I didn't, they wouldn't get milked that night, for Peter would be needed elsewhere.

Our first American baby, Lillian, was born right after midnight on August 24, 1890. After it was all over, Peter took Mrs. Meadows home, for she could not be spared from her own work. My baby and I went to sleep peacefully, all alone in the house except for the three little ones asleep on the floor in the other room. Peter had quite a time about all the chores, but mostly with the milking, for he never did learn to do it very well, but he did his very best. . . .[78]

Another woman who involved herself in the family business during the late nineteenth century was Mary Rosencrance of Franklin County, Washington:

I rode in many roundups, but the longest one was when I rode with 500 cowboys for that last roundup when the Big Bend was thrown open to settlement. Over 2,000 head of horses carried our brand, the Bar-X. We were four or five months in the saddle and the last great band of horses in Washington was taken off the range. We had to quit raising stock when the settlers came and didn't know how to do anything else.[79]

Despite the hard work involved, farm women often had fond memories of their days on the land. Gladys Hovet of the Red River Valley in North Dakota wrote this about her life on the farm during the early twentieth century:

I have worked in the fields haying, picking corn, shocking grain, and in the gardens with their bounty of produce. Cleaning chicken coops, setting hens and incubators, taking care of hundreds of baby chicks; milking cows and feeding calves and pigs, chickens, and turkeys. Crops and vegetables and fruits to be taken care of—the vegetables and fruits to be picked and canned all summer. The lovely strawberries to eat fresh with cream and sugar and the rest canned for winter use.

The shelves in the old stone cellar filled with glimmering red, gold, green, and violet food jars of jelly and jams, crocks of pickles, sauerkraut and carrots, bins of potatoes, cabbage, onions and turnips, cans of sour and sweet cream, crocks of butter and lard, making the dark old cellar more lovely than any mansion. Egg crates packed with eggs, 30 doz. to crate to be taken to town and exchanged for groceries, socks, shoes, dress materials, or anything needed. (Eggs bringing 9 cents in the 30's.)

Threshing time! Up at four o'clock, start the fire in the old cook stove and start a good breakfast for the men that will be working hard all day with the threshing; feed the hens and the chicks, and have breakfast ready. The children still asleep. I go down to the pasture to bring the milk cows home; and so many mornings seeing such a lovely sunrise, I cannot describe all the lovely colors, and the utter peace and quiet of the early morning. The only sound is the creaking of the old farm wagons, going down the road with the men, to work all day in the fields. . . .

Hard work and worries, yes! but lots of love and joy of life. God gave me strength.[80]

Other farm women were not so sanguine, however, either about work inside or outside the house. When asked in 1914 what could be done to help farmers, women in Colorado, Oregon, Oklahoma, and Texas bluntly stated their positions:

Colorado Farm Woman: Serving hot, substantial meals at 6 o'clock A.M., 12 o'clock noon, and 6 o'clock P.M., and clearing up the dishes, I leave the reader to figure out how much time a woman has to leisurely enjoy church, afternoon clubs, or social visiting, even with an automobile on the farm. The remedy for all the trouble is simple. Every wife should flatly refuse to labor for anyone outside of the family. That much is a duty, more is an imposition, considered all right by farmers because it has become customary. . . .

Some may argue that the daughters of the house share the work of the mother, or a hired girl lends her assistance. This may be true in some parts of the country. Most girls in the Rocky Mountain tier of States marry before they are 20. The unmarried daughter in the house is the exception to the rule. Hired girls are scarce for the same reason and do not care to work on farms.

Oregon Farm Woman: The farmer [could help] a great deal by sticking to the 10-hour labor system, which [would] lighten the labor of the woman on the farm. I know a great many farmers who will be in the field by 6 A.M. plowing, and they plow 13 hours. Of course the mother of the family must arise very early in order to prepare breakfast. The husband doesn't mind the long hours of labor because he thinks when he harvests the crop he will get his pay. The hired man gets paid for his work, but the tired housewife on the farm merely gets her board and clothing, the same as the farmer's work animals.

Oklahoma Farm Woman: Now, if you really wish to do something to help the farmers' wives you must work to get the Government to lend money direct to the farmers and their wives (not through the bankers or any one else) with which to buy themselves homes. . . .

The farmer gets only about one-half what the spinner pays for the cotton, and this causes the women and children to kill themselves from exposure and hard work to pay the bills. The banks of this country usually charge from 24 to 40 percent on money. . . . This causes these women to work and pay the graft . . . and our children are going uneducated and dying from exposure and women dying from consumption, where, if we had our just rights, we could live and let live. . . .

Texas Ranch Woman: Many farm women don't get off their own premises more than a dozen times a year. The fathers get so accustomed to the mothers' staying at home, they seem to forget that they might enjoy a little rest and recreation and really feel that she must stay at home "to keep the ranch going," as I have heard them express it. And the mother gets so accustomed to it, she, too, seems to forget she is human. The more intelligent and broader-minded men become, the more they appreciate woman and understand that she is equal in all things. But the men in the country realize this far less than the men in town. . . .[81]

4.2
Gainfully Employed

Census takers categorized men, and some women, as gainfully employed if they earned a direct income (such as a farmer did) or a cash wage (such as a factory worker might). This census designation reflected the standards of an industrializing society that judged people by the money they earned. If a person earned a wage, he or she worked; if a person didn't earn money, census takers and other statisticians excluded him or her from the classification "worker."

During the nineteenth century and the early twentieth century, the classification of wage-earner was far more applicable to men than to women. Male farmers, laborers, mechanics, merchants, and entrepreneurs won bread for their families by earning cash for their labor. Many women worked just as hard, yet no cash wage—no paycheck—rewarded their industry. As a result, they fell outside the category "gainfully employed."

Women's field labor, family business labor, make-extra-goods-for-sale labor, slave labor all contributed to a family's sustenance, but society generally considered the woman performing the work as unemployed. According to Susan La Flesche, "a Western woman has to know how [to] do everything that a man does besides her own work, for she has to be ready for any emergency that may occur when men are not around." La Flesche added, "I had to do anything that came to my hands to do, from measuring land for a pasture fence, harnessing horses, raking hay, doing housework, cooking, sewing, reading medicine, and nursing."[82] Yet La Flesche did not receive remuneration.

Thousands of other case histories demonstrate that women's labor expanded beyond domestic duties, yet such women received no cash and none of the privileges that came with being a "worker."

Mary Jane Megquier, a Winthrop, Maine, woman who accompanied her husband to the California Gold Rush, went back to Maine, then returned to San Francisco on her own, is a case in point. In letters to her family and a friend, she explained that her husband had urged her to go to California with him "as it is very difficult to get any thing done [there] in the way of women's help." After they reached San Francisco, Dr. Thomas Megquier earned as much as fifty dollars a day practicing medicine, while Mary Jane took in boarders, made pickles and other items for sale, helped in her husband's store, and cooked for twenty people, often without hired help and always without pay.[83] In a letter written in 1850 to her daughter, she described her work:

> We have a store the size of the one we had in Winthrop, in the morning the boy gets up and makes a fire by seven o'clock when I get up and make the coffee, then I make the biscuit, then I fry the potatoes then broil three pounds of steak, and as much liver, while the woman is sweeping, and setting the table, at eight the bell rings and they are eating until nine. I do not sit until they are nearly all done. . . . after breakfast I bake six loaves of bread (not very big) then four pies, or a pudding then we have lamb . . . beef, and pork, baked, turnips, beets, potatoes, radishes, sallad, and that everlasting soup, every day, dine at two, for tea we have hash, cold meat bread and butter sauce and some kind of cake and I have cooked every mouthful that has been eaten excepting one day and a half that we were on a steamboat excursion. I make six beds every day and do the washing and ironing. . . . if I had not the constitution of six horses I should been dead long ago. . . . I am sick and tired of work.[84]

Sarah Royce described her unpaid labor in a California mining camp in a similar fashion. When she and her husband arrived in Weaverville, a number of men convinced her husband to join them in opening a store. According to Sarah, two of the men continued mining because "it had not been thought necessary for all the men of the firm to devote their time to the store." As a consequence, when the store attracted a large number of customers," Sarah's husband called upon her for assistance. According to her, she agreeably "helped to serve them." Writing later, she found nothing unusual or exploitative in their request. Rather, she saw her additional duties as "an opportunity to see most of the dwellers in Weaverville, and observe in a small way their behavior to each other."[85]

An African American woman from Yakima, Washington, provides yet another example of a wife who contributed to the family business as a matter of course. When she was a young girl her guardian taught her the barbering trade and employed her in his shop. She married one of the other barbers, and they relocated to Seattle where she helped in his shop, contributing to the family business but drawing no wage.[86]

A Durant, Oklahoma, woman married to a Choctaw missionary also assisted her husband in earning the family income without direct remuneration. During the 1870s, he earned only $400 a year. She helped him in his duties. To improve his income, he also taught a subscription school. She helped him teach. He then opened an orphanage housing up to ten Native American children in his home. She "helped" by caring for the children and teaching them to speak English. She also remembered that when shipments of cast-off clothing arrived from other missions, she cut and sewed for days, remaking the scraps into acceptable clothes for the orphans. Despite her vital participation, she referred to the orphanage as her "husband's business."[87] An El Reno, Oklahoma, woman also assisted her missionary husband in his work with Kiowa and Comanche Indians. She frequently nursed sick Indians and recalled that during the late 1890s she rode horseback ten or twelve miles on cold winter nights to attend to ailing patients. She too described her labors as "helping" her husband.[88]

A woman newly arrived at Portland, Oregon, also used some interesting terms in describing her family's two-month stay with the hospitable Brown family in 1850: "I remained a guest as long as we were there, something over two months, but I did not remain idle, for I was a good seamstress and they needed my services as badly as the mens, for Mr. Brown had been in the California gold mines nine months . . ."[89] One can only wonder at her definition of the word "guest": she was an unpaid seamstress.

She went on to comment tellingly on the upkeep of Brown family farm while the male breadwinner was off in California in search of gold: "Mrs. Brown and her children had raised the crop and her family was in rags. The crop was sold for four thousand dollars. We saw the money paid over to Mr. Brown (not Mrs. Brown). A schooner from New Bedford, Massachusetts, landed at Mr. Brown's door and our men put the vegetables aboard so I know what I am saying.[90]

Women also contributed unpaid labor by playing hostess to their husbands' business associates. Mary Ronan of Montana noted that after her husband accepted the position of agent at the Flathead Indian Reservation she "was never again alone" in her own home with her family. Although she had no servants to assist her, she attempted to act as a "gracious hostess almost continually to members of Indian commissions, Senatorial commissions on appropriations for the Reservation Transcontinental Surveys and Railroad commissions, Special Agents of the Government, General of the Army and other officers, a Papal Ablegate, archbishop, bishops and priests, an English and an Irish earl, a French count and other sportsmen from abroad and the East and West, scientists, millionaires, journalists in search of a story, celebrities, friends, relatives, Indians—chiefs, tribesmen, squaws with their papooses."[91]

When necessary, women even worked as unpaid field hands. In Nebraska, for example, a number of women explained that women and children made the planting of the first crops possible by chopping holes with axes in the resistant prairie sod. A Gallatin Gateway, Montana, woman remembered that she "helped hay, and . . . stack grain and anything that had to be done on the farm." She also "worked with the cattle." In her case, however, she explained this was not a hardship, for she liked farm work. In fact, she insisted that she liked "to be doing the work outside more so than in the house."[92]

Slave women performed another kind of unpaid labor. African American slave women worked in the fields, helped build roads and cut down stands of timber, and performed the domestic labor necessary on plantations. A former Texas slave remembered that her mother was the plantation cook during the 1850s. "She cooked it all in the same place for white folks and us," she remarked. "We ate the same, when the white folks was finished." She also recalled her mother baking pies and bread in an oven, and hanging ham, sausage, and other meats in a huge fireplace to dry. At the time of emancipation, this girl's mistress was training her to do "handwork, knittin' and such." She didn't mind the work; in her case, she hoped she herself would somehow become white by working with "white folks" who lived in the "big house."[93]

Most young women—whether slave or free—expected to work without pay. Because social attitudes of the time defined women as unpaid family laborers, most women accepted what we might today term exploitation. For example, a young woman living in the mining town of Index in Washington state remembered working in her father's log cabin hotel without remuneration. "I was then only 11 years old," she explained, "but a very busy small girl." She cleaned and refilled washbowls and pitchers every morning, cleaned and refilled kerosene lamps, made beds, helped wash on the board a mountain of dirty linen daily, and helped in the dining room at mealtimes. "There was little time for play," she remarked, seemingly without rancor.[94]

An eighteen-year-old Wyoming girl similarly detailed a workload that prepared her to be a productive and well-trained family member, and eventually an efficient marital partner. One Friday morning in 1911, she noted in her diary, "I begun ironing this morning at half past seven quit at 12:00 began again after dinner and finished at half past three, then made a cake, helped freeze ice-cream, etc. No time for music today." In other entries, she revealed that she routinely performed the family washing, ironing, baking, cleaning, and shopping with little assistance from other family members. Surprisingly, she only occasionally mentioned that she took to her bed with a backache or a headache.[95]

Young women did not always work at home, however. Frequently, their families "hired them out" to other families in the neighborhood. If their employers paid any part of a girl's wages in cash, her family collected it and applied it to the upkeep of the rest of the family and of the family home. Olive Deahl of Wyoming recalled her "working-out" days as busy ones. According to Deahl, she "took care of the baby" and "helped anywhere they wanted me," including milking the cows. Fortunately for her, she liked to milk the six or seven cows she tended to every morning and evening because it gave her a rare opportunity to be outside the house for awhile.[96]

Another peculiarity is that the census listed as "farmer" only those women who farmed on their own. A married woman who was running the family farm while her husband worked elsewhere, for example, was not usually counted as a farmer.[97] Nor were women who worked on family farms alongside their fathers, brothers, and husbands classified as farmers or as gainfully employed—most people would have called them farm wives, daughters, sisters, or mothers instead. Census-takers also tended to overlook women ranchers and trail hands, although anecdotal evidence reveals that both single and married women engaged in both occupations. In Montana, Wyoming, and Texas, documented cases exist of women who ran ranches and drove their cattle to market, or worked as partners with their husbands, doing everything from cooking to wrangling cattle.[98]

Undoubtedly, census takers overlooked other hard-working and productive women because they worked in their own homes or in those of other people. Even if they earned a small amount of money for their labors, they would have escaped notice because their work was not regarded as important. During the early 1800s, for example, a young woman named Apolinaria Lorenzana taught the daughters of well-to-do California women in their homes. Apparently, she earned room and board. She began teaching in the home of Doña Tomasa Lugo, where she lived and schooled young girls in reading and religious doctrine. Later she lived and taught in the home of Doña Josefa Sal who, after her husband died, opened a school where both she and Apolinaria taught. After leaving there, Apolinaria taught Alferez Don Ignacio Martinez's three daughters and Doña Tomasa Lugo's niece. According to her, "many others learned their first letters and to sew with me," a fact that would have been overlooked by census takers.[99]

Given the number of laboring women the census overlooked, it is little wonder that figures indicate that the number of working women in the West was low compared to that of working men. For instance, in 1870, the workforce in the Dakotas comprised 160 women and 5,727 men. The figures rose for women and men between 1870 and 1910, with occasional gains in ratios of women to men. By 1910, 28,714 women and 190,363 men held jobs in South Dakota; 29,046 women and 188,372 men did so in North Dakota.

Figures for other trans-Mississippi states are as follows:

	California, 1870		California, 1910
women	13,780		174,916
men	224,868		932,752

	Colorado, 1870		Colorado, 1910
women	436		53,641
men	17,147		285,083

	Kansas, 1870		Kansas, 1910
women	6,509		80,694
men	117,343		540,639

	Nebraska, 1870		Nebraska, 1910
women	1,894		63,303
men	41,943		377,811

	Nevada, 1870		Nevada, 1910
women	443		4,375
men	26,468		40,535

	New Mexico, 1870		New Mexico, 1910
women	3,080		15,079
men	26,381		106,418

	Montana, 1870		Montana, 1910
women	171		18,851
men	13,877		159,896

	Oregon, 1870		Oregon, 1910
women	683		40,473
men	29,968		264,697

	Utah, 1870		Utah, 1910
women	1,075		18,427
men	20,442		113,113

	Washington, 1870		Washington, 1910
women	236		66,126
men	95,234		455,375

	Wyoming, 1870		Wyoming, 1910
women	300		6,013
men	6,345		67,593[100]

Of the women recognized by the census as "gainfully employed" perhaps the most well-known category was the country or cowtown schoolteacher. Certainly, the western teacher is still one of the most widespread stereotypes of working women in the American West. Frequently reincarnated in literature, on the stage, and in film, western teachers ranged from sweet to tough and even perverse. Of course, the schoolmarm in the movie *Butch Cassidy and the Sundance Kid* won viewers' hearts by combining all three of these qualities.

As with many stereotypes, the western schoolteacher image had some basis in fact, for a large proportion of employed women did work as teachers. Because most people tended to see teaching as a logical extension of women's child-care skills, they frequently accepted the notion of women being paid for work in western classrooms. Women teachers, who received lower pay than most men were willing or able to accept, outnumbered men teachers throughout the West.[101]

Reformer Catharine Beecher was one of the earliest and most vocal supporters of women teachers in the West. Beecher believed that women had a mission to migrate westward to teach children, immigrants, and the unschooled lower classes. She thus raised funds and embarked on speaking tours to promote the acceptance of women teachers. She also founded such seminaries as the Dubuque (Iowa) Female Institute, which offered teacher training to women already living in the West. Another result of Beecher's campaign was the founding of the Board of National Popular Education, a non-sectarian group organized in 1847. This organization gave teachers brief training in Hartford, Connecticut, before sending them West.[102]

Teaching demanded much from women, including accepting lower wages than male teachers, seasonal employment during winter and summer terms, discipline problems, poor working conditions, lack of equipment, and responsibility for cleaning and maintaining the schoolhouse. The case of Laura Brown, who began her teaching career in Custer County, Montana, in 1886, is representative. A local rancher who was also a member of the school board, lent Brown a horse and set her pay at $65 per month. Her board cost her $12 per month. "Was I ever thrilled," she recalled, "seventeen years old and earning so much!" She added, "I earned it all right." Homemade benches, a blackboard, and a teacher's desk were the only equipment in her classroom, and she took pride in keeping the sparsely furnished chamber exceedingly clean. Despite rumors of Indian problems, warnings from local military officers to stay home, and an exceptionally hard winter, she finished her four-month term with a sense of pride in her work.[103]

A teacher in Olympia, Washington, remembered that she received $75 per month, but had to take a 15 percent "discount," leaving her $63.75, or $573.75 for a year's work. She rationalized that she was better paid than elementary school teachers and that "the district was in debt for the new buildings and they had to economize somewhere." She also enjoyed teaching; she especially took an interest in the highly motivated students determined to better themselves.[104]

To offset their low wages, many women teachers combined teaching with other economic endeavors. Sarah Jane Price of Nebraska saved money from her small salary and bought a farm. She ran the farm and continued to teach.

Other teachers were also homesteaders; one even became a cook on a trail drive to North Dakota during the summer of 1885.[105]

To improve their teaching skills, many women also attended college and university programs during off-terms. A young Nebraska woman taught summer term so she could attend classes at a Chicago music conservatory during the winter months. From there, she went on to pursue college-level work. But, like so many women of her day, she chose to marry rather than finish her degree.[106]

Many other women's careers also ended when they married. Numerous school districts required women to resign when they married, although some did not. Married women teachers were especially common in areas plagued by teacher shortages and in families experiencing financial trouble. A Washington state woman explained that when she accompanied her husband to Spokane in 1888, "those were boom times in the Coeur d'Alene mining district." They crossed Lake Pend Oreille in a steamer, with the Big Chief Mine as their destination. But after the Big Chief "swallowed" their savings, she and her husband both took teaching jobs to "get money enough to go on with."[107] When necessary, some married women lied about their marital status, but others found many school boards willing to bend the rules, at least for a term or two.

Although historical accounts of western teachers have tended to focus upon white women teachers, the profession attracted African Americans as well. Local census records are only one source indicating that black women became teachers. For instance, the 1850 census of Bloomington, Illinois, showed that of the twenty-three black males in the county, none was a teacher. Of seventeen black females, however, one was a twenty-year-old teacher born in Kentucky. Newspapers are yet another source. One early Kansas newspaper noted that there was at least one African American woman teacher in the Exoduster town of Nicodemus in 1878.[108] Yet other evidence indicates that throughout the West, educated black women typically became teachers, especially in segregated schools or in schools they founded.

Less is known about Mexican American and Asian American teachers, although anecdotal evidence indicates that many existed in the West. We have discussed Apolinaria Lorenzana who, as a young woman, taught daughters of leading families in Santa Barbara, California, probably sometime during the 1820s. When illness paralyzed her left hand, priests took her into their mission hospital. This move ended her career as a teacher, but not her life of usefulness to others.[109]

It must also be noted that female teachers often taught children of racial or ethnic backgrounds different from their own. Numerous Anglo women, for example, taught in Mexican American and Native American schools. Many of them believed they were serving as religious and cultural missionaries as well. Sometimes, however, they ended up learning more than they taught. As a young woman, Grace Pritchett of northern New Mexico accepted a nine-month teaching appointment in a rural, adobe school in Placitas. She later speculated,

"I was probably the first *American* many of those little ones had ever seen. Quite possibly they had been told that *Americans* ate bad little children." She added, "There had not been much intermingling between the Anglos and Spanish because of a certain amount of racial prejudice, not all of which was on one side." She learned, however, to appreciate Mexican culture and to speak Spanish with a fair degree of fluency. People of two different cultures had met and understood, but only briefly, for Pritchett soon moved on. According to her, "the pasture was greener, the salary better on the other side of the fence."[110]

Women also served as teachers in Native American schools. Thisba Hutson Morgan, for instance, taught Ogallala Sioux children at the United States Government Boarding School on Pine Ridge Agency in South Dakota between 1890 and 1895. Hutson cut her students' hair, bathed them, dressed them in "white" clothing, and forced them to wear what she called the "awful brogans" supplied by the U.S. government. Because she spoke no Indian dialects, Hutson created her own sign language to communicate with children who spoke no English. As she taught English and other subjects decreed by government policy, Hutson often found visitors observing her work. These ranged from Chief Spotted Horse to inspectors from the Indian Office in Washington, D.C.[111]

In spite of the supposed timidity of nineteenth- and early twentieth-century women, some were willing to travel great distances to teach native children. In 1916, the Bureau of Indian Affairs hired May Wynne to teach village children in Akiak, Alaska. As Wynne traveled to her new post, other travelers bombarded her with questions about her motives for going to Alaska. One even warned her about the predatory men in Alaska, but Wynne found them "genuine bighearted, chivalrous characters with no visible signs of selfishness, shallowness, or hell-bound ways." She was equally pleased with her students who "enjoyed attending school" and were "truly thankful to advance."[112]

Other women who taught in Native American schools were missionaries, Indian teachers, and women religious. During the latter half of the nineteenth century, members of Irish religious orders in particular migrated to the United States to minister to Native Americans. The Presentation Sisters arrived in Dakota Territory in 1880, the Sisters of St. Francis taught in the South Dakota Indian missions between 1885 and 1910, and the Grey Nuns worked at Fort Totten Indian Reservation in Dakota Territory between 1874 and 1900. Farther west, Mother Mary Baptist Russell helped found the Sisters of Mercy, an order that built both hospitals and schools in Sacramento, California.[113]

In addition to teaching, women also held appointive and elected offices in education. They especially served as county superintendents of schools, a demanding job that required frequent travel for inspecting outlying schools and teachers. In Park County, Montana, women held the job of superintendent from the county's beginning in 1887. In another Montana county during the 1880s, Mary Johnstone served first as principal and then as county superintendent. Mary's sister accompanied her on trips in a one-horse light buggy. The two traveled over dangerous roads and through inclement weather, boarding with ranch families along their route. In Sacramento, California, Sarah Mildred Jones, an African American teacher, was also appointed to a position of leadership. Despite the racist attitudes that confronted her at every turn, Jones persevered and achieved success in her chosen profession.[115] Clearly, the usual image of the western woman teacher is a narrow and inaccurate one. Women of all ages, religious beliefs, ethnicity, and races taught in a wide variety of schools in the American West. Only further (and long overdue) research will reveal the similarities and differences that existed among these women.

Western women who entertained men—from women who worked as hurdy-gurdy girls to those who were prostitutes—have been similarly and widely stereotyped. Because society disdains women who sell companionship and sexual services to men, we often forget that this kind of work constitutes gainful employment. During the years that May Wynne taught in Alaska, she came to think of prostitutes as "loose-living girls, whose morals have long since died." But even though some people prefer to ignore such women as immoral beings, we must remember that entertaining men was an activity frequently undertaken out of economic necessity. Although some historians argue that these women were exploited, others believe they were capitalists and entrepreneurs who took advantage of profitable opportunities.[115]

One variety of female entertainer was the ubiquitous hurdy-gurdy girls who appeared from Montana to California. A California woman recalled her impressions of the first hurdy-gurdy girls she saw in mining camps during the 1850s. She described them as "more decent" than dance hall girls. She explained that a hurdy-gurdy troupe consisted of "four girls with a man to play the violin. . . . [they were] mostly German." Troupes moved from gold camp to gold camp; for a stiff fee, the girls drank and danced with men deprived of female company. In her words, "instead of drinking strong liquor, they drank something light. This was necessary because every dance brought to the house fifty cents for drinks and fifty-cents to the girl. Each and every dance cost the miner one dollar. But dollars were plentiful in those days." She concluded that these women provided "diversion" for a class of miners "that wore no evening suits, that never danced in respectable society."[116]

As implied by her remarks, dance hall girls were usually prostitutes. Throughout the West, prostitutes worked in dance halls, hotels, boardinghouses, brothels, and tiny houses called cribs. The majority of these women were typically, but not always, unmarried, usually in their teens and twenties. Census data, police records, newspapers, and other sources demonstrate that the calling attracted both white women and women of color.

In cattle towns, prostitutes often arrived in early spring, just at the beginning of cattle-shipping season, and left in September, when the season ended. In such towns as Abilene, Wichita, and Dodge City, Kansas, males outnumbered females by two or three to one, a situation that fostered prostitution. Although prostitution was illegal, officials seldom enforced the laws. Instead, they "taxed" prostitutes through fines which prostitutes paid regularly to avoid arrest. The fines provided revenue to town governments and allowed the women to work without serious hindrance.[117]

Brothel districts, often called tenderloins, developed in other kinds of towns as well. In the railroad town of Grand Island, Nebraska, evidence from newspapers, court dockets, plat maps, and city directories indicates that prostitution thrived during the late nineteenth-century. Sometime in the mid-1880s, a husband-wife team built the first brothel. Grand Island's "burnt district" soon grew and flourished. Around the turn of the century, however, city officials enacted restrictive laws, and the ranks of prostitutes thinned as the twentieth century advanced.[118]

This was apparently a common pattern. In other mining towns on the Plains, prostitution grew during the mid- to late nineteenth-century, then declined. In Helena, Montana, between 1865 and 1886, prostitution provided the largest source of paid employment for women. Some women worked Helena during the summer months when the mines were open; others worked the town throughout the year under the protection of "fines." In addition, hurdy-gurdy halls and infamous "dancing saloons," such as "Chicago Joe" (Josephine) Welch's Red Light Saloon, operated without interference during the boom years. When the Northern Pacific Railroad reached Helena in 1883 and began to bring in families and entrepreneurs, legislation and reform campaigns emerged. By the early twentieth century, prostitution had gone underground. In Butte, the city attorney's office responded to a similar anti-vice campaign by shutting down the town's tenderloin district in 1917.[119]

Teachers and female entertainers, including prostitutes, have clearly been the subject of both myth and media over the years, while other working women have gone virtually unnoticed. The western woman physician, unlike the schoolmarms and soiled doves, is invisible in the mythology of the West. Literature, theater, and movies have portrayed the kindly country doctor, the hardy, bewhiskered old gentleman who made his rounds on horseback through dust storms and blizzards, extracting a bullet here and delivering a baby there. Yet few can imagine his female counterpart because women physicians have received especially short shrift in the history of the American West. But exist they did. In the Dakota Territory, German-born and trained Friede Feige practiced medicine during the 1880s, while her minister husband homesteaded. Another, Abbie Ann Jarvis, had acquired medical training at the Women's Medical College in Chicago, where she graduated fourth in a class of twenty-four in 1898. Jarvis was reportedly the first licensed woman doctor and pharmacist in South Dakota. In Nebraska, Dr. Georgia Arbuckle Fix's husband occasionally drove her to house-calls in his buckboard wagon before she divorced him in the early 1900s. On the West Coast, Lavinia Goodyear Waterhouse became a successful hydropathic physician in Sacramento. She also fought for woman suffrage and regularly served as a delegate to state suffrage conventions in San Francisco during the 1870s and 1880s. In addition to their medical practices, these women were wives and mothers; Waterhouse herself bore ten children.[120]

Farther west, Dr. Kong Tai Heong was the first Chinese woman doctor to practice in Hawaii. Trained in the Canton Medical School, she and her husband, Dr. Li Khai Fai, emigrated to Hawaii in 1896. The couple established the first Chinese hospital in Honolulu, then went into private practice in 1910. Although many of her patients mistrusted Asian-trained physicians and female doctors, she soon established herself as a trusted obstetrician in Honolulu's Chinese community.[121]

A twentieth-century example of a female physician is Dr. Mary Perkins of Steilacoom, Washington, who began her medical practice in 1903. She was on call twenty-four hours a day, not just for the white community, but for the African American community and residents of the islands near Steilacoom as well. After her husband died in 1911, she continued her practice in Tacoma and raised her three children alone. She received support during those hard years from a group of women who met at the Tacoma Hotel, including at least six women doctors, two osteopaths, and several nurses. Today, Perkins Park in Steilacoom memorializes this woman's life and work.[122]

This overview of the paid and unpaid work of western women only hints at the vastness and diversity of their labor. Besides working in their own homes and fields, or the homes of others, often without a wage, women also worked in a tremendous variety of paid jobs. In their ranks were agricultural laborers, artists and illustrators, blackjack and monte dealers, domestic workers, environmental advocates, lawyers, midwives, ministers, morticians, novelists and journalists, nurses, photographers, postmistresses, proprietors and managers of boardinghouses and hotels, seamstresses and milliners, shop clerks and shop owners, waitresses, and telegraph operators.[123]

The motivations of women who pursued gainful employment outside their homes were many. Of course, economic need or desire was, as now, a powerful force. Some women stated that they wished to be independent of other people. Still other women held paid employment outside the home because of men—fathers, brothers, husbands, sons—who were, as we would say today, supportive, or at least accepting. Other men inadvertently pushed women into employment—by their inability or unwillingness to earn a living, or by desertion, divorce, illness, or death. Women who had never thought about earning a formal wage were forced to do so after the defection or death of a husband. For every one of the women who became part of the formal records, there were hundreds, perhaps thousands more who held some form of gainful employment during part, or all, of their adult lives. As one African American woman in Washington state who had held a range of jobs commented, "I've worked all my life, hard work . . ."[124]

When numbers of women who held paid employment are added to those who worked but were not directly paid, the record becomes impressive indeed. Neither census data nor stereotypes can be trusted to reveal the extent and importance of women's labor in the American West. Women's own words reveal a far more diverse, extensive field of labor than these traditional, limited, and too-long trusted sources. If the formal data had included ignored or forgotten women laborers, we would have a sharper picture of those women who had been excluded from the category "gainfully employed" and a much better idea of what they actually contributed to their families, neighborhoods, states—and to the West itself.

Of course, as the previous essay makes clear, not all women worked at home or took the socially accepted route of teaching school. During the early twentieth century, a Texas author, Adina de Zavala, helped preserve Mexican heritage and values in such pieces as The Margil Vine:

At the first Christmas season celebrated at Mission San Antonio de Valero (The Alamo), in 1718, the good Padres made the Crib of Bethlehem as realistic as possible, and the Indian children and neophytes were taking part in adorning the crib and bringing gifts to the Christ-Child.

Some brought beads and hung them where the lights would make them glisten; others, pretty colored stones or pebbles, others, bits of bright Indian blankets—everything and anything that to the crude Indian mind seemed beautiful. And the padres did not chide them, for their intention was to honor the Christ-Child. One afternoon as the Venerable Anthony Margil was reentering the Mission from a visit to a sick Indian not far away, he came upon a wee Indian boy sobbing. "What has made you sorrowful, little Shavano, at this happy time of the coming visit of the little Christ-Child?" "That is the very trouble," answered little Shavano, "all the rest have a gift for Him, and I can find nothing." "O, never mind that, little Shavano, the Christ sees into your heart and mind; you wish to love, obey and serve Him, do you not?". . . .

But little Shavano would not be satisfied, he sought the tangible gift; and the good Padre, touched by his grief, and sympathizing with his aspirations, said to him: "Bring a wide-mouthed olla, Shavano, and I shall help you find a gift." The wee Indian lad did as he was bid, and not far outside the Mission gate, on the acequia, was found a vine with triform green leaves and dark green berries. "We will take this to the little Christ-Child," said the Venerable Anthony Margil. "It is not very pretty," said little Shavano. "Never mind, it will be pretty to the Christ-Child; He will make it pretty," replied the Padre. And so consoled, little Shavano helped to dig the vine and planted it in the olla. They carried it to the crib, and setting the olla on one side, twined and festooned the vine over the front of the crib. Little Shavano decided that it was better than nothing, and asked the Christ-Child to be satisfied with the best he could do, and promised to do all in his power during the coming year to serve Him faithfully. The next morning as he renewed his promises to the Christ-Child, he was gazing on the vine wishing that his gift had been pretty like some of the others, when lo! the dark leaves began to glisten, and the green berries turned to a beautiful scarlet, and festooned as they were about the front of the crib, delighted the boy beyond measure. He ran for the Padre, excitedly exclaiming, "The Christ-Child did make my gift beautiful! Come and see it!"

The Venerable Anthony Margil, who was in one sense only a visitor at this mission, took the happy little Indian boy by the hand, and together they joined the procession just then winding through the arcaded galleries surrounding the patio, leading to the chapel, and which followed acolytes with lighted candles. The joyous paean of the "Adeste Fideles" was borne upward as they moved forward, and these two, the venerable, noted, and learned man and the wee Indian boy, with grateful hearts united their voices with the chorus of praise.

This vine is still of spontaneous growth around San Antonio and is called by those of the old days the "Margil Vine." From that early time its bright red berries come to do honor to the season of the Christ-Child.[125]

This baker *in California during the early 1850s described how she made a small fortune from her work:*

I have made about $18,000 worth of pies—about one third of this has been clear profit. One year I dragged my own wood off the mountains and chopped it, and I have never had so much as a child to take a step for me in this country. $11,000 [worth] I baked in one little iron skillet, a considerable portion by a campfire, without the shelter of a tree from the broiling sun. But now I have a good many "Robinson Crusoe" comforts about me . . . I bake about 1,200 pies per month and clear $200. . . . I intend to leave off work the coming spring, and give my business into the hands of my sister-in-law. Not that I am rich, but I need little, and have none to toil for but myself . . .[126]

A blackjack dealer *and* head waitperson *in Montana explained how she helped her husband raise a stake so they could begin to work the claim he filed in 1910 near Fort Benton, Montana:*

Our first stop after Joe and Bill had returned from filing their claims, was in Harlowtown, Montana. Here we obtained jobs at the Harlowtown Hotel. This was a new hotel and well furnished. I was asked to take over the Cigar counter, which meant I would have to play the card game Black Jack. I knew absolutely nothing about cards, but I put up a brave front, so I thought. . . .

It seemed there was a salesman who stopped at the hotel often, and the minute he walked in, he would park himself at the cigar counter and play Black Jack with me. Finally Mr. Smith, a close friend of ours, came over to the counter and said, "My dear little woman, that salesman is a card shark and he is dealing off the bottom of the deck and before long you won't have any cigars left. He is boasting around the lobby that he has his suitcases filled with cigars." Upon his advice, I resigned my position.

Our next stop was at Billings, Montana. I felt that with my four weeks experience as cigar girl in Harlowtown, I was ready for a similar position at the Northern Hotel. This was another fine hotel and I held the same position until Joe decided to go to the coast with the Billings Band. It was at this time I was offered a position as head waitress. I talked it over with Joe but he didn't go along with the idea. . . . However, I accepted the job, so Joe had some rubber heels put on my oxfords and away I went.

The work looked easy. All the head waitress did was to seat the guests and smile. Well, I could do both, but I soon found out there was more to the work than I thought. . . . I saved $80.00 and deposited it in the bottom of my trunk. In that time $80.00 was quite a stake. Joe had saved a little too. . . . I remained at the hotel for about two months as head waitress during which time I took plenty of rough treatment from the girls, but I knew our time there was short and we would soon be headed for the homestead. . . . Before I left they presented me with gifts and my employer packed a huge box of clothing, bedding, and dishes to help us in our new home. . . .[127]

A boardinghouse keeper *in a California mining company wrote home in 1849, explaining her business venture:*

I have ten boarders, two of which we board for the rent. . . . I assure you I have to work mighty hard—I have to do all my cooking by a very small fireplace, no oven, bake all my pies and bread in a dutch oven, have one small room about 14 feet square, and a little back room we use for a storeroom about as large as a piece of chalk. Then we have an open chamber over the whole, divided off by cloth. The gentlemen occupy the one end, Mrs. H—— and daughter, your father and myself, the other. We have a curtain hung between our beds, but we do not take pains to draw it, as it is no use to be particular here.

The gentlemen of whom we hire the house has been at housekeeping; he loaned us some few things, but I assure you we do not go into luxuries. We sleep on a cot without any bedding or pillow except our extra clothing under our heads. . . .

. . . it is nothing but gold, gold—no social feelings—and I want to get my part and go where my eyes can rest upon some green things.[128]

A book agent *in California between 1868 and 1874 related her experiences in trying to keep her ailing husband and her children from poverty:*

. . . I passed the bookstore of H. H. Bancroft, then on the corner of Montgomery and Merchant streets. In the window I noticed a card, with the words "Agents Wanted" on it. Stepping into the store a gentleman advanced to meet me. I asked him, "Do you employ ladies [as] agents?" "Yes", he replied, "allow me to take you to the Subscription Department." There I was shown to the gentleman in charge. I found him to be a frank kind-hearted gentleman.

Will I ever forget him, for it was he who cheered me with his pleasant words. After talking for a few moments, he showed me an engraving of [General Ulysses S.] Grant and his Family, in upright form; told me his terms, what to sell it for, and how much commission I would get . . . we made a bargain; he giving me a book to take orders in, and two of the pictures, told me to go on Montgomery street. I left the store with more elastic steps than I had since my arrival in California. I started up the street, but did not have the courage to stop until I reached Mr. M. on Washington street; he bought the two and gave me the coin for them. How I thanked him; I think if he had refused, I should not have had courage enough to ask any one else. I hastened back to the store, paid Mr. S. for them, and had four more rolled up for me. . . .

Taking them on my arm, order-book in my hand, I started up Montgomery street, calling on one and all, up stairs and down, in every room. Some looked at me curiously, others with pity, and some few with contempt, while I endeavored, in my embarrassment, and in an awkward way, to show the picture. . . .

Eight o'clock every morning would find me in the street-car on my way to the business part of the city. . . . It was now just before Grant's election [as President of the U.S.], and great excitement concerning it prevailed. . . . In almost every room, in front of every store or business house, and on every street corner, I would find gentlemen in groups, whispering or conversing in low tones . . . while others were loud and boisterous in expressing their opinions. It was a great trial for me to know just how to approach them, for the one almost frightened me, and the others so grave and solemn, still I did not pass any of them; with a heavy heart I would step up, unroll the picture, saying, "Gentlemen, I have a fine engraving of General Grant and his family."

After they had looked at it, which they very seldom failed to do, I would present my order-book, take them in rotation, and insist upon one and all to subscribe, and was generally very successful. They would treat me kindly, and were very polite, with the exception of some few ruffians who seemed to have forgotten "their mother was a woman.". . .

I went into a lawyer's office on Montgomery street. . . . Here I met a gentleman from the country, who was trading at one of the wholesale houses; he seemed very angry to think a woman should be selling pictures among so many men. He said I looked old enough to be married and have a family, and ought to be at home taking care of them. I told him I knew I looked old, but he need not remind me of it; that I had a family and was trying to make an honest living for them, at the same time telling him I presumed he was a bachelor, who would not know how to appreciate a wife if he had one. The proprietor laughed heartily, and said, "Madam, you guessed right." As I was wasting time I left him. . . .

I . . . was now canvassing on Third street, not succeeding very well. An old man was standing in the door-way of his shop; I spoke to him, unrolled the picture and asked him to subscribe. He was a strong Democrat and was not long in letting me know it. "You d—— women think you will rule the country. There is a clique of you who go prowling around, having secret meetings, lecturing all over the country on women's rights; here you are roaming around with that d—— picture of that loafer Grant. There was one of your clique in here the other day, lecturing on temperance. I told her in plain English to leave my shop; I would have no women's rights around me."

I replied, "Thank you for your hint; I am not in your shop, nor do not intend crossing your door-way, for fear I might become polluted, for you certainly are the most profane ruffian I ever met." At this he became very angry, and I think he would have struck me, had he dared. . . .[129]

A cannery worker in California raised her younger brothers and sisters and participated in thirty-five strikes:

We came in 1922, and I was 17. About June of that year, I went to work in the Libby Cannery in Sunnyvale. I was canning cherries. My mother passed away two years before that, and I was the oldest of 7 children. To provide for us, my father's wage when he began to pick cherries in this valley was about 35 cents an hour. So all of us had to bring in a supplement, if we were going to live. . . .

I worked in the cannery. . . . It was piece work; but if you didn't make up to 29 cents an hour, they wouldn't keep you. Even if you were doing piece work, you had to make the equivalent of that minimum amount in boxes of fruit. You see, cherries used to come in 50 pound boxes. Apricots came in 50 pound boxes; peaches and pears, too. You were checked when you were given this box of uncut fruit, and if you didn't finish it in a certain length of time, equivalent to 29 cents an hour, well, then, they gracefully sort of eased you out. . . .

Towards finishing time, if you weren't done, the other women would help you finish. It was cooperative. There were women who would like to finish that extra box. They'd help you finish one night, and you'd help them finish another night. But if, by the third evening you found out that a woman deliberately tried to finish an extra box, you wouldn't help, so she wouldn't finish it. . . . there was no discussion about it, but there was a general understanding that you helped each other out. Yet, if someone became too hoggish, you just ignored them. . . .

There were mothers that worked who had practically new-born babies. They'd just have some child in the neighborhood take care of their younger ones. . . . It was a hardship. If you had 5 or 6 children and tried to get them to the cannery, then get them fed at noon, get back to work again in half an hour, and then try to lug them home at night—it was hard. And they were large families in those days. It wasn't one or two children. It was 5 or 6, 7, and 8 children. . . .[130]

A clerk and telegraph operator in California remembered traveling for the Southern Pacific Railroad:

I grew up at Marysville and on October 23, 1872 married W. C. Gray. We immediately went to Redding, where Mr. Gray had the previous year built and was then operating the Redding hotel. In 1874, Mr. Gray sold the hotel and entered the service of the Southern Pacific railroad as a construction superintendent on the line between Oakland and Martinez. I was with him on all this work and was employed by the company as his clerk and telegraph operator. . . .[131]

A cook's story is told by her daughter. In 1910, the family migrated from Korea to Hawaii, and in 1911 to California:

Life in Hawaii was not much different from that in Korea because all the people I came in contact with were Orientals. I don't remember seeing white people, at least not face to face. There was a small group of Koreans in Oahu, where we lived, and a small church. . . . [Father] must have done hoeing or seeding; since he had not had any farming experience, he could not do specialized work such as picking. . . . Father was desperate, always writing to friends in other places, trying to find a better place to live. Finally, he heard from friends in Riverside, California who urged him to join them. . . .

In those days, Orientals and others were not allowed to live in town with the white people. The Japanese, Chinese, and Mexicans each had their own little settlement outside of town. . . . We had reached Riverside without any plans and with very little money, not knowing what we could do for a living. After much discussion with friends, it was decided that Mother should cook for about thirty single men who worked in the citrus groves. Father did not like her to work, but it seemed to be the only way we could make a living for ourselves. She would make their breakfast at 5 A.M., pack their lunches, and cook them supper at 7 P.M. But my parents did not have the cooking utensils we needed, so Father went to the Chinese settlement and told them of our situation. He could not speak Chinese but he wrote hanmun, the character writing that is the same in Korean and Chinese. He asked for credit, promising to make regular payments from time to time. They trusted him and agreed to give us everything we needed to get started: big iron pots and pans, dishes, tin lunch pails, chopsticks, and so forth. They also gave us rice and groceries.

The Korean men went to the dumpyard nearby and found the materials to build a shack large enough for our dining area. They made one long table and two long benches to seat thirty men. Father made a large stove and oven with mud and straw, and he found several large wine barrels to hold the water for drinking and cooking. That was the start of our business. . . .[132]

An entrepreneur *who left Japan to marry when she was 17 built a successful business in Honolulu, Hawaii:*

My husband was nearly forty. He was much like my father, kind but worried. He had a small tailor shop and hoped that a wife could help him build it into a stable business. I bore him seven children, but never learned to love him. That wasn't important; I respected him as he was fair and a hard-worker.

I saw that there was a need in Honolulu for traditional Japanese clothes so I began to sew and embroider custom garments. Within a few years, I apprenticed two young Japanese women. My husband continued to tailor shirts and suits for men. And so the years passed. We lived comfortably for almost two decades.

Then my husband fell ill. His heart had weakened from worry and long hours bending over his needle. He was soon confined to his bed and business matters were left to me. Although I grieved for my husband's condition, I was overjoyed to have control of the business. No longer did we produce shirts and suits. We only made traditional Japanese garments. I redecorated the shop in Japanese style, with mats on the floors and sliding panel walls and an inner courtyard garden. . . .

By the time my husband died nearly five years later, I owned three more shops patterned after the first. My success was due to the Japanese people living in and around Honolulu. They wanted their children to remember the homeland and its traditions. They didn't seem to mind trading with a woman. They had adjusted to the new world enough to accept me as a shopkeeper and businesslady. . . .[133]

An African American field worker *in Texas was taken West by her owner when she was a baby. After emancipation, she soon began to work for herself:*

I's good size when Old Cap'n calls us in and say we's free, but nobody tell me how old I is and I never found out. I knows some of us stays and works for somethin' to eat, 'cause we didn't know no one and didn't hab nowheres to go.

Den one day, Cap'n come out in de field with 'nother man and pick me and four more what's workin' and say we's good workers. Dat was

Mr. Jack Adams what have a place clost to Stafford's Run. He say if we wents to work on his place he feed us and give quarters and pay us for workin', and dat how come I leaves old Cap'n. . . .

I works in de field for Mr. Jack and dat where Wes Marshall, what I marries, works, too. After we gits married we gits a piece of ground and stays on de same place till Mr. Jack die and we come to Houston. . . .[134]

A journalist in Nevada portrayed life in the silver mining region in a light vein for The Overland Monthly *in 1869:*

John is superintendent of the "Great Bamboozle" now, and is besides a member of the Legislature, so of course we move in the best society. I spent a week with him in Carson a little while ago—when they were attempting to pass a bill by which a wife might insure her husband's life without his knowledge or consent. The bill did not pass, though fair notes from fair ladies entreated the suffrages of the honorable senators. . . .

The roads are not good, but in Nevada horses are not expected to be particular about the state of the roads over which they travel, and so one day we drove over to Washoe Valley to see the palatial residence of a man who was created a millionaire in the early days—now six or seven long years ago—and who died in poverty some eight or nine months since. Poor fellow, he is buried behind the house which stands as his monument and that of the wild speculations and excitements amid which this young State was born.

In its present condition it is emblematical of the unsettled and unfinished state of the country—a speck of civilization and grandeur dropped upon illimitable waste of savagery. . . .

Balls and levees here are the same in most countries, though perhaps here you will see more ungloved men and bejewelled women than in any other place. You are surprised that Mrs. ———, who wore such magnificent diamonds last night, should live in so small and plain a house. But the fact is the house is their own. None but wealthy companies build grand houses here. Persons are not judged by the places they live in. Ladies may envy me for living in the stone mansion of the Great Bamboozle company, but nevertheless they are not ashamed to receive me in their cloth and paper dwellings. . . .

The entire religious and social life of Nevada is conducted by ladies. The lords of creation are merely money-making machines, with apparently no other human attributes than a hasty appreciation of a good dinner, the hope of a fortune, and of a home "at the bay," or in the dimly remembered East. . . .[135]

A land commissioner in Washington took her job in 1908 at her father's urging and with her husband's encouragement:

My father never asked favors of me but one day father asked if I would take his job as Land Commissioner [at Fort Colville]. I didn't want to, as I had never had an education along that line but thought I would talk it over with my husband. He said, "Your father has never asked a favor of you before, and I think you should consider it seriously." My youngest child was 10 years old, and I thought my place was in the home. Thinking it over, realizing what my husband said was true, I accepted the position of United States Commissioner. I acted as Land Commissioner for fifteen years. I wanted to resign from my position after a short time, but they begged me to stay. Of course, I had pride enough in my work not to make mistakes. I didn't have any regular salary, just a fee, depending upon the work that came in.

Part of my work was holding court. I presided in all Federal cases and sometimes with a jury. At the age of 65 years, I resigned because there were many bootlegging cases and I didn't like them. Too close to the Canadian border and was very disagreeable. I did lots of espionage work and it was very dangerous. For this work I received my diploma . . .[136]

A Mexican midwife *in San Diego, California related the value people placed on her services between 1812 and 1820:*

I lived eight years in San Diego with my husband, Miguel Antonio Guillén, who continued his service in the garrison of the [Loreto] presidio, and I attended women in childbirth. I had relatives in the vicinity of Los Angeles and even farther north, and asked my husband repeatedly to take me to see them. My husband didn't want to come along, and the Comandante of the presidio didn't want me to go, either, because there was no other woman who knew midwifery. In San Diego everyone seemed to like me very much, and in the most important homes they treated me affectionately. Although I had my own house, they arranged for me to be with their families almost all the time, even including my children. . . .[137]

A migrant laborer in California came to the United States in 1922 with hopes of returning to Japan, but never did so:

We made money washing and packing asparagus [near Liberty, California]. We put about $2000 in the Sumitomo Bank and kept about $1000 on hand. Papa [her husband] said let's go home because we had the fare and only one child. He said, "A country like America, it takes a long time to save money. We have been here one year and we have saved this much. We also have money back in Japan, so let's go home." But I didn't want to go back yet. I thought we could work just a little longer, make more money, then return home.

Pear picking started in Walnut Grove. I said, "Let's go." After pears came peach packing in Marysville. In Marysville the air was so stifling hot that we would arise at three in the morning and quickly pick the peaches before the sun's rays reached their peak. We lived in a vacated schoolhouse and fetched water from a well. Since there was no kitchen, we dug a hole in the earth and placed two metal bars over the hole to cook our food.

Apple picking came next, in Watsonville. I was the cook there. My, I did all the farm work there was to do in America. . . . Papa and I and the children going from place to place. To move was easy. All I had to do was roll up the blankets and say, "Let's go," and soon after, we were gone. Issei [Japanese immigrants]—it was the same for all of them. They would bring their children everywhere. "Sa-a!" and they would wrap their children in blankets and go.

From Watsonville we moved on to Pismo. We stayed in a house behind a grocery store owned by a hakujin [white person]. He felt sorry for us living in the camps and he let us live there free. It was the first time I lived in a house since coming to America. . . .

We worked for Masuoka-san picking peas. He planted them on the mountain's slope because they grew faster, away from the ocean fog, yet warmed from the gentle salt air. The view from the mountains was breathtaking. We would leave Nesan in the car and let her sleep while we picked peas on slopes so steep that you slipped with each step. Already my stomach bulged big with child. I worked up to the day Hana was born. . . .[138]

A miner and saloon-keeper in California and Colorado during gold rush days was known as "Mountain Charley" because she masqueraded as a man to find work after her husband died:

At length, after casting over in my mind everything that presented itself as a remedy, I determined upon a project, which, improbable as it may appear to my sex . . . I actually soon after put into execution. It was to dress myself in male attire, and seek for a living in this disguise among the avenues which are so religiously closed against my sex.

My first essay at getting employment was fruitless; but after no small number of mortifying rebuffs from various parties to whom I applied for assistance, I was at last rewarded by a comparative success. In my assumed character, I made the acquaintance of some River men, and among others, that of the captain of the *Alex. Scott*—a steamer plying between St. Louis and New Orleans. I made known my desire of obtaining a situation, and he offered me that of cabin boy, at a salary of $35 per month.

The many rebuffs I had met with in searching for a situation though bitter at the moment, were in the end of benefit, for they removed to a large extent that timidity which accompanied my advent as a member of the stronger sex. I found myself able after a little, to address people without that tell-tale blush that at first suffused my countenance, and also to receive a rude reply without that deep mortification which in the beginning assailed me with terrible force. In short, I found myself able to banish almost wholly, the woman from my countenance. . . .

The duties of my new position, although menial in their character, were light. The captain, if he ever suspected my secret, as I have some reason for believing, respected it and never betrayed me with any degree of harshness, such as is too frequently to be found in the relations between the head and inferiors of a Mississippi steamboat. I quietly attended to my own business, and although never shunning to a marked extent the company and conversation of others, I avoided them when it could be done without exciting remark. . . .

I remained on the *Alex. Scott* nearly a year, and at the end of that time I obtained a situation on the *Champion* as second pantryman. At the end of six months I changed to the *Bay State*, plying between St. Louis and Memphis; and labored in the capacity of second waiter. I did not remain long on this boat, for an opportunity soon offered itself for me to procure a situation under my old captain on the *Alex. Scott*, and of this I gladly availed myself. . . .

My friend the captain died soon after my return, and not caring to remain under any other, I left the boat and determined to try my fortune on the land. With this view, I engaged a situation as brakeman, on the Illinois Central Railroad. This was in the spring of 1854, and I had been on the river nearly four years. It is needless for me to deny that during this time I heard and saw much entirely unfit for the ears or eyes of woman, yet whenever tempted to resume my sex, I was invariably met with the thought—what then? I was obliged to pay a certain amount weekly for the education and support of my children; and the chances were but few in case I resumed my other character, that I would be able to command the amount necessary for their support, without at all having reference to my own living. Besides this, as the sensitiveness which greeted my new position wore away, I began to rather like the freedom of my new character. . . .

Just then the California fever had not fully subsided and I was determined to gratify my curiosity by a visit to the Land of Gold. A company was about forming to proceed thither, and I, upon becoming acquainted with some of the men composing the party, determined to form one of them. I invested a portion of my means in an outfit and left St. Louis to go to California by the overland route in the spring of 1855. . . .

I staid . . . till the Pike's Peak fever broke out, when I came back to the States, and spent a few weeks with my children. I then started for Pike's Peak, going by the Santa Fe Mail route, and reached Pike's Peak in the spring of 1859. . . . I immediately went to prospecting for gold, and continued at that for about three months and met with no success. About this time gold was discovered by Gregory in the mountains, and following in the wake of the excitement which the event produced, I went thither and located myself about forty-two miles from Denver City. Finding nothing better to do I opened a Bakery and Saloon. I met with good success, and was making money rapidly, when in the Fall I was taken sick with the mountain fever, and was most unwillingly obliged to give up my business and go back to Denver.

After getting better I rented a saloon known as the "Mountain Boys Saloon," which I kept during the winter. I also took up several claims but never made anything in particular out of them. In the spring of 1859 I grew somewhat tired of the Saloon, and went to Tarry All—a place about one hundred miles from Denver, on the Blue River. I here worked a claim with six hands, and made during that summer about two hundred dollars, clear of all expenses. I then left Tarry All and went to Cache Le Poud, a place on a River of the same name, at the mouth of the Platte. I was there some two months, but meeting with no particular success I determined to leave. I did so, and returned to Denver City and bought my old Saloon and kept it during the winter of 1859.

I continued in my male attire . . . and kept my saloon during the winter of 1859–60. I had a bar-keeper, named H. L. Guerín, whom I married, and in the spring we sold out the saloon and went into the mountains where we opened a boardinghouse and commenced mining. . . .[139]

A Mexican mission matron *near Los Angeles, California, during the 1820s tells of her arduous, but enjoyable, work before the American takeover:*

When I came to San Gabriel the last time, there were only two women in this part of California who knew how to cook. One was Maria Luisa Cota, wife of Claudio López, superintendent of the mission; the other was Maria Ingacia Amador, wife of Francisco Javier Alvarado. She knew how to cook, sew, read and write, and take care of the sick. She was a good healer. She did needlework and took care of the church vestments. She taught a few children to read and write in her home, but did not conduct a formal school. . . .

The priests wanted to help me out because I was a widow burdened with a family. They looked for some way to give me work without offending the other women. Fathers Sánchez and Zalvidea conferred and decided that they would have first one woman, then the other, and finally me, do the cooking, in order to determine who did it best, with the aim of putting the one who surpassed the others in charge of the Indian cooks so as to teach them how to cook. With that idea in mind, the gentlemen who were to decide on the merits of the three dinners were warned ahead of time. . . . On the days agreed upon for the three dinners, they showed up. . . .

I made several kinds of soup, a variety of meat dishes, and whatever else happened to pop into my head that I knew how to prepare. The Indian cook, named Thomas, watched me attentively, as the Father had told him to do. At dinner time those mentioned came. When the meal was concluded, Father Sánchez asked for their opinions about it, beginning with the eldest, Don Ignacio Tenorio. This gentleman pondered awhile, saying that for many years he hadn't eaten the way he'd eaten that day—that he doubted that they ate any better at the King's table. The others also praised the dinner highly. . . .

Because of all this, employment was provided for me at the Mission. At first they assigned me two Indians so that I could show them how to cook. . . . The Fathers were very satisfied; this made them think more highly of me. . . . After this, the Fathers conferred among themselves and agreed to hand over the mission keys to me. This was in 1821, if I remember correctly. . . .

The duties of the housekeeper were many. In the first place, every day she doled out the rations for the mess hut. To do this she had to count the unmarried women, bachelors, day-laborers, vaqueros—both those with saddles and those who rode bareback. Besides that, she had to hand out daily rations to the heads of households. In short, she was responsible for the distribution of supplies to the Indian population and to the Fathers' kitchen. She was in charge of the key to the clothing storehouse where materials were given out for dresses for the unmarried and married women, and children. Then she also had to take care of cutting and making clothes for the men.

Furthermore, she was in charge of cutting and making the vaqueros' outfits, from head to foot. . . . They put under my charge everything having to do with clothing. I cut and fitted, and my five daughters sewed up the pieces. When they couldn't handle everything, the Father was told, and then women from the town of Los Angeles were employed and the Father paid them.

Besides this, I had to attend to the soap-house, which was very large, to the wine-presses, and to the olive-crushers that produced oil, which I worked in myself. Under my direction and responsibility, Domingo Romero took care of changing the liquid. Luis the Soap-maker had charge of the soap-house, but I directed everything. I handled the giving out of leather, calf-skin, chamois, sheepskin, Morocco leather, fine scarlet cloth, nails, thread, silk, etc.—everything having to do with the making of saddles, shoes, and what was needed for the belt- and shoe-making shops.

Every week I delivered supplies for the troops and Spanish-speaking servants. These consisted of beans, corn, garbanzos, lentils, candles, soap, and lard. To carry out this distribution, they placed at my disposal an Indian servant named Lucio, who was trusted completely by the Fathers. When it was necessary, some of my daughters did what I couldn't find the time to do. . . .[140]

A novelist in California, Mary Austin, explained in her autobiography, Earth Horizon, *how she became an Indian advocate during the 1890s and early 1900s:*

There is a large campody at Bishop and the largest Indian school in the valley. It was from the teacher, a more than ordinarily competent and intelligent woman, that [I] began to learn the sort of thing that made of [me] a fierce and untiring opponent of the colossal stupidities, the mean and cruel injustices, of our Indian Bureau. . . . At the same time that my contemporaries were joining labor organizations and aligning themselves with wage-strikers, I took to the defense of Indians because they were the most conspicuously defeated and offended against group at hand. . . .

What set me off on that trail was dreadful enough, a flagrant instance of a local pastime, known as mahala chasing. Many of the younger Indian women were employed in the town as household help, and it was no uncommon experience for them, on their way home unattended, to be waylaid by white men—in this instance two young girls, who had lingered behind to sweep the schoolhouse, and were afterward captured and detained for the greater part of the night by a gang of youths, of whom the only extenuating thing that can be said is that they were still very young, and instigated by an older man not a native of the community.

The Indian girls closed their part of the episode by eating wild parsnip root—the convulsions induced by that bane being mercifully shorter than the sufferings already endured—and though the community did actually take measures to prevent the recurrence of such incidents, nothing was done to the offenders, who were sons, some of them, of the 'best families.'. . .[141]

A poet in Dallas, Texas, during the early part of this century also spent a good deal of time in New York City. In "Song From the Traffic" she evinced her love of the West:

> The black haw is in flower again,
> The red bud's rosy tide
> Splashes the wood and stains the shade
> Where dog-tooth violets hide.
> (Manhattan—Manhattan—I walk your streets today,
> But I see the Texas prairies bloom a thousand miles away!)
>
> Primroses burn their yellow fires
> Where grass and roadway meet.
> Feathered and tasseled like a queen,
> Is every old mesquite.
> (It's raining in the barren parks, but on the prairie-side,
> The road is shining in the sun for him who cares to ride!)

> The plum tree's arms are burdened white,
> And where the shrubs are few
> Blue bonnets fold the windy ways—
> Is any blue so blue?
> (Clouds of them, crowds of them, shining through the grey,
> Blue bonnets blossoming a thousand miles away!)
>
> How could I live my life so far
> From where March plains are green,
> But that my gallivanting heart
> Knows all the road between?
> (Manhattan—Manhattan—when you jostled me today,
> You jostled one a-galloping a thousand miles away!)[142]

A woman who ran a post office in Washington state, probably during the late 1870s, remembered difficult working conditions:

At Silver Creek, the post office was owned and operated by an old man, Mr. Tucker, and he kept his mail and postal supplies under the bed. After a time, I started a store at Silver Creek, and I applied for and got the post office. I was postmistress there for several years . . . the mail was carried in by horseback every other day. The mail had to be weighed each day and the average weight was approximately four hundred pounds.[143]

A rancher in Montana, newly widowed in 1886, tried a variety of ranching ventures to support herself and her children. Her daughter describes her mother's efforts:

Our good neighbors and friends gave Mother all kinds of advice. Some said stay in Missoula with her six children and keep them in school. Others, to go back to the ranch, "the city" (a few hundred population) wasn't the place for us. . . . So the old waggan with all our earthly possessions was loaded up and far away we trucked into the wilderness. . . .

We managed to struggle on, raised a crop of wheat and oats, and a vegetable garden. . . . George and Jennie helped our neighbor round up his cattle and brand the increase for extra work on our ranch. John Byrd, a former neighbor of Mr. McClintic, came from Missouri. He helped us get out rails for a fence and other odd jobs. Jim Vance came about that time also and worked off and on for Mother in exchange for his keep. . . .

A sheepman traveling over from Glendive that fall came to see if Mother wanted to sell the ranch which she did, and took the advice of relatives to buy cattle and move on up to Ross Hole and go into the cattle business. Mother, hardly knew a cow from a steer, moved on farther out of civilization, no schools, churches, or doctor. She gave this relative a checkbook and free hand to go down the valley and buy some cows and heifers. . . . In about two weeks here came a herd of sixty of the oldest, sorriest looking cows one could pick.

February 19, 1888, the waggan was packed once more with our worldly possessions and away we went to make our fortune or get started before the cattle died of old age. There weren't any bridges on the East Fork and we had to ford the river twenty-one times from our ranch to Ross Hole, cutting out the ice from each ford. George and a man named Willie Tolan had built a cabin for us and I can still see the place all covered with snow and ice. We were marooned there for six weeks without seeing another person. . . . In August, 1888, a family by the name of Waugh drove over the hill from Idaho and bought the place lock, stock, and barrel, as the saying goes.

Our next move was to a ranch at Rye Creek. We lived there until April, 1890. . . . A man came over from Gibbonsville and told Mother he would sell her a hotel he had there and as Gibbonsville was a very lively mining camp, she could make money there. So once again our worldly possessions were loaded into two four-horse waggans and we set forth to make our fortune. . . . We landed there in the spring of 1895. Got the hotel furnished and ready for business in a short time and all the roomers and boarders we could take care of. Was "coining money" as the miners wanted the best of food and willing to pay for it. In October, the bottom fell out of the mine and the town turned into a ghost town, so we had to move quick in order to get out before we were snowed in. Had to leave all the furniture and heavy things. . . . The next spring she sold the place for a mere song.

Mother said "We arn't licked yet." She put on her bonnet and cape and drove to Hamilton. It was just starting up at that time. Billy Tool was the General Manager of the Daly Haggen Co. and one of the finest men we ever met. Mother told him her woes—so he took her over to their store and gave orders for them to load up the waggan with everything Mother needed, beds, bedding, carpets, lamps, wash bowls, pitchers, pots, range and heaters, etc. So we were soon back in business. . . .[144]

The story of a restaurateur from Mexico who established her own business in San Antonio, Texas, is told by her daughter:

Papa died in 1911. The doctor said it was heat prostration and a stroke. We were near San Antonio at the time. Mama tried to get a job in town. She said she wanted her children out of the field and in a home. But she couldn't find anything. I had known about discrimination against Mexicans for a long time. We were born in America. But I didn't expect it to be so strong in San Antonio. I remember mother crying the day a gringo told her to sell her daughters to men who wanted to lay with them.

Finally, Mama began selling Mexican specialties from a cart with wheels that my brother made out of scrap lumber. Soon, the older children took over, while she stayed in our one-room shack and cooked. I tried to help her and ran errands for her. Although I was only eight, I did all the marketing for her.

After two years of this, she had put by enough money to rent a small adobe near a main street. She opened a cantina in the front and we lived in the back. She called it Antonia's after her mother. . . . what I learned most from these years was what a strong woman my mother was. . . . I learned from her that a woman can do what she needs to, or what she wants to. Mama died in 1916, but I've never forgotten that lesson.[145]

A seamstress in Wyoming during the late 1880s explained the arduous process involved in making a dress:

I came to Wyoming in 1887. . . . I lived with my sister and sewed in the Laramie dress shop with Mrs. Goodale and Kate Fulton. For awhile we had our shop over the First National Bank, then over the post office. . . . From there we moved our shop into the basement of the Simons building, across from the Converse building. . . . In those days it took much more time and money to have a new dress; the entire dress was lined and interlined; it would usually take two or three days at the least to finish a dress. Materials cost from one dollar to five dollars a yard. For my work here I earned a dollar and a quarter a day. . . .[146]

An African American waitperson and field worker in Oklahoma described her mother's work, probably as a domestic, during the 1890s and her own work after the death of her husband in 1900:

They [the narrator's parents] chartered space on a train from Memphis, Tennessee and came to Oklahoma in 1889, with a whole train load of colored folk. All of them secured claims in Blaine, Canadian and Kingfisher counties. Most of them built dugouts and small log houses to live in. They lived hard. Sometimes the women would go to El Reno and get a few days work and the men would stay at home and grub out the blackjacks so that they could have more land to farm. . . .

I came with my daughter . . . on the train to Geary in 1900. There was plenty of work then and I went to work in the Silver Front restaurant for Mrs. Blevens, who was the proprietor. I got $5.00 a week and my board. I paid one dollar a week for a room to sleep. . . .

Sometimes I went out and picked cotton for fifty to seventy-five cents a hundred. I was not used to picking cotton in a sack. In Tennessee cotton was always picked in tall baskets. . . .[147]

A woman religious in Trinidad, Colorado and later in Santa Fe, New Mexico, during the 1870s, wrote to a friend and colleague of her trials:

Oh, the immense field of work there is in this place! I've not mentioned the location of Trinidad and its consequent results. It is the rendezvous for the outlawed, who take to the Santa Fe Trail, and an equal protector for those who use the "Statute of Limitation" from the Territory of New Mexico. The boundary line between Colorado and New Mexico is just twelve miles from Trinidad. . . .

Easter week—Here is a tragedy which took place this week. An elderly lady and gentleman—Americans—residing a few miles from Trinidad, were found murdered in their home. . . . One posse trailed four Mexicans, and because they would not acknowledge the deed, were hanged on the first tree to which they came. Afterwards the corpses were huddled into a wagon, brought to Trinidad in triumph and thrown into an old vacant adobe hut, twelve feet from the graveyard near the Convent. Can you imagine how we felt! Two days later the real murderers were captured and confessed their crime. They were outlawed Americans! . . .

Grave problems are ahead of us. The A.T. and Santa Fe road is working its way toward Santa Fe. What of the great number of men employed on the work? Some will succumb to the climate, others to accidents, and only one hospital within a radius of five hundred miles. The sick or injured will have to be taken either to Phoenix, Denver, or Santa Fe. Our hospital is the central point. Figure this out for us who are trying to do the most good with the least amount of money. . . .

Progress is in sight—so is disaster to a certain portion of our native [Mexican and Mexican American] population. The labor of our pioneer missionaries on our natives will be destroyed by money-making schemes. Deceit and dishonesty will rob the poor natives of everything. . . . Nothing too bad for the natives—nothing too good for the land-grabbers. Understand, dear Sister Justina, those I designate as land-grabber are not representative Americans, but restless characters who wish to get away from law and order and make their own rulings. Among my forebodings I foresee the disastrous effects on the spiritual life of our people. . . .[148]

While it is true that women worked in a wide variety of jobs, they often did so for less pay than men. Also, no words can describe the heartbreak caused by such window signs as "No Females Need Apply," "No Mexicans Hired Here," and "No Chinese Wanted" to women desperate for jobs. Although all forms of discrimination hurt, economic discrimination was and is a ruthlessly effective way of keeping a group of people down.

For Further Reading

Barnhart, Jacqueline Baker. *The Fair But Frail: Prostitution in San Francisco, 1849–1900.* Reno: University of Nevada Press, 1986.

Butler, Anne M. *Daughters of Joy, Sisters of Misery: Prostitutes in the American West, 1865–1890.* Urbana: University of Illinois Press, 1985.

García, Mario T. "The Chicana in American History: The Mexican Women of El Paso, 1880–1910—A Case Study." *Pacific Historical Review* 49 (May 1980), 315–37.

Guerín, E. J. *Mountain Charley, or the Adventures of Mrs. E. J. Guerin, Who Was Thirteen Years in Male Attire.* Norman: University of Oklahoma Press, 1986.

Jordan, Teresa. *Cowgirl: Women of the American West.* New York: Anchor Press, 1982.

King, Evelyn. *Women on the Cattle Trail and in the Roundup.* Bryan, Texas: Brazos Corral of the Westerners, 1983.

Lamb, May Wynne. *Life in Alaska: The Reminiscences of a Kansas Woman, 1916–1919.* ed. Dorothy W. Zimmerman. Lincoln: University of Nebraska Press, 1988.

Lecompte, Janet. "The Independent Women of Hispanic New Mexico, 1821–1846," *Western Historical Quarterly* 12 (January 1981), 17–35.

Lecompte, Janet, ed. *Emily: The Diary of a Hard-Worked Woman.* Lincoln: University of Nebraska Press, 1990.

Locke, Mary Lou. "Out of the Shadows and into the Western Sun: Working Women of the Late Nineteenth-Century Urban Far West." *Journal of Urban History* 16 (February 1990), 175–204.

Olds, Sarah E. *Twenty Miles from a Match: Homesteading in Western Nevada.* Reno: University of Nevada, 1987.

Moynihan, Ruth B., Susan H. Armitage, and Christiane Fischer Dichamp. *So Much to Be Done: Women Settlers on the Mining and Ranching Frontier.* Lincoln: University of Nebraska Press, 1990.

Peterson, Susan B., and Courtney Ann Vaughn-Roberson. *Women with Vision: The Presentation Sisters of South Dakota, 1880–1985.* Urbana: University of Illinois Press, 1988.

Petrik, Paula. *No Step Backward: Women and Family on the Rocky Mountain Mining Frontier, Helena, Montana, 1865–1900.* Seattle: University of Washington Press, 1986.

Ruiz, Vicki L. *Cannery Women, Cannery Lives: Mexican Women, Unionization, and the California Food Processing Industry.* Albuquerque: University of New Mexico Press, 1987.

Schrems, Suzanne H. "Teaching School on the Western Frontier: An Acceptable Occupation for Nineteenth-Century Women," *Montana: The Magazine of Western History* 37 (Summer 1987), 54–63.

Vaughn-Roberson, Courtney Ann. "Having a Purpose in Life: Western Women Teachers in the Twentieth Century," *Great Plains Quarterly* 5 (Spring 1985), 107–24.

Wunder, John R., ed. *At Home on the Range: Essays on the History of Western Social and Domestic Life.* Westport, Conn.: Greenwood Press, 1985.

24. MEXICAN GIRL

SECTION

5

Women, Adaptation, and Change

Gender norms and expectations affected all types of western women—African American, Native American, Asian American, Anglo, and Spanish-speaking—in some way. Yet many women pushed at customary boundaries and tested limits. Sometimes they had feminist intentions, but other times they sought to fulfill their own needs, talents, and desires. As a result, women turned up everywhere, and often in unexpected places: holding jobs, fighting for the right of suffrage, forming labor organizations, and divorcing their spouses at a higher rate than women in any other region of the country.

Other women, who are less obvious in the historical record, fought against other forms of injustice—prejudicial attitudes and discriminatory practices. Although historical accounts often present women of color only as victims of oppression and exploitation, in reality they frequently resisted and developed their own ways to live in an often hostile world. A wide variety of resources gave women of diverse races and ethnic backgrounds the strength to live in a West composed of groups of people who persistently belittled and shunned other groups who differed from them.

5.1
Women's Responses to the Challenges of Plains Living

The Great Plains region is an especially revealing case study of women's adaptation and survival in the West. Here, women, as in other western regions, carried the primary responsibility for home and family. Not only wives and

5.1: Adapted from Glenda Riley, "Women's Responses to the Challenges of Plains Living," *Great Plains Quarterly* 9 (Summer 1989), 174–84. Used by permission. Photo: A Mexican girl, c. 1890. Courtesy of Museum of New Mexico, Santa Fe.

mothers, but all women, young or old, single or married, white or black, Asian or Hispanic, whether employed outside the home or not, were expected to attend to, or assist with, domestic duties. In addition, women helped with the family enterprise and often held paid employment outside the home. They were also socially, and sometimes even politically, active. In all these realms, women had to deal on a daily basis with the particular limitations imposed upon them by the harsh and demanding Plains environment. This essay examines how the Plains affected women's duties and concerns, and how the majority of women triumphed over these exigencies.

Between the early 1860s and the early 1910s the Great Plains attracted much controversy. It had vehement boosters and equally determined detractors. Land promoters and other supporters were quick to claim that a salubrious climate, rich farming and grazing lands, and unlimited business opportunities awaited newcomers. This "boomer" literature presented an attractive image that did not always seem completely truthful to those men and women who actually tried to profit from the area's purported resources.

Particularly during the early years of settlement, many migrants widely bemoaned the lack of water and relatively arid soil as well as their own inability to grapple effectively with these natural features of the Plains. At times their hardships were so severe that special relief committees and such groups as the Red Cross and the United States Army had to supply food, clothing, and other goods to help them survive.[1] Consequently, twentieth-century historical accounts have often focused on the ongoing struggles of existence. Until recently, only a few of these studies documented or analyzed the special problems that the Plains posed to women. Fortunately, a growing sensitivity to women's roles in history has led to an examination of women's own writings. This analysis of diaries, letters, and memoirs has clearly and touchingly revealed the details of their lives.[2]

The challenges that confronted women on the Plains can be grouped into three categories: the natural environment; political upheavals over such crucial issues as slavery, racism, and economic policy; and personal conflict with other people, including spouses. Obviously, all these factors also affected men, but they had a particular impact upon women.

The Natural Environment

The physical environment of the Plains created numerous difficulties for women. They showed, for instance, tremendous creativity and energy in obtaining the water that constantly was in such short supply. They carried water in pails attached to neck yokes or in barrels on "water sleds." They melted snow to obtain cooking and wash water. They used sal soda to 'break' the alkali content of water. Women also helped build windmills and dig wells. And in their desperation they even resorted to hiring a 'water-witch' or diviner to help them locate a vein of water.[3]

The aridity of the Plains created another problem for women—horribly destructive prairie fires. Men feared these fires because they endangered the animals, crops, and buildings that were largely their responsibilities, but women thought first of their children and homes as well as their cows, pigs, and chickens. In 1889 a fire in North Dakota destroyed one man's horses and barn and also claimed his wife's precious cows and chickens. Four years later, another fire in Fargo, North Dakota, burned to the ground both the shops where primarily men labored and the homes where primarily women worked. Recalling her childhood, a Kansas woman explained that because most buildings were made of wood, the "greatest danger" they faced was fire. She added that her father immediately turned all stock loose in the face of an oncoming fire because the animals instinctively headed for the safety of the river valley, while her mother placed her in the middle of the garden on the presumption that fire would not "pass into the ploughed land." Other women described the deafening noise and blinding smoke of the fires that threatened their families and homes.[4]

In addition, many women claimed that the Plains climate plagued them and interfered with their work. Destructive storms and blizzards were a constant threat, while summer heat and winter cold were regular annoyances. A Norwegian woman confronted her cold kitchen each winter morning dressed in overshoes, heavy clothing, and a warm head-scarf. Another woman simply wrote in her journal, "the snow falls upon my book while I write by the stove."[5]

Ever-present insects and animals also challenged women at every turn. Grasshoppers not only demolished crops, but could destroy homes and household goods as well. The "hoppers" gnawed their way through clothing, bedding, woodwork, furniture, mosquito netting, and stocks of food. Bliss Isely of Kansas claimed that she could remember the grasshopper "catastrophe" of 1874 in vivid detail for many years after its occurrence. As she raced down the road trying to outrun the "glistening white cloud" of grasshoppers thundering down from the sky, she worried about the baby in her arms. When the grasshoppers struck, they ate her garden to the ground, devoured fly netting, and chewed a hole in her black silk shawl. "We set ourselves to live through a hungry winter," she remembered. In the months that followed, she "learned to cook wheat and potatoes in every way possible." She made coffee from roasted wheat and boiled wheat kernels like rice for her children. Another Kansas woman who survived the grasshopper attack bitterly declared that Kansas had been "the state of cyclones, the state of cranks, the state of mortgages—and now grasshopper fame had come!"[6]

Political Upheaval
As if the physical environment wasn't enough to discourage even the hardiest and most determined women, another problem, political conflict, beset them as well. The ongoing argument over slavery especially affected the Kansas Territory when in 1856 an outbreak of violence between free-staters and proslavery factions erupted. "Border ruffians" added to the chaos by crossing frequently into "Bleeding Kansas" from Missouri in an attempt to impose slavery on the territory by force. Sara Robinson of Lawrence felt terrorized

by frequent "street broils" and saw her husband imprisoned during what she termed the "reign of terror" in Kansas. Another Kansas woman lamented that there was no respite between this convulsive episode and the Civil War, which plucked men out of homes for military service. Women not only lost the labor and income of their men, but they feared the theft of food and children and the threat of rape for themselves and their daughters at the hands of raiders, thieves, and other outlaws made bold by the absence of men. In addition, the departure of men caused the burden of families, farms, and businesses to fall on the shoulders of already beleaguered women.[7]

The disputes that followed in the wake of the Civil War continued to disrupt women's lives. The period of Reconstruction between 1865 and 1877 included, for example, the chaotic entry of Exodusters (former slaves) into Kansas and other Plains states. In turn, prejudice against Exodusters created difficulties for African American women who had hoped they were migrating to a more hospitable region than the American South. Also during this period, economic unrest and dissatisfaction with federal and state government policies resulted in Populist agitation through the Plains during the 1880s and 1890s. By 1900, it seemed to many women that their lives had been entangled in a long series of political upheavals.

Personal Conflict

Women experienced personal conflict as well. Prejudice against Catholics, Jews, and people of other faiths led to intolerance at best and violence at worst. Ethnic and racial groups also received their share of distressing treatment. African American, Asian, and Mexican women were expected to work in the most menial, low-paid jobs, were barred from shops and other businesses, and were personally treated with disdain by many other migrants. This situation was especially difficult for women because they were frequently told that they were to be the arbitrators of society, yet they felt helpless to right this situation. Women also wanted desperately to shield their children from such treatment.

Some women also faced trouble within their own homes. Anecdotal evidence demonstrates that some husbands were domineering, demanding, and physically or verbally abusive. A young Jewish woman whose father had insisted that his family migrate to North Dakota remembered continual strife between her mother and father. "How can one bring the close, intimate life of the Russian *shtetl* to the vast open wilderness of the prairie?" she asked. But her mother tried. According to her daughter, "she rose early and cooked and baked and washed and scrubbed and sewed. She prayed and observed the fast days and holidays by making special dishes." Yet she also regretted and complained. Unable to understand her sorrow or offer her some much-needed sympathy, her husband argued and remonstrated. One day, much to his daughter's relief, he ran from the house storming and raging. Jumping into a buggy and seizing the reins, he shouted, "Goodbye, goodbye—I am leaving. This is more than human flesh can bear. . . . This is the end. I can take no more. It is beyond enduring. Goodbye, goodbye." When he soon returned, her joy dissipated: "My father had not kept his promise to go away and leave us in peace. He had returned. We were all trapped."[8]

On the Plains, and throughout the West, thousands of women deserted such husbands or sought relief in divorce courts. Census figures indicate that western women sought and received a higher proportion of divorces than women in other regions of the country. Whether economic opportunities encouraged this proclivity to divorce or whether western women had a spirit that sought independence is as yet unclear.[9]

Given the many difficulties that beset women, a reasonable person might ask why they stayed on the Plains. In fact, many did not stay. They and their families returned to former homes or moved onward to try life in another western region or town. After spending two years in Kansas, Helen Carpenter was delighted to become a new bride about to migrate to California. In 1857, Carpenter began her trail journal by going "back in fancy" over the two years she had spent in Kansas. She recalled the initial "weary journey of three weeks on a river boat" when all the children fell ill. Then, she wrote, it was "the struggle to get a roof over our heads . . . then followed days of longing for youthful companions . . . and before the summer waned, the entire community was stricken with fever and ague." Just as she finally made some friends and established something of a social life, "such pleasures were cut short by border troubles and an army of 'Border Ruffians' . . . who invaded the neighborhood, with no regard for life or property." She admitted that Kansas was "beautiful country" with its tall grass and lush wildflowers, but added that "the violent thunderstorms are enough to wreck the nerves of Hercules and the rattlesnakes are as thick as the leaves on the trees, and lastly 'but not leastly,' the fever and ague are corded up ever ready for use." Given the nature of her memories, it is not surprising that Carpenter concluded, "in consideration of what we have undergone physically and mentally, I can bid Kansas Good Bye without a regret." Another Kansas woman whose family left the region said that her father had taken sick and that her "Auntie wanted to get away from a place always hideous in her eyes."[10]

Fortunately, not all women felt so strongly about the drawbacks of their environment. Many women had already experienced a demanding life and, as Laura Ingalls Wilder put it, they saw the rigors of the Plains as "a natural part of life." They hung on because they had hope for the future, or according to one migrant, because they didn't expect the hard times to last. Often, their optimism was rewarded, and conditions did improve. Innovative technology gradually conquered the arid Plains, and economic booms occasionally appeared. A Nebraska woman of the early 1900s summed up her triumph in a pithy way when she wrote, "we built our frame house and was thru with our old leaky sod house. . . . We now had churches, schools, Telephones, Rural Mail."[11]

Still we must ask: did the women who remained on the Plains suffer disillusionment and despair, growing old and ill before their time? Did they blame

their menfolk who had seen economic opportunity in the Plains for their mis-
fortunes? The answer is "yes": many women who stayed on the Plains did
so with resentment and hostility. Their writings tell of crushing work loads,
frequent births, illnesses and deaths, recurring depression, loneliness, homesickness, and fear. A common complaint was the absence of other women;
Plains women also longed for family members who had stayed at home. A
Wyoming woman even claimed that the wind literally drove her crazy and that
she could no longer bear to spend long winters on a remote ranch with no
other women.[12]

Some women's lamentations were unrelenting, but others gradually included more pleasant observations. They noted that other people, including
women, soon moved in and that often members of their own families joined
them. Gradually, the depression of many hostile women ebbed and was replaced by a sense of affection for their new homes. Even the Wyoming woman
who feared for her own mental stability later maintained that "those years on
the Plains were hard years but I grew to like the West and now I would not
like to live any other place."[13]

Numerous women did blame men for their circumstances. But it is often
difficult to determine which women had fair cause to lay blame. Because
women were hesitant to record personal troubles in journals or letters sent
back home, it is not always clear how responsible men were for women's
difficulties. Certainly, sad stories do exist of men who verbally or physically
abused women or who were alcoholic, lazy, financially inept, or generally irresponsible. In the patriarchal family structure of the time, men were often
slow to recognize the importance of women's labor, allow women a voice in
family decisions, and extend understanding for women's concerns. As early
as 1862, the U.S. Commissioner of Agriculture's annual report suggested that
the supposedly prevalent insanity of plainswomen resulted more from the
harsh treatment doled out by their own men than from the Plains climate,
family finances, or infant mortality. In following years, newspaper reports of
wife-beating or journal accounts of alcoholic husbands gave credence to his
assertion.[14]

Here again, the negative testimony is balanced by other accounts. Countless women wrote about the energy, responsibility, support, community participation, and kindness of fathers, brothers, husbands, and sons. Women
spoke of men's "cheerful spirits," patience, thoughtfulness, sympathy, and
companionship. Army wives Ada Vogdes and Elizabeth Custer both felt that
the hardships of their lives as women in western forts were greatly offset by
the courtesy and consideration of their husbands, other officers, and enlisted
men. More important, a considerable number of plucky women faced challenges with creativity, energy, optimism, and motivation. They battled the circumstances of their environment by confronting the necessities of each day
while maintaining hope for a better future. They met political upheaval and
violence with religious faith and a commitment to help establish order. And
they endured conflict with family members, neighbors, and members of other

cultural groups by persevering and seeking the companionship of others, especially other women.

A Kansan of the 1880s, Flora Moorman Heston, is one example of a woman who confronted poverty, hard work, loneliness, and other problems with buoyant spirits. In a letter home, she maintained that "we have the best prospect of prosperity we ever had and believe it was right for us to come here." She added that "I have a great deal more leasure [sic] time than I used to have it dont take near the work to keep one room that it does a big house."[15] Like women in the Midwest, Southwest, and Far West, plainswomen relied on their inner strength and kept a positive outlook. Although these qualities are often forgotten in conventional descriptions of the darker side of Plains living, they did indeed exist.

How Women Adapted

Most women who ventured to the Plains states were highly motivated. They sought wealth, health, a more promising future for their children, lower taxes, and end to slavery, less prejudice or more freedom from governmental control. During the hard times and disasters, their hopes sustained them. When their fathers, brothers, or husbands talked of moving elsewhere, they often reminded the men of the particular dream that had brought them to the Plains in the first place. Others relied upon religious faith, or clung to their belief that they were civilizing a raw region, or some other commitment to keep them strong in the face of adversity.

Many women migrants created rich and varied social lives out of limited opportunities. They relieved their own isolation by writing in cherished journals or penning letters to friends and family. A young Nebraska woman who lamented the lack of women in the neighborhood wrote daily in her journal. "What should I do without my journal!" she exclaimed on one of its pages. Yet, as time passed, her entries became less frequent while her apologies to her neglected journal increased.[16]

Women also turned to the books and newspapers they had brought with them, borrowed from others, or had purchased with hoarded butter-and-egg money. Bliss Isely explained that even when she and her husband could "not afford a shotgun and ammunition to kill rabbits" they subscribed to newspapers and bought books. She made it a personal rule that "no matter how late at night it was or how tired [she] was, never to go to bed without reading a few minutes from the Bible and some other book." Other women wrote of their longing for more books, of feeling settled when their books were unpacked, and of borrowing books from others. Faye Cashatt Lewis poignantly wrote: "Finishing the last book we borrowed from the Smiths, and having it too stormy for several days to walk the mile and a half to return it and get more, was a frequent and painful experience. Seeing the end of my book approaching was like eating the last bite of food on my plate, still hungry, and no more food in sight."[17]

Music also provided solace and sociability. Frequently women insisted upon bringing guitars, pianos, and miniature parlor organs to the Plains. Despite the fact that Ada Vogdes and her husband were transported from fort to fort in army ambulances with limited space, she clung to her guitar. In her journal, she frequently mentioned the pleasure that playing that guitar and singing along brought to her and others.[18] Vogdes, like many others, also depended upon mail to keep her amused and sane. When a snowstorm stopped the mail for two long weeks, Vogdes proclaimed that she could not wait much longer. To many women, the arrival of the mail provided a lifeline to home and family and brought news of the larger world through magazines, journals, ethnic and other newspapers, and books.[19]

The coming of the railroad had great social implications. Not only did railroad companies bring additional people, but they sponsored fairs and celebrations and provided ties with other regions of the country. An Indian agent's wife in Montana wrote that "the coming of the Northern Pacific Railroad in 1883 brought us in closer touch with civilization, with kin and friends, with medical and military aid, but put an end to the old idyllic days." In 1907, a Wyoming woman was delighted to see the railroad come into her area and claimed that its very existence alleviated her depression. She explained that with "no trees and few buildings" to hamper her view of passing trains, she felt that she kept "in touch with the outside pretty well."[20]

Women also became effective instigators and organizers of a huge variety of social events including taffy pulls, oyster suppers, quilting bees, dinners, picnics, box suppers, church "socials," weddings and chivarees, spelling bees, dances, theatricals, song fests, puppet shows, and readings. Perhaps most important were the celebration of such special holidays as Thanksgiving, Hanukkah, Christmas, and the Fourth of July. The menus concocted by women on special occasions often confounded other women. After a particularly splendid dinner, one woman wrote, "however she got up such a variety puzzled me, as she cooks by the fireplace and does her baking in a small covered skillet."[21]

A third way in which women adapted was in their belief that they were family and cultural conservators. Women often derived great satisfaction and a sense of significance by establishing "real" homes for their families, preserving traditional values, folkways, and mores, passing on family and ethnic traditions, contributing to local schools and churches, and establishing women's organizations. Many would have probably agreed with the poetic woman who said of them, "Without their gentle touch, this land/Would still be wilderness." Certainly, women spent a good deal of time and energy recording and relating their cultural activities.[22]

In this role, women placed a great deal of emphasis on material goods. They preserved, but also used, family treasures. Some insisted on fabric rather than oilcloth table coverings, served holiday eggnog to cowhands in silver goblets, and used their best silver and chinaware whenever the occasion arose. Years after coming to the Plains, Faye Lewis still proudly displayed her mother's Haviland china. She explained that "Father had urged strongly that this china be sold, but the thought was so heartbreaking to mother that he relented and helped her pack it." Lewis perceptively saw that her mother's china was "more than a set of dishes to her, more than usefulness, or even beauty. They were a tangible link, a reminder, that there are refinements of living difficult to perpetuate . . . perhaps in danger of being forgotten." Certainly Mary Ronan felt this way. On an isolated Indian reservation in Montana, she still regularly set her dinner table with tablecloths and ivory napkin rings. She explained that "heavy, satiny damask" cloths gave her "exquisite satisfaction" although her children did not like them. She added that she had "one beautiful set of dishes" but used them only on "gala occasions."[23]

Rituals such as the celebration of Christmas were also important. In the early years, the Christmas trees in many Plains homes were scraggly, ornaments few and homemade, and Christmas dinner far from lavish. But as their situations improved financially, women provided more festive trees, elaborate presents, and special foods. They placed trees decorated with nuts, candy, popcorn balls, strings of cranberries, wax candles, and homemade decorations in schools and churches. They then surrounded the trees with gifts for family and friends as well as presents for poor children who might otherwise be deprived of a Christmas celebration. Often music, singing, speeches, and prayers preceded the arrival of a local man dressed as Santa Claus.[24]

It is important to note that women contributed to a diversity of cultural patterns because of their own mixed ethnic and racial stock. European, Native American, African American, Mexican, and Asian women who desired to preserve their own rich heritages subscribed to a variety of newspapers and magazines in their own languages, continued to wear traditional clothing, practiced their customary holiday rituals, and added their own words, foods, and perspectives to the evolving society. A Norwegian woman in Nebraska continued to speak Norwegian in her home, sent her children to parochial school, and cooked Norwegian food. African American women were another group who added their folkways to the cultural blend, especially after the Civil War when significant numbers of them migrated to Plains states as Exodusters.[25]

Jewish women were yet another group who brought their own culture to the Plains. Although many Jewish settlers first came to the Plains as members of agricultural communities, particularly under the auspices of the Jewish Colonization Association and the Hebrew Emigrant Aid Society, they soon relocated in such cities as Omaha, Nebraska, and Grand Forks, North Dakota. Here they established businesses and communities that could support rabbis and supply other religious needs. This relocation was important to many Jewish women who despaired of their inability to provide their children with religious education and keep a kosher home when separated from a sizable Jewish community.[26]

A fourth, and crucial, factor that aided many women in their adaptation to life on the Plains was their ability to bond with other women and to create what we would today call supportive networks. On the Plains, as elsewhere, women turned to each other for company, encouragement, information, and help in times of need. Women's longing for female companionship is clearly revealed by their laments about the lack of other women. One of only three known women migrants in a remote region of North Dakota stated simply, "Naturally I was very lonely for women friends."

Consequently, women frequently overcame barriers of age, ethnicity, social class, and race in forming friendships. Arriving in Oklahoma Territory in the early 1900s, Leola Lehman formed an extremely close friendship with a Native American woman whom she described as "one of the best women" she had known in her lifetime. A Kansas woman similarly characterized an African American woman who was first a domestic, then a confidante and friend, as "devoted, kind-hearted, hard-working." Still other women told how they found a way around language barriers in order to gain companionship from women of other races and cultures.[27]

Typically, women began a friendship with a call or chat. Lehman was hanging out her wash when the Indian woman who became her friend quietly appeared and softly explained, "I came to see you. . . . I thought you might be lonesome." The company of other women was especially important in male-dominated military forts, where a woman began receiving calls upon arrival. Ada Vogdes recorded her gratitude for being whisked off by another officer's wife the moment she first arrived at Fort Laramie. Her journal overflowed with mention of calls, rides, and other outings with women friends. When her closest friends left the fort, Vogdes described herself as feeling "forsaken and forlorn" and overwhelmed by an aching heart. Some years later, Fanny McGillycuddy at Fort Robinson in South Dakota also logged calls and visits with other women and noted their great importance to her.[28]

Women also established friendships, gave each other information and support and passed on technical information, often through quilting bees and sewing circles. Bliss Isely remembered that as a young woman she was always invited to the "sewings and quiltings" held by the married women in her neighborhood. On one occasion, she invited them in return and was pleased that "they remained throughout the day." Isely felt that these events gave her invaluable training in much-needed domestic skills and that the women had "a good time helping each other" with their work.[29]

Older women lavished new brides with maternal attention and were often very generous in sharing their time, energy, and skills with the novice. In 1869 the *Bozeman Chronicle* quoted a recent bride as saying, "In all there were just fourteen women in the town in 1869, but they all vied with each other to help us and make us welcome." This hospitality even included much-needed cooking lessons for the seventeen-year-old wife. A decade later, another bride arriving in Miles City, Montana, recalled that she met with a similar welcome: "Ladies called. . . . I wasn't at all lonely."[30]

Women were also quick to offer their services to other women in times of childbirth, illness, and death. Such aid in time of need created strong bonds between women that often stretched beyond racial, ethnic, and class lines. In

1871, the *Nebraska Farmer* quoted a settler who claimed that such women acted "without a thought of reward" and that their mutual aid transformed women into "unbreakable friends." During the early 1880s, a Jewish woman in North Dakota explained that when a woman was about to give birth she would send her children "to the neighbors to stay for the time" so that she "could have rest and quiet the first few days, the only rest many of these women ever knew." She added that "the rest of us would take home the washing, bake the bread, make the butter, etc." Other women said that in time of illness or death they would take turns watching the patient, prepare medicines, bring food, prepare a body with herbs, sew burial clothes, organize a funeral, and supply food.[31] The crucial nature of another woman's assistance in time of physical need was perhaps best expressed by Nannie Alderson, a Montana ranch wife during the 1880s. When she was ill, male family members and ranch hands strongly urged her to call a doctor from Miles City. Her reply: "I don't want a doctor. I want a woman!" When the men surrounding her failed to understand her need, they again pressed her to call a doctor. She sent for a neighbor woman instead. After her recovery, she justified her action by saying, "I simply kept quiet and let her wait on men, and I recovered without any complications whatever."[32]

As the number of women increased in an area, women began to join together in the public arena as well as in private. They formed a myriad of social, educational, and reform associations. Women's literary clubs studied books and started libraries. Temperance societies—the most famous of which was the national Women's Christian Temperance Union—attempted to help control the evil of alcoholism that was so damaging to women and children who were economically dependent upon men. And woman suffrage groups fought for the right to vote. Nebraskan Clara Bewick Colby, suffragist and editor of *The Woman's Tribune*, noted again and again that the Plains states were particularly fertile ground for suffrage reform.[33]

Plainswomen split, however, on the issue of suffrage. Nebraskan Luna Kellie explained that she "had been taught that it was unwomanly to concern oneself with politics and that only the worst class of women would ever vote if they had a chance." But when a tax reform proposed to cut the length of the school term, Kellie, a mother of several small children, "saw for the first time that a woman might be interested in politics and want a vote." With her father's and husband's help, she promoted a campaign that resulted in woman suffrage in local school elections. Kellie's husband urged her to continue her efforts to obtain women's right to vote in general elections.[34] In 1888, one Kansas women placed a cap bearing presidential candidate Belva Lockwood's name on her daughters head. Still, many women opposed the suffrage cause, maintaining that the vote should belong to men only. These women believed that women should focus on their homes and families rather than on making political decisions. Some of these women even organized anti-suffrage associations.[35]

But advocates of woman suffrage were not so easily deterred. After the National Woman Suffrage Association was organized in 1869 (the same year that Wyoming Territory granted women the right to vote), Elizabeth Cady Stanton and Susan B. Anthony traveled through the West promoting suffrage. Stanton thought that Wyoming was a "blessed land . . . where woman is the political equal of man." Although Esther Morris is usually given credit for bringing woman suffrage to Wyoming Territory and was later called the Mother of Woman Suffrage, some people dispute the centrality of her role. Evidently, many women worked to convince the Democratic legislature to adopt a Women's Rights Bill in December 1869 and persuaded Republican governor John A. Campbell to sign the bill on December 10, 1869.[36]

In addition to suffrage organizations, thousands of other women's clubs and associations existed, including hospital auxiliaries, housekeepers' societies, current events clubs, musical groups, tourist clubs, world peace groups, Red Cross units, and Women's Relief Corps chapters. By the 1880s, so many organizations existed that one Wyoming woman termed the era "the golden age of women's clubs." One leading Oklahoma clubwoman established or led over forty associations during her life.[37]

Unfortunately, much of the sharing that had existed during the early days of a region now began to dissipate. Many women's clubs were segregated; women of color formed their own groups and fought for suffrage or reforms in their own way. For instance, African American women worked energetically within their own communities to provide medical care, playgrounds, and better educational facilities.

Some men's organizations also invited women (usually only white women, however) to join their membership and support their causes. A few even expanded their platforms to include women's issues. As a result, women joined the Patrons of Husbandry (the Grange), the Farmers' Alliance, and the Populist party. Annie La Porte Diggs of Kansas, for example, was an active Populist speaker and writer known for her religious liberalism. Of course, the most famous Populist woman orator was Mary Elizabeth Lease, a woman who was admitted to the Kansas bar in 1885 and who gave in 1890 over 160 speeches in support of the Populist cause. She became famous for her admonition to farmers to "raise less corn and more hell" and was dubbed by the media "Mary Yellin'." So many other women spoke from wagons and platforms, carried banners, and marched in parades that political humorist Joseph Billings wrote, "Wimmin is everywhere."[38]

Women also began to run for office on the Populist ticket. They had long held elected positions on local, county, and state school boards so the idea was not totally unacceptable to many women and men. In 1892, Ella Knowles, a Montana lawyer who in 1889 successfully lobbied for a statute allowing women to practice law in the state, ran unsuccessfully for attorney general. She was, however, appointed to a four-year term as assistant attorney general, and during the mid 1890s was a delegate to Populist conventions and a member of the Populist National Committee. During this period, Olive Pickering

Rankin served as the only woman on the school board in Missoula, Montana. She was also the mother of Jeanette Rankin, the first woman to serve in the U.S. Congress and the person who introduced the "Anthony Amendment" for woman suffrage into the U.S. House of Representatives.[39]

Many men also supported women in other areas of life. Cases of supportive, helpful, sympathetic men who offered a helping hand and a listening ear when needed abounded in all communities. Faye Cashatt Lewis, whose mother so plaintively complained that the great trouble with North Dakota was that "there is nothing to make a shadow," claimed that her father was her mother's "saving support" throughout her various travails. Lewis said that her mother "could never have felt lost while he was by her side."[40] Children too offered assistance, company, and comfort to the older women of a family. While the men were gone in the fields, working in a shop, practicing a profession, or making trips, children were often women's solace, friends, and helpers. According to Lewis, she and her siblings were not only her mother's assistants, but her friends and confidantes as well.[41]

The ability of many women to concentrate on their hopes and dreams, create and enjoy socializing, serve as cultural conservators, and form strong bonds with others—both female and male—helped them triumph over the innumerable demands of the West. Although the Plains was an especially difficult environment for women, they were not generally disoriented, depressed, or in disarray. Rather, the majority of them managed to maintain homes and families, carry out domestic functions, and perpetuate the many values associated with the home. While depression, insanity, or bitterness characterized some women's lives, many more were able to respond to the challenges and hardships involved in Plains living in ways that insured survival and often brought contentment and satisfaction as well.

Although the preceding essay focuses on the Great Plains, the testimony of women makes it very clear that they faced problems no matter where they lived in the American West. Something as simple, but aggravating, as poor housing could cause distress. This Wyoming woman was rather sanguine about the shack she lived in during 1903:

There was a make-shift of a log house on the place we bought, we made it our quarters for the first year as there were other improvements that had to be taken care of. . . . The house was a habitat for pack rats, they are a curious little animal, when everything is quiet they come out of hiding to investigate. If I was sitting quietly at my work I would keep the 22 rifle at my side, there were plenty of holes in the old house for them to come in, at night they would run along the logs above the bed, it was a little too much for peaceful rest, I would get up and place a chair in the middle of the room, light the lamp and would wait for the rat with the 22 rifle across my knees, not long until I had my rat, the shot seemed to scare the others away, we had no fine furniture or plastered walls so it made no difference where the bullet hit. . . .[42]

Often, as suggested in the previous essay, a woman's problems could be ones that threatened property, stock, and human lives. A North Dakotan wrote home in 1889 about what she called the fire-fiend:

I write to tell you the "Fire-Fiend" has again visited us early this morning we were awakened by a man pounding on the door, yelling "fire"! I jumped out of bed and looked toward the barn—and saw the awful sight—that our new and pretty barn was all on fire—the flames just bursting through the roof on the northwest corner. . . . Hub, Oliver and our man ran out, almost naked, and tried to save the poor stock, but were too late. . . . One horse had got loose and got nere the door and fell—when Hub tried to pull him out he too fell and came nere losing his life. Nothing could be done, except to pull the chickens out of their coop close by and then some of them flew back into the fire. . . . Poor Hub! he just cried aloud when he saw the poor things dieing in the Fire. . . . Shep-dog was also burned. . . .[43]

Wars, of course, also threatened property and lives. A woman recalled how women in Victoria, Texas, during the late 1830s responded to the pressure of a likely war with Mexicans who opposed American rule in Texas:

War was being agitated and shortly after developed. Placido Benevidas organized a company. The women all met at the home of Mrs. John Linn to mold bullets and in other ways to assist the cause espoused by their husbands. . . . The company joined Fannin at La Bahia, every man going who could shoulder a gun. Fannin, finding the invading army was very immense, detailed the men of families to move their families out of danger before the arrival of the Mexican forces. Mr. Quinn [the author's stepfather] was one of these. . . .

Many frights were had through rumors of the return of the Mexican army or of the Indians. On one occasion all the families were brought to Market Square for better protection. . . . They were home but a short time—the same year—when another order came for the families to leave. [We] again went across the Navidad and spent Christmas near Mr. Wilde's place on the Carancahua. Again [we] took possession of the Coleman house, coming back from Carancahua, and spent the remaining part of the winter there—1837. Mr. Quinn farmed, making a fine crop of corn. While [we] lived here the Texas army was camped at Red Bluff, one mile below Coleman's ranch. . . .[44]

American determination to seize the entire Southwest also kept Mexican women in a state of worry and despair. A Mexican woman recollected her feeling about the American take-over of California:

I told the Padre that I wanted to go to San Juan Capistrano where the family of Forster was. I was very sad about the capturing of the country by the Americans, and for this reason, I did not want to return to San Diego.

Then the Padre told me, "Well, yes, you can go to San Juan. I will go there too." We went first to Santa Margarita, and we remained there about eight days. . . . I was obsessed with the thing about the Americans. I don't know what I imagined, perhaps through my going away the Americans would go away too. . . .

The Padre and I were returning carrying seeds, corn, chile, and other things, and we had arrived at Santa Margarita on the way to San Diego when Señor Don José Joachin Ortega who, bound for Los Angeles, had stopped at Santa Margarita, arrived. . . . he had talked with someone that had arrived from Los Angeles who had told him that it was going to make war and that the people of the pueblo were gathering to see if they could put the Americans out of our country. . . . We stayed at the mission [of Santa Margarita] about two months. . . .

The family of Doña Juana Moreno, which was going approximately in the direction of Los Angeles where their relatives were, had arrived. They told us that all the families were abandoning San Diego. . . .

When the American forces came by the Colorado River (I believe it was in 1830 or 31) Captain Magruder arrived with them. He asked Señor Forster who owned Rancho Jamacha. Forster told him that it was mine and that he was in charge of it. Magruder asked him if he might borrow it to put there the herds of the troop, and Señor Forster, acting with the trust I had placed in him, lent the ranch to him. I never saw my ranch again, nor did I know anything about it because Don Juan Forster went to a rancho of his own, and I did not see him again. When the Americans had won the war, Señor Magruder came to San Juan Capistrano where I was staying and spoke to me about the rancho. He asked if I wanted to lend it to him again. It is certain that I received nothing for the use of the rancho and that finally someone, perhaps Señor Magruder, took possession of my rancho. He, the second time that he wanted to borrow it, insisted that I should sell it, and I refused. . . . The other two ranchos were taken from me in some manner. Thus it is after having worked so many years, of having possessed properties of which I did not dispose by sale or by any other means, I find myself in the greatest poverty, living by the favor of God, and them that give me a morsel to eat. . . .[45]

Even though the Civil War was not fought in the West, it menaced women in a number of ways. States and territories split apart. This Kansas woman had bitter memories of her state's support of the Union in what she called "the great struggle":

Then came the great struggle between Freedom and slavery. . . . [Colonel James H.] Lane and others travelled over the territory all the time raising one regiment after another until it looked as though all of Kansas were hurrying to the front. . . . G. W. Packard [her future husband] left all his chances for wealth and joined the 9th Kansas and lived in the saddle for three years and a half. His time was spent escorting trains and hunting out bushwackers. Many left their families and joined the army. Harrison Hannahs, an enterprising farmer from Vermont, left his wife and two little ones with friends in Topeka and hurried away to the army. She was sick at the time but as soon as she could travel went east with her brother, but was taken worse on the way and died before reaching home. . . .

We made butter and cheese for sale and began about this time to sell milk. The Lawrence raid was in 1863 when more than 120 were butchered in cold blood. The Price raid was in the last part of the summer of 1864. The militia were called out. All men between 18 and 45 were hurried away to the front and those between 14 and 18 and 45 and 60 were ordered to guard the towns. They patrolled every road with gun and sabre. . . .

Our men came home all right, but 16 of the men from Shawnee Co. were left on the battlefield of the Blue. . . . G. W. Packard arrived at home in March 1866, and we were married April 19 of the same year. . . . He served in the army 4 years and 3 months and when mustered out his health was so broken that he never was well again. . . .[46]

Texans, who fought on the side of the Confederacy, also had troubles during the Civil War. A Texas woman talked about the ways in which women in Indianola on Matagorda Bay responded to the privations of the war:

Texas seceded from the Union on the 4th day of March 1861. The U.S. troops on the frontier were ordered back North. A company came to Indianola to embark. They marched with lively steps to the tune of Yankee Doodle, down to the wharf, where they boarded a vessel and started on their way rejoicing. They had not proceeded far when they were overtaken by Col. Van Dorn of the Steamer Rusk, joined by volunteers, some of them from Indianola, captured and brought back to the city where they were paroled and allowed to proceed on their way. . . .

We soon began to feel the privations which war entailed upon us, but we met them with brave hearts for we were full of patriotism in those days. Mrs. D. C. Proctor and other ladies took the lead in carding cotton, spinning thread, knitting and making comforts for our soldier boys. Companies were being formed and men drilled in military tactics. . . . Some people were quite optimistic, but they little knew.

The saying "Necessity is the mother of invention" was certainly exemplified in war times. Father bought a side of tanned leather for our shoe soles, the uppers were made of an old cloak of his, very heavy black material. Mother made a pair of pants out of a parlor table cover of wool, dyed it with the rind of pomegranates. . . . I made hats for the boys out of shucks or palmetto and mother made them cloth caps for winter wear. After the Yankees left a great deal of cast-off clothing was found. Mother boiled it in lye water, rinsed it thoroughly and dyed it with pomegranate rinds or pecan hulls and made it into clothes for the boys.

An iron mortar and pestle was used for pounding various things, as coarse salt, cloves, mustard, etc. Our bread was usually made of cornmeal as flour was scarce, but occasionally mother would make a batch of biscuits and we would count them to see how many there would be apiece. During the war we made tallow candles. . . .

Soon a company of negro soldiers was stationed near us. They seemed to be turned loose at first and went shouting around our places like a lot of demons; presently they began driving off our hogs, when father went out to protest and threatened to report them at headquarters, they picked up sticks and told him they would beat his brains out if he moved a step farther. . . . In the meantime mother had gone out through the grapevine arbor and on to camp where she reported their depredations to their white officers. Immediately two of them mounted their horses and came dashing up to the house. At the sight of them the negroes fled like chaff before the wind. That night the two young officers came to our house to apologize for the conduct of their men . . . the soldiers annoyed us so much we were obliged to apply for a guard. . . . Finally, mother took an officer and his wife to board with us, as she felt we would be more secure with them in the house. . . .[47]

Violence was not only associated with wars, however. A Colorado woman told in a matter-of-fact way of witnessing hangings in Denver in 1860 and 1869:

One day a man came down riding on a white horse and tied the horse to a large cottonwood tree just in front of the school house. . . . The man was George Steele, a notorious character, and had ridden to town to make William N. Byers, the editor of the *Rocky Mountain News*, retract some statements regarding this man Steele's career. This Mr. Byers refused to do. Mother wrapped sister, brother and myself in buffalo robes and put us in the attic so that no stray bullets could touch us, since friends of Steele had gathered close to our home, prepared to fight for him. Afterwards Steele was shot and killed at Bradford's Corner, now known as Larimer and Sixteenth Streets.

About the same time a young man, named Jim Gordan, who, when under the influence of liquor, was very quarrelsome, had killed a young German. After several trials he was acquitted under the flimsy excuse of "No Jurisdiction." This angered the Germans and they took it into their own hands and hung Gordan on a Saturday in July, 1860. I witnessed this hanging.

Nine years later, 1869, I saw Musgrove hung under the Larimer Street bridge. He was a stock thief, a general outlaw. . . .[48]

Other women recalled their lives as ones of constant fear. A Hispanic woman recounted several upheavals she experienced while living on a ranch near the San Pedro River at Tanque Verde in Arizona during the 1880s and 1890s:

Living on ranches meant constant fear. There was a saloon near by where the Texans occasionally visited. My husband had a narrow escape once; one of the laborers brought him a horse and he left before breakfast. Arriving at the ranch he found a big fire going on burning the Texans' masks which they had taken off. . . .

In 1881 we heard the terrible powder-house explosion distinctly at the ranch, the detonation was most terrible, horrifying; even the Chinese in Tucson we were told ran to the church crying, "Me Catoleek." My brother-in-law had a mine at Tierras Flojas, and when on the way to it we used to pass the powder-house. The man in charge disappeared; no one heard of him again. . . .

It was customary in those days to celebrate "La Fiesta de San Agus-tín" at Levin's Park (where the Womans Club is located now.) They used to have a dancing platform. Once it happened that an Apache squaw called Luisa was dancing, when Petrita Santa Cruz came along, and looking at the Apache squaw said "That is enough get out, we went to dance." The Apache squaw replied "I am a person too. . . ."[49]

Because the mad rush for gold brought thousands of people into California before law and governments could be established, California especially suffered outbreaks of violence during the late 1840s and 1850s. A California woman stated her position on the situation:

In the early part of '53 strict laws and the vigilantes sent an ever moving stream of human microbes from the cities—gun men, gamblers, blacklegs, and all the new class of the sporting element (men and women) to this county. They considered our hard-working miners lawful prey; and immediately introduced methods to reap the harvest. They used the method unsparingly, mercilessly and thoroughly, introducing all kinds of new gambling games. In the most unexpected places they started groggeries, where both men and women lived, sold whiskey, and gambled; sometimes with music and dancing. . . . as we all know, whiskey makes a confused and helpless fool out of a man. The honest, hard-working miner entered these dens of vice, to be robbed of his gold, his health, and often his life. . . .

Every succeeding year brought thousands to California. . . . Conditions changed for the people, and not for their betterment,—men wore guns and shot to kill. Not only conditions of the Pioneers changed, but the faces of nature was fain to confess the superior predatory capacity of the newcomers. Denuded hillsides, banks of gravel, tail-races, ditches, tailings, and stumps and boulders were in evidence, wherever gold could be found. . . .

In the Fall of 1854 my father moved from Shaws Flat to an unbroken wilderness, where feet of white men had seldom trod, and never those of a white woman. . . . In June, 1856, without warning of the awful shadow of death that was hovering over our peaceful home, my father was shot to death in French Bar, now known as La Grange. Oh, the awful sorrow and desolation of that bereft home! Another cold-blooded murder . . .[50]

Trouble erupted within families as well. A California woman of the early 1910s described her husband's verbal abuse:

While in the company of others, Papa [her husband], overflowed with laughter, but the minute he came home, he became yakamashi [stern, fault-finding]. At home he disciplined the children. He got angry if they used one word of English: "Use Japanese!" he admonished. . . . Even if I wanted to speak English, I couldn't. He wouldn't let me. "The children will naturally learn English," he said. Therefore at home they received discipline in Japanese: the language, social graces, practical wisdom.

He was severe. If I sat around not taking care of the household chores after coming home from work, he would say, "Don't go to work. After the household chores are taken care of, then go to work." He believed that a woman should never be idle for one minute. In the mornings, if I didn't come to the kitchen with my hair fixed neatly, he would get angry. Or if I came with slippers, he would say, "Go back into the bedroom and fix your hair and get dressed before you come out again." After marrying Papa, I have never risen after the sun was up. Even now, past four in the morning I can't stay in bed.

It has been that way between Papa and me ever since we got married. He never treated me well . . . birthdays . . . presents . . . clothes . . . who ever heard of such things? If I went into town, it was because my children were sick—not to have fun. But once I got married, I never entertained the thought of divorce. As long as he brought home enough to feed the children, I didn't care. Even if he was gone for a month, I didn't complain as long as my children could eat. . . .[51]

An Alaska woman, whose family settled in Fairbanks in 1906, recalled that her father was physically abusive when he was drinking:

Father was a big six-footer with red hair and blue eyes. He had a grand voice for singing Irish tunes and was very charming when so inclined. But Father had another side which he reserved mostly for family life. We never knew when he would go off on a week's drinking spree. . . . When

Mother heard him coming she hid Adolph and me under the bed. Poor little Mother, many a black-and-blue mark she tried to cover up and pretend it never happened.

A few days after Thanksgiving that first winter in Fairbanks, Father hooked up his dog team to a large basket sled, loaded it with his winter camping outfit, and took off. That was after he had cleaned out the food in the cabin and the money Mother had managed to save. Just before he cracked the whip over the back of the malamutes, he said to Mother, "Get busy and rustle a job so you can feed the kids."

The nicest things I can remember about Father were his absences. Mother took in sewing, nursed the sick, or waited on table to earn a few dollars. . . . Adolph and I were delighted to be left alone with Mother. . . .[52]

Abuse also came from men other than husbands. A former slave in Texas portrays her master's cruel treatment:

Dere am one thing Massa Hawkins does to me what I can't shunt from my mind. I knows he don't do it for meanness, but I allus holds it 'gainst him. What he done am force me to live with dat nigger, Rufus, 'gainst my wants. After I been at he place 'bout a year, de massa come to me and say, "You gwine live with Rufus in dat cabin over yonder. Go fix it for livin'." I's 'bout sixteen year old and has no larnin', and I's jus' ingo'mus chile. I's thought dat him mean for me to tend de cabin for Rufus and some other niggers. . . .

I's took charge of de cabin after work am done and fixes supper. Now, I don't like dat Rufus, 'cause he a bully. He am big and 'cause he so, he think everybody do what him say. We'uns has supper, den I goes here and dere talkin', till I's ready for sleep and den I gits in de bunk. After I's in, dat nigger come and crawl in de bunk with me 'fore I knows it. I says, "What you means, you fool nigger?" He say for me to hush de mouth. "Dis am my bunk, too," he say.

"You's teched in de head. Git out," I's told him, and I puts de feet 'gainst him and give him a shove and out he go on de floor 'fore he knew what I's doin'. Dat nigger jump up and he mad. He look like de wild bear. He starts for de bunk and I jumps quick for de poker. It am 'bout three feet long and when he comes at me I lets him have it over de head. Did dat nigger stop in he tracks? I's say he did. He looks at me steady for a minute and you's could tell he thinkin' hard. Den he go and set on de bench and say, "Jus wait. You thinks it am smart, but you's am foolish in de head. Dey's gwine larn you something."

"Hush yous big mouth and stay 'way from dis nigger, dat all I wants," I say and jus' sets and hold dat poker in de hand. He jus' sets, lookin' like de bull. Dare we'uns sets and sets for 'bout an hour and den he go out and I bars de door. De nex' day I goes to de missy and tells her what Rufus wants and missy say dat am de massa's wishes. She say, "yous am de portly gal and Rufus am de portly man. De massa wants you-uns for to bring forth portly chillen."

I's thinkin' 'bout what de missy say, but say to myse'f, "I's not gwine live with dat Rufus." Dat night when him come in de cabin, I grabs de poker and sits on de bench and says, "Git 'way from me, nigger, 'fore I busts yous brains out and stomp on dem." He say nothin' and git out. De nex' day de massa call me and tell me, "Woman, I's pay big money for you and I's done dat for de cause I wants yous to raise me chillens. I's put yous to live with Rufus for dat purpose. Now, if you doesn't want whippin' at de stake, yous do what I wants. . . ."

Dere it am. What am I's to do? So I 'cides to do as de massa wish and so I yields. . . . I never marries, 'cause one 'sperience am 'nough for dis nigger. After what I does for de massa, I's never wants no truck with any man. De Lawd forgive dis cullud woman, but he have to 'scuse me and look for some others for to 'plenish de earth.[53]

But even if African American women were free, they still suffered discriminatory treatment. A Roslyn, Washington, woman who migrated to the state in 1888 explains one reason:

I am a descendent of one of the members of the group of Negroes who came out to break the strike against the N.W.I. Company during the years 1888–1889. The term N.W.I. stands for North Western Improvement Company, which is a subsidiary of the Northern Pacific Railroad Co. . . .

The first group was recruited in Breakwood, Illinois, by Jim Sheppardson. They came out on the train as far as Cle Elum, Washington, and they were put on another train and sent up the Roslyn Spur. Rumors were that strikers in Roslyn were to blow up the train and if my memory serves me right, being told by older people who came out at the same time, dynamite was found along the tracks. The newcomers came through Roslyn with shotguns, revolvers, and so forth, loaded to protect the families and other people on the train. The newcomers were allowed to stay in Roslyn for a number of years but made their home at Jonesville, later named Ronald, Washington, also known among the settlers as Number 3. . . .

The reason was not so much that they were prejudiced against Negroes, but just the fact that they were strike breakers. . . . they had come out to break the strike, to work in the mines where the Caucasians were unable to do this because they were on a strike. And I started to say that also they would come down and they had to be protected when they went in the mines and they had to be protected when they came in to Roslyn to buy their food supply. But in later years, and it was a very short period of time, when the strike was over, the Negroes settled in

Roslyn. They brought homes, some of them continued to work in the mines. . . .[54]

Clearly, women everywhere in the West faced difficulties, some transitory and others long-term. How they dealt with these problems is a story in itself, one that is characterized by perseverance, adaptability, and creativity, but also sometimes by pain and suffering. But most women did whatever had to be done and pushed into whatever realm of life necessary to achieve their goals. A determination to have a better life helped women through difficult situations. In this excerpt, a missionary who worked with Narcissa Whitman in Washington during the 1830s revealed the zeal that was her reward for going West:

Nov. 29, 1836, Nez Perces Mission. Yesterday reached this desirable spot, where we expect to dwell the remainder of our earthly pilgrimage. As yet our dwelling is an Indian lodge. . . .

Jan. 27, 1837. By the blessing of God we are now in a comfortable dwelling, and in circumstances to devote a few hours daily to instructing the natives, who really appear eager to receive instruction—may we who have the privilege of being with the people in the capacity of teachers, be faithful and enabled to impart instruction to them which will be blest to the salvation of their precious souls. . . .

March 20, 1837. Our prospects of usefulness among this people appear very promising, they seem to manifest an increasing interest in instruction, particularly the story of the cross. I have prepared some paintings representing several important events recorded in Scripture, these we find a great help in communicating instruction to ignorant minds, whose language, as yet we speak very imperfectly. The children, in particular, are interested in learning to read, several are beginning to read in the Testament. . . .

June 15, 1837. We feel happy and satisfied with our situation and employment, though it removes us far from almost all we hold dear on earth. The privilege of laboring to introduce the blessings of the Gospel of our adorable Redeemer among the destitute heathen will more than compensate for all we have laid aside for this blessed object. We find this people anxious to receive instruction and to have their children into our family—as yet they appear promising. We hope to come into circumstances soon to do more to benefit the children, for they are our hope of the nation. . . .[55]

A Montana woman was so delighted to have escaped factory work and slum-living in Chicago in 1917 she was willing to learn whatever she needed to survive in the West:

When I came out to Montana I didn't see 500 people in the 21 years I lived on the ranch. But after walking to and from work a distance of 7 miles a day for ten years—walking after a breaking plow was a pleasure to me and just to be out in the fresh air and sunshine was heaven. And to have an eight-room house all to myself after living in a tenement building that had 23 families and three stores in it, it was more than I ever again hoped to have. . . .

I knew nothing about cooking or building a fire in a cookstove, nor could I keep it going after my husband started a fire for me. That lignite coal had me stumped. . . . it was a blessing he knew how to cook or we would have both starved to death. . . .

I had never made a garden or never seen one. I did not know radishes from cucumbers when I did go over to my neighbors and she sent me down to dig some potatoes. I looked high and low, pulled up a beet and a turnip, looked up in the plum trees, gooseberry bushes and no potatoes. I told my neighbor, she had no potatoes left, why she said they had in an acre of potatoes, so she came down to the garden, took a hoe and chopped off the tops (some of the potatoes were still blooming) I thought she was angry at me for not bringing the potatoes, so she was chopping down the pretty flowers. She took a spade, dug down and turned the ground over and lo and behold there were the potatoes. I said no wonder I couldn't find them, way down deep in the ground like they were. I told her I had never seen them grow before. I made my own garden and as I looked on the package of seed I thought that little tiny seed won't made a radish or cucumber or turnip. So I'd throw the whole package down in one place. . . .

I decided to wash clothes one day and the water would not suds and the clothes looked so yellow. I told my neighbor about it, and she told me I had to break the water that was hard. I had never heard of breaking water, so I thought she was crazy too, and let it go at that. . . .

Came time to raise chickens, and my husband only had a few hens at that time I thought that I'd raise a lot of them so that I could have fried chicken every day. I had a neighbor ask me if I had ever set a hen, when I answered all I knew about chickens was that you bought them at the butchers, he decided to have some fun, and fun he did have. He told me I had to have a cluck to set. When I asked what that was, he said a hen that wants to set, he said she made a clucking noise, and you gave her a batch of eggs, put a rock on her back and that was all there was to it. . . . I walked over to my neighbors and got all the eggs they could spare (which was a 15 dozen crate) I couldn't wait for it to get dark so the hens would go to roost so I could go and get those clucks and set them. So when the hens were all on the roosts I went down to the chicken house and gave each hen a poke, if she made a noise, she was a cluck, of course they all made a noise, so I got busy. I gathered boxes and baskets and set all 15 dozen eggs, put a rock on each hen's back (our place had a lot of shale rock on it), and I would hardly wait for morning to come. You see I thought those chickens would hatch overnight. So 4:00 a.m. I

was up and down to the chicken house and out came all the hens. The
rocks had slipped off and smashed the eggs. Naturally, I stood there
crying. So when the neighbor came over later that day I would hardly
speak to him and I finally told him what I thought of him and I showed
him the smashed eggs and when he saw the mess, did he ever laugh! He
told me the hens had to cover the eggs to keep them warm for 21 days
before they hatched, and I made up mind he was crazy too. . . .

I was willing to learn and I was bound to show my neighbors that
where there's a will there's a way. So learn I did. I learned to do all the
field work—plowing with a sulky plow and three horses, stacking hay,
shocking, mowing, milking, raising chickens, make garden and the
hundred and one other things. I even helped my husband break broncs. I
held on to the trip rope. . . . I learned to like the wide open spaces and
would not go back to live in Chicago if they gave me the entire city with
a fence around it. . . .[56]

*A southern Oregon woman who migrated with her husband to the Rogue River
Valley in 1853 dreamed of economic prosperity:*

Friday, May 20. Pleasant weather, alternate sunshine. Clouds and show-
ers. Mr Butler [her husband] breaking prairie . . . as to myself I am maid
of all traids, sweeping dusting churning ironing baking bread and pies
dishwashing &c. . . .

Monday, May 23. The men are weeding their garden, fine growing
weather, hope to raise a great many vegetables as we anticipate a large
emigration this year and thereby have aplenty for them to eat. I am attending to my domestic duties as usual

Tuesday, May 24. Acceptionally warm this forenoon, quite a pretty
little shower this afternoon accompanied with hard thunder and a change
of the atmosphere. Quite a number of packtrains this week for Wyre[ka]
three today. Provisions cheap

Wednesday, May 25. This is one of Mays bright and beautiful day, all
hands are busily employed and our crop looks very flourishing. The prospect is good, what the final resul[ts] will be we cannot tell. . . .[57]

*Other women hoped that improved health would be their reward for moving to
the American West. An Englishwoman described the health-seekers she saw in
Colorado in 1873:*

I have made the acquaintance of all the careworn, struggling settlers
within a walk. All have come for health, and most have found or are
finding it, even if they have not better shelter than a wagon tilt or a blanket on sticks laid across four poles. The climate of Colorado is considered
the finest in North America, and consumptives, asthmatics, dyspeptics,
and sufferers from nervous diseases, are here in hundreds and thousands,

either trying the "camp cure" for three or four months, or settling here permanently. People can safely sleep out of doors for six months of the year.... The air, besides being much rarefied, is very dry. The rainfall is far below the average, dews are rare, and fogs nearly unknown. The sunshine is bright and almost constant, and three-fourths of the days are cloudless. The milk, beef, and bread are good. The climate is neither so hot in summer nor so cold in winter as that of the States, and when the days are hot the nights are cool....[58]

Social life was important also to women's survival. Many women knew, or soon learned, how to create or maximize social opportunities. A Montana woman explains that their entertainment during the early 1890s was sometimes rough:

Nearly everyone went to the dances which were the center of our social life. Balls were infrequent, but a *dance*, that was different.... With a fiddler, possibly a guitar player, a good caller, and a crowd of neighbors, the fun went on until morning. Square dances were the most popular, because more of the men could dance them. The waltz was a little difficult for many ...

Once in awhile, a traveling show came to town and performed in the Opera House. *Uncle Tom's Cabin* was played annually. The first real drama that I can remember here was Ibsin's [sic] "A Doll's House," played by a brave little troupe from somewhere. Between acts, one of their number came out and sang, "On the Road to Mandalay," and it was the talk of the town for months....

Our local entertainment was sometimes rough. Charivaris are considered relics of the Dark Ages, but the whole town enjoyed one the wedding night of the "Heart and Hand" bride. Serenaders swept all through town, gathered at the Mayor's house, and kept going until morning. Times must have changed, because we read in the papers about correspondence marriages turning out wrong, but this one is still a success....[59]

Other women turned to the natural environment for entertainment during good weather and relied upon visitors during the bad. A Wyoming woman who homesteaded on her own around 1910 describes her adventures:

I must tell of one expedition we had to the canyons.... Bessie and I ... hitched up Maude, a pretty buckskin mare, young and just broke to harness, weighing possibly 1500 pounds, to the spring wagon; loaded up the lunch and ourselves and drove out to the brakes. Locating a spring we decided on that spot as a suitable place to prepare and partake of our dinner. With stones we soon built a fireplace and in a short time the cabbage was cooking in a pail, eggs and coffee had their turns. Oh! we had a grand dinner and a grand time! What fun we had scrambling over the rocks and peeking into caves. . . .

We took other interesting trips later—one to Cedar Canyon and to Box Elder Canyon, Maude taking us over each time in the little wagon. On one trip we encountered rattlers—Jennie would break their backs with the buggy whip and the rest of us would kill them, by crushing their heads and lastly placing a rock on each of the mutilated members. . . . We wandered about enjoying the rocks, trees, grass, creek and contrasting scenery with that of the plains. Nearing noon hour we prepared dinner, cooking it over an old abandoned camp stove. . . . During the afternoon we saw on an opposite ledge a nest made of sticks and some large birds resembling eagles circling over it. Late mid afternoon we returned to our several homes tired but happy. . . .

In January I was granted a very pleasant surprise by having my mother come to see me. She chanced a hazardous trip into the West by starting out from Eagle Grove [Iowa] immediately after a heavy snowstorm. Late trains brought her into Omaha [Nebraska] unable to make good connections for Burns, Wyoming, where she spent a few days attempting the final run to Chugwater. . . . after a ride through snow coach high, reached Chugwater—tired and with a lame back. . . .

How appropriate for me, to have Mother select this shut in season, as the time for her visit. I had been quite alone these days. . . . Indeed it was wonderful for me to have Mother here, but how would it be for Mother? She, however adapted herself to conditions and surroundings. . . .

Ere we realized it six weeks of Mother's visit had passed by, and she thought she must return home. On February 18, a mild Sabbath day we attended church services. We were invited to a neighbor's for dinner. Late in the afternoon we walked homeward—twas snowing softly, the air was calm and quiet, the sky was gradually becoming grayer, some subconscious feeling gave us the urge to seek shelter and protection. We returned to the shack, brought in an extra supply of fuel and the shovel. The snow continued to fall, it was coming down thick when we retired. For six weeks Mother and I were truly "shut ins." It would snow at intervals, then the wind would pile the snow into great drifts. . . . Neighbors would watch mornings for smoke to emit from our stove pipe, that would indicate that "All's Well" with Mother and me. We did not carry water these days but melted snow for cooking, drinking and washing. . . .

Mother returned to Iowa the latter part of March. Instead of six weeks as the had planned, her stay covered a period of nearly twelve weeks. To be sure I would miss her but was comforted by the fact that in two months I could make final proof of my homestead. . . . It was a joy to live in this great, broad, newly awakened, out-of-doors again. The birds were returning, the gophers too, whistled greetings to me. . . .[60]

Women took their duties as family and cultural conservators seriously. Many believed they had a mission in the new land—to preserve their ethnic and racial heritages, to perpetuate family traditions, and to establish churches and schools. An Oklahoma woman tells how she organized the first Sunday school and helped build the first church in her area:

I came to the Chickasaw Nation, August, 1897, and located near Marietta; then one year later I moved to the Seminole Nation on a farm near Wewoka. When I moved here there were no churches but I soon organized a Sunday School in my own home for the colored people. I soon had several in attendance; we used old quarterlies that I had had for several years.

My home became too small for the Sunday School; an old Indian lady, Aunt Lesser Bowleg, had a large corn-crib made of logs. She told me we could have the building to meet in, so on the following Monday morning I arose before daybreak and moved all the corn from the building, then we went to the woods and cut logs and split them for seats, made a table from a box and the new location was ready for worshipping the next Sunday. I finally got the aid of a publishing Company and wrote them about ordering the literature and we soon had $15.00 in donations.

We then organized a colored Methodist Church which was the first Methodist Church organized for the colored people. . . .[61]

Other women sowed seeds of religion wherever they happened to be. An army wife on her way to join her husband in a western fort in 1866 wrote her family about this incident:

I am spending Sunday in one of these mushroom western towns [Odin, Texas]. . . . This is rather a heathenish place; none of the servants at the tavern knew where a church was. However, I discovered one at last and attended it. It was a square brick building—two storied. In the upper part was held the "Church of the Disciples," as I was told. The ground floor was devoted to the Presbyterians. We had a curious sermon full of western expressions—the shorter catechism was "as full of bible truths as an egg is of meat." I found a class without a teacher at the Sunday school before church and sowed a little seed by the wayside.[62]

Even women who were not especially religious often felt they had to take a stand of some sort. A Wyoming woman who migrated with her family to the vicinity of Worland in 1909 explained her position:

Now, when I write that "we have been to church today" do not think that I went because I was "good." I go, because I must take a stand in this careless, Godless country, and stand for the influences which I wish my children to grow to maturity under. This is a confession—I am always glad and relieved when something turns up (perhaps the weather) to make it inadvisable to go to church so far . . .[63]

Other women were interested in education—in building schools, expanding education, and in taking advantage of the trend toward coeducation in the West. A Mexican American woman in Wyoming relates how she was able to help educate Spanish-speaking children beginning around 1930:

After I finished high school I did some substitute teaching children Spanish. A Spanish class at the high school. And then, of course, I wanted to go to college but that was out of the question because we were poor. . . . in later years, I had the opportunity of teaching a family of four boys, I think they were from Mexico. The whole family came over and they didn't know a bit of English. And right here at Lincoln School I taught them English. . . . So you see when I did this teaching I could, well I knew how to get started, I knew what was more important. I could identify with their needs. And one of the teachers said, "Well, how did you do that? How did you get these children?" Now they don't need a teacher. And they're speaking English . . . that was satisfying . . .[64]

Another influence that helped women adapt to the West was their ability to reach out to each other—to effectively network. They assisted each other with their daily work and with more serious matters as well. When her husband died in 1893, this North Dakota woman was relieved that her neighbors came to help:

. . . at 4:00 o'clock in the afternoon he passed away. You can perhaps imagine our terrible plight when the Doctors closed the house, and the children and I had to stay all night in the kitchen. We did not have even a quilt or pillow, so the children slept on grain sacks; there were six of them—the baby was fourteen months old. . . . The undertaker came about twelve o'clock midnight with the casket and next morning at ten o'clock they took the body to Forest River and laid it away in a new cemetery. My baby was very ill and I could not go to the burial. However, our neighbor women came and opened up the house and white-washed the walls, and some of them washed bed clothes and got the house cleaned up and we moved in. Oh! but it was so lonely and I was prostrated and had to give up. Mrs. Kearns took my baby over to her house for ten days and kept her—she was not weaned at that time—she was a nursing baby. We were all sick and right here I will say the support and sympathy I received from my neighbors and friends I will never forget. . . .[65]

Problems other than death weighed on women's minds. When a young Mexican woman met with language difficulties and discriminatory treatment after her family's move to Laramie around 1920, she turned to other women to help ease her situation:

I was four years old when I came to Laramie, my brother was 6 years old. . . . he waited until I was 6 years old, in those days we could start [school] when we were six, we didn't have to wait until we were 7. And so he waited until I would be able to start with him. . . . And we had a teacher, her name was Bert White. . . . I often wondered how she could teach us English when we knew none at all. . . . I remember one time she sent me downtown with some money to buy some thread and some needles and that way I could use the language, bring what she wanted and also work with, you see with money. [We] often marveled how that woman taught us. . . . I was the first Mexican to graduate from this town. And that was very satisfying.

I'd like to speak about communication between different people in different cultures. When we were going to here to Lincoln School, there was the family that lived right here on Thompson in the second house from the corner. Well, [their two boys] were always picking on my brother and I when we were coming home. They would pick on us continuously. They'd throw rocks at us and insults and like, beat us up, you know. Well we'd come home and cry to mother and dad, well, they didn't speak much English so they weren't going to get involved. And one day I got up the courage and I said, "Now Joe, I'm going to speak to [their mother] about this, this is enough." And she said, "Consuelo, why didn't you come tell me? I didn't know this was going on," she said. "This is going to be corrected."

I'm bringing this up to show that sometime there's a link, a failure in a line of communication. And if there is communication some of these prejudices will be erased. You know, although we've had a hard time. The Mexican people at that time, there was a lot of discrimination. . . .[66]

Other women also reached out across ethnic and racial lines. An Anglo woman in New Mexico gave her view of her relations with Mexican women in Santa Fe in 1846:

This morning a Mexican lady, Doña Juliana, called to see me. She is a woman poor in the goods of this world, a great friend to the Americans and especially to the Magoffins whom she calls a mui bien famile [muy buena familia—very good family]. Though my knowledge of Spanish is quite limited we carried on conversation for half an hour alone, and whether correct or not she insists that I am a good scholar. . . .

Una Señora [a lady] called to see me today, mi alma [my husband] was in and interpreted for me, so my tongue was vale nada [no account]. Her name I do not know as yet, but her lengua [tongue] I do, for she kept in constant motion all the time of her visit, which lasted an hour and a half, very fashionable! She is a good lady I dare say; speaks in favour of the foreigners. . . .

Una Señora called this morning, and as usual when mi alma is out. I talked a good deal, she thinks I both speak and understand bastante [sufficiently]. What an inquisitive, quick people they are! Everyone must know if I have una madre un padre, hermanos e hermanas [a mother, father, brothers, and sisters], their names &c. They examine my work if I am engaged at any when they are in, and in an instant can tell me how it is done, though perhaps 'tis the first of the kind they have ever seen. . . .

What a polite people these Mexicans are, altho' they are looked upon as a half barbarous set by the generality of people. This morning I have rather taken a little protege, a little market girl. Sitting at the window and on the look out for vegetables, this little thing came along with green peas . . . she came in and we had a long conversation on matters and things in general, and I found that not more than six years old she is quite conversant in all things. On receiving her pay she bowed most politely, shook hands with a kind "adios" and "me alegro de verte bien" [I am glad to see you in good health], and also a promise to return tomorrow. . . .

A little Mexican boy of nine or ten years came this morning to mi alma to buy him. His story though affecting is soon told. Three years since the Apache Indians, beside depredations to other families, murdered his father (his mother was then dead) and carried him off prisoner. After three years of hard servitude among them, the little fellow ran off and found his way to the house of an old Mexican, who resides here on the bank of the River in a lone hut the picture of misery. Here this boy has been for two months under the fostering care of the old compadre [godfather], but growing weary of this life, which was not better than that with the Indians, he now wishes to be bought with the sum of $7.00 which he owes the old man for his protection. Tomorrow the money is to be paid & hence forth Francisco is our servant. . . .

. . . the old gentleman's single daughter Doña Josefita, [is] a very interesting and lady-like girl of twenty two years, she is affable, perfectly easy in her manners, and I think if some of the foreigners who have come into this country, and judged of the whole population from what they have seen on the frontiers, would, to see her a little time, be entirely satisfied of his error in regard to the refinement of the people. . . . The more I see of this family the more I like them, they are so kind and attentive, so desirous to make us easy, so anxious for our welfare in the disturbances of the country. I can't help loving them. The old gentleman remarked at breakfast this morning, that he sympathized—for the experience of many years has taught him that sympathy is a soothing balm—much with me in the troubles, dangers, and difficulties I have been in, those I am now in, and those that I may be in, but with all he says I am learning a lesson that not one could have taught me but experience, the ways of the world. . . .

This morning I have been to mass—not led by idle curiosity, not by a blind faith, a belief in the creed there practiced, but because tis the house of God, and whether Christian or pagan, I can worship there within myself, as well as in a protestant church, or my own private chamber. . . .[67]

Western women not only learned about other cultures from their relationships with other women, but also about political and social issues. A California woman of the 1890s and early 1900s explains that her ideas concerning women's roles and rights were changed by some of the leading women of the era, many of whom traveled and spoke of their causes in the West:

By no process that can be recalled or reasoned out, [I] found the pointers on [my] own trail going in the direction of women who desired the liberation of women for its own sake; not for its symbolic values nor for any subsidiary propagandist advantage; women touched with the same profound solicitude for the spiritual communion of mankind that moved Frances Willard, but manifesting it by achieved freedoms of their own. They dressed and wore their hair as it pleased them; declined to admit marriage as a bar to public careers; refused on every side to admit the pertinence of personal behavior to public appeal. There were such women beginning to appear on [my] horizon: Susan B. Anthony, whom once [I] heard; Dr. Anna Howard Shaw; Charlotte Perkins Stetson; Jane Addams. It was in the direction of these women that [I] felt invisibly drawn. Without previous contact [I] counter myself in on their claims on the reasonable conclusions of mankind. Without preamble or collusion, [I] found [myself] adopting their characteristic renunciation of charm as a means of establishing a personal advantage, the charm which they freely exercised on behalf of an audience. They could charm an audience . . . but the mark that they set between self-aggrandizement through the quality of that charm was clearly and deliberately thought. Mother Jones, when she came along in her turn, was, in that particular, precisely of their stripe; she could beguile the judge and the jury, or a hall full of the more or less contentious friends of labor; gray-haired and of ample girth, she would diddle newspaper reporters out of their most hard-boiled convictions, or abase her jailers to the condition of adolescent embarrassment; and she would have clouted any one of them on the head for hinting that he could win such concessions of entertainment from her on behalf of his being a male.

It was at this point that Frances Willard, great woman as she was, lost continuity with the purpose and intent of the woman's revolt. What she envisaged, what she almost achieved, was the remaking of society from the Hearth as the Sacred Middle; what those others hazarded was a remaking of the pattern in which the Hearth itself should be reformed, should itself be made to revolve about a Middle whose true name was as yet undiscerned, but as the lodestone of their compass deeply felt.[68]

Women also formally worked together in hundreds of types of clubs and organizations. From helping others to fighting for woman suffrage, women joined together to reach their goals. A Mormon woman who migrated first to Utah in

1860 and then to Nevada in 1891 felt that she derived more than she gave from the relief society and temple work she did all of her adult life:

In recent years, I have enjoyed working in the St. George temple. I am so happy to be able to do good in this way. I have found no other work that gives me so much satisfaction now that my children are grown and have families of their own. . . .

I have spent as much time as possible in Temple work, and have great joy in doing good in this way. . . .

On "Mother's Day," May 8th, [1938] I was honored at a special program in Sunday School and in Church. The Bishopric and members of the Relief Society had planned it. . . . The Singing Mothers (a group of Relief Society members) sang three beautiful numbers. . . . a group of about twenty little grandchildren marched up to where I sat and sang, "Happy Birthday to You, Dear Grandma," when two of them . . . placed on my head a wreath of roses that had been prepared by Sisters Annie E. Cox and Luella Leavitt. . . . Brothers Harmon Tobler and Thomas Adams each told of incidents in their lives when I had been of assistance to them in times of trouble, but which I had entirely forgotten. All in all it was a very pleasant occasion and I felt that I had many friends. . . .[69]

A final factor that enabled western women to persevere was the help and support of men and children. A Norwegian woman migrated to South Dakota with the help of a man in 1875 and also learned to speak and read English with the help of three children and their father:

I was seventeen years old when I came here. I came all alone. I had an uncle in South Dakota, just a little ways out of Vermillion. He sent my ticket and I came to him. He was a farmer. I didn't know much about America when I came. . . . We came out by train. I didn't speak English. . . . My first impression of United states was that I didn't like it. . . .

The family that I came to work for had three little girls and they had some of those first readers, and I got a hold of them and they loved to help me learn it. He [the girls' father] gave me plain stories to read. I got by very nicely. I liked to read. It was harder to learn to read, I think, than it was to learn to speak. . . .[70]

This California woman acquired a fortune during the early 1850s with the help of her father. Her story was told by a Marysville woman:

She was married very young, and in opposition to the wishes of her parents. Unfortunately, her married life proved miserable in the extreme. After a lapse of years, she returned penniless, with one child, to the home of her youth, where she received a hearty welcome from her father; but the gentle, loving mother, whom she had forsaken, had gone long since to the spirit-land. . . . She told her father that if he would furnish her with means, she would seek her fortune in California. . . .

She commenced keeping a boarding-house. She soon had thirty or forty boarders, for each of which she received twelve dollars per week. One day as she was sweeping her floor,—which, by the way, was nothing but the earth,—she saw something glitter. Upon examination, it proved to be a lump of gold. She searched farther, and found the earth was full of particles of gold. She . . . moved the table, benches, and stove. Upon the last-named utensil, a dinner was in progress; but who would think of preparing dinner, even if it were near the dinner hour, should they suddenly find themselves in possession of such rich diggings. This land, which she had appropriated to her own use, was situated in a central part of the town of Downieville. It had never been prospected, for the very reason that its appearance betokened nought to impress the beholder with the idea that gold existed there in such quantities. That day they two took from the kitchen floor, as she termed it, five hundred dollars, mostly in lumps. Every day witnessed similar success. . . .[71]

There were even some relatively kind slave owners in the West. A former Texas slave described her master in favorable terms:

Everybody call my massa Jedge Turner, but him am a Baptist preacher and have de small farm and gen'ral store. My pappy and mammy don't live together, 'cause pappy am own by Massa Jack Hooper. Massa Turner done marry dem. Mostest de cullud folks jus' lives together by 'greement den, but massa have de cer'mony.

Us live in log cabins with de dirt floor and no windows, and sleep on straw ticks. All de cookin' done in de eatin' shed but when pappy come over twict de week, mammy cooks him de meal den. Let me tell yous how de young'uns cared for. Massa give dem special care, with de food and lots of clabber and milk and pot-liquor, and dey all fat and healthy. . . .

Massa Turner wants de good days work and us all give it to him. Every Saturday night us git de pass if us wants to go to de party. Us have parties and dancin' de quadrille and fiddles and banjoes. On Sunday massa preach to us, 'cause he de preacher heself. He preach to de white folks, too.

I 'member dat surrender day. He call us round him. I can see him now, like I watches him come to de yard, with he hands clasp 'hind him and he head bowed. I know what he sayd, "I likes every one of you. You been faithful but I has to give you up. I hates to do it, not 'cause I don't want to free you, but 'cause I don't want to lose you all." Us see de tears in he eyes. . . .[72]

Nor were women always excluded from men's activities. Here a North Dakota woman told how women and men built a church together during the mid 1880s:

The women had a share in the enterprise. They provided a good meal when the men gathered to work. They made an autograph quilt on which people paid to have their names embroidered in red on white patches. Proceeds from that quilt made possible the final payment on the building so it was dedicated free of debt. A diary kept by the church treasurer records that local funds raised came to $100.00 which was a lot of money for those times and circumstances. It was dedicated December 1886 by the Rev. D. C. Plannette, a Methodist Presiding Elder from Grand Forks.[73]

Groups of men also came to women's assistance when necessary. A California woman who feared life in the diggings in 1849 soon discovered that the miners looked out for her and her child:

And now began my first experience in a California mining camp. . . . like a child fixing a play-house I sang as I arranged our few comforts in our tent. . . . Still, there was a lurking feeling of want of security from having only a cloth wall between us and out of doors. I had heard the sad story (which, while it shocked, reassured us) of the summary punishment inflicted in a neighboring town upon three thieves, who had been tried by a committee of citizens and, upon conviction, all hung. The circumstances had given to the place the name of Hang-Town. We were assured that, since then, no case of stealing had occurred in the northern mines; and I had seen, with my own eyes, buckskin purses half full of gold-dust, lying on a rock near the roadside, while the owners were working some distance off. So I was not afraid of robbery; but it seemed as if some impertinent person might so easily intrude, or hang about, in a troublesome manner.

But I soon found I had no reason to fear. Sitting in my tent sewing, I heard some men cutting wood up a hill behind us. One of them called out to another "Look out not to let any sticks roll that way, there's a woman and child in that tent." "Aye, aye, we won't frighten them" was the reply, all spoken in pleasant, respectful tones. A number of miners passed every morning and afternoon, to and from their work; but none of them stared obtrusively. One, I observed, looked at Mary [her small daughter] with interest a time or two, but did not stop, till one day I happened to be walking with her near the door, when he paused, bowed courteously and said, "Excuse me madam, may I speak to the little girl? We see so few ladies and children in California, and she is about the size of a little sister I left at home." "Certainly," I said, leading her towards him. His gentle tones and pleasant words easily induced her to shake hands, and talk with him. He proved to be a young physician, who had not long commenced practice at home, when the news of gold discovery in California induced him to seek El Dorado, hoping thus to secure, more speedily, means of support for his widowed mother and the younger members of the family. His partner in work was a well educated lawyer;

and another of their party was a scientist who had been applying his knowledge of geology and mineralogy, in exploring. . . . Here, then, was a party of California miners, dressed in the usual mining attire, and carrying pick, shovel and pans to and from their work; who yet were cultured gentlemen.

. . . Merchants, mechanics, farmers were all there in large numbers. So that in almost every mining camp there was enough of the element of order, to control, or very much influence, the opposite forces. These facts soon became apparent to me, and, ere long, I felt as secure in my tent with the curtain tied in front, as I had formerly felt with locked and bolted doors. There was, of course, the other element as elsewhere; but they themselves knew that it was safer for law and order to govern; and, with a few desperate exceptions, were willing, to let the lovers of order enjoy their rights and wield their influence. . . .[74]

An especially interesting example of adaptive and innovative women are those who were active in developing the land on their own. Far from being afraid of the land, as some historians have maintained, these women conquered it. Although they are often overlooked in historical accounts, a surprising number of western women homesteaded alone:

5.2
"Girl" Homesteaders

Beginning in the latter half of the nineteenth century, an army of women homesteaders marched onto the Great Plains. "Girl homesteaders," as they were often called, have received only slight attention from historians. Yet land office data clearly demonstrate their existence. Records in Lamar, Colorado, and Douglas, Wyoming, for example, indicate that in the years 1887, 1891, 1907, and 1908, an average of 11.9 percent of the homestead entrants were women.[75]

Despite the fact that creating a farmstead was regarded as a "male" occupation, women homesteaders were not thought oddities in their own time. Spurred on first by the Homestead Act of 1862 that offered to homesteaders 160 acres, and later by the Kincaid Act of 1904 that upped the stakes to 320 acres, women enthusiastically flocked to the Plains. They were seeking investments, trying to earn money to finance additional education for themselves, looking for husbands, or hoping to find a way to support themselves and sometimes several children after the loss of a spouse through death, divorce, or desertion. As the beneficiaries of a slowly liberalizing attitude

5.2: Adapted from the "Introduction" to Edith Eudora Ammons Kohl's, *Land of the Burnt Thigh* (St. Paul: Minnesota Historical Society Press, 1986 reprint edition), ix–xxxiii. Used by permission.

toward women during the late nineteenth and early twentieth centuries, they were spared widespread criticism by their contemporaries.

Numerous young, single (and primarily white) women claimants were initially more intent upon establishing ownership of a piece of land in the West then spending their lives living on it and developing it. For example, the Ammons sisters, Edith Eudora and Ida Mary, both unmarried and in their twenties at the time, seemed to be looking for a wise financial investment that might bring them profit in the near future. When they made their initial homestead claim in South Dakota in 1907, they seemed to be afflicted by what Enid Bern, a member of a North Dakota homesteading family, later termed a "strange malady"—the desire to homestead—that seized all types of people. Bern believed that the unmarried women and men homesteaders "formed an interesting segment of the population" and that "their presence added zest to community life, perhaps because of their youthfulness and varied personalities."[76]

Although a large number of women homesteaders were young, single women like Edith and Ida Mary, there were many widowed and divorced ones as well. "Widow Fergus," homesteading with her young son, was the first woman to visit the Ammons sisters and soon became one of their dearest friends. Other examples abound. A widow with two small children became a homesteader in the early 1880s when she learned that a number of her friends were leaving for Kansas to enter timber claims. She recalled, "I jumped up, saying, 'I am going to Kansas.' In a few minutes I left the door with my collar in my mouth and putting on my cuffs, and I was soon on the train to join the western party."[77] A divorced woman with a four-year-old daughter boarded a train for Montana, where she chose a 360-acre homestead, while another joined an Oklahoma land run to obtain a homestead to support herself and her four-month-old child.[78]

It was also not unusual for women to retain and work their claims on their own after marriage. Although Ida Mary Ammons left her share of the claim to Edith after her marriage to Imbert Miller in 1909, many others wanted to add to a husband's farm or ranch through their own homesteading efforts. Former Denver washwoman Elinore Pruitt continued to hold her Wyoming claim after she married cattle rancher Clyde Stewart in 1910. Because the boundary line of her claim ran within two feet of Stewart's house, her claim shack was erected as an addition to his home. Despite this joint housing, Elinore Pruitt Stewart insisted that she did not allow her husband to help her with her claim, for she wanted the "fun and experience" herself.[79]

While the need to improve their financial situations clearly attracted women of all ages and marital statuses to the Plains, they were also drawn by what Enid Bern called the "enchantment of the prairie" and Edith Ammons described as the "wild adventure" of homesteading.[80] Abbie Bright, a single homesteader in Kansas, claimed that her "desire to cross the Mississippi and a love of traveling" lured her to a homestead. In 1904, Martha Stoecker of Iowa enthusiastically accepted her brother's invitation to join a party of homesteaders;

after giving the matter more thought, she realized that the "thrill" of taking up land on her own fascinated her. She also thought that the undertaking was a great opportunity to see Dakota, "that awfully barren state we'd heard so much about in the song 'Dakota Land' "—a dubious inducement, since the song ended with the lines, "We do not live, we only stay/We are too poor to get away."[81]

The costs of homesteading seemed relatively modest to most women, although expenses varied depending upon the region, era, improvement level of the claim, and perceived needs of the individual. The Ammons sisters figured that their land, claim shack, food, fuel, and other necessities would total approximately $300.00. They held costs down by claiming a "relinquishment" or "improved" homestead that a bachelor forfeited after building a claim shack on it because he could not endure the loneliness. In 1887, twenty years before the Ammons migrated to South Dakota, homesteader Susan Carter paid only $21.75 for her Nebraska claim and its shack, which included a stove and rudimentary furniture. She then spent another $5.10 on flour, groceries, and soap, $3.75 on dishes and a lamp, $3.00 on a cupboard and chairs, and $.35 on thread and needles, for a total capital investment of $33.95.[82] Another woman's homestead expenses in 1909 were about $15.00 for transportation to South Dakota, $14.00 for the initial filing fee, $4.00 an acre to have sod broken, $50.00 for a shack, and $80.00 in additional fees if "proving up" in fourteen months rather than in five years. It did not take her long to decide that the "five year plan" with its minimal proving-up fee was for her.[83] A Wyoming woman of the same period saved receipts showing that she paid $23.48 in claim filing fees, $.48 for a pound of bacon, $.15 for a container of milk, and $.15 for two Hershey bars.[84]

Once on their claims, women frequently discovered that the low costs and aura of adventure were more than offset by the hard work involved. Edith Ammons declared her sister and herself to be "wholly unfitted for the frontier" having "neither training nor physical stamina for roughing it." Yet they were far from alone in their predicament, for while many women homesteaders came from farm backgrounds, many also came from towns and cities. Despite their lack of preparation, the women rallied an unbelievable store of courage as well as a willingness to tackle chores and master new skills. One Nebraska woman learned to use a rifle, once killing a "pesky gopher" and another time "5 little birds to make broth of."[85] Anna and Ethel Erickson, sisters who homesteaded in North Dakota, not only learned to use rifles, but became adept at carpentry and hanging wallpaper as well.[86]

Women homesteaders turned to men for help when confronted by tasks that were beyond their strength or ability. The Ammons sisters relied upon neighboring homesteaders and cowpunchers for occasional aid while other women sought help from fathers, brothers, friends, and hired hands. Although Nebraska homesteader Susan Carter planted her own corn and beans, she hired a man to dig her well; her future husband broke sod for her.[87] Similarly, Abbie Bright of Kansas planted her own corn, hoed her beans and peas, and made improvements on her claim shack, but paid to have a dugout bored into a hillside and relied upon her brother Phillip to do the heavy work of the claim.[88] Bess Corey of South Dakota had no male friend or relative to call upon, so she hired men to break sod, construct fencing, erect her frame shack, and build a dam.[89]

Primitive housing also presented a problem to women homesteaders. Horrified reactions to their first claim shacks was a common one among women who were dismayed by the crude state of their homes and furnishings. Dimensions of these shacks were typically nine by twelve feet, twelve feet square, or twelve by fourteen feet. They ranged from frame shacks, covered inside and out with tarpaper or flattened tin cans (for protection from the harsh winds and cold of the Plains), to dugouts in hillsides or huts made of strips of sod ripped from the ground with plows. Furniture was wooden and often homemade; a cupboard made of wooden boxes, painted or wallpapered and hung with muslin curtains, was a universal feature. Bedticks were stuffed with cornhusks, hay, or slough grass while small cookstoves burned "cats" of twisted hay, buffalo "chips," or scarce wood and coal. A precious clock, rocking chair, or mirror, carefully transported across the Plains by a determined owner, sometimes supplemented these sparse furnishings. The rooms were completed by curtains, a crucial household item for most women, who made them of muslin, petticoats, or old sheets. Inventive women created other household items: a table with two loose boards was designed to serve as an ironing board, or an old trunk placed outdoors was used as a refrigerator.[90]

Women expressed great pride in the improvements they added to their claim shacks, shanties, sod huts, and dugouts. Edith Ammons explained that "from the moment we began to make improvements, transforming the shack, it took on an interest for us out of all proportion to the changes we were able to make." In other words, women quickly began to invest part of themselves in these strange dwelling places, turning them bit by bit into homes that functioned as effective workplaces, sometimes even boasting a small touch of elegance. The things that could be accomplished by a determined woman within the walls of a diminutive claim shack were often remarkable. A Kansas homesteader of 1886 recalled that she dug a cellar under her twelve-foot-square shack where she stored her fuel "to keep it from blowing away," furnished her abode with a bed, trunk, bookcase, wardrobe, cookstove, and cupboards made of "goods-boxes," and on one occasion entertained twenty-two people with a dinner of boiled ham, baked beans, brown bread, pickled eggs, potato salad, and cake.[91]

Homelike as they may have become, homesteads still presented a number of inconveniences and even threats to their owners' safety. The Ammons sisters responses to the numerous Native Americans they encountered after they moved to their claim on the Lower Brule Indian Reservation in 1908 were typical. Edith related sentiments that today seem naïve, racist, or totally laughable. Yet, placed in the context of their time, and given other women's reactions to native peoples, the Ammons sisters' judgments were not unusual.

There were few women who did not feel a shiver of dread on their first contact with Native Americans. Before Edith and Ida Mary moved to their claim on the Lower Brule Reservation, the only Native American they had ever seen had been a performer in a Wild West show. Terrified when a group of natives approached on horseback, they locked themselves in their shack, peering in fright through a crack in the blind. They heard "savage mutterings," including the phrase "How kill 'em?" Finally, the sisters emerged from their hiding place to confront the "savage-looking creatures" who, it turned out, wanted to trade a horse for sugar, tobacco, and other staples. Obviously well-schooled in the alarmist rumors, titillating captivity narratives, and terrifying stories of scalping that abounded in the nineteenth century, these two young women could not have reacted sensibly. Women similarly steeped in anti-Indian prejudice and wild tales of Native American "atrocities" shared the Ammons sisters' feeling of terror. Allie Busby, a young woman visiting the quiet Mesquakis at the Tama Agency in Iowa in 1886 admitted that when she saw what were her "first" Native Americans, "wild visions of tomahawk or scalping knife arose, while the Indian of romance disappeared altogether" from her mind.[92] The Ammons sisters fell into another common trap when they let the joshing and frightening stories of a cowhand called Sourdough convert their fears into outright panic. Imploring him to keep watch outside their door, they spent a miserable night awaiting certain scalping and death. In the morning, with hair intact, they ventured outdoors only to learn that Sourdough had laughingly abandoned them and ridden off to watch his herd instead.[93]

Once intimidated, women were often unable to make wise decisions with or about Native Americans. In their fright, the Ammons sisters accepted a corral full of debilitated horses—"the lame, the halt and the blind"—in trade from the Native Americans they were so sure were about to attack them. They were not the first women, made vulnerable by their own anxieties, to discover the business acumen of Native Americans.[94]

Gradually, however, women homesteaders began to see another side of Native Americans as they came to know them; sometimes they even came to like them. The Ammons sisters realized that Native Americans did not want to harm them, that the Indians' problems were not all self-induced, and that many of these visitors were kind and generous. From an educated Native American who spoke English proficiently, Edith learned that rather than saying "How kill 'em?" the Native Americans were offering the greeting "How Kola." She seemed tickled to see enterprising Native Americans who strolled about in full native dress, posing for pictures at fifty cents apiece. At the same time, Ida Mary became an adept trader and gained a reasonable knowledge of native dialects. And when the sisters were burned out in 1909, their native friends were among the first to bring corn, meat, shawls, blankets, moccasins, and other supplies.[95]

Indigenous animals and insects also frightened women homesteaders until they learned how to handle them. Ida Mary Ammons once remarked that deadly rattlesnakes were "taking the country." These snakes were a potentially lethal nuisance for all women homesteaders, who soon learned to carry weapons and exercise great care in picking up anything. Bess Corey depicted her South Dakota claim as "a regular rattlesnake den," insisting that "it's nothing to kill half a dozen just crossing it."[96] A Nebraska woman "formed the habit of taking a garden hoe" with her whenever she walked "since it was an unwritten law that no rattler should be allowed to get away."[97] Martha Stoecker had a particularly sobering contact with rattlers on her claim when she fell asleep outdoors: "When I awoke there was a big rattler coiled up on top of the bank of dirt thrown up against the shack rattling like fury, about 10 or 12 feet away. I was frightened, got up and went inside and loaded my rifle. I took aim and fired, hit it in the middle, and how it rattled and hissed. I waited a little while until I was calm and quit shaking and then fired again and blew its head to bits. I took the hoe and chopped the rattles off. There were nine. I still have them." Stoecker never slept outdoors again.[98]

Myriad other problems faced women homesteaders. One Nebraska woman in 1909 recalled with distaste "gumbo mud," scarce water, and torrential spring rains.[99] Others disliked the scorching sun, the drying effect of the wind and hard water on their faces, the high prices, the lack of flowers and trees, and the ever-present dust that no amount of housecleaning could remove.[100]

Edith Ammons particularly sympathized with homesteaders terrorized by searing droughts, and she plaintively described the experience. People were forced to keep close watch over their combustible crops and to haul water for drinking, cooking, and washing over long distances, either in pails attached to ill-fitting wooden neck yokes or in barrels on cumbersome water sleds. As debates raged concerning the possibilities of irrigation or on the fallowing method of planting, women and men worked together burrowing holes deep into parched soil in hopes that it would yield water. Like the homesteaders Ammons described, settlers all over the Plains prayed fervently, searched the skies in desperation for a sign of rain, and, when it finally appeared, ran out into the downpour to literally drink it in.[101]

Even more dramatic and impressive is Ammon's vivid depiction of the prairie fires that resulted when homes, out-buildings, and fields became parched. These huge conflagrations turned the sun red, whipped the wind into a deafening roar, and sent blinding billows of smoke over the land.[102] Fires posed a menace to crops, stock, and farm buildings as well as to homes, children, and small animals. One North Dakota man cried aloud in 1889 when he saw his barn and horses destroyed by fire, while his wife fought in vain to save the cows and chickens. The Ammons sisters struggled valiantly but unsuccessfully to salvage part of their claim, businesses, and home from the raging fire that wiped them out in 1909, just as they were to make final their claim on the Lower Brule.[103]

Fierce rains and snowstorms were another scourge. Torrential downpours, floods, and blizzards often caught women alone in homes or in schoolrooms with small children to protect. Edith Ammons remembered simply as "The Big

Blizzard" a furious storm that caught her and Ida Mary without adequate fuel, forcing them out on the snowswept Plains in search of help. Others wrote of rain, hail, snowstorms, and cyclones that knocked down stovepipes, broke windows, caved in roofs, flooded houses, ruined furniture, destroyed gardens, killed chickens, quickly reduced scanty stocks of food, and even froze brothers, husbands, sons, and grandfathers to death.[104]

Perhaps the most common, long-lasting problem, however, one that plagued homesteaders regardless of gender or marital status, was raising the cash necessary to hold on to and prove up their claims. Married couples solved the problem in a variety of ways. Husbands frequently sought employment away from their claims as farm hands, railroad laborers, or construction workers, while their wives and children "held down" the family farm by living on it and often farming it themselves. One example was Christine Ayres, a German woman who not only stayed alone on the Wyoming homestead that she held with her husband, but raised pigs and horses, "broke" eighty acres, and planted all the crops.[105]

But single women homesteaders had to rely upon their own labor to bring in the necessary money. Hundreds of them became schoolteachers. Martha Stoecker, for example, began teaching in 1904 in a single room furnished only with "a fine, big hard coal stove, old rickety table, a chair, two planks and four boxes."[106] When Ida Mary Ammons decided to establish a post office and store, she was pursuing another popular way of raising money. Other women, such as Kansas homesteader Abbie Bright, who wrote for the *Wichita Tribune*, worked as part-time journalists. Still others became skilled typesetters and printers.[107] Edith Ammons displayed an extra measure of grit and talent by producing her own newspaper. When Edith took over the *McClure Press*, a recently founded local paper largely composed of public notices that were necessary to prove up a claim, she worked for western newspaper magnate Edward L. Senn, known as the "Final-Proof King." She later described Senn as having helped tame the West "with printer's ink instead of six-shooters." She used the experience she gained in working for Senn to establish and publish her own newspaper, the *Reservation Wand*, after she moved to the Lower Brule in 1908.[108]

The difficulties involved in homesteading overwhelmed some women who could think only of returning to their former homes. One woman explained that she was fond of life on the Plains but was not able to secure an adequate living from her land. With her old job awaiting her in Chicago, she reluctantly proved up her claim as a future investment and left South Dakota. Assessing her homesteading years, she later wrote: "From a business standpoint the whole venture was a losing game, since I did not realize enough from my holding to cover what I had spent. But I have always considered it a good investment. . . . I had a rested mind and a broadened outlook. I always say—and mean it—that I would not give up my pioneering experience for a fortune."[109] Others simply felt that life on the Plains was too different from the homes and lives they had known. In 1911, Anna and Ethel Erickson decided that they did not want to live permanently in North Dakota: "It's too much of a change." Although the sisters liked the state, they longed for all the amenities of their Iowa home.[110]

In spite of the hardships, however, many other women clung to their dreams and slowly discovered homesteading experiences to enjoy and cherish. They waxed eloquent on the beauty of the countryside, remarked upon the friendliness of their neighbors, and emphasized the opportunities available to them. Many found the camaraderie of homesteading to be especially satisfying. Myrtle Yoeman, a homesteader in South Dakota in 1905, was pleased that her grandmother's, father's, and aunt's claims all lay within a few miles of her own.[111] Mary Culbertson and Helen Howell, friends homesteading together in Wyoming in 1905, settled on adjoining claims and built one house straddling both pieces of land in which they both lived, each sleeping on her own side of the property line.[112] The Ammons sisters also recognized the importance of such collegiality. They undertook their land gamble in "west-river" South Dakota, that is, west of the Missouri River, as a team. When they felt disillusioned and despairing upon first viewing their "improved" claim with its ten-foot-by-twelve-foot tarpaper shack, they found their spirits buoyed and their resolution restored by other women homesteaders in the area. These women seemed to have little self-pity.[113]

The Ammons sisters also came to recognize the many advantages offered women by homesteading. Soon after they arrived in South Dakota, they realized that although women homesteaders worked hard, they also led satisfying lives, took delight in the countryside, and frequently lost their desire to return to their former homes. Edith and Ida Mary began "making friends, learning to find space restful and reassuring instead of intimidating, adapting [their] restless natures to a country that measured time in seasons" and sinking their own roots into "that stubborn soil." Although the environment was demanding, Edith Ammons came to believe that a woman "had more independence here than in any other part of the world." When she was told "the range is no place for clingin' vines, 'cause there hain't nothin' to cling to," she felt she was learning to meet the challenge. For her, the hardships "were more than compensated for by its unshackled freedom. . . . The opportunities for a full and active life were infinitely greater here. . . . There was a pleasant glow of possession in knowing that the land beneath our feet was ours."[114]

More evidence has been unearthed of the rewards women reaped by homesteading: expanded responsibilities and power within the family and community, a rapidly improving standard of living, great possibilities for future economic gains, and greater equity, new friendships, and mutual reliance between women and men. These opportunities spurred on large numbers of women to participate in such land runs as those staged in Oklahoma during the 1890s and early 1900s. Despite the incredible tension and even violence associated with these contests, women were greatly in evidence: hundreds of their names appear in the lists of claimants later registered in the land offices.[115] A high proportion of these women claimants remained on the land—approximately forty-three percent of women "proved up" their claims as opposed to only thirty-seven percent of men. The women homesteaders who remained persevered despite overwhelming odds, cared effectively for themselves and their claims, made money through a wide variety of jobs and enterprises, and formed fast friendships with people of all backgrounds, ages, educational levels, marital statuses, cultures, and races. They ceased pining for home; indeed, their homesteads became home to them. Their hearts belonged to the West, and their feet were firmly planted on its sod.

This Oklahoma woman depicted homesteading around the turn of the twentieth century as adventurous and at times humorous:

Since I was of age, my father, feeling the call of the West and he, being too old to file, persuaded me to do so. Father had a brother living at Tecumseh at the time of the Kiowa-Comanche Drawing so he came on down before I did, visiting and looking over the country. His glowing accounts of the beautiful prairie, wild flowers, tall grass, wonderful streams of water and the possibilities in a new country, put adventure in my blood, too, so I decided to come down and try my luck at drawing for a claim. . . .

We went to El Reno where I registered and I drew one of the early claims but didn't even know I had been so lucky until everyone else in town knew about it. I didn't hear about it until a young fellow brought his outfit, got down in front of me and with many flourishes started to shine my shoes. Upon being questioned as to the reason for this unusual service he told me that I had drawn a claim. Then the letters began pouring in—men wanting to marry me, men all the way from twenty-one to seventy-five. They had the money and I had the claim. However, I did not take advantage of any of the offers.

We came down on the train as far as Richard's Spur and by stage from there to Lawton. The stage was one of those big old wagons, board sides and canvas over the top. We reached Lawton Saturday afternoon and Sunday we rode all over the country trying to locate my claim. . . . We lived in a tent hotel where there were cots for the ladies on one side, and cots on the other side for the men.

We finally located the farm and went back to the town of Tecumseh for a while, returning in January, 1902, at which time we built a house on the farm, a little two-room shack. The lumber was hauled from Lawton on a lumber wagon and it took all day to make the trip as there were no roads, just a sort of a dim trail. . . . After a week my father and I took up our abode on the new claim and living was hard in winter months. We nearly froze to death for the only stove we had was a small cook stove. Water was carried from a spring a quarter of a mile from the house. . . . The first night my father and I were sitting playing dominoes, when we heard a knock at the door. Since there were no neighbors within miles we wondered who in the world it could be. Thinking only of wild Indians come to scalp us, my father whispered to me to get the shotgun while he went to the door. Imagine our embarrassment when the door was opened, to see standing there a young man from Kansas by the name of Sheridan. He had drawn a claim that day and someone hauled him out there with a load of lumber and left him. He saw our light and came to it. . . .

I used to come into Lawton and back either on horseback or on a bicycle, for at home there was nothing to do but sit and look around over the prairie. Every once in awhile we would see Indians coming over the hill dressed in bright blankets or sometimes only a G-string. They wore brightly-painted war feathers and bonnets. We would run for the house, bar the doors and windows and wait for the war whoop but none ever came and finally we were not so afraid of them, becoming well acquainted with dozens of bucks and squaws in later years and counting them as some of our best friends.

To fence the farm my father and I went to the timber, up in the mountains, and cut logs from which we made posts and fenced my claim. I handled one end of a cross-cut saw for it was too lonely to stay at the house by myself. . . . Money was scarce in those days, therefore, part of the time we would not have much to eat, especially if the weather was bad and we could not get to town for weeks.

The day I filed, a man said he would pay me $1,000 for my relinquishment but my father said I had no intention of relinquishing it under any circumstances. As for myself, I wasn't so sure whether I wanted to stay and homestead that claim or not, but did. There is something about a new country that makes one want to stay and grow up with it. . . .[116]

In 1909, Elinore Pruitt, a widow living in Denver, left her position as "washlady" and moved with her small daughter to become a homesteader in Wyoming. Here she wrote back to her former employer in Denver:

When I read of the hard times among the Denver poor, I feel like urging them every one to get out and file on land. I am very enthusiastic about women homesteading. It really requires less strength and labor to raise plenty to satisfy a large family than it does to go out to wash, with the added satisfaction of knowing that their job will not be lost to them if they care to keep it. Even if improving the place does go slowly, it is that much done to stay done. Whatever is raised is the homesteader's own, and there is no house-rent to pay. This year Jerrine [her daughter] cut and dropped enough potatoes to raise a ton of fine potatoes. She wanted to try, so we let her, and you will remember that she is but six years old. We had a man to break the ground and cover the potatoes for her and the man irrigated them once. That was all that was done until digging time, when they were ploughed out and Jerrine picked them up. Any woman strong enough to go out by the day could have done every bit of the work and put in two or three times that much, and it would have been so much more pleasant than to work so hard in the city and then be on starvation rations in the winter.

To me, homesteading is the solution of all poverty's problems, but I realize that temperament has much to do with success in any undertaking, and persons afraid of coyotes and work and loneliness had better let ranching alone. At the same time, any woman who can stand her own company, can see the beauty of the sunset, loves growing things, and is willing to put in as much time at careful labor as she does over the wash-tub, will certainly succeed; will have independence, plenty to eat all the time, and a home of her own in the end.

Experimenting need cost the homesteader no more than the work, because by applying to the Department of Agriculture at Washington he can get enough of any seed and as many kinds as he wants to make a thorough trial, and it doesn't even cost postage. Also one can always get bulletins from there and from the Experiment Station of one's own State concerning any problem or as many problems as may come up. . . . I am only thinking of the troops of tired, worried women, sometimes even cold and hungry, scared to death of losing their places to work, who could have plenty to eat, who could have good fires by gathering the wood, and comfortable homes of their own, if they had the courage and determination to get them. . . .[117]

Women received grants of land from agencies other than the U.S. Congress. A Mexican woman talked about the ranches she owned in California during the 1830s and 1840s and how she dealt with conflicts with Native Americans:

I still had my three ranchos then, one that I had bought called Capistrano de Secua, which was located half-way between my other two ranchos. . . . The other two had been given me years before by the governor. . . . I recall the sad happenings at Rancho Jamul, Pío Pico's ranch, which occurred, I believe, in 1838. . . . When the incident occurred at Jamul I had been at my ranch, Jamacha, for two days. . . . the house Indians instigated the entire episode [at Jamul]. . . . The aborigines set the house ablaze. . . .

The one that first arrived at my rancho was José Antonio. . . . My comadre Nieves, the wife of my mayordomo, and I were near a pond, cleaning it with an Indian. The other Indians were working with the mayordomo. José Antonio directed himself to Nieves, relating the condition of his mother [Doña María de Los Angeles] and asking her to send his mother something with which to cover herself. Nieves ran to the house to look for whatever she might find. . . .

I directed the Indian to stop work and ordered him to go call my mayordomo and all the people. They came right away as the Indian told them what had happened at Jamul. . . . When the mayordomo, Valentín, came to the house with the Indians, I directed one of them to race on horseback to the ranchería of the Indians at Secua. . . . I directed the servant to tell them to come at once with their arms. Three of my servants were from the mission of San Diego and nearly all the rest were from Secua. . . . About eight or ten of those of Secua came in addition to those that were here before. All were well armed with their bows and arrows and ready to defend us if the hostiles came to attack us. . . .

I sent to a friend of mine . . . saying that she should send me the gunpowder and shot that I kept [at the mission] . . . and asking for the directions for making cartridges. All came to me without delay. . . . Sergeant Macedonio González was sent for. He came with some troops from Baja California, and to these were joined some residents of San Diego. . . . The troops killed a few Indians, but . . . after several futile attempts, Macedonio González and his troops were forced to retreat. . . . Doña María de Los Angeles suffered mortal anguish the rest of her life.[118]

Clearly, many western women were adaptive and innovative, no matter how desperate the situation. Women's motivations, inner resources, and help from others all contributed to their ability to cope with, and sometimes triumph over, the challenges of western life. Still, many deeper questions remain unanswered, especially regarding the differing experiences of women from diverse racial, ethnic, and class backgrounds. Why were so many women discriminated against in the West, which was supposedly the home of the free and the egalitarian? Why was it place to grow for some but not for others? At this time, all we can conclude with certainty is that although the history of western women is being written, it is far from complete.

For Further Reading

Armitage, Susan H., and Elizabeth Jameson, eds. *The Women's West*. Norman: University of Oklahoma Press, 1987.

Blair, Karen J. *Women in Pacific Northwest History: An Anthology*. Seattle: University of Washington Press, 1988.

Beeton, Beverly. *Women Vote in the West: The Woman Suffrage Movement, 1869–1896*. New York: Garland Press, 1986.

Berman, David K. "Male Support for Woman Suffrage: An Analysis of Voting Patterns in the Mountain West." *Social Science History* 11 (Fall 1987), 281–94.

Edwards, G. Thomas. *Sowing Good Seeds: The Northwest Suffrage Campaigns of Susan B. Anthony*. Portland, Oregon: Oregon Historical Society Press, 1990.

Foote, Cheryl. *Women of the New Mexico Frontier, 1846–1912*. Niwot, Colorado: University Press of Colorado, 1990.

Griswold, Robert L. *Family and Divorce in California, 1850–1890: Victorian Illusions and Everyday Realities*. Albany: State University of New York Press, 1982.

Jameson, Elizabeth. "Women as Workers, Women as Civilizers: True Womanhood in the American West." *Frontiers* 7 (1984), 1–8.

Jeffrey, Julie Roy. *Frontier Women: The Trans-Mississippi West, 1840–1880.* New York: Hill & Wang, 1979.

Jensen, Joan M., and Darlis A. Miller, eds. *New Mexico Women: Intercultural Perspectives.* Albuquerque: University of New Mexico Press, 1986.

Levy, Joann. *They Saw the Elephant: Women in the California Gold Rush.* Hamden, Conn.: Archon Books, 1990.

Mathes, Valerie Sherer. "Annie E. K. Bidwell: Chico's Benefactress." *California History* 68 (Spring/Summer 1989), 14–25, 60–64.

Myres, Sandra L. *Westering Women and the Frontier Experience, 1800–1915.* Albuquerque: University of New Mexico Press, 1982.

Pascoe, Peggy. *Relations of Rescue: The Search for Female Moral Authority in the American West, 1874–1939.* New York: Oxford University Press, 1990.

Riley, Glenda. *The Female Frontier: A Comparative View of Women on the Prairie and the Plains.* Lawrence: University Press of Kansas, 1988.

Robertson, Janet. *The Magnificent Mountain Women: Adventures in the Colorado Rockies.* Lincoln: University of Nebraska Press, 1990.

Schaffer, Ronald. "The Problem of Consciousness in the Woman Suffrage Movement: A California Perspective." *Pacific Historical Review* 45 (Fall 1976), 469–94.

Schlissel, Lillian, Vicki L. Ruiz, and Janice Monk, eds. *Western Women: Their Land, Their Lives.* Albuquerque: University of New Mexico Press, 1988.

Scharff, Virginia. "The Case for Domestic Feminism: Woman Suffrage in Wyoming." *Annals of Wyoming* 56 (Fall 1984), 29–37.

Webb, Anne B. "Minnesota Women Homesteaders: 1863–1889." *Journal of Social History* 23 (Fall 1989), 115–36.

Wold, Jo Anne. *This Old House: The Story of Clara Rust, Alaska Pioneer.* Anchorage: Alaska Northwest Books, 1989.

CONCLUSION

The phrase "cultural diversity" has become something of a glib watchword during the late 1980s and early 1990s. The term appears everywhere—from university catalog descriptions to titles of articles, books, and conferences. Yet we would be foolish to dismiss cultural diversity as a mere cliché, or worse yet, to denigrate its significance in our pursuit of the meaning of the American West. The women's words in this book demonstrate the complexity of their presence in the West. Customary images and assumptions demand further rethinking and reinterpretation—and cultural diversity itself demands further investigation—if we are to understand fully the region that played, and still plays, such an important role in shaping the American people and nation.

There is an old maxim that says a problem is like a circle; where you stand on its perimeter determines what you see. Change your position, and you see the problem differently. The same can be said of history—change your place and your viewpoint changes as well. From the white American perspective, for example, successful entrepreneurs, courageous soldiers, and industrious settlers were the heroes of the nineteenth-century West. The exploits of entrepreneurs like David Jacks or of generals John C. Frémont and Stephen Watts Kearney were the stuff from which legends grew.

But let's move to another part of the circle. From the Mexican viewpoint these same men were invaders, crooks, and ne'er-do-wells. For instance, in 1874, a Californio named Dorotea Valdez described David Jacks as a "very mean man, a cunning rascal, a pious hypocrite." She hoped that some "smart lawyer" would help her people divest Jacks of the land he held in Monterey, California—land that was her people's former pueblo, "land which no person had the right to give away, because said land did not belong to the American authorities" who sold it. Instead, she argued the land was "the property of every man, woman and child born in our town." She concluded that Jacks was "an innate enemy of everything having relation to our ancient history."[1]

Valdez also held a low opinion of Frémont—no doubt shaped by her observation of events during the Mexican War of 1846–48. She thought him no more than the leader of "rabble" who "stole horses, saddles, *aguardiente,* and everything else they could lay their hands upon." A Sonoma woman, Rosalia Leese, agreed. She referred to Frémont's band, who attempted to establish the Bear Flag Republic in Sonoma on June 14, 1846, as "desperadoes," "ruffians," and "robbers." In her eyes its leader Frémont was "the man who had planned the wholesale robbery of California." She added that although he was an officer of the U.S. army, he "was afraid to compromise the honor of his government if his party pursues their thieving operations under the flag that lovers of liberty through the world hold dear, hence his reason for resorting to the adoption of a flag unknown to civilized nations."[2]

Both Valdez and Leese spoke of the bitterness that remained in their hearts after Americans took over California. But Leese added that "those men inspired me with such a large dose of hate against their race that . . . not being desirous of coming in contact with them I have abstained from learning their language.[3]

When the Mexican War ended in 1848, the Treaty of Guadelupe Hidalgo formally awarded the areas of California, Arizona, and New Mexico to the U.S. government. In anticipation of victory, the American general Kearney marched into Santa Fe in 1846. One Mexican woman was so distraught by the American takeover of Santa Fe and its aftermath that she eventually left the United States. In the following letter, she explains to her daughter why she went to Mexico to die:

October 1, 1910, Monterey, México
My dearest daughter,

Now that distance lies between us and the impersonality of writing-paper makes my task somewhat easier, I would like to tell you the truth about what lay behind my decision to go to México to finish my life.

As you already know, I grew up in northernmost México. I lived in a gracious city that lay in a beautiful valley. A river ran through the city and a lovely plaza graced its center. I was the youngest daughter of a moderately well-to-do family. Every morning, Mamá, my sisters, and I went to Mass. I loved to hear the bells pealing above the town and watch Mamá's heavy lace mantilla swaying in front of me.

We would often cross the plaza on returning home. On one side was a government building with a wide veranda and on the others were shops and adobe dwellings. Our house was also built of adobe. Each room opened onto a courtyard with a fountain in the center. Around the fountain were brightly colored pots of flowers and many trees. After our lessons and then dinner—which always included boiled meats, vegetables, fruits, tortillas, tortas, candies, wine, brandy, and coffee—we each went into our rooms, darkened the chamber by closing the wooden shutters, and had a siesta.

It was a wonderful way of life for me—a little girl—and I thought it would continue forever. Every weekend there was a fandango and the dancers seemed so happy, I could not envision despair entering our lives.

But things changed. In 1848, México lost a great war to the United States, and with it northernmost México. Our lovely, old city of Santa Fé was to become American. In August of that year, an American general named Kearny marched into the city and claimed it for the United States. He brashly claimed the former governor's office, and even his chair, as his own. Soon his men erected a flag pole in the plaza and flew the American colors from it. Although I was only fifteen at the time, I remember these events well and have related them to you before.

But, now, for the part of the story that has lain silently in my heart for these many years. Mamá was extremely upset. She said she feared for her family's future. There were many rumors that a Mexican general was gathering troops for an attack on Santa Fé. We were afraid that if México took over Santa Fé we would be regarded as traitors for having remained there under the American regime. Yet we were afraid to help the Mexican troops for fear the Americans would see us as traitors. Soon, one of the American leaders began to arrest Mexicans. He even arrested women and priests. Some of our friends fled from the city and we never saw them again.

Soldiers were stationed on the plaza and all around the city. The peace of our courtyard was shattered by their shouting, oaths, and bugles. We no longer ventured out to Mass. Instead, we gathered in the parlor and, kneeling together, said the rosary. Mamá grew more pale and thin each day.

Then, one morning an American soldier arrived with an order for the arrest of my Papá. Oddly enough, neither Mamá nor Papá disputed the justice of the order, but Mamá begged the soldier to allow Papá one more day with his family. The soldier said that he would return in the morning. Mamá lay in bed without moving and hardly breathing the rest of the day. That evening she died. At the time, I thought it was from grief, but later I thought it must have been from a heart attack.

The next morning, after a sleepless, tearful night, I arose early to say goodbye to Papá before the soldier arrived to take him to prison. I finally found Papá in the storeroom, his neck encased in the loop of a rope he had flung over a wooden beam. He had been dead for several hours.

My eldest brother—your Uncle Alexandro—became the head of the family. He told us that as far as he knew, Papá had committed no crime. We never spoke of those occurrences again. As you know, we have always said that Mamá and Papá died young, as a result of accidental happenings. We later sold out and moved to Albuquerque where you were born. I am proud of you for becoming a loyal American and a successful teacher. But as much as I have tried I never lifted this burden—the image of my dead parents—from my soul. I lived in New Mexico, but I want to die in old México. I hope that in these last days of my life you will give me understanding and forgiveness for having left you and the others.

With the abiding affection of a mother's heart,
Your Mamá[4]

Mexican women were generally active, influential, and well-regarded throughout the Southwest before the Americans arrived. As another woman, Fabiola Cabeza de Baca, explained, wives of Mexican ranchers "held a very important place in the villages and ranches on the Llano." According to Baca, these women were "a great social force in the community. . . . life on the Llano would have been unbearable without their guidance and labor." Although their influence remained great, these women's lives changed as, in Baca's words, American migrants "marched toward the Utopia of their dreams."[5] As the migrants marched, they pushed aside some Mexicans, while they trod upon or used others. It is little wonder, then, that many Mexican women have their own particular view of the "settlement" of the West.

Of course, there are other perspectives well, including those of African American, Native American, and Asian women. This is not to suggest that the experience of white American women is without value. Rather, I would argue that it must be leavened and balanced by the accounts of other groups. To accomplish this, we need a new conceptualization of western history. At the moment, whether historians write "old" or "new" western history, they tend to employ paradigms that remain basically unchanged. Most historians—indeed, most Americans—still see the American West as having been there for the taking. Even the so-called new western historians still debate the same old issue—the meaning and legacy of Anglo conquest.[6]

This focus on conquest leads to an inordinate emphasis on the West's "settlement" period. Just as we tend to begin studying and teaching American history with the arrival of Anglo explorers and settlers, we also begin studying and teaching western history with the arrival of white explorers and settlers. As a result, in many peoples' minds, the eighteenth- and nineteenth-century West *was* the West. Consequently we routinely ignore the thousands of years of history and development that preceded the arrival of Americans and Europeans. We also overlook twentieth-century developments; all but a few historians give the contemporary American West short shrift.

This limited focus not only compresses western history into basically two centuries, but it also diminishes western history as an era that is over, finished, a nostalgic memory at best. It is little wonder that many easterners still envision the West as a vast colony, or that a recent atlas maker omitted maps of South and North Dakota to save space, or that many Americans fail to recognize that the West has more large cities, more land area, more population, and more natural resources than any other region of the country. It also helps explain why so many histories of American women continue to omit western women.

Yet, when we stop to think about it, we know the West existed before American explorers and settlers "discovered" it. It had peoples and cultures before Anglos colonized it; it continues to have distinctive peoples and cultures today. Perhaps we would understand the West better if we made the story of its conquest a single chapter rather than the entire book.

I suggest that we embrace a "holistic" view of western history, a view that encompasses the centuries before "conquest" *and* the contemporary West as well. With such an expanded perspective, we might discover a rich new field for investigations of cultural diversity. We might also come to understand continuity and change. Certainly, a larger view would help us revise our muddled ideas about "the frontier." Perhaps most important, a holistic outlook would help us recognize that the West's heritage is one of diversity; seeing the region from this angle would constantly remind us that explorers, conquerors, and "pioneers" were only one part of the story.

We can only establish the significance of the American West—and answer such questions as whether the West offered women a place to grow—by enlarging our conception of western history, by integrating into the overall picture the thousands of years of human history that preceded Anglo settlement and the hundred years that followed its end. Only by developing a holistic panorama of western history can we effectively analyze and understand its smaller parts.

CHECKLIST OF PRIMARY DOCUMENTS

This descriptive checklist of the primary documents contained in *A Place to Grow* can be used to relocate individual documents or types of documents found throughout the text. The documents are also cited in full in the Notes, which begin on page 255.

Section 1

Section 2

Section 3

Section 4

Section 5

Conclusion

NOTES

Abbreviations used in the notes:
BCYU—Beinecke Collection, Yale University, New Haven, Connecticut
BL—Bancroft Library, Berkeley, California
BTHC—Eugene Barker Texas History Center, University of Texas, Austin
CSLS—California State Library, Sacramento
HL—Huntington Library, San Marino, California
IPP—Indian-Pioneer Papers, Western History Collections, University of Oklahoma Library, Norman
KHS—Kansas State Historical Society, Topeka
MHS—Minnesota Historical Society, St. Paul
MHSA—Montana Historical Society Archives, Helena
MSU—Montana State University Library Special Collections, Bozeman
Miss. Coll.—Joint Collection of the University of Missouri/Western History Society of Missouri Manuscripts, Columbia
NDOH—State Historical Society of North Dakota, Oral History Project, Bismarck
NHS—Nebraska State Historical Society, Lincoln
SDHRC—South Dakota Historical Resource Center, Pierre
SHSI—State Historical Society of Iowa, Iowa City
SHSND—State Historical Society of North Dakota, Bismarck
WAHC—University of Wyoming American Heritage Center, Laramie
WSAMHD—Wyoming State Archives, Museum, and Historical Department, Cheyenne

Introduction

1. Stella M. Drumm, ed., *Down the Santa Fe Trail and Into Mexico: The Diary of Susan Shelby Magoffin, 1846–1847* (New Haven: Yale University Press, 1926), 120–21. Magoffin was far from alone in her negative portrayals of Mexicans. See W. W. H. Davis, *El Gringo; or, New Mexico and Her People* (New York: Harper & Brothers, 1857); Lewis H. Garrard, *Wah-To-Yah and the Taos Trail* (Glendale, Calif.: Arthur H. Clark Co., 1938); and Cecil Robinson, *With the Ears of Strangers: The Mexican in American Literature* (Tucson: University of Arizona Press, 1963).

2. Fray Angélico Chávez, "Doña Tules, Her Fame and Her Funeral," *El Palacio* 57 (August 1957), 230–32.

3. For discussions of an expansion of images of Hispanic women see Antonia I. Castañeda, "Gender, Race, and Culture: Spanish-Mexican Women in the Historiography of Frontier California," *Frontiers: A Journal of Women's Studies* 11 (1990), 8–20; Frances R. Conley, "Martina Didn't Have a Covered Wagon: A Speculative Reconstruction," *The Californians* 7 (March–August 1989), 48–54; and Beverly Trulio, "Anglo-American Attitudes Toward New Mexican Women," *Journal of the West* 12 (April 1973), 299–339.

4. The idea of colonizing groups of women was discussed by Antonia Castañeda in a paper titled "Decolonization or Recolonization" on October 19, 1990, at the Western History Association's annual meeting in Reno, Nevada.

5. For a fuller discussion of the invented American woman's applicability to specific groups of women, especially women of color, see Glenda Riley, *Inventing the American Woman: A Perspective on Women's History, 1607 to the Present* (Arlington Heights, Illinois: Harlan Davidson, Inc., 1986). The quotation is from Elizabeth Fox-Genovese, "Between Individualism and Fragmentation: American Culture and the New Literary Studies of Race and Gender," *American Quarterly* 42 (March 1990), 9–10.

6. For the concept of the virtual past see Donald Ostrowski, "The Historian and the Virtual Past," *The Historian* 51 (February 1989), 201–20. For an examination of history as a relevant topic to contemporary issues, as a search for the truth, as narrative, and as a study of concepts see Jeffrey B. Russell, "History and Truth," *The Historian* 50 (November 1987), 3–13. See also Gene Wise, *American Historical Explanations: A Strategy for Grounded Inquiry* (Minneapolis: University of Minnesota Press, 1980, rev. ed.). For an appraisal of "old" and "new" perspectives see Gertrude Himmelfarb, *The New History and the Old: Critical Essays and Reappraisals* (Cambridge, Massachusetts: Belknap Press, 1987) and Peter Novick, *That Noble Dream: The "Objectivity Question" and the American Historical Profession* (Cambridge: Cambridge University Press, 1988), especially 573–629.

7. For a discussion of the use of deconstructionism in women's history see Louise A. Tilly, "Gender, Women's History, and Social History"; Gay L. Gullickson, "Comment on Tilly: Women's History, Social History, and Deconstruction"; Judith M. Bennett, "Comment on Tilly: Who Asks the Questions for Women's History?"; and Louise Tilly, "Re-

sponse," *Social Science History* 13 (Winter 1989), 439–80.

8. According to recent scholarship, domesticity, or woman's sphere, was probably more of a model for white middle- and upper-class women than for other classes and races. For an expansion of this argument see Riley, *Inventing the American Woman.*

9. Maggie Humm, *The Dictionary of Feminist Theory* (Columbus: Ohio State University Press, 1990), 117–18. For a fuller discussion of the meaning and implication of liberation and equality see Ellen Carol DuBois, et al, *Feminist Scholarship: Kindling in the Groves of Academe* (Urbana: University of Illinois Press, 1985), 126–53.

10. See for example Lancaster Pollard, "The Pacific Northwest," in Merrill Jensen, ed., *Regionalism in American* (Madison: University of Wisconsin Press, 1965), 187–206, and W. Eugene Hollon, *The Southwest: Old and New* (Lincoln: University of Nebraska Press, 1962), 3–21.

11. Another recent study exploring the issue of gender and region will soon be published. In it, rural sociologist Deborah Fink reports the findings of extensive interviews conducted with Nebraska rural women. These findings reaffirm the idea that gender expectations continue to shape women's lives in at least one region of the Great Plains.

12. See for example Humm, *The Dictionary of Feminist Theory.*

13. Horace Austin, letter to "My dear Madam," (Mrs. W. C. Dodge), March 14, 1870, in Horace Austin Family Papers, Minnesota Historical Society [hereafter MHS], and Carl Ross and K. Marianne Wargelin Brown, *Women Who Dared: The History of Finnish American Women* (St. Paul: Immigration History Research Center, University of Minnesota, 1986).

14. Julia K. S. Hibbard, Reminiscences, 1856–68, n.d., and Kathryn Stover Hicks Moody, "Territorial Days in Minnesota," 1960, both at MHS. See also Catherine Bissell Ely, Diary, 1835–39, which is one of the earliest accounts of Minnesota rural women's work, although the diary focuses on child care after the birth of Ely's first child.

15. Mary Carpenter, letter to "Dear Cousin Laura," August 18, 1871, in Mary E. Lovell Carpenter and Family Papers, MHS.

16. Mary Burns, "The Bright Side of Homesteading," 1923, MHS.

17. Abby Fuller Abbe, "Account of Trip West in 1854," n.d., and Clippings, "The Fuller Family Letters," both in Abby Fuller Abbe Family Papers, MHS. Quotes are from Charlotte Van Cleve, *"Three Score Years and Ten": Life-Long Memories of Fort Snelling, Minnesota, and Other Parts of the West* (Minneapolis: Harrison and Smith, 1888), 161.

18. Advocates of women as teachers stressed their capacity for affection and maternal instincts, qualities that would create greater rapport with students than would be possible or proper for "the other sex," as men were often called during the nineteenth century. See Kathryn Kish Sklar, *Catharine Beecher: A Study in American Domesticity* (New York: Norton, 1976), 113–15, 168–83, and Polly Welts Kaufman, "A Wider Field of Usefulness: Pioneer Women Teachers in the West, 1848–1854," *Journal of the West* 21 (April 1982), 16–25; and *Women Teachers on the Frontier* (New Haven, Connecticut: Yale University Press, 1984).

19. Marion Louisa Sloan, Reminiscences, 1926, 1936, 1937, and Maude Baumann Arney, "Earliest History of School District Number 64," n.d., both at MHS. For a Swedish woman who moved her family to the loft so that a school and its teacher could occupy the lower level of their home, see "Mor Hetteen of Roseau County," 1975, Minnesota American Mothers Committee Inc. Biographies, MHS.

20. A description of a woman's group to help migrants is found in Abby Bucklin, "Just Indians," n.d. For an account of an early church relief group see First Congregational Church, Marine (Minnesota) Sewing Society Minute Book, 1857, MHS. Another early group, which claimed to be the oldest philanthropic organization in Minnesota, was the Woman's Christian Association of Minneapolis; see its Minutes, 1866–67, MHS. The Civil War spurred the formation of a number of other women's groups. See "Interviews with Some of the Early Pioneers of Mankato, Minnesota," c. 1943, MHS.

21. Emily Veblen Olsen, Memoirs, 1941, MHS describes improved housing. In order to see the continuing domestic focus of women before and after the evolution of a market economy, it is helpful to compare women's writings to those of Minnesota men. Unlike his wife's diary, Edmund Ely's diary seldom mentions his young daughter. See Edmund F. Ely, Diary, 1838–39, MHS. In a letter written in 1858, another man advises his brother to keep his wife "in oven wood & tea and there wont be much trouble." He adds, "be carful [sic] & not let her get your pants on for if you do it will make a fus [sic] in the family." (Rufus W. Payne, letter to "Dear Brother," December 12, 1858, MHS.) Other similar and interesting sources are E. Grahame Paul, Reminiscences, 1880, which describes an English colony in Minnesota; Charles V. Kegley, Interview, December 31, 1934, in which he and his wife describe their taking up land near Lydia; and Claude E. Simmonds, "George Davies—Wright County Pioneer," 1946, which tells of George and Maria Davies's settlement in Minnesota, especially near Lake Pulaski, all at MHS.

22. Lucia B. Johnson, Memoir, August 28, 1963, and Gertrude Vandergon, Reminiscences, 1940–41, both at MHS.

23. Agnes Mary Kolshorn, "My Parents, Henry Kolshorn and Mary Teitge," 1983, MHS. For another description of washing on the board during the early 1880s see Vandergon, Reminiscences, MHS.

24. Lydia M. Sprague Scott, Diary, 1878–1910, and Kolshorn, "My Parents," both at MHS.

25. Kolshorn, "My Parents," MHS. Keeping animals in early towns was not an uncommon practice. One retired farm couple in Northfield during the 1880s kept not only a cow, but a horse and pig as well, while the Fuller sisters kept chickens in St. Paul. See Emily Veblen Olsen, Memoirs, 1941; Sarah Fuller, letter to "Dear Lizzy," June 12, 1852, in Clippings, Abby Fuller Abbe Family Papers, all at MHS.

26. Minnesota *Pioneer*, May 2, 1850, and October 24, 1850, and Scott, Diary.

27. For the diary of a hotel maid in Renville, Minnesota, see Louisa Wanner, Diary, 1903–04, in Elizabeth Hampsten, comp., *To All Inquiring Friends: Letters, Diaries and Essays in North Dakota, 1880–1910* (Grand Forks: University of North Dakota, 1979), 275–83. For the presence of milliners, seamstresses, and needleworkers see issues of the Minnesota *Pioneer* (for example on February 5, 1852) for it frequently carried their advertisements. For the diary of a seamstress see Abbie T. Griffin, Diary, 1882–85; for an account of a tailor and seamstress see Daisy Barncard Schmidt, "History of the Jacob Zed Barncard Family," 1960; of a dressmaker see Bernice P. Jenkins, "Life of Jennie Atwood Pratt," 1949, all at MHS. For an account of several teachers, one of whom was also a part-time milliner, see Sloan, Reminiscences, MHS. For another teacher's experiences see Hattie Augusta Roberts Eaton, Reminiscences, c. 1934, MHS. The minister was Josephine Lapham; see Susan B. Anthony, letter to "Dear Friend" (Josephine Lapham), June 22, 1868, MHS. For the story of a woman doctor see Winston U. Solberg, "Martha G. Ripley: Pioneer Doctor and Social Reformer," *Minnesota History* 39 (Spring 1964), 1–17. See also Nellie N. Barsness, "Highlights in Careers of Women Physicians in Pioneer Minnesota," 1947, MHS.

28. *Ninth Census of the United States, 1870*, Vol. 1, *Population and Social Statistics* (Washington, D.C.: Government Printing Office, 1872), 670; *Eleventh Census of the United States, 1890*, Part 2 (Washington, D.C.: Government Printing Office, 1897), 302; and *Thirteenth Census of the United States, 1910*, Vol. 4 (Washington, D.C.: Government Printing Office, 1914), 111.

29. *Ninth Census of the United States 1870*, Vol. 1, 677, 678; *Eleventh Census of the United States 1890*, Part 2, 319; and *Thirteenth Census of the United States 1910*, Vol. 4, 123.

30. *Ninth Census of the United States, 1870*, Vol. 1, 677, 687; *Eleventh Census of the United States, 1890*, Part 2, 319; and *Thirteenth Census of the*

United States, 1910, Vol. 4, 120. For the story of Minnie Mary Lee, who wrote sketches and articles for newspapers and journals after 1850 and well into the 1900s, see Henry S. Wood, *A Woman of the Frontier*, n.d., MHS.

31. An example of a woman who maintained that the women of her family enjoyed farm work is Johnson, Memoir, MHS.

32. Quote from Helen E. Howie, "The Historical Background of the Dundas Methodist Church," 1955, MHS. For another ladies' aid society see First Universalist Church, Minneapolis, Bylaws, 1878, MHS.

33. Described in Minutes, Hebrew Ladies' Benevolent Society, St. Paul, 1891–99, MHS. For a Jewish woman's account of life in Dubuque, Iowa, and St. Paul, Minnesota, see Florence Shuman Sher, Reminiscences, 1976, MHS. For the Minnesota WCTU see Minnesota Women's Christian Temperance Union, Minutes, 1866–67, in its Records, 1866–1983, MHS. For the Scandinavian WCTU see Scandinavian Young Women's Christian Temperance Union, Minute Book, 1885, MHS. A Minnesota experiment with a temperance colony is described in "The Story of the National Colony," c. 1943, MHS. The story of the Schubert Club is found in Aylpha Morton, "A Brief History of the Schubert Club, 1882–1962," c. 1962, MHS. For accounts of a few of the numerous other women's clubs see "The Woman's Club, Fergus Falls, 1897–1925," n.d., and Mrs. E. L. Lowe, "Accounts of Various Clubs," 1927, MHS.

34. Federation of Women's Clubs, "Some Special Dates and Events," 1954; Alvin Guttag, "Mrs. Margaret Jane Evans Huntington," n.d.; and Obituary, St. Paul *Pioneer Press*, October 18, 1925, in Huntington Family Papers, all at MHS. For the narrative of another woman who was active in church and other organizations, see "Mrs. Anna Partridge of Owatonna," 1975, Minnesota American Mothers Committee Inc. Biographies, MHS.

35. Ely's graduation is reported in a clipping from the *Winona Daily Republican*, June 9, 1875, in Orrin Smith Papers, MHS. Another example of a woman who attended college (Carleton) found in Olsen, Memoirs, MHS. A few educated women even went on to become college instructors, including Matilda Jane Wilkin of St. Anthony, who became an instructor at the University of Minnesota, and Margaret Jane Evans Huntington, who became Lady Principal (dean of women) at Carleton College. For Wilkin's career see Matilda Jane Wilkin, "Autobiography," 1923, and for Huntington see Guttag, "Mrs. Margaret Jane Evans Huntington," both at MHS.

36. Susie Stageberg, Correspondence and Other Papers, 1881–1938, and "Susie W. Stageberg of Red Wing," 1975, Minnesota American Mothers Committee Inc. Biographies, both at MHS. Ac-

counts of two suffrage workers are found in Sloan, *Reminiscences*, and Eugenia B. Farmer, "A Voice from the Civil War," 1918, both at MHS.

37. One woman even masqueraded as a man in order to get a more remunerative job to support her two children. See Kathryn O'Connell, "A Lensboro Report of 1864," 1965, MHS. For other recent descriptions of the continuing gender separation in women's and men's work see John Mack Faragher, *Sugar Creek: Life on the Illinois Prairie* (New Haven: Yale University Press, 1986); Deborah Fink, *Open Country, Iowa: Rural Women, Tradition and Change* (Albany: State University of New York Press, 1986); and Joan M. Jensen, *Loosening the Bonds: Mid-Atlantic Farm Women, 1750–1850* (New Haven: Yale University Press, 1986); Glenda Riley, *The Female Frontier: A Comparative Perspective of Women of the Prairie and on the Plains* (Lawrence: University Press of Kansas, 1988); and Carolyn Sachs, *"The Invisible Farmers": Women in Agricultural Production* (Totawa, New Jersey: Rowman and Allenheld, 1983).

38. For the argument that modernization has less effect on women than on men see Esther Boserup, *Women's Role in Economic Development* (New York: St. Martin's Press, 1970); Judith van Allen, "Modernization Means More Dependency," *Center Magazine* (May/June 1974), 60–67; and Helen Safra and June Nash *Sex and Class in Latin America* (New York: Praeger, 1975).

39. For the argument that gender roles were adhered to less often than usually thought, see Anne B. Webb, "Forgotten Persephones: Women Farmers on the Frontier," *Minnesota History* 50 (Winter 1986), 134–48. See also Nancy Grey Osterud, "She Helped Me Hay It as Good as a Man: Relations among Women and Men in an Agricultural Community," in Carol Groneman and Mary Beth Norton, eds., *"To Toil the Livelong Day": America's Women at Work, 1780–1980* (Ithaca: Cornell University Press, 1987).

40. See Scott and Tilly, *Women and Work*, for an expanded discussion of this argument.

41. Virginia Sapiro, *Women in American Society* (Palo Alto, California: Mayfield Publishing Company, 1986), 434. See also Lynne B. Iglitzin and Ruth Ross, eds., *Women in the World: A Comparative Study* (Santa Barbara, California: Clio Books, 1976). For a pioneering comparative study see D'Ann Campbell, "Was the West Different? Values and Attitudes of Young Women in 1943," *Pacific Historical Review* 47 (August 1978), 453–63.

Section 1

1. Glenda Riley, "European Views of White Women in the American West," *Journal of the West* 21 (April 1982), 71–81.

2. The term "squaw" was probably a European corruption of a Native American word. Its connotation of a demeaned slave seems to have existed originally only in the minds of non-Indians (Susan Gouge, "Let's Ban the Word 'Squaw'," *Ohoyo: Bulletin of American Indian-Alaska Native Women* 9 [July 1981], 10). See also Jean C. Goodwill, "Squaw is a Dirty Word," in Norman Scheffe, ed., *Issues for the Seventies: Canada's Indians* (Toronto: McGraw-Hill, 1970), 50–52, and Lillian Schlissel, *Women's Diaries of the Westward Journey* (New York: Schocken Books, 1982), 85.

3. For a thorough discussion of the genesis and evolution of these concepts, see Robert F. Berkhofer, Jr., *The White Man's Indian: Images of the American Indian from Columbus to the Present* (New York: Random House, 1979), and Ray A. Billington, *Land of Savagery, Land of Promise: The European Image of the American Frontier in the Nineteenth Century* (New York: W. W. Norton and Company, 1980).

4. Karl May, *Winnetou* (New York: Seabury Press, 1977), xii–xiv.

5. James Axtell, ed., *America Perceived: A View from Abroad in the 17th Century* (West Haven, Conn.: Pendulum Press, 1974), 69.

6. Rupert Brooke, *Letters From America* (London: Sidgwick and Jackson, Ltd., 1931), 143.

7. Alice H. Finckh, ed., "Gottfried Duden Views Missouri, 1824–1827," Part 2, *Missouri Historical Review* 44 (October 1949), 22; Paul Wilhelm, *Travels in North America: 1822–1824* (Norman: University of Oklahoma Press, 1973), 318; Louis-Phillippe, King of France, *Diary of My Travels in America* (New York: Delacorte Press, 1977), 85; Franz von Loher, *Land und Leute in der Alten und Neuen Welt* (Gottingen: G. H. Wigand, 1855–1858), 173; John V. Cheney, ed., *Travels of John Davis in the United States of America, 1789–1802* (Boston: privately printed, 1910), 62.

8. Jean-Bernard Bossu, *Travels in the Interior of North America, 1751–1762* (Norman: University of Oklahoma Press, 1962), 131; Friedrich Gerstacker, *Wild Sports in the Far West: The Narrative of a German Wanderer beyond the Mississippi, 1837–1843* (Durham, N.C.: Duke University Press, 1968), 108; Eduard de Montule, *Travels in America, 1816–1817*, trans. Edward D. Seeber (Bloomington: Indiana University Press, 1951), 155–56.

9. Frederick Marryat, *The Travels and Romantic Adventures of Monsieur Violet among the Snake Indians and Wild Tribes of the Great Western Prairies*, 3 vols. (London: Longman, Brown, Green, and Longman, 1843), 1: 111–12, 131–32.

10. Alexis de Tocqueville, *Journey to America*, ed. J. P. Mayer, trans. George Lawrence (New Haven: Yale University Press, 1960), 133.

11. Louis L. Simonin, *The Rocky Mountain West in 1867* (Lincoln: University of Nebraska Press, 1966), 92; Marian Schouten, "The Image of the American West Evoked in the Netherlands" (unpublished manuscript, Huntington Library, San Marino, California [hereafter HL]), 36–37; J. C. Beltrami, *Pilgrimage in Europe and America*, 2 vols. (London: Hunt and Clarke, 1828), 2: 145–46.

12. Isaac J. Weld, *Travels Through North America and the Province of Canada . . . 1795–1797*, 4th ed. (New York: Augustus M. Kelley, 1970), 228.

13. Paul Wilhelm, *Erste Reise nach dem nordlichen Amerika in den Jahren 1822 bis 1824* (Stuttgart: J. G. Cotta, 1835), 179; Jacob H. Schiel, *Journey through the Rocky Mountains . . . to the Pacific Ocean,* ed. and trans. Thomas N. Bonner (Norman: University of Oklahoma Press, 1959), 96–97; John T. Irving, *Indian Sketches, Taken During an Expedition to the Pawnee and Other Tribes of American Indians,* 2 vols. (London: J. Murray, 1835), 1: 170.

14. Reuben Gold Thwaites, ed., *Early Western Travels, 1748–1846,* 2 vols., published as Vol. 23 of a 32-vol. set (Cleveland, Ohio: Arthur H. Clark Co., 1906), 23: 223, 271, 325.

15. Byron Y. Fleck, "The West as Viewed by Foreign Travellers, 1783–1840" (Ph.D. diss., University of Iowa, 1950), 233–34.

16. Weld, *Travels,* 235–36.

17. Cheney, *Travels of John Davis,* 62; Alexander Sandor Farkas, *Journey in North America* (Philadelphia: American Philosophical Society, 1977), 122, 136.

18. Wilhelm, *Travels,* 318, and Farkas, *Journey,* 122.

19. John Xantus, *Letters From North America,* ed. and trans. Theodore Schoenman and Helen Benedek Schoenman (Detroit: Wayne State University Press, 1975), 34.

20. Percy B. St. John, *The Trapper's Bride* (London: J. Mortimer, 1845), 81–82.

21. Mayne Reid, *The Scalp Hunters* (London: C. J. Skeet, 1851), 277–79, and Sygurd Wisniowski, *Ameryka, 100 Years Old* (Cheshire, Conn.: Cherry Hill Books, 1972), 64.

22. Gustave Aimard, *Stronghand: A Tale of the Disinherited* (London: J. and R. Maxwell, 1878), 98.

23. Charlotte Lennox, *Euphemia,* 4 vols. (London: T. Cadell and J. Evans, 1790), 3: 190–91; Gustave Aimard, *The Indian Scout* (London: Ward and Lock, 1865), 229, and *The Trappers of Arkansas* (New York: T. R. Dawley, 1858), 186; D. L. A. Ashliman, "The American West in 19th Century German Literature" (Ph.D. diss., Rutgers University, 1969), 154.

24. Martin J. Evans, *America: The View From Europe* (San Francisco: San Francisco Book Company, 1976), 108–10.

25. Finckh, ed., "Gottfried Duden," 2: 22; and Marryat, *Narrative,* 126.

26. Marryat, *Narrative,* 126.

27. Friedrich von Raumer, *Die Vereinigten Staaten von Nordamerika* (Leipzig: F. A. Brockhaus, 1845), 144. See also Lydia Maria Child, "The Indian Wife," in *Coronal: A Collection of Miscellaneous Pieces* (Boston: Carter and Hendee, 1832), 162–80, which was widely reprinted in Germany.

28. Weld, *Travels,* 221, and Hodgson, *Remarks,* 271.

29. Tivador Acs, ed., *A Számüzöttek* (Budapest, 1943), 245–56.

30. Mor Jókai, *Vándoroljatok Ki!* (Budapest, 1848), 29, 50.

31. Wisniowski, *Ameryka,* 67–68.

32. Count Francesco Arese, *A Trip to the Prairies and in the Interior of North America, 1837–1838* (New York: Cooper Square Publishers, 1975), 66, 72.

33. Loher, *Land und Leute,* 174.

34. Richard H. Cracroft, "The American West of Karl May," (Master's thesis, University of Utah, 1963), 57.

35. Arese, *Trip to the Prairies,* 72.

36. Bossu, *Travels,* 77; Chateaubriand, *Travels,* 88; Louis-Phillippe, *Diary,* 71; Gustave Aimard, *The Bee-Hunter* (London: J. A. Berger, 1868), 79, and Aimard, *The Pirates of the Prairies* (London: Ward and Lock, 1861), 62; Arese, *Trip to the Prairies,* 164–65.

37. Louis-Phillippe, *Diary,* 72, and von Raumer, *Die Vereinigten Staaten,* 281–82.

38. Heinrich Luden, ed., *Reise Seiner Hoheit des Herzogs Bernard zu Sachsen-Weiner-Eisenach durch Nord-Amerika in den Jahren 1825 and 1826,* 2 vols. (Weimar: W. Hoffman, 1828), 2: 33, and Fredrika Bremer, *The Homes of the New World: Impressions of America,* 2 vols. (New York: Harper and Brothers, 1853), 2: 33.

39. Bossu, *Travels,* 131.

40. Wilhelm, *Travels,* 198.

41. Fleck, "The West as Viewed," 242–56, and Weld, *Travels,* 187.

42. Bremer, *America of the Fifties,* 232.

43. See for example, Marryat, *Narrative,* 2: 12–13, and James A. Jones, *Traditions of the North American Indians,* 3 vols. (London: Colburn and Bentley, 1830), 2: 131–40.

44. Wisniowski, *Ameryka,* 64–65.

45. Marryat, *Diary,* 234; Marryat, *Narrative,* 2: 111–12; Wilhelm, *Travels,* 316.

46. Frances Brooke, *The History of Emily Montague,* 4 vols. (London: J. Dodsley, 1769), 1: 18–19.

47. Bossu, *Travels*, 132, 171, and Louis-Phillippe, *Diary*, 72.

48. Axtell, *America Perceived*, 54–55.

49. Bradbury, *Travels*, 168.

50. Bossu, *Travels*, 171.

51. Oscar Handlin, ed., *This Was America* (Cambridge, Mass.: Harvard University Press, 1949), 10–13; Chateaubriand, *Travels*, 88.

52. Chateaubriand, *Travels*, 32.

53. Bremer, *Homes of the New World*, 593.

54. Montule, *Travels*, 161.

55. Gerstacker, *Wild Sports*, 1: 356–57.

56. Wilhelm, *Travels*, 338, and Fleck, "The West as Viewed," 236–44.

57. Acs, ed., *Számüzöttek*, 245–46.

58. Cheney, ed., *Travels of John Davis*, 68.

59. Pulszky, *White, Red, Black*, 6.

60. Hodgson, *Remarks*, 265.

61. Weld, *Travels*, 290.

62. von Raumer, *Die Vereinigten Staaten*, 138.

63. Napoleon A. Murat, *America and the Americans* (New York: W. H. Graham, 1849), 212.

64. Bradbury, *Travels*, 89.

65. John U. and Donna M. Terrell, *Indian Women of the Western Morning: Their Life in Early America* (Garden City, N.Y.: Doubleday, 1976), 38–40; Karen O. Kupperman, *Settling With the Indians* (Totowa, N.J.: Rowman and Littlefield, 1980), 60–63; Margot Liberty, "Hell Came With Horses: Plains Indian Women in the Equestrian Era," *Montana: The Magazine of Western History* 32 (Summer 1982), 10–17. For a more thorough discussion of these issues, see Patricia Albers and Beatrice Medicine, *The Hidden Half: Studies of Plains Indian Women* (Washington, D.C.: University Press of America, 1983). For a review of images of Native American women in folklore, theater, art, and vernacular culture, see Rayna Green, "The Pocahontas Perplex: The Image of Indian Women in American Culture," *Massachusetts Review* 16 (Autumn 1975), 698–714.

66. Rayna Green, "Native American Women," *Signs* 6 (Winter 1980), 250. For a somewhat different interpretation, see Sylvia Van Kirk, *Many Tender Ties: Women in Fur-Trade Societies, 1670–1870* (Norman: University of Oklahoma Press, 1980), and Jacqueline Peterson, "The People in Between: Indian-White Marriage and the Genesis of a Metis Society and Culture in the Great Lakes Region, 1680–1830" (Ph.D. diss., University of Illinois, Chicago, 1981).

67. Sue Armitage, "Western Women: Beginning to Come into Focus," *Montana: The Magazine of Western History* 32 (Summer 1982), 4–5; Green, "Native American Women," 248, 255, 260, 262; Liberty, "Hell Came With Horses," 18–19; and

Valerie S. Mathes, "Native American Women in Medicine and the Military," *Journal of the West* 31 (April 1982), 41–47.

68. Karen Sacks, "State Bias and Women's Status," *American Anthropologist* 78 (September 1976), 565–69; Liberty, "Hell Came With Horses," 12; and Mathes, "Native American Women," 41.

69. Marryat, *Diary*, 248.

70. Terrell and Terrell, *Indian Women*, 37, and Mathes, "Native American Women," 41.

71. Gerstacker, *Wild Sports*, 110, and Bradbury, *Travels*, 146.

72. Jones, *Traditions*, 1: 255–68; Gustave Aimard, *White Scalper: A Story of the Texan War* (London: Ward and Lock, 1861), 125–38; and Marryat, *Narrative*, 1: 130–36.

73. Bossu, *Travels*, 132; Weld, *Travels*, 259; David J. Jeremy, *Henry Wansey and His American Journal, 1794* (Philadelphia: American Philosophical Society, 1970), 51; Balduin Möllhausen, *Diary of a Journey from the Mississippi to the Coasts of the Pacific* (New York: Johnson Reprint Corp., 1969), 98.

74. Thwaites, ed., *Early Western Travels, 1748–1846*, 22: 352.

75. Terrell and Terrell, *Indian Women*, 71–90, and Liberty, "Hell Came With Horses," 13–15.

76. Jerzy Jedlicki, "Images of America," *Polish Perspectives* 18 (November 1975), 26–28.

77. William Baillie-Grohman, *Camps in the Rockies* (New York: Charles Scribner's Sons, 1910), 23.

78. Isabella L. Bird, *The Englishwoman in America* (Madison: University of Wisconsin Press, 1966), 143.

79. William Cobbett, *A Year's Residence in the United States of America* (Carbondale: Southern Illinois University Press, 1964); Tocqueville, *Journey*; and Dr. Albert C. Koch, *Journey Through a Part of the United States of North America in the Years 1844 to 1846* (Carbondale: Southern Illinois University Press, 1972).

80. Billington, *Land of Savagery*, 30.

81. An Old Scout, *The White Boy Chief; or, The Terror of the North Platte* (New York: Frank Tousey, 1908), 3–4, 11, 20, and F. A. Briggs, *Buffalo Bill's Witchcraft; or, Pawnee Bill and the Snake Aztecs* (New York: Street and Smith, 1911), 8.

82. Interview #12079, Indian-Pioneer Papers, Western History Collection, University of Oklahoma Library [hereafter IPP], Vol. 89, 265–78. Used by permission.

83. Gilbert A. Wilson, ed., *Buffalo Bird Woman's Garden* (St. Paul: Minnesota Historical Society Press, 1987) 9, 33. In public domain.

84. Interview with Nellie Quail, August 1, 1967, Fort McDowell Indian Reservation, held by Arizona

State Museum, University of Arizona, Tucson. Used by permission.

85. Interview, Walter Running Legs, May 27, 1977, at Pipestone National Monument, Pipestone, Minnesota. Original in author's possession. Used by permission.

86. Primary literature used here includes Tivador Acs, ed. *Hungarian Pioneers in the New World* (Budapest: Lathatar Kiadasa, 1942); Robert Barclay-Allardice, *Agricultural Tour in the United States and Upper Canada, with miscellaneous notices* (Edinburgh: W. Blockwood and Sons, 1842); Magnus Bech-Olsen, *My Trip to America* (Copenhagen: J. L. Wulff, 1900); William Abraham Bell, *New Tracks in North America*, 2 vols. (London: Chapman and Hall, 1869); Giacomo Constantino Beltrami, *Pilgrimage in Europe and America*, 2 vols. (London: Hunt and Clark, 1828); William N. Blane, *An Excursion Through the United States and Canada, during the Years 1822–23* (London: Baldwin, Cradock, and Joy, 1824; Jean-Bernard Bossu, *Travels in the Interior of North America, 1751–1762* (Norman: University of Oklahoma Press, 1962); John Bradbury, *Travels in the Interior of America* (Ann Arbor: University Microfilms, Inc., 1966); Fredrika Bremer, *The Homes of the New World: Impressions of America*, 2 vols. (New York: Harper and Brothers, 1853); Fredrika Bremer, *America of the Fifties: Letters of Fredrika Bremer* (New York: The American-Scandinavian Foundation, 1924); J. P. Brissot de Warville, *New Travels in the United States of America, 1788* (Cambridge: Belknap Press, 1964); Moritz Busch, *Travels Between the Hudson and the Mississippi, 1851–1852* (Lexington: University Press of Kentucky, 1971); Michael Chevalier, *Society, Manners and Politics in the United States: Being a Series of Letters on North America* (Philadelphia: Carey and Hart, 1846); William Cobbett, *A Year's Residence in the United States of America* (Carbondale: Southern Illinois University Press, 1946); Chateaubriand, *Travels in America* (Lexington: University of Kentucky Press, 1969); Charles Dickens, *American Notes for General Circulation* (London: Chapman and Hall, 1842); C. Ax Egerstrom, *Travel is Great, But There is No Place Like Home* (Stockholm: A. Bromier, 1859); Alexander Farkas, *Journey in North America* (Philadelphia: American Philosophical Society, 1977); W. Faux, *Memorable Days in America: Being a Journal of a Tour to the United States* (New York: AMS Press, 1969); Henry Bradshaw Fearon, *Sketches of America: A Narrative of a Journey of Five Thousand Miles Through Eastern and Western States* (New York: Benjamin Blum Inc., 1969); James Flint, *Letters From America* (Edinburgh: W. and C. Tait, 1822); Friedrich Gerstacker, *Narrative of a Journey Round the World*, 3 vols. (London: Hurst and Blackett, 1853); Friedrich Gerstacker, *Wild Sports of the Far West: The Narrative of a German Wanderer Be-*

yond the Mississippi, 1837–1843 (Durham, N.C.: Duke University Press, 1968); Francis J. Grund, *The Americans in their Moral, Social, and Political Relations* (New York: Johnson Reprint Corp., 1968); Mattie Austin Hatcher, *Letters of an Early American Traveller: Mary Austin Holley, Her Life and Works, 1784–1846* (Dallas: Southwest Press, 1933); Henri Herz, *My Travels in America* (Madison: The State Historical Society, 1963); Adam Hodgson, *Remarks During a Journey Through North America in the Years 1819, 1820, 1821* (Westport, Conn.: Negro Universities Press, 1970); Dr. Albert C. Koch, *Journey Through a Part of the United States of North America in the Years 1844 to 1846* (Carbondale: Southern Illinois University Press, 1972); Louis-Philippe, King of France, *Diary of My Travels in America* (New York: Delacorte Press, 1977); Charles Lyell, *Travels in North America; with Geological Observations on the United States* (London: J. Murray, 1845); Frederick Marryat, *Narrative of the Travels and Adventures of Monsieur Violet, in California, Sonora, and Western Texas*, 3 vols. (London: Longman, Brown, Green, and Longman, 1843); Harriet Martineau, *Retrospect of Western Travel*, 2 vols. (London: Saunders and Ottley, 1838); Harriet Martineau, *Society in America*, 3 vols. (New York: AMS Press, 1966); Balduin Möllhausen, *Diary of a Journey from the Mississippi to the Coasts of the Pacific* (New York: Johnson Reprint Corp., 1969); Eduard de Montule, *Travels in America, 1816–1817* (Bloomington: Indiana University Press, 1951); Simon A. O'Ferrall, *A Ramble of Six Thousand Miles Through the United States of America* (London: E. Wilson, 1832); Francis and Theresa Pulzsky, *White, Red, Black: Sketches of Society in the United States During the Visit of Their Guest*, 3 vols. (New York: Negro Universities Press, 1968); Ole Munch Raeder, *America in the Forties: The Letters of Ole Munch Raeder* (Minneapolis: University of Minnesota Press, 1929); Charles Sealsfield, *The United States of North America As They Are* (New York: Johnson Reprint Corp., 1970); Charles Sealsfield, *The Americans As They Are* (New York: Johnson Reprint Corp., 1970); Patrick Shirreff, *A Tour Through North America: With a comprehensive view of the Canadas and United States as adapted for agricultural emigration* (Edinburgh: Simpkin, 1835); Alexis de Tocqueville, *Journey to America* (New Haven: Yale University Press, 1960); Alexis de Tocqueville, *Democracy in America* (London: Oxford University Press, 1953); Frances Trollope, *Domestic Manners of the Americans* (New York: Dodd, Mead and Co., 1927); Charles Victor Crosnier de Varigny, *The Women of the United States* (New York: Dodd, Mead, and Co., 1895); Henry Wansey, *The Journal of an Excursion to the United States of North America in the Summer of 1794,* (New York: Johnson Reprint Corp., 1969); Isaac J. Weld, *Travels Through North America and the Provinces of Canada, 1795–1797* (New York:

Augustus M. Kelley, 1970); Paul Wilhelm, Duke of Wurttemberg, *Travels in North America, 1822–24* (Norman: University of Oklahoma Press, 1973); Frances Wright, *Views of Society and Manners in America* (Cambridge: Belknap Press, 1963); John Xantus, *Letters From North America* (Detroit: Wayne State University Press, 1975).

Primary sources in published collections include Robert G. Athearn, *Westward the Briton* (New York: Charles Scribner's Sons, 1953); James Axtell, ed., *America Perceived: A View from Abroad in the 17th Century* (West Haven, Conn.: Pendulum Press, 1974); James Axtell, ed., *America Perceived: A View from Abroad in the 18th Century* (West Haven, Conn.: Pendulum Press, 1974); William J. Baker, ed., *America Perceived: A View from Abroad in the 19th Century* (West Haven, Conn.: Pendulum Press, 1974); H. Arnold Barton, *Letters From the Promised Land, 1840–1914* (Minneapolis: University of Minnesota Press for the Swedish Pioneer Historical Society, 1975); Mary R. Beard, ed., *America Through Women's Eyes* (Westport, Conn.: Greenwood Press, 1969); Isabella Lucy Bird, *The Englishwoman in America* (Madison: University of Wisconsin Press, 1966); Theodore Christian Blegen, *The Land of Their Choice: The Immigrants Write Home* (Minneapolis: University of Minnesota Press, 1955); Henry Steele Commager, *America in Perspective: The United States Through Foreign Eyes* (New York: Mentor Brooks, 1947); Alan Conway, ed., *The Welsh in America: Letters From the Immigrants* (Minneapolis: University of Minnesota Press, 1961); Jane Louise Mesick, *The English Traveller in America, 1785–1835* (New York: Columbia Press, 1922); Richard L. Rapson, *Britons View America* (Seattle: University of Washington Press, 1971); Marilyn M. Sibley, *Travelers in Texas, 1761–1860* (Austin: University of Texas Press, 1967); Andrew J. Tirriellei, *Italian Opinion on America as Revealed by Italian Travelers, 1850–1900* (Cambridge, Mass.: Harvard University Press, 1941).

Novels include several titles by Gustave Aimard: *The White Scalper: A Story of the Texan War* (London: Ward and Lock, 1861); *Stronghand: A Tale of the Disinherited* (London: J. and R. Maxwell, 1878); *The Trappers of Arkansas, or, The Loyal Heart* (New York: T. R. Dawley, 1858); *The Pirates of the Prairies: Adventures in the American Desert* (London: Ward and Lock, 1861); *The Border Rifles, A Tale of the Texan War* (Philadelphia: T. B. Peterson and Brothers, 1840); *The Indian Scout: A Story of the Aztec City* (London: Ward and Lock, 1865); *The Bee-Hunter: A Tale of Adventure* (London: J. A. Berger, 1868); Mrs. Frances Brooke, *The History of Emily Montague*, 4 vols. (London: printed for J. Dodsley, 1769); Thomas Campbell, *Gertrude of Wyoming: A Pennsylvania Tale* (London: Longman, Hurse, Rees, and Orme, 1809); François-René de Chateaubriand, *Atala* and *René* (London: Oxford University Press, 1963); Edward S. Ellis, *Hurricane*

Gulch, A Tale of the Asota and Bufferville Trail (New York: P. F. Collier, 1892); Edward S. Ellis, *Seth Jones; or, The Captives of the Frontier* (London: Beadle and Co., 1861); Wilhelm Frey, *The Apaches on the Rio Grande* (Mulheim on the Ruhr: J. Bagel, n.d.); Wilhelm Frey, *In the Hands of the Indians* (Mulheim on the Ruhr; J. Bagel, 1892); Karl May, *The Treasure of Silver Lake* (Braunschweig: Graff, 1873); Karl May, *Winnetou* (New York: The Seabury Press, 1977); Mayne Reid, *The Scalp Hunters; or, Romantic Adventures in Northern Mexico* (London: C. J. Skeet, 1851); Henri Reviol Benedict, *Le Bivouac des Trappeurs* (Paris: Brunet, 1864); Percy B. St. John, *The Trapper's Bride* (London: J. Mortimer, 1845); Henryk Sienkiewicz, *Western Septet: Stories of the American West* (Cheshire, Conn.: Cherry Hill Books, 1973).

87. Quoted in *Pioneer Stories Written by People of Nelson County, North Dakota* (Lakota, N.D.: American Press, n.d.).

88. Mary Annetta Coleman Pomeroy, "My Life Story," 1939, Arizona Historical Society, Tucson. Used by permission.

89. Doña Jesús Moreno de Soza, Reminiscences, 1939, Antonio Soza Papers, Arizona Historical Society, Tucson. Used by permission.

90. Quoted in Evelyn Nakano Glenn, *Issei, Nisei, War Bride: Three Generations of Japanese American Women in Domestic Service* (Philadelphia: Temple University Press, 1986) 47, 260 n. 5.

91. Era Bell Thompson, *American Daughter* (1946; reprint, St. Paul: Minnesota Historical Society, 1986).

92. Examples of historians who have attempted to reconstruct western black history but have included little or no material on black women are Jean I. Castles, "The West: Crucible of the Negro," *Montana: The Magazine of Western History* 19 (Winter 1969), 83–85; William L. Katz, *The Black West* (Garden City, New York: Doubleday, 1971); Kenneth W. Porter, *The Negro on the American Frontier* (New York: Arno Press and the New York Times, 1971); Lawrence D. Rice, *The Negro in Texas, 1874–1900* (Baton Rouge: Louisiana State University Press, 1971); W. Sherman Savage, *Blacks in the West* (Westport, Conn.: Greenwood Press, 1976). Richard White, "Race Relations in the American West," *American Quarterly* 38 (Bibliography edition, 1986), 397–416, has very little on blacks and nothing on black women. A recent and refreshing collection of original essays and photographs of western African Americans that reflects the existence of women throughout is Marguerite Mitchell Marshall, et al., *An Account of Afro-Americans in Southeast Kansas, 1884–1984* (Manhattan, Kansas: Sunflower University Press, 1986). For a discussion of the historiography of black women, see Gerda Lerner, *The Majority Finds Its Past: Placing Women*

in History (Oxford: Oxford University Press, 1979), 63–82. Regarding racism, sexism, and African American women, see Diann Holland Painter, "The Black Woman in American Society," *Current History* 70 (May 1976), 224–27, 234.

93. Tish Nevins, American Mothers Bicentennial Project, 1975–1976, Montana Historical Society Archives, Helena [hereafter MHSA].

94. Sudie Rhone, interview, November 8, 1979, University of Wyoming Heritage Center, Laramie [hereafter WAHC]. Another useful collection is the Black Oral History Interviews, Holland Library, Washington State University, Pullman.

95. Sara J. Bernson and Robert J. Eggers, "Black People in South Dakota History," *South Dakota History* 7 (Summer 1977), 247, 251–52. See also Quintard Taylor, "Blacks in the West: An Overview," *Western Journal of Black Studies* 1 (March 1977), 4–10. Suggestions for locating African American women's sources can be found in Deborah Gray White, "Mining the Forgotten: Manuscript Sources for Black Women's History," *Journal of American History* 74 (June 1987), 237–42.

96. Sue Armitage, Theresa Banfield, and Sarah Jacobus, "Black Women and Their Communities in Colorado," *Frontiers* 2 (1977), 45–51.

97. Lawrence B. de Graaf, "Race, Sex, and Region: Black Women in the American West, 1850–1920," *Pacific Historical Review* 49 (May 1980), 289, 291, 296–97, 313. For an analysis of black women in the Far West before the Civil War, see Michael S. Conray, "Blacks in the Pacific West, 1850–1860: A View from the Census," *Nevada Historical Society Quarterly* 28 (Summer 1985), 90–121.

98. Glenda Riley, *Frontierswomen: The Iowa Experience* (Ames: Iowa State University Press, 1981), 88–91. The mob violence in Grinnell was described by Sarah Parker, letter to "Dear Mother," March 10, 1860, State Historical Society of Iowa, Iowa City [hereafter SHSI]. For a discussion of contradictory attitudes toward blacks, see Eugene H. Berwanger, *The Frontier Against Slavery: Western Anti-Negro Prejudice and the Slavery Extension Controversy* (Urbana: University of Illinois Press, 1967).

99. Sandra L. Myres, *Westering Women: The Frontier Experience, 1800–1915* (Albuquerque: University of New Mexico Press, 1982), 85–86.

100. Katz, The Black West, 50, 54, 284. For a contrasting view of attitudes toward African Americans in west Texas, see George R. Woolfolk, "Turner's Safety-Valve and Free Negro Westward Migration," *Journal of Negro History* 50 (July 1965), 185–97. For discussions of blacks in Iowa, see Leola M. Bergmann, *The Negro in Iowa* (Iowa City: State Historical Society of Iowa, 1969); Paul W. Black, "Lynchings in Iowa," *Iowa Journal of History and Politics* 10 (April 1912), 151–254; Louis Pelzer, "The Negro and Slavery in Early Iowa," *Iowa Jour-*

nal of History and Politics 2 (October 1904), 471–84; Morton M. Rosenberg, *Iowa on the Eve of the Civil War: A Decade of Frontier Politics* (Norman: University of Oklahoma Press, 1972); Joel H. Silbey, "Proslavery Sentiment in Iowa," *Iowa Journal of History and Politics* 55 (October 1957), 289–318; Jacob Van Eck, "Underground Railroad in Iowa," *Palimpsest* 2 (May 1921), 129–93.

101. Riley, *Frontierswomen*, 94–99.

102. Fred Lockley, "Some Documentary Records of Slavery in Oregon," *Oregon Historical Quarterly* 17 (June 1916), 108; John E. Briggs, *History of Social Legislation in Iowa* (Iowa City: State Historical Society, 1915), 34–35.

103. Howard County, Missouri, Registry for Free Negroes, 1836–1861, and Cooper County, Missouri, United States Census, 1850, Vol. 1, manuscript census unpaginated, both in the Joint Collection of the University of Missouri/Western History Society of Missouri Manuscripts, Columbia [hereafter Miss. Coll.]; McLean County, United States Census, 1850, McLean County Historical Society, Bloomington, Illinois, manuscript census unpaginated.

104. For studies regarding African Americans that draw on census data, see Daniel M. Johnson and Rex R. Campbell, *Black Migration in America: A Social Demographic History* (Durham: Duke University Press, 1981); Elmer R. Rusco, *"Good Times Coming?": Black Nevadans in the Nineteenth Century* (Westport, Conn.: Greenwood Press, 1975); Douglas Henry Daniels, *Pioneer Urbanites: A Social and Cultural History of Black San Francisco* (Philadelphia: Temple University Press, 1980).

105. Castles, "The West," 83; David Vassar Taylor, "The Blacks," in *They Chose Minnesota: A Survey of the State's Ethnic Groups*, ed. June Drenning Holmquist (St. Paul: Minnesota Historical Society Press, 1981), 73; Richard B. Morris, ed., *Encyclopedia of American History* (New York: Harper and Row, 1961), 159.

106. Eliza Byer Price, "Recollections of My Father, Samuel Dyer, 1905," Miss. Coll. For a discussion of the westward migration of southern slaveholders, see James Oakes, *The Ruling Race: A History of American Slave Holders* (New York: Alfred A. Knopf, 1982), 73–95.

107. Myres, *Westering Women*, 119; Adrienne Christopher, "The Story of Daniel Yoacham, Westport Pioneer Innkeeper," n.d., Delia Richerson McDaniel, diary, 1841, and James A. Ward, "Autobiography," n.d., University of Missouri, Columbia.

108. Burlington *Tri-Weekly Telegraph* (Iowa), August 27, 1850.

109. Ruth A. Gallaher, "Slavery in Iowa," *Palimpsest* 28 (May 1947), 158–60.

110. Silbey, "Proslavery Sentiment in Iowa," 189–91; Rosenberg, *Iowa on the Eve of the Civil War*, 14.

111. Pelzer, "The Negro and Slavery in Early Iowa," 471; Briggs, *History of Social Legislation in Iowa,* 34–35; William M. Donnell, *Pioneers of Marion County* (Des Moines: Republican Steam Printing House, 1872), 70–75.

112. Taylor, "The Blacks," in Holmquist, *They Chose Minnesota,* 73–74.

113. See Shirley J. Carlson, "Black Migration to Pulaski County, Illinois, 1860–1900," *Journal of the Illinois Historical Society* 80 (Spring 1987), 37–46; Roy Garvin, "Benjamin, or 'Pap,' Singleton and His Followers," *Journal of Negro History* 33 (January 1948), 7–23; Glen Schwendemann, "Wyandotte and the First 'Exodusters' on the Missouri," *Kansas Historical Quarterly* 26 (Autumn 1960), 233–49; "The 'Exodusters' on the Missouri," *Kansas Historical Quarterly* 29 (Spring 1963), 25–40; Nell Irvin Painter, *Exodusters: Black Migration to Kansas After Reconstruction* (New York: Alfred A. Knopf, 1977), 108–17; Robert G. Athearn, *In Search of Canaan: Black Migration to Kansas, 1879–1880* (Lawrence: The Regents Press of Kansas, 1978); George H. Wayne, "Negro Migration and Colonization in Colorado, 1870–1930," *Journal of the West* 15 (January 1976), 102–20; Mozell C. Hill, "The All-Negro Communities of Oklahoma: The Natural History of a Social Movement," *Journal of Negro History* 31 (July 1946), 254–68; Arvarh E. Strickland, "Toward the Promised Land: The Exodus to Kansas and Afterward," *Missouri Historical Review* 69 (July 1975), 376–412; Harold M. Rose, "The All-Negro Town: Its Evolution and Function," *Geographic Review* 55 (July 1965), 362–81; Nudie E. Williams, "Black Newspapers and the Exodusters of 1879," *Kansas History* 8 (Winter 1985–1986), 217–25.

114. Anne E. Bingham, "Sixteen Years on a Kansas Farm, 1870–1886," *Kansas State Historical Society Collections* 15 (1919–1920), 520–21.

115. Quoted in Glen Schwendemann, "Nicodemus: Negro Haven on the Solomon," *Kansas Historical Quarterly* 34 (Spring 1968), 14, 26. For a discussion of contemporary media images that usually represented Exodusters as male, see George R. Lamplugh, "The Image of the Negro in Popular Magazine Fiction, 1875–1900," *Journal of Negro History* 57 (April 1972), 177–89.

116. William C. Sherman, *Prairie Mosaic: An Ethnic Atlas of Rural North Dakota* (Fargo: North Dakota Institute for Regional Studies, 1983), 14; Ava Day, two letters to "Nebraska Historical Society," March 28 and May 23, 1964, Nebraska State Historical Society, Lincoln [hereafter NHS]; "A Colored Man's Experience on a Nebraska Homestead," *Omaha World Herald,* February 11, 1899; Kathie Ryckman Anderson, "Era Bell Thompson," *North Dakota History* 49 (Fall 1982), 11–18; Era Bell Thompson, interview, September 16, 1975, State Historical Society of North Dakota, Oral History Project, Bismarck [hereafter NDOH]. See also Minnie Miller Brown,

"Black Women in American Agriculture," *Agricultural History* 50 (January 1976), 202–12; Bernson and Eggers, "Black People in South Dakota History," 245–53.

117. Patricia C. Harpole, ed., "The Black Community in Territorial St. Anthony: A Memoir," *Minnesota History* 49 (Summer 1984), 42–55.

118. Eva Neal, Family Papers, 1881–1963, Minnesota Historical Society, St. Paul, [hereafter MHS]; Helen Johnson Downing, Interview, September 16, 1976, NDOH. See also Taylor, "The Blacks," in Holmquist, *They Chose Minnesota,* 73–91.

119. De Graaf, "Race, Sex, and Region," 296; Katharine T. Corbett and Mary E. Seematter, "Black St. Louis at the Turn of the Century," *Gateway Heritage* 71 (Summer 1986), 44. For a discussion of African American expectations of women, see James Oliver Horton, "Freedom's Yoke: Gender Conventions Among Antebellum Blacks," *Feminist Studies* 12 (Spring 1986), 51–76.

120. Painter, Exodusters, 153; W. Sherman Savage, "The Negro in the Westward Movement," *Journal of Negro History* 25 (October 1940), 532–33; David M. Katzman, *Seven Days a Week: Women and Domestic Service in Industrializing America* (Urbana: University of Illinois Press, 1978), 82–85, 289–90.

121. Anna Ramsey, letter to "My Darling Children," March 31, 1876, and to "My Dear Daughter," February 2 and December 8, 1876, Alexander Ramsey Family Papers, MHS; *Bloomington Bulletin* (Illinois), January 26, 1899.

122. Phillip T. Drotning, *A Guide to Negro History in America* (New York: Doubleday, 1968), 67; Georgiana Packard, "Leaves from the Life of a Kansas Pioneer, 1914," Kansas State Historical Society, Topeka [hereafter KHS]; Mattie V. Rhodes, Family Papers, 1968, MHS.

123. "Mary Ellen Pleasant," in *Notable American Women, 1607–1950,* 3 vols., ed. Edward T. James and Janet W. James (Cambridge, Mass.: Belknap Press, 1971), 3: 75–76; Bernson and Eggers, "Black People in South Dakota History," 250; D. Cheryl Collins, "Women at Work in Manhattan, Kansas, 1890–1910," *Journal of the West* 21 (April 1982), 33–40; Nevins, "Montana American Mothers," MHSA; "Washwomen, Maumas, Exodusters, Jubileers," in *We Are Your Sisters: Black Women in the Nineteenth Century,* ed. Dorothy Sterling (New York: W. W. Norton & Company, 1984), 355–94; Sylvia Lea Sallquist, "The Image of the Hired Girl in Literature: The Great Plains, 1860 to World War I," *Great Plains Quarterly* 4 (Summer 1984), 168.

124. "Sarah Breedlove Walker," in James, *Notable American Women,* 3: 533–34. For some other cases of black women entrepreneurs, see William L. Lang, "The Nearly Forgotten Blacks of Last Chance Gulch, 1900–1912," *Pacific Northwest Quarterly* 70 (April 1979), 54–55.

125. Donna Mungen, *Life and Times of Biddy Mason: From Slavery to Wealthy California Laundress* (n.p., 1976); Kathleen Bruyn, *"Aunt" Clara Brown: Story of a Black Pioneer* (Boulder, Colorado: Pruett Publishing Company, 1970); Bernson and Eggers, "Black People in South Dakota History," 251.

126. Savage, *Blacks in the West,* 168–81; E. Wilburn Bock, "Farmer's Daughter Effect: The Case of the Negro Female Professions," *Phylon* 30 (Spring 1969), 17–26. For the "sex loophole" that helped daughters get education, see Lerner, *The Majority Finds Its Past,* 69–70.

127. See Delilah L. Beasley, *The Negro Trail Blazers of California* (Los Angeles: Times Mirror Printing and Binding House, 1919), 123, 173–78; "California Colored Women Trail Blazers," in *Homespun Heroines and Other Women of Distinction,* ed. Hallie Q. Brown (Xenia, Ohio: Aldine Publishing Company, 1926), 241–42; Rudolph M. Lapp, *Blacks in Gold Rush California* (New Haven, Conn.: Yale University Press, 1977), 184; Corbett and Seematter, "Black St. Louis," 48. For African American women who practiced nursing see Day, letters, NHS; Elizabeth Cochran, "Hatchets and Hoopskirts: Women in Kansas History," *Midwest Quarterly* 2 (April 1961), 235; "Black Women in Colorado: Two Early Portraits," *Frontiers* 7 (1984), 21. For an African American woman physician, see Armitage, Banfield, and Jacobus, "Black Women and Their Communities," 46; Susan H. Armitage, "Reluctant Pioneers," in *Women and Western American Literature,* ed. Helen Winter Stauffer and Susan J. Rosowski (Troy, New York: Whitston Publishing Company, 1982), 47.

128. See Era Bell Thompson, interview, September 16, 1975, NDOH; James T. Abajian, comp., *Blacks in Selected Newspapers, Censuses and Other Sources: An Index to Names and Subjects,* 3 vols. (Boston: G. K. Hall, 1977), 1: 221–22, 649, 716; "Charlotta Spears Bass," *Notable American Women: The Modern Period,* ed. Barbara Sicherman (Cambridge, Mass.: Belknap Press, 1980), 61–63; Gerald R. Gill, " 'Win or Lose—We Win': The 1952 Vice-Presidential Campaign of Charlotta Bass," in *The Afro-American Woman: Struggles and Images,* ed. Sharon Harley and Rosalyn Terborg-Penn (Port Washington, New York: Kennikat Press, 1978), 109–18.

129. For a fascinating study of African American women convicts, see Anne M. Butler, "Still in Chains: Black Women in Western Prisons, 1865–1910," *Western Historical Quarterly* 20 (February 1989), 19–35.

130. Thompson, interview, September 16, 1975, NDOH. For an analysis of the development of black women's sexual image, see Winthrop D. Jordan, *White Over Black: American Attitudes Toward the Negro, 1550–1812* (Chapel Hill: University of North Carolina Press, 1968), 150–51.

131. Bernson and Eggers, "Black People in South Dakota History," 247; Kenneth W. Porter, "Negro Labor in the Western Cattle Industry," *Labor History* 10 (1969), 327; Erwin N. Thompson, "The Negro Soldier and His Officers," in *The Black Military Experience in the American West,* ed. John M. Carroll (New York: Liveright, 1971), 182; Lang, "The Nearly Forgotten Blacks of Last Chance Gulch," 55. Nevins, "Montana American Mothers," MHSA, is an example of a black woman who detested a madam, Mammy Smith, reportedly the only other black in Hamilton, Montana. For African American women's views of the myth of the "bad" black woman, see Gerda Lerner, ed., *Black Women in White America: A Documentary History* (New York: Vintage Books, 1973), 164–72.

132. Thompson, interview, September 16, 1976, NDOH; Armitage, "Reluctant Pioneers," 47–48; Armitage, Banfield, and Jacobus, "Black Women and Their Communities," 46.

133. Day, letters, NHS. See also Downing, interview, September 16, 1976, NDOH.

134. Anderson, "Era Bell Thompson," 11–12.

135. Sudie Rhone, interview, November 8, 1979, WAHC.

136. Armitage, Banfield, and Jacobus, "Black Women and Their Communities," 46.

137. Willard Gatewood, "Kate D. Chapman Reports on 'The Yankton Colored People,' 1889," *South Dakota History* 7 (Winter 1976), 28–35; Spann, Black Pioneers; Nellie Bush, interview, IPP, Vol. 14, 53.

138. "A Brief Resume of History," Pilgrim Baptist Church, ca. 1977, MHS. See also Elizabeth Lindsay Davis, *Lifting As They Climb* (Chicago: National Association of Colored Women, 1933); Marilyn Dell Brady, "Kansas Federation of Colored Women's Clubs, 1900–1930," *Kansas History* 9 (Spring 1986), 19–30; Gerda Lerner, "Early Community Work of Black Club Women," *Journal of Negro History* 59 (April 1974), 158–67.

139. Mrs. Laurence C. Jones, "The Desire for Freedom," *Palimpsest* 7 (May 1927), 153–63.

140. Rhone, interview, November 8, 1979, WAHC.

141. Harpole, "The Black Community," 44; Neal, Family Papers, MHS; Rhone, interview, November 8, 1979, WAHC.

142. Savage, *Blacks in the West,* 187–88. See also Lerner, *The Majority Finds Its Past,* 83–93; Lerner, *Black Women in White America,* 437–78.

143. Susan H. Armitage and Deborah G. Wilbert, "Black Women in the Pacific Northwest: A Survey and Research Prospectus"; Armitage, "Black Women in the Pacific Northwest." The author thanks Sue Armitage for sharing this research. Particularly useful sources on African American women in the Pacific Northwest are Quintard Taylor, "The Emergence of Black Communities in the

Pacific Northwest, 1864–1910," *Journal of Negro History* 64 (Fall 1979), 346–51; Elizabeth McLagan, *A Peculiar Paradise: A History of Blacks in Oregon, 1788–1940* (Portland, Ore.: Georgian Press, 1980); Esther Mumford, *Seattle's Black Victorians, 1852–1910* (Seattle: Ananse Press, 1980). In addition, Melissa Hield and Martha Boethel, *The Women's West Teaching Guide: The Multicultural History of Women in the Nineteenth Century American West,* is available from the Women's Studies Program at Washington State University, Pullman.

144. Anna Ramsey to "My Dear Daughter," June 27, 1875, Alexander Ramsey Family Papers, MHS; Susan D. Vanarsdale, Diary, 1847, Miss. Coll.

145. Interview with Mandy Morrow in George P. Rawick, ed., *The American Slave* (Westport, Conn.: Greenwood Press, 1972), 138–39. Used by permission.

146. Interview with Susan Merritt, in Rawick, *The American Slave,* 75–78. Used by permission.

147. Interview #7838, October 15, 1937, IPP, Vol. 7, 386–88. Used by permission.

Section 2

1. Allan G. Bogue, "Social Theory and the Pioneer," *Agricultural History* 34 (January 1960), 24.

2. See for example John Faragher and Christine Stansell, "Women and Their Families on the Overland Trail to California and Oregon, 1842–1867," *Feminist Studies* (1975), 150–66; John Faragher, *Women and Men on the Overland Trail* (New Haven: Yale University Press, 1979); Dorys C. Grover, "The Pioneer Women in Fact and Fiction," *Heritage of Kansas: A Journal of the Great Plains* 10 (Spring 1977), 35–44; Emerson Hough, *The Passing of the Frontier* (New Haven: Yale University Press, 1921), especially 93–94; Georgia Willis Read, "Women and Children on the Oregon-California Trail in the Gold Rush Years," *Missouri Historical Review* 34 (October 1944), 1–23; Lillian Schlissel, "Women's Diaries on the Western Frontier," *American Studies* 18 (Spring 1977), 87–100; Page Smith, *Daughters of the Promised Land* (Boston: Little, Brown and Company, 1970), especially 223; Christine Stansell, "Women on the Great Plains, 1865–1890," *Women's Studies* 4 (1976), 87–98. For a discussion of images and their development see Glenda Riley, "Images of the Frontierswomen: Iowa as a Case Study," *Western Historical Quarterly* 3 (April 1977), 189–202, and "Women in the West," *Journal of American Culture* 3 (Summer 1980), 311–29; and Beverly J. Stoeltje, "'A Helpmate for Man Indeed': The Image of the Frontier Woman," *Journal of American Folklore* 88 (January–March 1975), 25–41.

3. Allan G. Bogue, *From the Prairie to the Corn Belt: Farming on the Illinois and Iowa Prairies in the Nineteenth Century* (Chicago: Quadrangle

Books, 1968): 22–33; Martin Ridge, "Why They Went West," *The American West* 1 (Summer 1964): 40–57; *Iowa Census of 1880,* 57, 168–170.

4. Joanna Harris Haines, "Seventy Years in Iowa," ed. Frank Herriott, *Annals of Iowa* 27 (October 1945), 98.

5. Abbie Mott Benedict, "My Early Days in Iowa," *Annals of Iowa* 17 (July 1930), 331.

6. Edith H. Hurlbutt, "Pioneer Experiences in Keokuk County, 1858–1874," *Iowa Journal of History* 52 (October 1954), 327–28.

7. B. J. Zenor, "By Covered Wagon to the Promised Land," *The American West* 11 (July 1974), 32–33.

8. Kitturah Penton Belknap, Reminiscences, SHSI.

9. Ibid.

10. Ibid.

11. Zenor, "By Covered Wagon," 37.

12. Belknap, Reminiscences; Mary Alice Shutes, Diary, Iowa Historical Museum and Archives, Des Moines; Catherine Margaret Haun, "A Woman's Trip Across the Plains," HL.

13. Katharine Horack, "In Quest of a Prairie Home," *Palimpsest* 5 (July 1924), 252–53.

14. Shutes, Diary, and Belknap, Reminiscences.

15. Shutes, Diary.

16. Quoted in Bruce E. Mahan, "The Iowa Pioneers," *Palimpsest* 49 (July 1968), 247.

17. Horack, "In Quest of a Prairie Home," 254.

18. Ibid; Shutes, Diary.

19. Bessie L. Lyon, "Grandmother's Story," *Palimpsest* 5 (January 1924), 4; Haines, "Seventy Years in Iowa," 103–4.

20. Mary Ann Ferrin Davidson, "An Autobiography and a Reminiscence," *Annals of Iowa* 37 (Spring 1964), 245; Horack, "In Quest of a Prairie Home," 250.

21. Kathryn Kish Sklar, *Catharine Beecher: A Study in American Domesticity* (New York: W. W. Norton & Company, Inc., 1976), 97–98, 102; John B. Newhall, *A Glimpse of Iowa in 1846; or, the Emigrant's Guide* (Iowa City: State Historical Society, 1957), 61.

22. See for example Faragher and Stansell, "Women and Their Families on the Overland Trail," 153, and Stansell, "Women on the Great Plains," 90. For a different view, see Julie Roy Jeffrey, *Frontier Women: The Trans-Mississippi West, 1840–1880* (New York: Hill and Wang, 1979), 32–34.

23. Lydia Arnold Titus, "From New York to Iowa," ed. Bruce E. Mahan, *Palimpsest* 2 (October 1921), 319; Haines, "Seventy Years in Iowa," 104.

24. Shutes, Diary; Horack, "In Quest of a Prairie Home," 254.

25. Belknap, Reminiscences.

26. Shutes, Diary.

27. Titus, "From New York to Iowa," 319; E. Mary Lacey Crowder, "Pioneer Life in Palo Alto County," *Iowa Journal of History and Politics* 46 (April 1948), 162; Horack, "In Quest of a Prairie Home," 254.

28. Jane Augusta Gould, Diary, SHSI.

29. Robert L. Munkres, "Wives, Mothers, Daughters: Women's Life on the Road West," *Annals of Wyoming* 42 (October 1970), 198.

30. Gould, Diary.

31. Faragher and Stansell, "Women and Their Families on the Overland Trail," 156; see Read, "Women and Children on the Oregon-California Trail," for a discussion of the number of women and children on the Overland Trail.

32. Titus, "From New York to Iowa," 318–19; Margaret E. Archer Murray, "Memoir of the William Archer Family," *Annals of Iowa* 39 (Fall 1968), 369.

33. Quoted in Ruth Barnes Moynihan, "Children and Young People on the Overland Trail," *Western Historical Quarterly* 6 (July 1975), 292; Shutes, Diary.

34. Crowder, "Pioneer Life in Palo Alto County," 156; Harriet Connor Brown, *Grandmother Brown's Hundred Years, 1827–1927* (Boston: Little, Brown and Company, 1929), 103.

35. Haun, "A Woman's Trip Across the Plains"; Belknap, Reminiscences; Lyon, "Grandmother's Story," 4–5.

36. Caroline Phelps, Diary, SHSI.

37. Shutes, Diary.

38. Francis E. Whitely, "Across the Mississippi," *Palimpsest* 15 (January 1934), 13–15.

39. Belknap, Reminiscences.

40. Titus, "From New York to Iowa," 315.

41. Faragher and Stansell, "Women and Their Families on the Overland Trail," 160; Stansell, "Women on the Great Plains," 87–90.

42. Gould, Diary; Shutes, Diary; Gould, Diary.

43. Cowles, *Early Algona,* 123; Horack, "In Quest of a Prairie Home," 253; Haines, "Seventy Years in Iowa," 104; Mrs. E. A. Hadley, Journal, SHSI.

44. Crowder, "Pioneer Life in Palo Alto County," 156.

45. Belknap, Reminiscences.

46. Lucy Rutledge Cooke, *Covered Wagon Days: Crossing the Plains in 1852* (Modesto, California: privately published, 1923), 7–37, 41–44.

47. Ibid., 49, 60–70.

48. E. Allene Taylor Dunham, *Across the Plains in a Covered Wagon* (n.p., n.d.), 1–20.

49. Eliza Ann Egbert, "Travel Diary," California Historical Society, San Francisco, California.

50. Haun, "A Woman's Trip Across the Plains."

51. Ibid.

52. Virginia Wilcox Ivins, *Pen Pictures of Early Western Days* (Keokuk, Iowa: n.p., [c. 1905]), 52–69, 96, 101, 111, 114.

53. Ibid., 116–20.

54. Interview 10436, IPP, Vol. 101.

55. From Virginia Reed Murphy, "The Donner Party," *Century Magazine* 42 (July 1891), 409–26.

56. Minnie Lee Cardwell Miller, "The Road to Yesterday," 1937, Bancroft Library, Berkeley, California [hereafter BL]. Used by permission.

57. Mary Ann Hafen, Memoir, 1938, published as *Recollections of a Handcart Pioneer of 1860: A Woman's Life on the Mormon Frontier* (Lincoln: University of Nebraska Press, 1983), 23–26. In public domain.

58. Interview with Esther Easter in George P. Rawick, ed., *The American Slave* (Westport, Conn.: Greenwood Publishing Co., 1972), Vol. 7, 90–91. Used by permission.

59. Interview with Mary Grayson in Rawick, *The American Slave*, Vol. 7, 115–17. Used by permission.

60. Interview with Jenny Proctor in Rawick, *The American Slave,* Vol. 7, 209, 216–17. Used by permission.

61. Interview with Ophelia Salas by Glenda Riley, October 23, 1990, Milwaukee, Wisconsin. Transcript in author's possession. Used by permission.

62. A survey of the literature revealed no books or articles devoted to the topic of female migrants on the Panama route. On the other hand, a number of works focus in whole or part on women's migration experiences on the various overland roads. These include Jeffrey, *Frontier Women: The Trans-Mississippi West*; Sandra L. Myres, *Westering Women and the Frontier Experience, 1800–1915* (Albuquerque: New Mexico University Press, 1982); Glenda Riley, *Frontierswomen: The Iowa Experience* (Ames, Iowa: Iowa State University Press, 1981) and *Women and Indians on the Frontier, 1825–1915* (Albuquerque: University of New Mexico Press, 1984); Lillian Schlissel, *Women's Diaries of the Westward Journey* (New York: Schocken, 1982); Faragher and Stansell, "Women and Their Families on the Overland Trail"; and John Mack Faragher, *Women and Men on the Overland Trail.*

63. The women's documents used here were selected on the basis of their availability and completeness rather than their representation of various backgrounds and social classes. A limited number of Panama female migrants' writings are to be found in archives, and most of these were produced by middle- and upper-class women whose families tended to preserve such documents. It should be noted that not all female migrants travelling across Panama ended their journey in Califor-

nia. That some went on to other destinations such as Oregon is illustrated by Elizabeth M. Wilson, "From New York to Oregon, Via the Isthmus of Panama, in 1851," *Proceedings of the Oregon State Historical Society* (Salem, Ore., 1901), 99–113.

64. John Haskell Kemble, *The Panama Route, 1848–1849* (Berkeley: University of California Press, 1943), 149.

65. Oscar Lewis, *Sea Routes to the Gold Fields* (New York: Alfred A. Knopf, 1949), 35, 38–40, 61, 68.

66. Sandra Myres, *Ho for California! Women's Overland Diaries from the Huntington Library* (San Marino, Calif.: The Huntington Library, 1980), 6.

67. The *San Francisco Daily Bulletin* and *Daily Alta California* both published lists of arriving passengers. See also Victor Maximilian Berthold, *The Pioneer Steamer* California, *1848–1849* (Boston: Houghton Mifflin, 1932). For detailed passenger lists of Panama-bound steamers for this period, see Louis J. Rasmussen, *San Francisco Ship Passenger Lists* (currently 5 volumes with more scheduled, Colma, Calif.: San Francisco Historical Records & Genealogy Bulletin, 1965–), Vol. 1, 4–6, 8, 14–23, 28–31, 36–47, 50–51, 60–62, 64–82, 84–85, 89–96, 101–3, 106–8, 125–28, 130–38, 142–45, 152–55, 158–67.

68. Megquier to her friend Milton, Feb. 18 and May 14, 1849, California Letters, 1849–1856, Mary Jane Megquier Papers, HL.

69. Megquier to her daughter Ange, Feb. 24, March 13 and 20, May 12, 1849, Megquier Papers, HL.

70. Jessie Benton Frémont, *A Year of American Travel: Narrative of Personal Experience* (1878; San Francisco, 1960), 14, 26–28, 30, 32–34, 39.

71. Myres, *Ho for California*, 7–8.

72. DeWitt to Mr. and Mrs. Peter DeWitt, (no day or month) 1849, and DeWitt to Mrs. Peter DeWitt, July 30, 1849, Margaret DeWitt Letters, DeWitt Family Papers, BL.

73. Mary Pratt Staples, Reminiscences (c. 1886), BL.

74. John Xantus, *Letters from North America* (Detroit: Wayne State University Press, 1975), 171.

75. Sarah Merriam Brooks, *Across the Isthmus to California in '52* (San Francisco: C.A. Murdock & Co. Printers, 1894), 12.

76. Ibid., 57.

77. Eleanor Taylor, "Ross Kin: Early Settlers of the West" (1978), BL.

78. John Haskell Kemble, "The Gold Rush by Panama, 1848–1851," in John Walton Caughey, ed., *Rushing for Gold* (Berkeley: University of California Press, 1949), 46–47; Joseph W. Gregory, *Gregory's Guide for California Travellers via the Isthmus of*

Panama (San Francisco, reprinted by the Book Club of California, 1949), 9–13; George Alexander Thompson, *Handbook to the Pacific and California* (London: Simpkin and Marshall, 1849); and Joseph E. Ware, *The Emigrant's Guide to California*, ed. John W. Caughey (Princeton, N.J.: Princeton University Press, 1932).

79. See, for example, the *New York Times,* Jan. 20, 1863, and Aug. 15, 1887.

80. Megquier to her daughter Ange, Feb. 2, 1849, Megquier Papers, HL.

81. Brooks, *Across the Isthmus*, 8–10.

82. Hester Harland, Reminiscences (n.d.), California State Library, Sacramento [hereafter CSLS].

83. Lucy Sexton, *The Foster Family, California Pioneers* (Santa Barbara: Press of the Schauer Printing Studio, Inc., 1925), 250.

84. Julia S. Twist, Diary (1861), BL.

85. Kemble, "The Gold Rush," 49–56. See also William S. Ament, *By Sea to California* (Los Angeles: Powell Publishing Co., 1929), 392–94. Children, invalids, and sometimes women were carried in hammocks or in chairs fastened to Panamanian men's backs or heads. Myres, *Ho for California*, 27; Julia L. Hare, Reminiscences (n.d.), 4–5, CSLS. The other popular isthmian route, the one across Nicaragua, was similar to the Panama crossing in most respects. See, for example, Mary E. Durant to her cousins, Dec. 24, 1853, Durant Family Letters, BL; and Robert N. Searls, *The Diary of a Pioneer and Other Papers* (n.p., 1940), 71–90.

86. Alex Perez-Venero, *Before the Five Frontiers* (New York, 1978), 84–85.

87. Pereira Jimenez Bonifacio, *Historia de Panamá*, 2d ed. (Panama: Angencia Internacional de Publicaciones, 1963), 265–66.

88. Kemble, "The Gold Rush," 52; R. N. Otis, *History of the Panama Railroad* (New York: Harper & Brothers, 1867), and Joseph L. Schott, *Railroads across Panama* (Indianapolis: Bobbs-Merrill, 1967).

89. Xantus, *Letters*, 172.

90. Kemble, "The Gold Rush," 53–55.

91. Megquier to her daughter Ange, March 20 and 24, 1849, Megquier Papers, HL.

92. Myres, *Ho for California*, 9–32.

93. Frémont, *A Year of American Travel*, 56–63.

94. Mrs. Charles Wood, Diary (c. 1850), BL.

95. Mary Bean Ballou, Journal (1850–1851), Beinecke Collection, Yale University, New Haven, Connecticut [hereafter BCYU].

96. Brooks, *Across the Isthmus*, 16–17, 19, 21–22, 24, 38–40, 42–43.

97. Ibid., 44–45, 49, 51, 53, 63, 66, 70, 77. Although Brooks was impressed with the speed of her twenty-three-day trip from Panama to San

Francisco, a few years later it was no longer seen as unusual. See, for example, Mrs. E. Van Court, Reminiscences (March 26, 1914), BCYU.

98. Emeline Benson, Diary (1853–1854), CSL.

99. Emeline Hubbard Day, Journal (1853), BL. See also Martha M. Morgan, "A Trip Across the Plains in the Year 1849," 23–25, CSL.

100. Mrs. D. B. Bates, *Incidents on Land and Water* (Boston: James French & Co., 1857), 281, 286, 291–96, 301, 304–8.

101. Mallie Stafford, *The March of Empire through Three Decades* (San Francisco: Geo. Spaulding & Co., 1884), 13–15, 20–22, 24–25, 27, 29, 30–40, 42, 57, 65.

102. Fannie Wallace Reading to Mrs. Richard B. Lee, May 4, 1856, Pierson Barton Papers, BL; Sexton, *Foster Family*, 251; Mary Ann Meredith, Diary (1859), CSLS; Nellie Wetherbee, Diary (1860), BL.

103. Twist, Diary.

104. Angelina Harvey to Mary Ann Wheaton, Nov. 19, 1863, Harvey File, BL.

105. Hannah Bourn Ingalls to her husband, Oct. 5, 16, and 27, 1865, Bourn-Ingalls Family Papers, BL.

106. Gregory, *Gregory's Guide*, 9, 11.

107. *San Francisco Daily Evening Bulletin*, May 2, 1856, and San Francisco *Daily Alta California*, May 2, 1856.

108. Brooks, *Across the Isthmus*, 31.

109. Ida F. Fitzgerald, "Account of Life of Plummer Edward Jefferis Including Voyages from New York to California in 1850 and 1854," HL.

110. Brooks, *Across the Isthmus*, 35, 37; Day, Journal; Meredith, Diary; Sexton, *Foster Family*, 251; Mary Jane Megquier to her daughter Ange, March 20, 1849, Megquier Papers, HL; Bates, *Incidents*, 283.

111. Meredith, Diary; Day, Journal; Ballou, Journal; Hannah Ingalls to her husband, Oct. 6, 1865, Bourn-Ingalls Family Papers, BL; Stafford, *March of Empire*, 18; Wood, Diary; and Wilson, "From New York to Oregon, Via the Isthmus of Panama, in 1851," 106.

112. Staples, Reminiscences.

113. Twist, Diary.

114. Brooks, *Across the Isthmus*, 35.

115. Stafford, *March of Empire*, 43; Bates, *Incidents*, 284, 288, 308.

116. Megquier to her friend Milton, May 4, 1849, Megquier Papers, HL; see also Morgan, "A Trip across the Plains," 23–24.

117. Megquier to her daughter Ange, March 20, 1849, Megquier Papers, HL.

118. Frémont, *A Year of American Travel*, 27.

119. Meredith, Diary; see also Brooks, *Across the Isthmus*, 37; Hare, Reminiscences, 2–3; and Wood, Diary.

120. Brooks, *Across the Isthmus*, 37.

121. Stafford, *March of Empire*, 8, 20, 23, 25–26, 33–35, 38.

122. Harland, Reminiscences, 2; see also Sexton, *Foster Family*, 251.

123. Stafford, *March of Empire*, 39.

124. Day, Journal; see also Bates, *Incidents*, 315; and Wood, Diary.

125. Inga Sjolneth Kolloen, Crossing the Chilcoot Pass, March 9 to June 25, 1898, University of Washington Library, Manuscript Collection. Used by permission.

126. Georgia White, Diary, February 21 to September 29, 1898, Georgia White Collection, Yukon Archives, Whitehorse, Yukon Territory, Canada.

127. Letter from June Oshima to Glenda Riley, September 8, 1979, Honolulu, Hawaii. Original in author's possession. Used by permission.

Section 3

1. Harriet A. L. Smith, "My Trip across the Plains in 1849," CSLS.

2. Virginia Reed Murphy, "Across the Plains in the Donner Party (1846): A Personal Narrative of the Overland Trip to California," *Century Magazine* 42 (July 1891), 409.

3. Lucy H. Fosdick, "Across the Plains in '61," BCYU. See Emily K. Andrews, "Diary of Emily K. Andrews of a Trip from Austin to Fort Davis, 1874," Barker Texas History Center, University of Texas, Austin [hereafter BTHC].

4. Mabel Sharpe Beavers, Interview 6850, IPP, Vol. 6.

5. Mary Ellen Williams, Interview 6877, IPP, Vol. 98.

6. Elisha Brooks, *A Pioneer Mother of California* (San Francisco: Harr Wagner Publishing Co., 1922), 13–15.

7. Isaac Jones Wistar, *Autobiography of Issac Jones Wistar, 1827–1905: Half a Century in War and Peace* (New York, 1937), 74.

8. Mallie Stafford, *The March of Empire Through Three Decades* (San Francisco: Geo. Spaulding & Co., 1884), 126–27.

9. Lucena Pfeiffer Parsons, "The Women in the Sunbonnets" (1850), Stanford University Library, Stanford, California. See also Lydia Waters, "Account of a Trip across the Plains in 1855," *Quarterly of the Society of California Pioneers* 6 (March 1929), 65, 72; Helen Carpenter, Diary (1856), HL.

10. Margaret A. Frink, *Journal of the Adventures of a Party of California Gold Seekers* (Oakland, California: n.p., 1897), 28–29.

11. Thomas D. Clark, ed., *Off at Sunrise: The Overland Journal of Charles Glass Gray* (San Marino, California: The Huntington Library, 1976), 78; Jane

Augusta Gould, Diary (1862), SHSI; James A. Pritchard, *The Overland Diary of James A. Pritchard from Kentucky to California in 1849,* ed. Dale L. Morgan (Denver: The Old West Publishing Co., 1959), 58; Harriet Bunyard, "Diary of Miss Harriet Bunyard from Texas to California in 1868," *Annual Publications, Historical Society of Southern California* 13 (1924), 94, 97; David M. Kiefer, ed., "Over Barren Plains and Rock-Bound Mountains," *Montana: The Magazine of Western History* 22 (October 1972), 22, 26.

12. Helen Marnie Stewart Love, Diary (1853), HL. See also Louisa Miller Rahm, Diary (1862), BL; Ellen Tompkins Adams, "Diary of Ellen Tompkins Adams, Wife of John Smalley Adams, M.D." (1963), BL.

13. Fosdick, "Across the Plains."

14. Robert L. Munkres, "The Plains Indian Threat on the Oregon Trail before 1860," *Annals of Wyoming* 40 (October 1968), 212–15.

15. Catherine Amanda Stansbury Washburn, "Journal (1853) from Iowa to Oregon Territory," HL; Ward G. DeWitt and Florence S. DeWitt, *Prairie Schooner Lady: The Journal of Harriet Sherrill Ward, 1853* (Los Angeles: Westernlore Press, 1959), 46; Ada Millington, "Journal Kept While Crossing the Plains" (1862), BL; Fosdick, "Across the Plains"; Bunyard, Diary, 100.

16. Susan Thompson Parrish, "Westward in 1850," HL.

17. Mary Eliza Warner, Diary (1864), BL.

18. Millington, Journal.

19. Katherine Dunlap, Journal (1864), BL. See also Lucy Sexton, *The Foster Family, California Pioneers* (Santa Barbara, California: Press of the Schauer Printing Studio, Inc., 1925), 123; Emily McCowen Horton, *My Scrap-book* (Seattle: n.p., 1929), 17.

20. Mary Burrell, "Diary of a Journey Overland from Council Bluffs to Green Valley Cal., April 27 to Sept. 1, 1854," BCYU.

21. Margaret W. Chambers, *Reminiscences* (n.p., 1903), 13.

22. Charlotte Stearns Pengra, Diary (1853), HL. See also Lavinia H. Porter, *By Ox Team to California: A Narrative of Crossing the Plains in 1860* (Oakland: Oakland Enquirer Publishing Co., 1910), 65, 67, 69–70.

23. Unruh, *Plains Across,* 156, 175–76.

24. Sarah J. Cummins, *Autobiography and Reminiscences* (LaGrande, Oregon: LaGrande Printing Co., 1914), 28.

25. Margaret Hall Walker, *The Hall Family Crossing the Plains* (San Francisco, 1952), 13. See also Olivia Holmes, Diary (1873), BL.

26. Washburn, Journal.

27. Catherine M. Haun, "A Woman's Trip across the Plains, from Clinton, Iowa, to Sacramento, California, by way of Salt Lake City" (1849), HL.

28. DeWitt and DeWitt, *Prairie Schooner Lady,* 46.

29. Owen P. White, *A Frontier Mother* (New York: Minton, Balch, & Co., 1929), 68.

30. Milo M. Quaife, ed. *Across the Plains in Forty-Nine* (Chicago: Lakeside Press, 1948), 48–49; James Hewitt, ed. *Eye-Witnesses to the Wagon Trains West* (New York: Charles Scribner's Sons, 1973), 12.

31. Byron N. McKinstry, *The California Gold Rush Overland Diary of Byron N. McKinstry* (Glendale, California: Arthur H. Clark Co., 1975), 94.

32. Wistar, *Autobiography,* 74

33. Barry, comp., "Charles Robinson," 179–88; Gilbert Drake Harlan, ed., "The Diary of Wilson Barber Harlan," *Journal of the West* 3 (1964), 148.

34. Lydia M. Waters, "Account of a Trip," 61. See also DeWitt and DeWitt, *Prairie Schooner Lady,* 46.

35. Lucy Rutledge Cooke, *Covered Wagon Days: Crossing the Plains in 1852* (Modesto, California: privately published, 1923), 58. See also Sandra L. Myres, ed., *Ho for California! Women's Overland Diaries from the Huntington Library* (San Marino: The Huntington Library, 1980), 271.

36. See for example Ella Bird-Dumont, "True Life Story of Ella Bird-Dumont, Earliest Settler in the East Part of Panhandle, Texas" n.d., BTHC.

37. Unruh, *Plains Across,* 157, 169–70, 177.

38. Pauline Wonderly, *Reminiscences of a Pioneer* (Placerville, California: El Dorado County Historical Society, 1965), 4.

39. Porter, *By Ox Team,* 79.

40. Mary E. Hopping, "Incidents of Pioneer Life As I Remember and As I Have Been Told," 1962, CSLS.

41. Unruh, *Plains Across,* 177.

42. Carpenter, Diary.

43. Myres, *Ho for California!* 167, Nannie T. Alderson and Helena Huntington Smith, *A Bride Goes West* (Lincoln: University of Nebraska Press, 1969), 101.

44. Elsie Pearson, Interview 8538, IPP, Vol. 71; Harold F. Taggert, ed., "The Journal of David Jackson Staples," *California Historical Society Quarterly* 22 (June 1943), 146.

45. Abigail Malick to "My Dear Children," December 8, 1855, in Abigail Malick, Letter (1855), BCYU; Lily Klasner, *My Girlhood among Outlaws,* ed. Eve Ball (Tucson: University of Arizona Press, 1972), 86; M. A. Rogers, "An Iowa Woman in Wartime," Part 3, *Annals of Iowa* 36 (Summer 1961), 26–28; Mrs. Warren R. Fowler, "A Woman's Experience in Canon City" (1884), BL; Chambers, Reminiscences, 45–47; Mollie Dorsey Sanford, *Mollie: The Journal*

of Mollie Dorsey Sanford in Nebraska and Colorado Territories, 1857–1866 (Lincoln: University of Nebraska Press, 1976), 186–89; Bessie L. Lyon, "Hungry Indians," Palimpsest 9 (October 1928), 369.

46. Dorotea Valdes, Reminiscences, 1874, BL. Used by permission.

47. Bird-Dumont, "True Life Story." Used by permission.

48. Interview 10601, IPP, Vol. 4.

49. Jonaphrene Faulkner, "Prairie Home on the Frontier" n.d., BTHC. Used by permission.

50. Flora Spiegelberg, "The Tenderfoot Bride of the Santa Fe Trail Has Her First Indian Scare," n.d., University of New Mexico Library, Special Collections, Albuquerque. Used by permission.

51. "Early Reminiscences of a Nisqually Pioneer," in United States Works Progess Administration, Told by the Pioneers, Vol. 1 (1937), 166–84.

52. Apolinaria Lorenzana, "Recollections" n.d., San Diego Historical Society, California. Used by permission.

53. Roy Harvey Pearce, "The Significance of the Captivity Narrative," American Literature 19 (1947), 1–20; and Richard Van Der Beets, "The Indian Captivity Narrative as Ritual," American Literature 43 (1972), 548–62. One investigator has argued that these captivity narratives sold so well because they "focused on Indian brutality" which "served to justify the extermination of the Indian" who "still inhabited and defended the lands which whites coveted." James A. Levernier, "Indian Captivity Narratives: Their Functions and Forms" (Ph.D. diss., University of Pennsylvania, 1975), 27.

54. John Frost, Pioneer Mothers of the West; Or, Daring and Heroic Deeds of American Women (Boston: Lee and Shepard, 1875), 22.

55. Abie Gardner-Sharpe, The Spirit Lake Massacre and the Captivity of Miss Abie Gardner (Des Moines: Iowa Printing Co., 1885).

56. David T. Haberly, "Women and Indians: The Last of the Mohicans and the Captivity Tradition," American Quarterly 28 (Fall 1976), 431–43; and Donald L. Kaufman, "The Indian as Media Hand-Me-Down," in Gretchen M. Bataille and Charles L. P. Silet, The Pretend Indians: Images of Native Americans in the Movies (Ames: Iowa State University Press, 1980), 24–25.

57. Roy Harvey Pearce, The Savages of America: A Study of the Indian and the Idea of Civilization (Baltimore: Johns Hopkins University Press, 1965), 3–5; and Frederick Turner, "The Terror of the Wilderness," American Heritage 28 (1977), 59–62. See for example Robert F. Berkhofer, Jr., The White Man's Indian (New York: Alfred A. Knopf, 1978), 2, 23–28.

58. Berkhofer, The White Man's Indian, 28–30.

59. Ray Allen Billington, Land of Savagery, Land of Promise: The European Image of the American Frontier in the Nineteenth Century (New York: W. W. Norton, 1980), 5, 26, 30, 106; Nancy B. Black and Bette S. Weidman, eds., White on Red: Images of the American Indian (Port Washington, New York: Kennikat Press, 1976), 1–2; Billington, "Cowboys, Indians and the Land of Promise: The World Image of the American Frontier," Opening Address, 14th International Congress of Historical Sciences, San Francisco, August 22–29, 1975, 5.

60. Carl N. Degler, At Odds: Women and the Family in America from the Revolution to the Present (Oxford: Oxford University Press, 1980), 26–27, 30–31, 150–51, 283, 351–53; Ann Douglas, The Feminization of American Culture (New York: Alfred A. Knopf, 1979), 8–10, 45–48, 56–60, 68–76; John Mack Faragher, Women and Men on the Overland Trail (New Haven: Yale University Press, 1979), 94–97; Gerda Lerner, The Majority Finds Its Past: Placing Women in History (New York: Oxford University Press, 1979), 25–28, 162–65, 185–86; and Glenda Riley, "The Subtle Subversion: Changes in the Traditionalist Image of the American Woman," The Historian 32 (February 1970), 210–27, and The Origins of the Feminist Movement in America (St. Charles, Missouri: Forum Press, 1973), 1–13.

61. Leslie A. Fiedler, The Return of the Vanishing American (New York: Stein and Day, 1968), 24, 177; Julie Roy Jeffrey, Frontier Women: The Trans-Mississippi West, 1840–1880 (New York: Hill and Wang, 1979), 33–34; and Ronald J. Quinn, "The Modest Seduction: The Experience of Pioneer Women on the Trans-Mississippi Frontier" (Ph.D. diss., University of California-Riverside, 1977), i–iii, 8–9, 11, 15, 18, 23, 30, 39, 45–50.

62. Kate McDaniel Furness, "From Prairie to Pacific," CSLS; Sarah R. Herndon, Days on the Road: Crossing the Plains in 1865 (New York: Burr Printing House, 1902), 73; Mary Fetter Hite Sandford, "A Trip Across the Plains," 1853, CSLS; Reminiscences of Mary Pratt Staples, c. 1886, BL; Sallie Hester Maddock, "The Diary of a Pioneer Girl," 1849, CSLS; Margaret M. Hecox, California Caravan: The 1846 Overland Trail Memoir of Margaret M. Hecox (San Jose: Harlan-Young Press, 1966), 40; and Fleming Fraker, Jr., ed., "To Pike's Peak by Ox Wagon: The Harriet A. Smith Day-Book," Annals of Iowa 35 (Fall 1959), 132.

63. Journal of Caroline L. Richardson, 1856, BL; Leo M. Kaiser and Priscilla Knuth, eds., "From Ithaca to Clatsop Plains: Miss Ketcham's Journal of Travel," Part 2, Oregon Historical Quarterly 62 (December 1961), 368; Mrs. B. G. Ferris, The Mormons at Home (New York: Dix & Edwards, 1856), 13; Hecox, California Caravan, 32; and Maria J. Norton, "Diary of a Trip Across the Plains in '59," BL.

64. Maddock, "Diary of a Pioneer Girl"; Reminiscences of Mary Staples; and Mary Jane Guill, "The Overland Diary of a Journey From Livingston County, Missouri, to Butte County, California," 1860, CSLS.

65. Ferris, *Mormons at Home,* 68.

66. Angeline Jackson Ashley, "Diary Crossing the Plains in 1852," HL; Mrs. D. B. Bates, *Incidents on Land and Water* (Boston: James French and Company, 1857), 151–52; and Diary of Helen Marnie Stewart Love, 1853, HL.

67. Hecox, *California Caravan,* 29; and Thompson, "Summer of '77," 11.

68. Mary C. Fish, "Across the Plaines in 1860," BL; and Frances M. A. Roe, *Army Letters From an Officer's Wife, 1871–1888* (New York: D. Appleton & Co., 1909), 10.

69. Ellen Tomplins Adams, Diary, 1863, BL; Journal of Esther Bell Hanna, 1852, BL; and Guill, "Overland Diary."

70. Kaiser and Knuth, "From Ithaca to Clatsop Plains," 368.

71. Guill, "Overland Diary"; Norton, "Diary of a Trip"; DeWitt and DeWitt, *Prairie Schooner Lady,* 78; Diary of Marie Nash, 1861, CSLS; Diary of Helen Carpenter, 1856, CSLS; Millington, Journal.

72. Fish, "Across the Plaines"; Frances H. Sawyer, "Overland to California," 1852, BL; and Norton, "Diary of a Trip."

73. Mary Stuart Bailey, "A Journal of the Overland Trip From Ohio to California," 1852, HL; Horton, *My Scrap-book,* 17; Fraker, "To Pike's Peak," 134; Diary of Mary Warner; and letter from Catherine Jane Bell to Julia, October 31, 1859, Oroville, California, BL.

74. Millington, Journal; and Harriet Bunyard, "Diary of a Young Girl," 1868, HL.

75. Kaiser and Knuth, "From Ithaca to Clatsop Plains," 262; Miriam D. Colt, *Went to Kansas; Being a Thrilling Account of an Ill-Fated Expedition* (Watertown: L. Ingalls & Co., 1862), 61, 136; and Mary Jane Caples, "Overland Journey to California," 1911, CSLS.

76. Martha Ann Minto, "Female Pioneering in Oregon," 1849, BL; Emeline L. Fuller, *Left By the Indians. Story of My Life* (Mt. Vernon, Iowa: Hawk-Eye Steam Print, 1892), 29; Margaret W. Chambers, *Reminiscences* (n.p., 1903), 45; and Bates, *Incidents on Land and Water,* 156.

77. Diary of Georgia Willis Read, 1850, CSLS; Sexton, *The Foster Family,* 127–28; Diary of Helen Carpenter; Diary of Mrs. Nicholas Harrison Karchner, 1862, CSLS.

78. Sarah Royce, *A Frontier Lady* (New Haven: Yale University Press, 1932), 50; Augusta Tabor, "Cabin Life in Colorado," 1884, BL; Rebecca Hildreth Nutting Woodson, "A Sketch of the Life of Rebecca Hildreth Nutting Woodson and Her Family," 1909, BL; and Guill, "Overland Diary."

79. Journal of Mary Hall Jatta, 1869, BL; Haun, "A Woman's Trip Across the Plains"; and Diary of Helen Love.

80. Herndon, *Days on the Road,* 235.

81. Guill, "Overland Diary"; Stafford, *The March of Empire,* 117; Bunyard, "Diary of a Young Girl"; Journal of Catherine Washburn; Sawyer, "Overland to California"; Mattie Walker, "A Brief History of the William B. Walker Family," CSLS; Leo M. Kaiser and Priscilla Knuth, eds., "From Ithaca to Clatsop Plains: Miss Ketcham's Journal of Travel," Part 1, *Oregon Historical Quarterly* 62 (September 1961), 258; and Journal of Katherine Dunlap.

82. Hecox, *California Caravan,* 28; Haun, "A Woman's Trip"; Diary of Georgia Read; Diary of Charlotte Pengra, 1853, HL; and Lucy Rutledge Cooke, *Covered Wagon Days: Crossing the Plains in 1852* (Modesto, California: privately published, 1923), 30.

83. Eliza Spalding Warren, *Memoirs of the West: The Spaldings* (Portland, Oregon: March Printing Co., 1916), 13; Elizabeth L. Lord, *Reminiscences of Eastern Oregon* (Portland, Oregon: The Irwin-Hodgson Co., 1903), 42; Lodisa Frizzell, *Across the Plains to California in 1852* (New York: New York Public Library, 1915), 18.

84. Barsina French, "Journal of a Wagon Trip," 1867, HL; Cynthia J. Capron, "Life in the Army," *Journal of the Illinois State Historical Society* 13 (October 1920), 367; Diary of Charlotte Pengra; Journal of Katherine Dunlap; and Hecox, *California Caravan,* 33.

85. Parsons, "Women in the Sunbonnets"; Frizzell, *Across the Plains,* 25; Journal of Esther Hanna; see also Emma Shepard Hill, *A Dangerous Crossing and What Happened on the Other Side: Seven Lean Years* (Denver: Bradford-Robinson Printing Co., 1924), 82; Juliette Fish Walker, "Crossing the Plains," *Noticias* 16 (1970), 4; Susan S. Magoffin, *Down the Santa Fe Trail and Into Mexico: The Diary of Susan Shelby Magoffin, 1846–1847* (New Haven: Yale University Press, 1926), 68.

86. Diary of Rachel C. Rose, 1852, CSLS; Nancy A. Hunt, "By Ox Team to California," BL; Furness, "From Prairie to Pacific"; Sandford, "A Trip Across the Plains"; Walker, *The Hall Family,* 28; Journal of Esther Hanna; Porter, *By Ox Team to California,* (Oakland, California: Oakland Enquirer Publishing Co., 1910), 67.

87. Journal of Ada Adelaide Vogdes, 1866–1872, HL.

88. DeWitt and DeWitt, *Prairie Schooner Lady,* 87, 123, 144, 158, 166.

89. Glenda Riley, *Women on the American Frontier* (St. Louis: Forum Press, 1977), 3–4, and "Women in the West," *Journal of American Culture* 3 (Summer 1980), 314–18.

90. Journal of Elizabeth Julia Goltra, 1853, BL.

91. Jean Webster, "The Myth of Hardship on the Oregon Trail," *Reed College Bulletin* 24 (January 1946), 34.

92. Mary Hall Pelham, "The Indians," in Walker, *The Hall Family*, 29.

93. Polly Jane Purcell, "Autobiography and Reminiscence of a Pioneer," Newberry Library, Chicago; Sandford, "A Trip Across the Plains."

94. Susan H. Armitage, "Women's Literature and the American Frontier: A New Perspective on the Frontier Myth," in L. L. Lee and Merrill Lewis, eds., *Women, Women Writers, and the West* (Troy, New York: Whitston Publishing Company, 1979), 5–11.

95. Porter, *By Ox Team*, 56; Barbara Baker Zimmerman and Vernon Carstensen, "Pioneer Woman in Southwestern Washington Territory: The Recollections of Susanna Maria Slover McFarland Price Ede," *Pacific Northwest Quarterly* 66–67 (October 1976), 143, 147; and Bessie L. Lyon, "Hungry Indians," *Palimpsest* 9 (October 1928), 366.

96. French, "Journal of a Wagon Trip"; Christiane Fischer, "A Profile of Women in Arizona in Frontier Days," *Journal of the West* 16 (July 1977), 43; Diary of Eliza Ann Egbert, 1852, BL; Mary Ann Ferrin Davidson, "An Autobiography and a Reminiscence," *Annals of Iowa* 37 (Spring 1964), 256; and Susie P. Van De Wiele, "Travels and Experience in America with army and Indian reminiscences," Newberry Library.

97. Cummins, *Autobiography and Reminiscences*, 42; Saunders, "The Whitman Massacre"; Journal of Almira Neff Beam Enos, 1858–1866, BL; Mrs. M. S. Hockensmith, "Diary of a Trip Overland From the Mississippi to California," 1866, BL; Reminiscences of Julia L. Hare, CSLS; Hopping, "Incidents of Pioneer Life"; Frink, *Journal*, 46; Diary of Louisa Rahm; Sawyer, "Overland to California"; Guill, "Overland Diary"; and Journal of Catherine Washburn.

98. Cooke, *Covered Wagon Days*, 66; Mary Horne, "Migration and Settlement of the Latter Day Saints," 1884, BL; Martha M. Morgan, *A Trip Across the Plains in the Year 1849* (San Francisco: printed at Pioneer Press, 1864), 7, 12, 15–16; Ellen McGowen Biddle, *Reminiscences of a Soldier's Wife* (Philadelphia: J. B. Lippincott Co., 1907), 83; Cynthia J. Capron, "Life in the Army," 369; Sandra L. Myres, ed., *Cavalry Wife: The Diary of Eveline M. Alexander, 1866–1867* (College Station: Texas A&M University Press, 1977), 102; and Journal of Ada Vogdes.

99. Mary E. Ackley, *Crossing the Plains and Early Days in California* (San Francisco: privately printed, 1928), 66; Caroline D. Budlong, *Memories. Pioneer Days in Oregon and Washington Territory* (Eugene, Oregon: Picture Press Printers, 1949), 38; Fraker, "To Pike's Peak," 137.

100. Sandra L. Myres, ed., "Evy Alexander: The Colonel's Lady at Ft. McDowell," *Montana: The Magazine of Western History* 24 (Summer 1974), 32–34; and Diary of Caroline Phelps, 1830–1860, SHSI.

101. Rachel Elizabeth Wright, "The Early Upper Napa Valley," 1928, BL.

102. Diary of Malvina Virginia Manning, 1862, BL.

103. E. Allene Taylor Dunham, *Across the Plains in a Covered Wagon* (n.p., n.d.), 7; Ferris, *Mormons at Home*, 24.

104. DeWitt and DeWitt, *Prairie Schooner Lady*, 78.

105. Hopping, "Incidents of Pioneer Life"; Diary of Eliza Egbert.

106. Mary A. Hodgson, "The Life of a Pioneer Family," 1922, CSLS; Robert C. and Eleanor R. Carriker, eds., *An Army Wife on the Frontier: The Memoirs of Alice Blackwood Baldwin, 1867–1877* (Salt Lake City: Tanner Trust Fund, University of Utah Library, 1975), 79; Diary of Caroline Phelps; and Leola Lehman, "Life in the Territories," *Chronicles of Oklahoma* 41 (Fall 1963), 373–75.

107. Cummins, *Autobiography and Reminiscences*, 37; Saunders, "The Whitman Massacre"; Diary of Mary Richardson Walker, 1848, HL; and Wilhelmina B. Carrigan, *Captured by the Indians: Reminiscences of Pioneer Life in Minnesota* (Forest City, South Dakota: Forest City Press, 1907), 11, 16. For a similar account see Ruth S. Thompson, "The Tragedy of Legion Valley," 1928, BL.

108. Colt, *Went to Kansas*, 67.

109. Furness, "From Prairie to Pacific"; and Lord, *Reminiscences*, 142–45.

110. Diary of Mary Ann Tatum, 1870, SHSI.

111. Journal of Katherine Dunlap; Myres, *Cavalry Wife*, 117; Margaret E. Archer Murray, "Memoir to the William Archer Family," Part 1, *Annals of Iowa* 39 (Summer 1968), 368; Journal of Ada Vogdes; Lois L. Murray, *Incidents of Frontier Life* (Goshen, Indiana: Ev. United Mennonite Publishing House, 1880), 92–93.

112. Annie Argyle, *Cupid's Album* (New York: M. Doolady, 1866), 89; Mary Butler Renville, *A Thrilling Narrative of Indian Captivity* (Minneapolis: Atlas Company's Book and Job Printing Office, 1863), 43; Caples, "Overland Journey"; Eleanor Taylor, "Ross Kin: Early Settlers of the West," 1978, BL; Mrs. M. A. Rogers, "An Iowa Woman in Wartime," Part 1, *Annals of Iowa* 35 (Winter 1961), 525; Warren, *Memoirs*, 177; Dunham, *Across the Plains*, 11; "Narrative of Nancy N. Tracy," 1880, BL; and Ruth Peterson, comp., "Across the Plains in '57," told by Nancy Campbell Lowell, CSLS.

113. Journal of Maria Schrode; Alice C. Fletcher, *Historical Sketch of the Omaha Tribe of Indians in Nebraska* (Washington: Judd & Detweiler, 1885), 12; Letters from Annie K. Bidwell to Colonel Pratt

April 26, 1904, and to Senator George C. Perkins, March 11, 1904, in the Annie K. Bidwell Collection, CSLS; Ann Archbold, *A Book for the Married and Single, the Grave and the Gay: And Especially Designed for Steamboat Passengers* (East Plainfield, Ohio: printed at the Office of the "Practical Preacher," 1850), 168–69; Walker, Diary; and Allie B. Busby, *Two Summers Among the Musquakies* (Vinton, Iowa: Herald Book and Job Rooms, 1886), 19.

114. Margaret I. Carrington, *Ab-sa-ra-ka, Home of the Crows: Being the Experience of an Officer's Wife on the Plains* (Philadelphia: J. B. Lippincott & Co., 1868), 184, 219.

115. Other scholars who have also argued that the Plains Indian threat was vastly exaggerated are Robert L. Munkres, "The Plains Indian Threat on the Oregon Trail before 1860," *Annals of Wyoming* 40 (1968), 193–221, and John D. Unruh, *The Plains Across: The Overland Emigrants and the Trans-Mississippi West, 1840–1860* (Urbana: University of Illinois Press, 1979), 9, 135–36, 156–200, 386, 395–96, 408–09.

116. Although almost two-thirds of the women's sources showed evidence of favorable changes in female attitudes toward Indians, particularly good examples are Ackley, *Crossing the Plains*; Carriker and Carriker, *An Army Wife on the Frontier*; Cooke, *Covered Wagon Days*; DeWitt and DeWitt, *Prairie Schooner Lady*; Fraker, "To Pike's Peak"; Reminiscences of Julia Hare; Hodgson, "Life of a Pioneer Family"; Hopping, "Incidents of Pioneer Life"; Horne, "Migration and Settlement"; Ivins, *Pen Pictures of Early Western Days*; Diary of Rachel Rose; Van De Wiele, "Travels"; and Journal of Ada Vogdes.

117. Interview with Isadora, widow of the California Native American chief, Solano, April 10, 1874, BL. Used by permission.

118. Interview with Nellie Quail, July 31, 1967, Fort McDowell Indian Reservation, copy held by the Arizona State Museum, University of Arizona, Tucson. Used by permission.

119. Sarah Winnemucca Hopkins, *Life Among the Piutes: Their Wrongs and Claims* (New York: G. P. Putnam Sons, 1883).

120. Zitkala-Sa, "An Indian Teacher Among Indians," *Atlantic Monthly* 85 (March 1980), 380–86.

121. Originally appeared as Thomas B. Marquis, ed., "Red Ripe's Squaw," *Century Magazine* 118 (June 1929), 201–09.

Section 4

1. Laura Ingalls Wilder, *These Happy Golden Years* (New York: Harper & Bros., 1943), 119.

2. Everett Dick, *The Sod-House Frontier: A Social History of the Northern Plains from the Creation of Kansas & Nebraska to the Admission of the Dakotas* (New York: D. Appleton-Century Co., 1937), 233.

3. Harold E. Briggs, "The Settlement and Development of the Territory of Dakota, 1860–70," *North Dakota Historical Quarterly* 7 (Jan./Apr. 1933), 116, 118, 124–25.

4. Mary W. M. Hargreaves, *Dry Farming in the Northern Great Plains* (Cambridge, Mass.: Harvard University Press, 1957), 25–30. See also Briggs, "Settlement and Development," 127.

5. Briggs, "Settlement and Development," 129–39; Dick, *Sod-House Frontier*, 128; and Edith Eudora Kohl, *Land of the Burnt Thigh* (New York: Funk & Wagnalls Co., 1938), 88, 92, 94, 144–45.

6. Laura Ingalls Wilder, *The First Four Years* (New York: Harper & Row, 1971), 17.

7. Wilder, *These Happy Golden Years*, 114–22.

8. Kohl, *Land of the Burnt Thigh*, 38.

9. Sheryll and Gene Patterson-Black, "From Pack Trains to Publishing: Women's Work in the Frontier West," in Sheryll and Gene Patterson-Black, *Western Women in History and Literature* (Crawford, Nebr.: Cottonwood Press, 1978), 5–6. See also Sheryll Patterson-Black, "Women Homesteaders on the Great Plains Frontier," in *Western Women in History*, 15–31, and "Women Homesteaders on the Great Plains Frontier," *Frontiers* 1 (Spring 1976), 67–88.

10. Enid Bern, "The Enchanted Years on the Prairies," *North Dakota History* 40 (Fall 1973), 11. See also Enid Bern, ed., "They Had a Wonderful Time: The Homesteading Letters of Anna and Ethel Erickson," *North Dakota History* 45 (Fall 1978), 4–31.

11. Walker D. Wyman, *Frontier Woman: The Life of a Woman Homesteader on the Dakota Frontier* (River Falls: University of Wisconsin—River Falls Press, 1972), 22–23, 90–91, 113.

12. See for example Annie D. Tallent, *The First White Woman in the Black Hills* (Mitchell, S. D.: Educator Supply Co., 1923), and *The Black Hills; or, The Last Hunting Ground of the Dakotahs* (1899; reprint ed., Sioux Falls, S. D.: Brevet Press, 1974).

13. Fanny McGillycuddy, Diary, 1877–1878, Manuscript Division, South Dakota Historical Resource Center [hereafter SDHRC]. See also John R. Sibbald, "Camp Followers All: Army Women of the West," *American West* 3 (Spring 1966), 56–67, and Miller J. Stewart, "Army Laundresses: Ladies of the 'Soap Suds Row,'" *Nebraska History* 61 (Winter 1980), 421–36.

14. Elaine Goodale Eastman, Sister to the Sioux: *The Memoirs of Elaine Goodale Eastman, 1885–1891*, ed. Kay Graber (Lincoln: University of Nebraska Press, 1978); Thisba Hutson Morgan, "Reminiscences of My Days in the Land of the Ogallala Sioux," *South Dakota Historical Collec-*

tions 29 (1958), 21–62; Faye Cashatt Lewis, *Nothing to Make a Shadow* (Ames: Iowa State University Press, 1971), 119–23; and Susan Peterson, "Religious Communities of Women in the West: The Presentation Sister's Adaptation to the Northern Plains Frontier," *Journal of the West* 21 (Apr. 1982), 65–70, and "From Paradise to Prairie: The Presentation Sisters in Dakota, 1880–1896," *South Dakota History* 10 (Summer 1980), 210–22. See also the collection of church histories at the Dacotah Prairie Museum and the Archives of the Presentation Sisters of the Blessed Virgin Mary, both in Aberdeen, S. D.; the Archives of the Oblate Sisters of the Blessed Sacrament, Saint Sylvester's Convent, Marty; the Archives of the Benedictine Convent of Saint Martin, Rapid City; and the Archives of the Benedictine Sisters of the Sacred Heart Convent, Yankton.

15. Minnie Miller Brown, "Black Women in American Agriculture," *Agricultural History* 50 (Jan. 1976), 202–12, and Sue Armitage, Theresa Banfield, and Sarah Jacobus, "Black Women and Their Communities in Colorado," *Frontiers* 2 (1977), 45–51. The census of 1870 showed 94 black people in Dakota, while the 1880 census indicated an increase to 2,003 blacks. See Robert B. Porter, *The West: From the Census of 1880* (Chicago: Rand McNally & Co., 1882), 404. See also Sara L. Bernson and Robert J. Eggers, "Black People in South Dakota History," *South Dakota History* 7 (Summer 1977), 241–70.

16. Mrs. R. O. Brandt, "Social Aspects of Prairie Pioneering: The Reminiscences of a Pioneer Pastor's Wife," *Norwegian-American Studies* 7 (1933), 1–46; Lorna B. Herseth, ed., "A Pioneer's Letter," *South Dakota History* 6 (Summer 1976), 306–15; Barbara Levorsen, "Early Years in Dakota," *Norwegian-American Studies* 21 (1962), 158–97; Emily Lunde, *Uff Da* (Grand Forks, N. D.: privately published, 1974); Aagot Raaen, *Grass of the Earth: Immigrant Life in the Dakota Country,* Scandinavians in America Series (New York: Arno Press, 1979); Martha Reishus, *The Rag Rug,* no. 3 (New York: Vantage Press, 1955); Herbert S. Schell, *South Dakota: A Student's Guide to Localized History,* Localized History Series (New York: Teachers College Press, 1971), 41—42; Martha Thal, "Early Days: The Story of Sarah Thal," *American Jewish Archives* 23 (Apr. 1971), 47–62; and Mary Dodge Woodward, *The Checkered Years,* ed. Mary B. Cowdrey (Caldwell, Idaho: Caxton Printers, 1937), 41–42, 86–88, 239–40.

17. Kohl, *Land of the Burnt Thigh,* and Elizabeth ("Bess") Corey Papers, 1909–79, Manuscript Division, SDHRC.

18. Kohl, *Land of the Burnt Thigh,* 3–4, 26.

19. Elenore Plaisted, quoted in Brett Harvey Vuolo, "Pioneer Diaries: The Untold Story of the West," *Ms. Magazine* 3 (May 1975), 32.

20. Mary W. M. Hargreaves, "Women in the Agricultural Settlement of the Northern Plains," *Agricultural History* 50 (January 1976), 185.

21. Herseth, "A Pioneer's Letter," 309.

22. Wilder, *The First Four Years,* 16.

23. Plaisted, quoted in Vuolo, "Pioneer Diaries," 33.

24. Brandt, "Social Aspects of Prairie Pioneering," 15. See also p. 5.

25. Mary W. M. Hargreaves, "Homesteading and Homemaking on the Plains: A Review," *Agricultural History* 157 (Apr. 1973), 62. Vuolo, "Pioneer Diaries," 32.

26. Herseth, "A Pioneer's Letter," 310–11.

27. Brandt, "Social Aspects of Prairie Pioneering," 37, and Raaen, *Grass of the Earth,* 10–14.

28. Kate Roberts Pelissier, "Reminiscences of a Pioneer Mother," *North Dakota History* 24 (July 1957), 134–35.

29. Woodward, *The Checkered Years,* 238. For detailed descriptions of the skills and techniques involved in these tasks, see Glenda Riley, " 'Not Gainfully Employed': Women on the Iowa Frontier, 1833–1870," *Pacific Historical Review* 94 (May 1980), 237–64. See also Pioneer Daughters Collection, 1850–1955, Library, SDHRC.

30. Cora D. Babcock, Reminiscences, 1800–85, SDHRC.

31. Edeen Marten, "Frontier Marriages and the Status Quo," *Westport Historical Quarterly* 10 (Mar. 1975), 100.

32. Leo E. Oliva, "Our Frontier Heritage and the Environment," *American West* 9 (Jan. 1972), 45.

33. "One of the Knitters," *American-Scandanavian Review* 6 (July-Aug. 1918), 215.

34. Margaret Johnson Interview, "North Dakota Oral History Project Issue," *North Dakota History* 43 (Spring 1976), 78–79; Walter F. Peterson, ed., "Christmas on the Plains: Elizabeth Bacon Custer's Nostalgic Memories of Holiday Seasons on the Frontier," *American West* 1 (Fall 1964), 53–57; Woodward, *The Checkered Years,* 108–9, 152; Vuolo, "Pioneer Diaries," 33; and Herseth, "A Pioneer's Letter," 312.

35. John Mack Faragher, "History from the Inside-Out: Writing the History of Women in Rural America," *American Quarterly* 33 (Winter 1981), 540.

36. Margaret Johnson Interview, 78–79; Pelissier, "Reminiscences," 133; William Forrest Sprague, *Women and the West: A Short Social History* (Boston, Mass.: Christopher Publishing House, 1940), 239–40; and Julie Roy Jeffrey, *Frontier Women: The Trans-Mississippi West, 1840–1880,* American Century Series (New York: Hill & Wang, 1979), 59.

37. Gilbert C. Fite, *The Farmers' Frontier, 1865–1900* (New York: Holt, Rinehart, and Winston, 1966), 47. See also Jeffrey, *Frontier Women,* 60.

38. Babcock, Reminiscences.

39. Pelissier, "Reminiscences," 134–35

40. E. May Lacey Crowder, "Pioneer Life in Palo Alto County," *Iowa Journal of History and Politics* 46 (Apr. 1948), 181.

41. Emerson Hough, *The Passing of the Frontier* (New Haven, Conn.: Yale University Press, 1921), 93.

42. Carol Fairbanks, "Lives of Girls and Women on the Canadian and American Prairies," *International Journal of Women's Studies* 2 (Sept./Oct. 1979), 452.

43. Page Smith, *Daughters of the Promised Land* (Boston: Little, Brown & Co., 1970), 223.

44. Dee Brown, *The Gentle Tamers: Women of the Old Wild West* (New York: Bantam Books, 1974), 269.

45. Brandt, "Social Aspects of Prairie Pioneering," 5–6, 9; Kate Eldridge Glaspell, "Incidents in the Life of a Pioneer," *North Dakota Historical Quarterly* 8 (Apr. 1941), 184–90; Lewis, *Nothing to Make a Shadow,* 21–23, 40, 71, 73; Mabel Lorshbough Interview, "North Dakota Oral History Project Issue," 22–23; Pelissier, "Reminiscences," 130; Thal, "Early Days," 47–62; and Woodward, *The Checkered Years,* 28–30, 35, 38, 55, 58–59, 65, 80–81, 118, 142, 159–60, 222.

46. Jeannie McKnight, "American Dream, Nightmare Underside: Diaries, Letters and Fiction of Women on the American Frontier," in L. L. Lee and Merrill Lewis, eds. *Women, Women Writers, and the West* (Troy, N.Y.: Whitston Publishing Co., 1979), 25–40.

47. Thal, "Early Days," 53, and Vuolo, "Pioneer Diaries," 34.

48. Herseth, "A Pioneer's Letter," 308.

49. Woodward, *The Checkered Years,* 81, 127. See also pp. 75, 87–88, 121, 167, 175, 200–201, 224.

50. Wilder, *The First Four Years,* 1, 4, 6, 134.

51. H. Arnold Barton, *Letters from the Promised Land* (Minneapolis: University of Minnesota Press for the Swedish Pioneer Historical Society, 1975), 291.

52. Pelissier, "Reminiscences," 138.

53. Woodward, *The Checkered Years,* 52.

54. W. F. Kumlien, *Basic Trends of Social Change in South Dakota,* Vol. 3. *Community Organization, South Dakota Agricultural Experiment Station Bulletin,* no. 356 (Brookings: South Dakota State College, 1941), 4–17.

55. Henry Frawley and Anne Frawley, "Agriculture, Dairying, Ranching," in Lawrence County for the Dakota Territory Centennial, 1861–1961, ed. Mildred Fielder (Deadwood/Lead, S. D.: Lawrence County Centennial Committee, 1960), 105.

56. Brandt, "Social Aspects of Prairie Pioneering," 16–18, 23–25, and Glaspell, "Incidents," 188–90.

57. Edna LaMoore Waldo, *Dakota: An Informal Study of Territorial Days* (Bismarck, N. D.: Capital Publishing Co., 1932), 198–213. See also Martha Correll Interview, "North Dakota Oral History Project Issue," 86–87.

58. Lewis, *Nothing to Make a Shadow,* 14–15, 33–34, 48–49, 74–77, 94, 132.

59. Brandt, "Social Aspects of Prairie Pioneering," 30.

60. Woodward, *The Checkered Years,* 144.

61. Herbert S. Schell, *History of South Dakota,* 3d ed. (Lincoln: University of Nebraska Press, 1975), 219–22.

62. Hargreaves, "Women in the Agricultural Settlement of the Northern Plains," 187. For a discussion of how various kinds of South Dakota farm families allotted their income in the 1930s to items such as housing, clothing, food, and household accessories and facilities, including power washing machines, electric lights, inside water supply, and telephones, see W. F. Kumlien et al., *The Standard of Living of Farm and Village Families in Six South Dakota Counties, 1935, South Dakota Agricultural Experiment Station Bulletin,* no. 320 (Brookings: South Dakota State College, 1938), 5–49. A Lawrence County study claimed that as late as 1950 only 74 percent of farms in that heavily agricultural county had electric power and that in 1954 only 72 percent had running water. Frawley and Frawley, "Agriculture, Dairying, Ranching," 114.

63. June Sochen, "Frontier Women: A Model for All Women?" *South Dakota History* 7 (Winter 1976), 43.

64. Sue Armitage, "Housework and Farmwork: The Changing World of Farm Women," paper delivered at the Conference on the History of Women, St. Paul, Minn., May 2, 1982.

65. "One of the Knitters," 215.

66. Lewis, *Nothing to Make a Shadow,* 39.

67. Ibid., 38–40.

68. Lunde, *Uff Da,* 2, 6, 8, 10, 14–15, 17, 27.

69. Frances M. Wold, comp. and ed., "The Letters of Effie Hanson, 1917–1923: Farm Life in Troubled Times," *North Dakota History* 48 (Winter 1981), 20–43.

70. Waldo, *Dakota,* 202; Dorinda Riessen Reed, *The Woman Suffrage Movement in South Dakota,* 2d ed. (Pierre: South Dakota Commission on the Status of Women, 1975), 5–7, 11–14, 18–113; and Mary Kay Jennings, "Lake County Woman Suffrage Campaign in 1890," *South Dakota History* 5 (Fall 1975), 390–401. For a detailed discussion of Susan B. Anthony's role in the 1889–1890 campaign, see Cecelia M. Wittmayer, "The 1889–1890 Woman Suffrage Campaign: A Need to Organize," *South Da-*

kota History 11 (Summer 1981), 199–225. For fuller accounts of later suffrage crusades, see the Jane Rooker Smith Breeden Papers, 1886–1946, Manuscript Division, SDHRC; the Mrs. John (Mamie I. Shields) Pyle Papers, Richardson Archives, I. D. Weeks Library, University of South Dakota, Vermillion; and the Woman Suffrage Movement Papers, 1889–1925, Manuscript Division, SDHRC.

71. Wilder, *These Happy Golden Years,* 269.

72. Wold, "Letters of Effie Hanson," 33–34, 36, 41.

73. Joan M. Jensen, "Women and Agriculture in American History: An Overview," paper presented at the Conference on the History of Women, St. Paul, Minn., May 2, 1982.

74. See Faragher, "History from the Inside-Out," for a discussion of the effects of twentieth-century progressive farming on women's roles in work and life.

75. Jensen, "Women and Agriculture in American History." See also the South Dakota Oral History Project, Richardson Archives, I. D. Weeks Library, University of South Dakota, which includes many interviews with farm women. *Tales of the Early Days as Told to Mirandy* (Hollywood, Calif.: Oxford Press, 1938) is an example of an early published collection of oral history interviews.

76. Wilson Cape, "Population Changes in the West North Central States, 1900–1930," *North Dakota Historical Quarterly* 6 (July 1932), 276–91. See also Walter L. Slocum, *Migrants from Rural South Dakota Families, South Dakota Agricultural Experiment Station Bulletin,* no. 359 (Brookings: South Dakota State College, 1942), 3–17, and W. F. Kumlien, *Basic Trends of Change in South Dakota:* Vol. 2, *Rural Life Adjustments, South Dakota Agricultural Experiment Station Bulletin,* no. 357 (Brookings: South Dakota State College, 1941), 5–21.

77. As told to Gilbert L. Wilson in *Buffalo Bird Woman's Garden* (St. Paul: Minnesota Historical Society Press, 1987), 10–14, 119–20. In public domain.

78. From Bertha Josephson Anderson, Autobiography, c. 1940, MHSA. Used by permission.

79. Mary Rosencrance, "A Woman Rides the Range," in United States Works Progress Administration, *Told by the Pioneers* Vol. 2 (N.p., 1938), 135.

80. Gladys Hovet, Reflections, c. 1975, privately held by Grace Ann and Theodore Hovet, Cedar Falls, Iowa. Copy in author's possession. Used by permission.

81. From U.S. Department of Agriculture, *Social and Labor Needs of Farm Women. Report No. 103* (Washington, D.C.: U.S. Government Printing Office, 1914), 153–55.

82. Susan La Flesche to Sarah T. Kinney (probably written November 19, 1888), Sarah Thomson Kin-

ney Collection, Connecticut State Library, Hartford, Connecticut.

83. Robert Glass Cleland, ed., *Apron Full of Gold: The Letters of Mary Jane Megquier from San Francisco, 1849–1856* (San Marino, California: The Huntington Library, 1949), 3, 30.

84. Ibid., 43.

85. Sarah Royce, *A Frontier Lady: Recollections of the Gold Rush and Early California,* ed. Ralph Henry Gabriel (New Haven, Conn: Yale University Press, 1932), 85.

86. Interview with Mrs. LeEtta S. King, March 4, 1976, University of Washington Library, Manuscript Collection, Seattle, Washington.

87. Interview 7240, IPP, Vol. 68.

88. Interview 9068, IPP, Vol. 15.

89. Mary Hayden, *Pioneer Days* (Fairfield, Washington: Ye Galleon Press, 1979), 34.

90. Ibid., 35.

91. Margaret Ronan, ed., *Frontier Woman: The Story of Mary Ronan* (Helena: University of Montana Publications in History, 1973), 89.

92. Amelia Bruner Monroe, "Some Happenings in the Early Days," c. 1870, and Eva Klepper, "Memories of Pioneer Days," n.d., both at NHS; and Interview with Lillie Badgley, April, 9, 1982, NEHC Oral History Project, MHSA.

93. Interview with Hagar Lewis, George P. Rawick, ed., *The American Slave,* Vol. 5, Part 3 (Westport, Conn.: Greenwood Publishing Co., 1972), 5.

94. "Mrs. Persis Ulrich," in United States Works Progress Administration, *Told by the Pioneers,* Vol. 3 (n.p., 1938), 91.

95. Della M. Todd's Daily Journal, July 5, 1911–July 5, 1912, WAHC.

96. Interview with Olive B. Deahl, October 13, 1979, WAHC.

97. Jesse E. Mudgett, for example, farmed because her husband worked off the farm as a bridge builder. See Pioneer Memories Collection, Wyoming State Archives, Museum, and Historical Department, Cheyenne [hereafter WSAMHD].

98. Evelyn King, "Women on the Cattle Trail and in the Roundup," *Buckskin Bulletin* 18 (Spring 1984), 3–4, and *Women on the Cattle Trail and in the Roundup* (Bryan, Texas: Brazos Corral of the Westerners, 1983); Nannie T. Alderson and Helena Huntington Smith, *A Bride Goes West* (Lincoln: University of Nebraska Press, 1969), 271–73; Georgia Kelley, "A Courageous Homesteader—Edna N. Eaton," interview, 1936, and Eva Putnam, "Reminiscences of Pioneer Women," 1936, both WSAMHD; and Emily J. Shelton, "Lizzie Johnson: A Cattle Queen of Texas," *Southwestern Historical Quarterly* 50 (January 1947), 349–66.

99. From Apolinaria Lorenzana, Reminiscences, 1878, BL.

100. *Ninth Census*, Vol. 1: *Population and Social Statistics* (Washington, D.C.: Government Printing Office, 1872), 722–23, 725, 734, 744–46, 749, 753, 759, 762, 765, and *Thirteenth Census of the United States Taken in the Year 1910*, Vol. 4: *Population, Occupation Statistics* (Washington, D.C.: Government Printing Office, 1910), 438–42, 462–63, 484–87, 493, 501–2, 507–08, 518, 523, 527–29, 534.

101. Suzanne H. Schrems, "Teaching School on the Western Frontier: An Acceptable Occupation for Nineteenth-Century Women," *Montana: The Magazine of Western History* 37 (Summer 1987), 54–63. See also Courtney Ann Vaughn-Roberson, "Having a Purpose in Life: Western Women Teachers in the Twentieth Century," *Great Plains Quarterly* 5 (Spring 1985), 107–24.

102. Kathryn Kish Sklar, *Catharine Beecher: A Study in American Domesticity* (New York: Norton, 1976), 113–15, 168–83; *Burlington* (Iowa) *Weekly Hawk-Eye* April 6, 1849; Catharine Beecher, *Suggestions Respecting Improvements in Education* (Hartford: Packard & Butler, 1829), 12, and *The Evils Suffered by American Women and Children* (New York: Harper & Brothers, 1846), 12. For discussions of the Board of National Popular Education teachers see Polly Welts Kaufman, "A Wider Field of Usefulness: Pioneer Women Teachers in the West, 1848–1854," *Journal of the West* 21 (April 1982), 16–25, and *Women Teachers on the Frontier* (New Haven, Conn.: Yale University Press, 1984).

103. Laura Brown Zook, "Sketches of Laura Brown Zook's Early Life, 1869–1944," Montana State University Library Special Collections, Bozeman [hereafter MSU].

104. Mrs. George H. Funk, "Reminiscences of an Early Schoolteacher in Washington," 1956, Washington State Library, Olympia.

105. Sarah Jane Price, Diaries, 1878–95, NHS. For women teachers/homesteaders see Elizabeth Tyler, Reminiscence, 1954, Montana State Historical Society, Helena; Abbie Bright, Diary, 1870–71, KHS; and Bern, ed., "They Had a Wonderful Time." The teacher/trail drive cook is found in Mary Hethy Bonar, Diary, 1885, State Historical Society of North Dakota, Bismarck [hereafter SHSND].

106. Mrs. A. S. (Mary) Raymond, "My Experiences as a Pioneer," 1929, NHS.

107. "Mrs. Frank Reeves," in United States Works Progress Administration, *Told by the Pioneers*, Vol. 3 (n.p., 1938), 88.

108. Greg Koos, comp., Census of Bloomington, Illinois, 1850, McLean County Historical Society, Bloomington, Illinois, and Glen Schwendemann, "Nicodemus: Negro Haven on the Solomon," *Kansas Historical Quarterly* 34 (Spring 1968), 14, 26.

109. Apolinaria Lorenzana, Reminiscence, 1878, BL.

110. Grace Pritchett, *The Road Goes This Way and That Way* (St. Paul, Minnesota: Braun Press, 1981), i, 17, 95.

111. Thisba Hutson Morgan, "Reminiscences of My Days in the Land of the Ogallala Sioux," South Dakota Department of History, *Report and Historical Collections* 29 (1969), 21–62.

112. May Wynne Lamb, *Life in Alaska: The Reminiscences of a Kansas Woman, 1916–1919* (Lincoln: University of Nebraska Press, 1988) 59, 62, 64.

113. Susan C. Peterson, "Religious Communities of Women in the West," 65–70; "From Paradise to Prairie: The Presentation Sisters in Dakota, 1880–1896," *South Dakota History* 10 (Summer 1980), 210–22; "Challenging the Stereotypes: The Adaptation of the Sisters of St. Francis to South Dakota Indian Missions, 1885–1910," *Upper Midwest History* 4 (1984), 1–10; " 'Holy Women' and Housekeepers: Women Teachers on South Dakota Reservations, 1880–1910," *South Dakota History* 13 (Fall 1983), 245–60; "Doing 'Women's Work': The Grey Nuns at Fort Totten Indian Reservation, 1874–1900," *North Dakota History* 52 (Spring 1985), 18–25; "A Widening Horizon: Catholic Sisterhoods on the Northern Plains, 1874–1910," *Great Plains Quarterly* 5 (Spring 1985), 125–32; and Lisa Larrabee, Guest Curator, "Women of Sacramento," exhibit brochure, 1989, Sacramento History Center, 4, 6.

114. List of County Superintendents in "Park County Women," 1977, MSU; Mary Johnstone Powers, "A Pioneer Woman's Reminiscences," 1947, MSHA; Larrabee, "Women of Sacramento," 7.

115. Lamb, *Life in Alaska*, 66. For scholarly discussions of prostitution in the West see Jacqueline Baker Barnhart, *The Fair but Frail: Prostitution in San Francisco, 1849–1900* (Reno: University of Nevada Press, 1986); Anne M. Butler, *Daughters of Joy, Sisters of Misery: Prostitutes in the American West, 1865–1890* (Urbana: University of Illinois Press, 1985); Anne P. Diffendal, "Prostitution in Grand Island, Nebraska, 1870–1913," *Heritage of the Great Plains* 16 (Summer 1983), 1–9; Paula Petrik, "Capitalists with Rooms: Prostitution in Helena, Montana, 1865–1900," *Montana: The Magazine of Western History* 16 (Spring 1981), 28–41; and Elliott West, "Scarlet West: The Oldest Profession in the Trans-Mississippi West," *Montana: The Magazine of Western History* 31 (Spring 1981), 16–27.

116. Mrs. Lee Whipple-Halsam, *Early Days in California* (Jamestown, Calif.: n.p., 1924), 26.

117. Carol Leonard and Isidor Walliman, "Prostitution and Changing Morality in the Frontier Cattle

Towns of Kansas," *Kansas History* 2 (Spring 1979), 27–40, and Joseph W. Snell, *Painted Ladies on the Cowtown Frontier* (Kansas City, Missouri: Lowell Press, 1965), 3–5, 7–12.

118. Diffendal, "Prostitution in Grand Island, Nebraska," 1–5, and Paula Petrik, "Strange Bedfellows: Prostitution, Politicians and Moral Reform in Helena, Montana, 1885–1887," *Montana: The Magazine of Western History* 35 (Summer 1985), 2–13.

119. Petrik, "Capitalists with Rooms," 29–34; West, "Scarlet West," 16–27; and Petrik "Strange Bedfellows, 2–13. For Chicago Joe see Rex C. Myers, "An Inning for Sin: Chicago Joe and Her Hurdy-Gurdy Girls," *Montana: The Magazine of Western History* 27 (1965), 147–56. For Butte see Mary Murphy, "The Private Lives of Public Women: Prostitution in Butte, Montana, 1878–1917," *Frontiers* 7 (1984), 30–35. For a thoughtful, highly informed discussion of prostitution in the American West see Butler, *Daughters of Joy, Sisters of Misery.*

120. Friede Van Dalsem and Abbie Jarvis, Pioneer Daughters Collection, SDHRC; "Dr. Georgia Arbuckle Fix: Pioneer," in A. B. Wood, ed., *Pioneer Tales of the North Platte Valley* (Gering, Nebraska: Courier Press, 1938), 188–89; and "Lavinia Goodyear Waterhouse," Pacific Grove (California) Heritage Society *Newsletter* (February/March 1989).

121. Judy Yung, *Chinese Women of America: A Pictorial History* (Seattle: University of Washington Press, 1986), 39.

122. *The News Tribune,* Tacoma, July 18, 1976, E-4.

123. See Benay Blend, "Mary Austin and the Western Conservation Movement, 1900–1927, *Journal of the Southwest* 30 (Spring 1988), 12–34; Ann LaBastille, *Women and Wilderness: Women in Wilderness Professions* (San Francisco: Sierra Club Books, 1980), section one; Elizabeth C. MacPhail, *Kate Sessions: Pioneer Horticulturist* (San Diego: San Diego Historical Society, 1976); Sandra Lin Marburg, "Women and the Environment: Subsistence Paradigms, 1850–1950," *Environmental Review* 8 (Spring 1984), 7–22; and Carolyn Merchant, "Women of the Progressive Conservation Movement, 1900–1916," *Environmental Review* 8 (Spring 1984), 57–85.

124. Interview with Mrs. LeEtta S. King.

125. Adina de Zavala, "The Margil Vine," in Mabel Major and Rebecca W. Smith, eds., *The Southwest in Literature* (New York: The Macmillan Company, 1929), 159–61.

126. From *Boston Traveler,* quoted by *Merchant's Magazine and Commercial Review* 26 (1852), 777.

127. Susan Howell, "Recollections of a Busy Life," 1972, MHSA. Used by permission.

128. "Running a Boarding House in the Mines," *California Emigrant Letters* 24 (Dec. 1945), 347. Used by permission.

129. Mrs. J. W. Likins, *Six Years Experience as a Book Agent* (San Francisco: Women's Union Book and Job Printing, 1874), 53–57.

130. Quoted in "Elizabeth Nicholas: Working in the California Canneries," *Harvest Quarterly,* Nos. 3/4 (Sept.–Dec. 1976), 12–25. Used by permission.

131. "Mrs. W. C. Gray," in United States Works Progress Administration, *Told by the Pioneers,* Vol. 11 (n.p., 1937), 166, 169, 170. Used by permission.

132. Mary Paik Lee, *Quiet Odyssey: A Pioneer Korean Woman in America* (Seattle: University of Washington Press, 1990), 11, 14–15. Used by permission.

133. June Oshima, letter to Glenda Riley, September 8, 1979, from Honolulu, Hawaii, in author's possession. Used by permission.

134. George P. Rawick, ed., *The American Slave,* Vol. 5, Part 3 (Westport, Conn.: Greenwood Publishing Co., 1972), 47.

135. Louise Palmer, "How We Live in Nevada," *The Overland Monthly,* Vol. 2, No. 5 (May 1869), 457–62.

136. "Mrs. Katherine S. Ide," in United States Works Progress Administration, *Told by the Pioneers,* Vol. 1 (n.p., 1938), 65–66. Used by permission.

137. Eulalia Pérez, Reminiscences, 1877, BL.

138. Akemi Kikumura, *Through Harsh Winters: The Life of a Japanese Immigrant Woman* (Novato, Calif.: Chandler & Sharp Publishers, Inc., 1981), 31–32. Used by permission.

139. E. J. Guerín, *Mountain Charley; or the Adventures of Mrs. E. J. Guerín, Who Was Thirteen Years in Male Attire.* Norman, Okla.: University of Oklahoma Press, 1986. In public domain.

140. Pérez, Reminiscences. Used by permission.

141. Mary Austin, *Earth Horizon: Autobiography* (New York: Literary Guild, 1932), 231, 251–52, 266–67, 319–20.

142. Margaret Belle Houston, "Song from the Traffic," in Mabel Major and Rebecca W. Smith, eds., *The Southwest in Literature* (New York: Macmillan, 1929), 328–29.

143. "Margaret Jean Maloney," in United States Works Progress Administration, *Told by the Pioneers,* Vol. 3 (n.p., 1938), 144. Used by permission.

144. Stella Tanner Fowler, "The Tanner Family," c. 1970, MHSA. Used by permission.

145. Interview with Ophelia Salas by Glenda Riley, October 23, 1990, Milwaukee, Wisconsin. Transcript in author's possession. Used by permission.

146. Mary and George Baillie, "Recollections in the Form of a Duet," 1939, WSAMHD. Used by permission.

147. Interview 10521, IPP, Vol. 77. Used by permission.

148. Sister Blandina Segale, *At the End of the Santa Fe Trail* (Columbus, Ohio: The Columbian Press, 1932), 37, 41, 161. Used by permission.

Section 5

1. Gilbert C. Fite, "The United States Army and Relief to Pioneer Settlers, 1874–1875," *Journal of the West* 6 (January 1967), 99–107.

2. Louise Pound, *Pioneer Days in the Middle West: Settlement and Racial Stocks* (Lincoln: Nebraska State Historical Society, n.d.); Mary W. M. Hargreaves, "Homesteading and Homemaking on the Plains: A Review," *Agricultural History* 47 (April 1973), 156–63; Lillian Schlissel, "Women's Diaries on the Western Frontier," *American Studies* 18 (Spring 1977), 87–100, and Lillian Schlissel, "Mothers and Daughters on the Western Frontier," *Frontiers* 3 (1979), 29–33; Christine Stansell, "Women on the Great Plains, 1865–1900," *Women's Studies* 4 (1976), 87–98; John Mack Faragher and Christine Stansell, "Women and Their Families on the Overland Trail to California and Oregon, 1842–1867," *Feminist Studies* 2 (1975), 150–66; Glenda Riley, *The Female Frontier: A Comparative View of Women on the Prairie and the Plains* (Lawrence: University Press of Kansas, 1988).

3. See Myra Waterman Bickel, Lydia Burrows Foote, Eleanor Schubert, and Anna Warren Peart, Pioneer Daughters Collection, SDHRC; Abbie Bright, Diary, 1870–1871, KHS; Barbara Levorsen, "Early Years in Dakota," *Norwegian-American Studies* 21 (1961), 167–69; Kathrine Newman Webster, "Memories of a Pioneer," in *Old Times Tales*, Vol. 1, Part 1 (Lincoln: Nebraska State Historical Society, 1971); Bertha Scott Hawley Johns, "Pioneer Memories 1975," WSAMHD; Emma Crinklaw (interview by Mary A. Thon) "One Brave Homesteader of '89," 1989, WSAMHD. Regarding 'witching' for water in Kansas see Bliss Isely, *Sunbonnet Days* (Caldwell, Idaho: Caxton Printers, 1935), 176–79.

4. Ellen Stebbins Emery, letter to "Dear Sister Lizzie," December 31, 1889, from Emerado, SHSND (used by permission); "Prairie Pioneer: Some North Dakota Homesteaders," *North Dakota History* 43 (Spring 1976), 22; Adela E. Orpen, *Memories of the Old Emigrant Days in Kansas, 1862–1865* (New York: Harper & Brothers, 1928) 65–69; Florence Marshall Stote, "Of Such is the Middle West," n.d., KHS; Meri Reha, Pioneer Daughters Collection, SDHRC.

5. Amanda Sayle Walradth, Pioneer Daughters Collection, SDHRC, and Ada Vogdes, Journal, 1868–1872, HL.

6. Isely, *Sunbonnet Days*, 196–201, and Anne E. Bingham, "Sixteen Years on a Kansas Farm, 1870–1886," Kansas State Historical Society *Collections* 15 (1919/20), 516.

7. Sara Tappan Doolittle Robinson, *Kansas, Its Interior and Exterior Life* (Freeport, New York: Books for Libraries Press, 1856), 85, 249–69, 347; Georgiana Packard, "Leaves from the Life of a Kansas Pioneer," 1914, KHS; Marian Lawton Clayton, "Reminiscences—The Little Family," 1961, KHS.

8. From Sophie Trupin, *Dakota Diaspora: Memoirs of a Jewish Homesteader* (Lincoln: University of Nebraska Press, 1984), 35, 39, 41–42.

9. For a fuller discussion of western divorce see Glenda Riley, *Divorce: An American Tradition* (New York: Oxford University Press, 1991), ch. 4.

10. Helen M. Carpenter, "A Trip Across the Plains in an Ox Wagon," 1857, HL, and Orpen, *Memories of the Old Immigrant Days*, 8.

11. Laura Ingalls Wilder, *The First Four Years* (New York: Harper & Row, 1971), Mollie Dorsey Sanford, *Mollie: The Journal of Mollie Dorsey Sanford in Nebraska and Colorado Territories, 1857–1886* (Lincoln: University of Nebraska Press, 1976), 54; Eva Klepper, "Memories of Pioneer Days," n.d., in May Avery Papers, NHS.

12. Sarah Ettie Armstrong, "Pioneer Days," n.d., WSAMHD.

13. Ibid.

14. U.S. Commissioner of Agriculture, *Annual Report*, 1862, 462–70; *Laramie Sentinel*, October 10, 1885; Martha Farnsworth, Diary, 1882–1922, KHS. See also John Mack Faragher, "History from the Inside-Out: Writing the History of Women in Rural America," *American Quarterly* 33 (Winter 1981), 537–57, and Melody Graulich, "Violence Against Women in Literature of the Western Family," *Frontiers* 7 (1984), 14–20.

15. Flora Moorman Heston, " 'I think I will Like Kansas': The Letters of Flora Moorman Heston, 1885–1886," *Kansas History* 6 (Summer 1983), 92.

16. Sanford, *Mollie*, 38.

17. Isely, *Sunbonnet Days*, 180, and Lewis, *Nothing to Make a Shadow*, 76.

18. Vogdes, Journal.

19. Ibid.

20. Margaret Ronan, *Frontier Woman: The Story of Mary Ronan* (Helena: University of Montana, 1973), 123, and Mrs. Charles Robinson, "Pioneer Memories," 1975, WSAMHD.

21. Sanford, *Mollie*, 63. Descriptions of social events can be found in Nannie T. Alderson and Helen H. Smith, *A Bride Goes West* (Lincoln: University of Nebraska Press, 1969), 169; Mary and George Baillie, "Recollections in the Form of a Duet," 1939, WSAMHD; Enid Bennets, "Rural Pioneer Life," 1939, WSAMHD; Minnie Doehring, "Kansas One-Room Public School," 1981, KHS; W. H. Elznic, Pioneer Daughters Collection, SDSHRC;

Lottie Holmberg (recorder), Laura Ingraham Bragg, Recollections, n.d., WSAMHD; Lena Carlile Hurdsman, "Mrs. Lena Hurdsman of Mountain View," 1939, WSAMHD; Levorson, "Early Years in Dakota," 161; Alice Richards McCreery, "Various Happenings in the Life of Alice Richards McCreery," n.d., WSAMHD; Minnie Dubbs Millbrook, ed., "Rebecca Visits Kansas and the Custers: The Diary of Rebecca Richmond," Kansas Historical Quarterly 42 (Winter 1976), 366–402; Graphia Mewhirter Wilson, "Pioneer Life," 1939, WAHC.

22. Catherine E. Berry, "Pioneer Memories," 1975, WSAMHD. For discussions of women reconstructing their known lifestyle patterns on the Plains see James I. Fenton, "Critters, Sourdough, and Dugouts: Women and Imitation Theory on the Staked Plains, 1875–1910," in John R. Wunder, ed., At Home on the Range: Essays on the History of Western Social and Domestic Life (Westport, Conn.: Greenwood Press, 1985), 19–38; Jacqueline S. Reinier, "Concepts of Domesticity on the Southern Plains Agricultural Frontier," in Wunder, ed. At Home on the Range, 55–70.

23. Mrs. G. W. Wales, Reminiscences, 1866–1877, SHSND; Florence McKean Knight, "Anecdotes of Early Days in Box Butte County," Nebraska History 14 (April–June 1933), 142; Alderson and Smith, A Bride Goes West, 89; Lewis, Nothing to Make a Shadow, 71–72; Ronan, Frontier Woman, 115.

24. Lorshbough, "Prairie Pioneers," 78–79; Walter F. Peterson, "Christmas on the Plains," American West 1 (Fall 1964), 53–57; Anna Warren Peart, Pioneer Daughters Collection, SDHRC; Mabel Cheney Moudy, "Through My Life," n.d., WAHC.

25. Hannah Birkley, "Mrs. Iver O. Birkley," 1957, NHS. For descriptions of Exodusters see Roy Garvin, "Benjamin, or 'Pap' Singleton and His Followers," Journal of Negro History 33 (January 1948), 7–8; Glen Schwendemann, "Wyandotte and the First 'Exodusters' of 1879," Kansas Historical Quarterly 26 (Autumn 1960), 233–49, and "The 'Exodusters' on the Missouri," Kansas Historical Quarterly 29 (Spring 1963), 25–40; Arvarh E. Strickland, "Toward the Promised Land: The Exodus to Kansas and Afterward," Missouri Historical Review 69 (July 1975), 405–12; Nell Irvin Painter, Exodusters: Black Migration to Kansas after Reconstruction (New York: Alfred A. Knopf, 1977; reprint, Lawrence: University Press of Kansas, 1986), 108–17; George H. Wayne, "Negro Migration and Colonization in Colorado, 1870–1930," Journal of the West 15 (January 1976), 102–20; "Washwomen, Maumas, Exodusters, Jubileers," in We Are Your Sisters: Black Women in the Nineteenth Century, ed. Dorothy Sterling (New York: Norton, 1984), 355–94.

26. For descriptions of Jewish women and men on the Plains see Lipman Goldman Feld, "New Light on the Lost Jewish Colony of Beersheba, Kansas, 1881–1886," American Jewish Historical Quarterly 60 (December 1970), 159, 165–67; Susan Leaphart, ed., "Frieda and Belle Fligelman: A Frontier-City Girlhood in the 1890s," Montana: The Magazine of Western History 32 (Summer 1982), 85–92; James A. Rudin, "Beersheba, Kansas: 'God's Pure Air on Government Lands,' " Kansas Historical Quarterly 34 (Autumn 1968), 282–98; Elbert L. Sapinsley, "Jewish Agricultural Colonies in the West: The Kansas Example," Western States Jewish Historical Quarterly 3 (April 1971), 157–69; Lois Fields Schwartz, "Early Jewish Agricultural Colonies in North Dakota," North Dakota History 32 (October 1965), 217, 222–32; William C. Sherman, Prairie Mosaic: An Ethnic Atlas of Rural North Dakota (Fargo: North Dakota Institute for Regional Studies, 1983), 19–20, 53–54, 70, 112.

27. Mrs. W. M. Lindsay, "My Pioneer Years in North Dakota," 1933, SHSND; Leola Lehman, "Life in the Territories," Chronicles of Oklahoma 41 (Fall 1963), 373; Orpen, Memories of the Old Emigrant Days, 219; Lucy Horton Tabor, "An Old Lady's Memories of the Wyoming Territory," n.d., WSAMHD; Emma Vignal Borglum, "The Experience at Crow Creek: A Sioux Indian Reservation at South Dakota," 1899, SDHRC.

28. Lehman, "Life in the Territories," 373; Vogdes, Journal; Fanny McGillycuddy, Diary, 1877–78, SDHRC.

29. Isely, Sunbonnet Days, 78–79. For other descriptions of the importance of quilting see Mrs. Henry (Anna) Crouse, Reminiscence, January 12, 1939, MSU; Ellen Calder DeLong, "Memories of Pioneer Days in Cavalier County," n.d., SHSND; Agnes Henberg, Interview, September 6, 1979, WAHC; Olivia Holmes, Diary, 1872, KHS; Sarah Bessey Tracy, Diary, 1869, MSU.

30. Bozeman Chronicle, August 10, 1954; unidentified newspaper clipping, "Journey from Missouri to Montana in 1880 Great Adventure According to Mrs. Mary Myer," n.d., MSU.

31. Nebraska Farmer, December 8, 1934; Martha Thal, "Early Days: The Story of Sarah Thal, Wife of a Pioneer Farmer of Nelson County, N.D.," American Jewish Archives 23 (April 1971), 59; Mary Raymond, "My Experiences as a Pioneer," 1929, 1933, NHS; Allen, Diary; Lindsay, "My Pioneer Years"; Eleanor Schubert and Mary Louise Thomson, Pioneer Daughters Collection, SDHRC.

32. Alderson and Smith, A Bride Goes West, 205–06.

33. Clara Bewick Colby, Scrapbook of Clippings from The Woman's Tribune, 1883–1891, Clara Colby Collection, HL. See in particular pp. 24, 25, 257.

34. Luna Kellie, "Memoirs," n.d., NHS.

35. Catherine Wiggins Porter, "Sunday School Houses and Normal Institutes: Pupil and Teacher in

Northern Kansas, 1886–1895," KHS, and Bingham, "Sixteen Years on a Kansas Farm," 502.

36. Stanton is quoted in Beverly Beeton and G. Thomas Edwards, "Susan B. Anthony's Woman Suffrage Crusade in the American West," *Journal of the West* 21 (April 1982), 5. See also Virginia Scharff, "The Case for Domestic Feminism: Woman Suffrage in Wyoming," *Annals of Wyoming* 56 (Fall 1984), 29–37; Dr. Grace Raymond Hebard, "How Woman Suffrage Came to Wyoming," n.d., WSAMHD; Katharine A. Morton, "How Woman Suffrage Came to Wyoming," n.d., Woman Suffrage Collection, WSAMHD; Staff of the Library of the University of Wyoming, "Esther Hobart Morris and Suffrage," n.d., Woman Suffrage File, WAHC; and Mary Lee Stark, "One of the First Wyoming Women Voters Tells How Franchise Was Granted," n.d., WAHC.

37. Mathilda C. Engstad, "The White Kid Glove Era," n.d., SHSND, and Marilyn Hoder-Salmon, "Myrtyle Archer McDougal: Leader of Oklahoma's 'Timid Sisters,'" *Chronicles of Oklahoma* 60 (Fall 1982), 332–43.

38. Marilyn Dell Brady, "Populism and Feminism in a Newspaper by and for Women of the Kansas Farmers' Alliance, 1891–1894," *Kansas History* 7 (Winter 1984/85), 280–90; O. Gene Clanton, "Intolerant Populist? The Disaffection of Mary Elizabeth Lease," *Kansas Historical Quarterly* 34 (Summer 1968), 189–200; Katherine B. Clinton, "What Did you Say, Mrs. Lease?" *Kansas Quarterly* 1 (Fall 1969), 52–59; and Richard Stiller, *Queen of the Populists: The Story of Mary Elizabeth Lease* (New York: Crowell, 1970). See also Elizabeth Cochran, "Hatchets and Hoopskirts: Women in Kansas History," *Midwest Quarterly* 2 (April 1961), 229–49.

39. Richard B. Knowles, "Cross the Gender Line: Ella L. Knowles, Montana's First Woman Lawyer," *Montana: The Magazine of Western History* 32 (Summer 1982), 64–75, and Olive Pickering Rankin, Montana American Mothers Bicentennial Project, MHSA.

40. Stote, "Of Such is the Middle West," KHS; Bingham, "Sixteen Years on a Kansas Farm," 517; Alderson and Smith, *A Bride Goes West*, 206, 233–34; Elizabeth B. Custer, *"Boots and Saddles" Or Life in Dakota With General Custer* (New York: Harper & Brothers, 1885), 126, 145; Vogdes, Journal; Faye Cashatt Lewis, *Nothing to Make a Shadow* (Ames: Iowa State University Press, 1971), 33–34.

41. Lewis, *Nothing to Make a Shadow*, 33–34.

42. Mary Francis Baltzly, "Aunt Fannie," 1942, WSAMHD. Used by permission.

43. Emery, letter to "Dear Sister Lizzie." Used by permission.

44. Elizabeth McAnulty Owens, "The Story of Her Life," 1895, BTHC. Used by permission.

45. Apolinaria Lorenzana, Recollections, n.d., BL. Used by permission.

46. From Glenda Riley, ed., "The Memoir of Georgiana Packer," *Kansas History* 9 (Winter 1986–87), 186–89. Original held by KHS. Used by permission.

47. Eudora Inez Moore in *Indianola Scrap Book* (Victoria, Texas: Victoria Advocate Publishing Company, 1936).

48. Mrs. Charles A. Finding, "The Story of a Colorado Pioneer," *Colorado Magazine* 2 (1925), 52.

49. Doña Jesús Moreno de Soza, Reminiscences, 1939, Antonio Soza Papers, Arizona Historical Society, Tucson. Used by permission.

50. Mrs. Lee Whipple-Halsam, *Early Days in California* (n.p., c. 1924), 14–16.

51. Akemi Kikumura, *Through Harsh Winters: The Life of a Japanese Immigrant Woman* (Novato, Calif.: Chandler & Sharp Publishers, Inc., 1981), 32–33. Used by permission.

52. Quoted in Jo Anne Wold, *The Way It Was: Of People, Places and Things in Pioneer Interior Alaska* (Anchorage: Alaska Northwest Publishing Co., 1988). Used by permission.

53. George P. Rawick, ed., *The American Slave,* Vol. 5, Parts 3 and 4 (Westport, Conn.: Greenwood Publishing Co., 1972), 65–66, 174–78. Used by permission.

54. Interview with Liola McClean Cravens Woffort, n.d., Manuscript Collection, University of Washington Libraries. Used by permission.

55. From Eliza Spalding Warren, *Memoirs of the West, The Spaldings* (Portland, Ore.: March Printing Co., 1916), 56, 68–71.

56. Anna Caldwell Stiefvator, Reminiscences, 1954, MHSA. Used by permission.

57. Oscar Osburn Winther and Rose Dodge Galey, eds., "Mrs. Butler's 1853 Diary of Rogue River Valley," *Oregon Historical Quarterly* 41 (December 1940), 345–46. Used by permission.

58. Isabella L. Bird, *A Lady's Life in the Rocky Mountains* (Norman, Okla.: University of Oklahoma Press, 1960), 41–42. In public domain.

59. Mrs. Lee A. Jones, "Reminiscences of Early Days at Havre," n.d., MHSA. Used by permission.

60. From Ella Martfeld, "Homesteading Days," c. 1910, WSAMHD. Used by permission.

61. Interview 13738, IPP, Vol. 17.

62. Eveline M. Alexander, Diary, 1866–67, BL. Used by permission.

63. "Clara's Episodes. A Reflection of Early Wyoming, 1909–11," 1964, WSAMHD. Used by permission.

64. Interview with Consuelo Rocha, September 19, 1979, WAHC. Used by permission.

65. Mrs. W. M. Lindsay, "My Pioneer Years in North Dakota," 1933, SHSND. Used by permission.

66. Interview with Consuelo Rocha, WAHC.

67. Stella M. Drumm, ed., *Down The Santa Fe Trail and Into Mexico: The Diary of Susan Shelby Magoffin, 1846–1847* (New Haven: Yale University Press, 1926), 107, 109–10, 115, 130–31, 163, 205, 207, 209–10.

68. Mary Austin, *Earth Horizon: Autobiography* (New York: The Literary Guild, 1932), 278–80.

69. Mary Ann Hafen, *Recollections of a Handcart Pioneer of 1860: A Woman's Life on the Mormon Frontier* (Lincoln: University of Nebraska Press, 1983), 91, 95–97. In public domain.

70. "Mrs. Iver O. Birkley," NHS. Used by permission.

71. Mrs. D. B. Bates, *Incidents on Land and Water, or Four Years on the Pacific Coast* (Boston: E. O. Libby and Company, 1858), 210–12.

72. Interview with Louise Mathews in George P. Rawick, ed., *The American Slave*, Vol. 5, Part 3 (Westport, Conn.: Greenwood Publishing Co., 1972), 65–66. Used by permission.

73. Mary Elder Calder DeLong, "Memories of Pioneer Days in Cavalier County, c. 1950, SHSND. Used by permission.

74. Sarah Royce, *A Frontier Lady: Recollections of the Gold Rush and Early California*, ed. Ralph Henry Gabriel (New Haven, Conn: Yale University Press, 1932), 79–82.

75. Sheryll Patterson-Black, "From Pack Trains to Publishing: Women's Work in the Frontier West," in Sheryll and Gene Patterson-Black, *Western Women in History and Literature* (Crawford, Nebr.: Cottonwood Press, 1978), 5–6. See also Sheryll Patterson-Black, "Women Homesteaders on the Great Plains Frontier," in *Western Women in History*, 15–31, and "Women Homesteaders on the Great Plains Frontier," *Frontiers* 1 (Spring 1976), 67–88. Other historians who mention the prevalence of women homesteaders include Everett Dick, *The Sod-House Frontier, 1854–1890* (New York: Appleton-Century Company, 1937), 129; Dick, "Free Homes for the Millions," *Nebraska History* 43 (Dec. 1962), 221; and Mary W. M. Hargreaves, "Women in the Agricultural Settlement of the Northern Plains," *Agricultural History* 50 (Jan. 1976), 182.

76. Edith Eudora Kohl, *Land of the Burnt Thigh* (New York: Funk & Wagnalls, 1938), and Enid Bern, "The Enchanted Years on the Prairies," *North Dakota History* 40 (Fall 1973), 5, 11.

77. Serena J. Washburn, Autobiography, 1836–1904, MSU. For other examples, see Cora D. Babcock, Reminiscences, 1880–85, and Fanny Achtnes Malone, "The Experience of a Michigan Family on a Government Homestead in South Dakota," n.d., both in SDHRC; Mary Fox Howe, Montana American Mothers Bicentennial Project, 1975–76, MHSA; Margaret Matilda Mudgett, Pioneer Memories Collection, 1975, and Ethel Hamilton, "Ethel Hamilton of Mountain View," 1936, both in WSAMHD; Martha Ferguson McKeown, *Them Was the Days: An American Saga of the 70s* (Lincoln: University of Nebraska Press, 1961); and Kate Roberts Pelissier, "Reminiscences of a Pioneer Mother," *North Dakota History* 24 (July 1957), 138.

78. Kohl, *Land of the Burnt Thigh*, 21–22; Katherine Grant, Montana American Mothers Bicentennial Project, 1975–76, MSHA; Henry K. Goetz, "Kate's Quarter Section: A Woman in the Cherokee Strip," *Chronicles of Oklahoma* 61 (Fall 1983), 246–67.

79. Elinore Pruitt Stewart, *Letters of a Woman Homesteader* (Lincoln: University of Nebraska Press, 1961), 7, 77, 216.

80. Bern, "Enchanted Years," 7; Kohl, *Land of the Burnt Thigh*, 6–7. See also "Prairie Pioneers: Some North Dakota Homesteaders," *North Dakota History* 43 (Spring 1976), 40.

81. Glenda Riley, "The Memoirs of a Girl Homesteader: Martha Stoecker Norby," *South Dakota History* 16 (Spring 1976), 1–17. See also Sarah Schooley Randall, "My Trip West in 1861," in *Collection of Nebraska Pioneer Reminiscences* (Cedar Rapids, Iowa: Nebraska Society of the Daughters of the American Revolution, 1916), 211, and Mary Price Jeffords, "The Price Girls Go Pioneering," in Emerson R. Purcell, ed., *Pioneer Stories of Custer County, Nebraska* (Broken Bow, Nebr.: Custer County Chief, 1936), 74.

82. Kohl, *Land of the Burnt Thigh*, 8, and Susan Ophelia Carter, Diary, 1887, NHS.

83. Paul Corey, "Bachelor Bess: My Sister," *South Dakota Historical Collections* 37 (1974), 12.

84. Susan Strawbridge, Papers, 1913–28, Iowa State Historical Department, Division of Museum and Archives, Des Moines.

85. Kohl, *Land of the Burnt Thigh*, 6, and Carter, Diary.

86. Enid Bern, ed., "They Had a Wonderful Time: The Homesteading Letters of Anna and Ethel Erickson," *North Dakota History* 45 (Fall 1978), 15, 17, 19.

87. Carter, Diary

88. Abbie Bright, Diary, 1870–71, KHS.

89. Corey, "Bachelor Bess," 15, 18. For other examples see Mrs. William Bangs, "My Homesteading Days," n.d., MSHA; Monroe Billington, ed., "Pothook Pioneer, a Reminiscence by Ada Blayney Clarke," *Nebraska History* 39 (Mar. 1958), 45, 50–52; and Ella Martfeld, "Homesteading Days," n.d., WSAMHD.

90. Babcock, Diary; Bangs, "Homesteading Days"; Washburn, Autobiography.

91. Kohl, *Land of the Burnt Thigh*, 27, and Washburn, Autobiography. See also Angel Kwolek-Folland, "The Elegant Dugout: Domesticity and Move-

able Culture in the United States, 1870–1900,"
American Studies 25 (Fall 1984), 21–37.

92. Kohl, *Land of the Burnt Thigh*, 105–06, and Allie B. Busby, *Two Summers among the Musquakies* (Vinton, Iowa: Herald Book and Job Rooms, 1886), 75. See also Glenda Riley, *Women and Indians on the Frontier, 1825–1915* (Albuquerque: University of New Mexico Press, 1984), 83–126.

93. Kohl, *Land of the Burnt Thigh*, 107–09.

94. Ibid., 109

95. Ibid., 109, 151, 181, 262.

96. Ibid., 136, and Corey, "Bachelor Bess," 16.

97. Billington, ed., "Pothook Pioneer," 54.

98. Riley, "Memoirs of a Girl Homesteader." See also Elizabeth Ruth Tyler, Reminiscence, 1954, MHSA.

99. Billington, ed., "Pothook Pioneer," 46, 48–49. See also Frances Jacob Alberts, ed., *Sod House Memories* (Hastings, Nebr.: Sod House Society, 1972), 6, 51.

100. Bess Cobb to "Dear Helen," July 31, 1907, SHSND; Bern, ed., "They Had a Wonderful Time," 6, 8, 28; Charley O'Kieffe, *Western Story: The Recollections of Charley O'Kieffe* (Lincoln: University of Nebraska Press, 1960), 26; Roger L. Welsh, *Shingling the Fog and Other Plain Lies* (Chicago: Swallow Press, 1972), 126. See also Glenda Riley, "Farm Women's Roles in the Agricultural Development of South Dakota," *South Dakota History* 13 (Spring/Summer 1983), 55–62.

101. Kohl, *Land of the Burnt Thigh*, 268–79. See also Myra Waterman Bickel, Lydia Burrows Foote, Eleanor Schubert, and Anna Warren Peart, Pioneer Daughters Collection. c. 1850–1955, SDHRC; Bertha Scott Hawley Johns, Pioneer Memories Collection, 1975, WSAMHD; Levorsen, "Early Years in Dakota," 167–69; and Webster, "Memories of a Pioneer," in *Old Timer's Tales Collection.*

102. See also Florence Marshall, "The Early Life and Prairie Years of a Pioneer Wife and Mother," n.d., KHS; Meri Reha, Pioneer Daughters Collection, SDHRC.

103. Kohl, *Land of the Burnt Thigh*, 253–67, and Emily Stebbins Emery to "Dear Sister Lizzie," December 31, 1889, SHSND.

104. Kohl, *Land of the Burnt Thigh*, 185–98; Mrs. R. O. Brandt, "Social Aspects of Prairie Pioneering: The Reminiscences of a Pioneer Pastor's Wife," *Norwegian-American Studies* 7 (1933), 5, 9, 26–30; Venola Lewis Bivans, ed., "The Diary of Luna E. Warner, a Kansas Teenager of the Early 1870's," *Kansas Historical Quarterly* 35 (Autumn 1969), 296; Ida Kittelson Gullikson, Jennie Larson, and Mary Louise Thompson, Pioneer Daughters Collection, SDHRC; Carolyn Strong Robbins, Journal, 1887–88, KHS.

105. Lillie Goodrich, Interview, Sept. 19, 1979, WAHC.

106. Riley, "Memoirs of a Girl Homesteader." See also Bangs, "Homesteading Days"; Bern, ed., "They Had a Wonderful Time," 4–31; Bright, Diary; Carter, Diary; Corey, "Bachelor Bess," 14, 36, 46; Porter, "Sunday School Houses," KHS; Tyler, Reminiscence; Anne Wright, "Mary Alice Davis, Pioneer Woman," 1957, WSAMHD.

107. Bright, Diary; Lucie Emma Dickinson Lott, Reminiscences, n.d., and Jeanne L. Wuillemin, "A Homesteader's Letter," n.d., both at SDHRC.

108. Edith Eudora Kohl, "Frontier Crusader," *Rocky Mountain Empire Magazine,* Nov. 23, 1947, and *Land of the Burnt Thigh*, 36–45, 89–98. For more information on Edward L. Senn see Florence Dirks Anderson, "History of Lyman County, South Dakota" (Master's thesis, University of South Dakota, 1926), 77–78; Lawrence K. Fox, ed., *Fox's Who's Who among South Dakotans* (Pierre: Statewide Service Company, 1924), 178; and Robert F. Karolevitz, "With a Shirt Tail Full of Type: The Story of Newspapering in South Dakota," 42, 53, SDHRC.

109. Billington, ed., "Pothook Pioneer," 56.

110. Bern, ed., "They Had a Wonderful Time," 28.

111. Myrtle Yoeman to "Dear Grace," June 24, 1905, SDHRC.

112. Lottie Holmberg, "Experiences of Mary Culbertson," 1939, and Mrs. Ashby Howell, Biographical Sketch, 1936, both at WSAMHD. See also Bern, ed., "They Had a Wonderful Time," 6, 10–11, 14, 17, 25; Corey, "Bachelor Bess," 65; Martfeld, "Homesteading Days"; and Martha Suckow Packer, Memoirs, Sept. 20, 1880, to Jan. 21, 1970, MSU.

113. Kohl, *Land of the Burnt Thigh*, 2–7, 12–13, 21–23.

114. Ibid., 27, 38, 65, 84.

115. Katherine Hill Harris, "Women and Families on Northeastern Colorado Homesteads, 1873–1920" (Ph.D. dissertation, University of Colorado, Boulder, 1983), 257–64, and "Sex Roles and Work Patterns among Homesteading Families in Northeastern Colorado, 1873–1920," *Frontiers* 7 (1984), 43–49; Lonnie E. Underhill and Daniel F. Littlefield, "Women Homeseekers in Oklahoma Territory, 1889–1901," *Pacific Historian* 17 (Summer 1973), 36–47; Kohl, *Land of the Burnt Thigh*, 143–63. For other descriptions of women participating in land runs see B. B. Chapman, "The Land Run of 1893, as Seen at Kiowa," *Kansas Historical Quarterly* 31 (Spring 1965), 67–75; Goetz, "Kate's Quarter Section," 246–67; Charles Moreau Harger, "The Prairie Woman: Yesterday and Today," *The Outlook* 70 (Apr. 26, 1902): 1009; Lynette West, "The Lady Stakes a Claim," *Persimmon Hill* 6 (1976), 18–23.

116. Interview 9837, IPP, Vol. 67. Used by permission.

117. Stewart, *Letters of a Woman Homesteader,* 216. In public domain.

118. Lorenzana, Recollections, BL. Used by permission.

Conclusion

1. Dorotea Valdez, Reminiscences, June 26, 1874, BL.

2. Ibid., and Rosalia Leese, "History of the Bear Party," 1874, BL.

3. Valdez, Reminiscences, and Leese, "History of the Bear Flag Republic," 1874, BL.

4. Orginal letter in Spanish, privately held by the letter writer's granddaughter in Los Angeles, Calif.

Copy of English translation in Glenda Riley's possession, dated 1986. For obvious reasons, the family has asked that its name not be revealed.

5. Fabiola Cabeza de Baca, *We Fed Them Cactus* (Albuquerque: University of New Mexico Press, 1954), 60, 147, 153.

6. For reviews of western historiography see Michael P. Malone, ed., *Historians and the American West* (Lincoln: University of Nebraska Press, 1983); Roger L. Nichols, ed., *American Frontier and Western Issues: A Historiographical Review* (New York: Greenwood Press, 1986); and Brian W. Dippie, "American Wests: Historiographical Perspectives," *American Studies International* 38 (October 1989), 3–25.

SUBJECT INDEX

Note: This two-part index first lists names and concepts found in the author's text only, then lists Place Names found throughout the book. For location of the primary documents contained in *A Place to Grow,* consult the Checklist which begins on p. 251.

PLACE INDEX

A Place to Grow: Women in the American West was copyedited by Michael Kendrick and proofread by Michael Kendrick and Lucy Herz. The production editor was Lucy Herz. Alan Wendt designed the book. Impressions typeset the text, and Malloy Lithographing printed and bound the book.